Prairie Farmer
and WLS

Prairie Farmer
and WLS

The Burridge D. Butler Years

JAMES F. EVANS

UNIVERSITY OF ILLINOIS PRESS

Urbana   Chicago   London

1969

ACKNOWLEDGMENTS

The close of an effort such as this brings with it a keen awareness of the fact that completion rests upon more persons and other sources than I can recognize individually. Although most of them must go unnamed here, all have my sincere thanks.

Among those who have invested extraordinary amounts of time toward making the book as complete and meaningful as possible, the management of Prairie Farmer Publishing Company merits special appreciation. In particular, I am indebted to Paul C. Johnson, a most helpful source of ideas about where to find answers as questions emerged. George C. Biggar and Merrill C. Gregory also provided materials and insights which were invaluable, both in the information-gathering stage and as the manuscript took shape.

I wish to thank Professor Theodore Peterson for basic guidelines and perspectives which served me in this effort, Professor Hadley Read for his ideas and active support, Mrs. Bonita Depp for her competent editorial contributions, and my family for its encouragement.

Finally, I deeply appreciate the interest of the Chicago Community Trust, a grant from which allowed nearly 20,000 miles of travel that personal interviewing and other fact-gathering efforts required.

JAMES F. EVANS

CONTENTS

His Family Gathered

CHAPTER 1

Prairie Farmer and WLS had announced that their public picnic would begin shortly before noon, yet families were converging upon Noblesville, Indiana, before many farmers had finished morning chores. By 7 A.M. of that Sunday, July 30, 1939, 500 cars had entered Forest Park, forcing local planners to shift from fears of a slim crowd to visions of an overflow.

Cars were streaming through the stone gates bumper to bumper by 9 A.M., assuring Noblesville that it was due for the biggest crowd it had ever seen. Although many contained residents of Indiana—for this was in the heart of the state—license plates identified visitors from 15 other states.

Nine thousand cars soon filled the park to capacity and forced helpers to stop cars at the gate, after which another 3,000 cars lined the road more than a mile back to Noblesville. Twenty thousand persons were in the park by mid-morning and the rush was only starting. Traffic jammed miles outside of Noblesville, and by early afternoon state policemen halted cars seven miles from the town in all directions to tell people they should turn back and go home—there was no more room.

Friends throughout the midwest had accepted this invitation from *Prairie Farmer* and WLS to join in a Sunday picnic. Children lined up at slides and swings. The swimming pool was full. Farmers and wives visited wherever they could find unoccupied shade. When Dr. John Holland, staff pastor of *Prairie Farmer* and WLS, stepped to the microphone to conduct his Little Brown Church of the Air, he faced the largest congregation of his life. Holding a small Testament in his hand, he looked up the hill into a mass of clothes and faces which hid all signs of the grass-covered outdoor amphitheater except occasional shade trees which rose out of the long slope. Many churches in the area had dismissed regular services so their congregations could see the program which they had heard so many times over WLS.

The crowd was at its largest around one o'clock after perhaps the biggest farm picnic ever spread. By then 60,000 persons blanketed acres of space for a quarter of a mile along the hillside amphitheater. The spirit of this goodwill expression swept over the stars of the WLS National Barn Dance as they clowned and sang on the dwarfed stage at the foot of the slope. Patsy Montana, Maple City Four, Hoosier Sodbusters, Little Genevieve—strange names today, but they were old friends to the picnickers at Noblesville. In fact, these stars were almost like family members to the midwest farm people whose homes they entered daily as radio guests. The progression of songs, laughter, and encores engulfed both performers and viewers until a program planned for one hour extended to nearly three, ended only (as an editor of *Prairie Farmer* later put it) by the need to get about 50,000 cows milked on time.

Of all who took part in this event, none got more personal pleasure from it than a 71-year-old man who was not there. He was the host for this picnic: Burridge D. Butler, owner and patriarch of *Prairie Farmer* and WLS. To Butler the picnic at Noblesville was one of the greatest accomplishments of the 30 years that he had owned *Prairie Farmer*. He was on a business trip at the time, but his absence did not dampen his pleasure in this event. No one knows for sure why it touched him so because in many respects it was relatively modest. *Prairie Farmer* had been deeply involved in agricultural problems involving billions of dollars, helping farmers answer crucial questions of the times.

Even the collection of 60,000 persons could not have overwhelmed Butler. Less than a year earlier, the Illinois corn husking contest which *Prairie Farmer*–WLS sponsored had drawn 85,000. Four years earlier 100,000 people had watched the WLS Dinner Bell program broadcast from the corner of State and Madison Streets, Chicago, in a display of goodwill between farm and city. Butler was accustomed to having up to 75,000 visit his company's hospitality tents each year at the state fairs of Illinois, Indiana, and Wisconsin. His WLS National Barn Dance was beginning to anticipate its millionth paid customer. An average of about one million pieces of mail flooded the WLS mail center each year.

It seems likely that Butler's unusual pride in the picnic at Noblesville arose in part from what he thought it symbolized: *Prairie Farmer*–WLS and midwestern farm people as one big family— more specifically, perhaps, *his* family, to replace the one he never had. People came to Noblesville not for the thrill of a corn husking contest, a dollar's worth of entertainment, or out of idle curiosity. They came, Butler probably felt, because they liked being with each other and with his *Prairie Farmer*–WLS. At Noblesville they talked, ate, prayed, and laughed together as families after a week of hard work, thereby symbolizing Butler's idea of the perfect family life which had escaped him as a boy.

The crowd at Noblesville also may have fed Butler's unusually strong need to fill the role of father-protector. It may have given him occasion to see in himself part of what he admired in his idol, Abraham Lincoln—an emancipator of the oppressed. Butler was proud of farm people in 1939, for they were emerging, however battered, from a depression which had left rural communities limp with exhaustion. He was proud of his staff (by now calling him "Daddy") which had earned loyalty and respect among these farm people by defending them and promoting their causes.

Butler also may have found some reason for self-pride in the event at Noblesville. Under his direction, *Prairie Farmer* had outlived every high-powered newspaper that his partners in the old Clover Leaf League had started at the turn of the century. He had advanced the traditions of John S. Wright, who founded *Prairie Farmer* and left a well-defined shadow of which Butler was acutely aware.

Probably, Butler also felt some selfish pride of possession as a result of the picnic. More than once he had smashed office chairs and brought light fixtures crashing to the floor in violent demonstration that "all this is mine." According to the Butler mind, a family's rights and possessions remain in the hands of the father.

Striking 30-Year Contrast

Much had changed since that September of 1909 when Butler and his wife, Ina, had moved to Chicago from Minneapolis, anxious to "retire." Looking back, perhaps Butler could appreciate the irony of the fact that half again as many people attended his family picnic in 1939 as even subscribed to *Prairie Farmer* in 1909. The paper, with a circulation of more than 300,000 in 1939, had gained steadily under Butler's ownership. From a staff of nine in 1909, *Prairie Farmer* and WLS had grown to more than 200 in 1939, not counting subscription salesmen.

One would hardly recognize the *Prairie Farmer* of 1909 as being any kin to its successor, for when Butler bought the paper it was showing the strain of limited finance and muffled or missing editorial vigor. Thin 16-page issues appeared on low-quality newsprint, each containing no more than three photographs, none of them local. The editorial copy also lacked a strong local flavor. Canada seemed to get as much space as Illinois in the editorial columns, and the paper took copy wherever it found it: *Harper's Weekly, American Magazine,* Ontario Agricultural College, *Circle Magazine, Chicago Tribune,* and many others. As a result, articles were as likely to deal with "A Great Year for Sugar" or "The Latest in Umbrellas" as with items which probably were closer to the lives of farm readers in Illinois.

Some articles, appearing to be news items, lapsed without warning into advertisements. A reader attracted to an article entitled "At the Dawn of History" might find himself reading about the special advantages of a wagon box manure spreader or a certain brand of stock food.

Advertisers commonly got special favors in *Prairie Farmer* shortly before Butler took over. The paper had sold several front covers to advertisers, and a sizable advertising schedule by a Canadian railroad probably helped account for the strong editorial emphasis upon Canada during the same period.

Advertisers of health panaceas filled pages with promises in language more colorful (if more crude) than the editorial matter and clamored for the opportunity to cure readers of catarrh, deafness, or nearly any other ailment. Their suggested remedies ranged from medicines to "magic shields," which were vests containing tiny magnetic storage batteries to "keep the body bathed in a constant stream of magnetism, which floods the system with its life and energy."

Such cure-all advertising was gone within a year after Butler took over. By 1939 advertising stressed items such as fencing, fertilizer, and machinery which farmers used in their farming operations. Nearly all editorial content in 1939 was of local interest and written by staff members. Issues were larger and more attractive. Where a 16-page issue was normal in 1909, issues averaged 32 pages during 1939. A *Prairie Farmer* which ran two or three editorial photographs before Butler arrived was printing as many as 55 photographs an issue in 1939, not counting frequent pieces of art which the staff produced. By 1939, too, Butler was publishing more than one *Prairie Farmer*, an Illinois edition and an Indiana edition which began early in 1923.[1]

Finances were both cause and effect of this 30-year contrast. *Prairie Farmer* had lost money for at least five of the seven years before Butler took over. In 1939, coming out of the lean years of depression, *Prairie Farmer* was again earning a consistent profit and carrying assets many times those of 1909. WLS, in turn, was paying its stockholders dividends of 12 per cent annually and carrying rapidly rising assets of more than $500,000.

Butler's competition also had changed during the previous 30 years. When he came, *Prairie Farmer* was choking in the dust raised by four other general farm publications aimed at the Illinois market, but by 1939 it stood alone.

Butler had changed, too, in some ways. A proud, ramrod-straight young man standing six-feet-four had become slightly gnarled. Big, but not fat, he still was built like a boxer with long arms, wide shoulders and upper torso tapering down to a narrower waist. He still darkened doorways when he entered, sometimes having to hunch. But those broad shoulders, now slightly rounded, topped a long spinal column that was beginning to cause almost constant pain. Legs that had long supported more than 200 pounds were becoming unsteady. By now he walked rather heavily. His coarse

[1] *Prairie Farmer,* 95 (September 15, 1923), 8.

dark hair had whitened and largely disappeared from the top of his head, except for a sparse forelock that he parted to the right. Glasses with round gold frames accented the roundness of his face, seeming almost too small for the features surrounding them and making his nose and long ears even bigger by comparison. His dress, long ago improved by a wife with a fashionable taste, was conservative, yet somehow often rumpled.

Unchanged—The War Within

For all the transformation of 30 years, Butler in one respect defied change as long as he lived: his unpredictability. Employees and acquaintances often disagreed about Burridge Butler, but all could agree that he was inordinately complex. Years after his death, some still would break into a tirade against a man who they felt was crude, ruthless, and devoid of principles. Others could find only kind words to express their opinions about a warm, generous Butler.

Those closest to the man, however, considered him to be an unpredictable mixture from both extremes. His emotionalism produced many surprises. Pacing his office on the southeast corner of the second floor in the Prairie Farmer Building, he could step to the window, look southward as if to scan those broad prairies on which his farm people were busy working, and turn back to his associates with tears rolling down his cheeks. A voice normally brusque and gruff suddenly would quiver with emotion. Out would come a large white handkerchief to muffle a man-sized snort of released feeling.

Nothing could immobilize Butler more quickly than the memory of his mother and grandmother. He would break into tears at the very mention of his mother, and when he visited his aging grandmother, who lived to be 93, she could hardly say a word without drawing tears. Butler felt somewhat the same affection for employees. In his late years he cried at the sight of his "boys" leaving for service in World War II.

Also the poverty of farm people touched him deeply. Staff members learned to screen his mail carefully because letters from readers often stirred his emotions, especially letters that were rather long and handwritten on tablet paper. For example, one woman in southern Indiana who had walked three miles to a neighbor's home to hear a corn husking contest over WLS and who wrote Butler telling how much joy the broadcast had given her, received a new radio at his request. "I can't rest easy until I know that she has it," Butler explained.[2]

Butler could also be granite-hard, as salesmen sometimes learned. Once when a salesman upset him he pitched a chair the full length of the room. His wrath inevitably rose against outside threats to the autonomy of his editors (although he was not opposed to exerting some of his own influence). Employees fondly recall the time an executive with a farm cooperative came to Butler insisting that editors of *Prairie Farmer* should be horsewhipped for what they said about the cooperative and the executive himself. The visitor also threatened to remove some printing business from Prairie Farmer Publishing Company. One onlooker later assured another staff member: "I want you to know that Mr. Butler did not hit Mr. Cooke with any of the office furniture. We will, of course, have to have the glass repaired in his library because he cleared the decks before he took Mr. Cooke by the collar and necktie and waved him up and down . . . and then he said, 'Who is going to horsewhip who, Mr. Cooke?' "[3]

Sometimes Butler's violence had origins which were more petty. For example, he liked clean desks and insisted that piled-up desks were signs of sloppy housekeeping. Occasionally he felt compelled to renew his point by walking down the rows of desks with outstretched arms after employees had left for the day, sweeping everything onto the floor for their attention the next morning.

At times his eruptions surprised even himself. In an argument with an executive who was not knuckling under, Butler looked up at a bank of fluorescent lights overhanging them and blurted out in his frustration, "I could take those lights and smash them."[4] The uncompromising reply was, "Well, why don't you?" Whereupon Butler grabbed his cane and smashed all of the bulbs, which exploded and left everyone somewhat in shock—including Butler.

This line between violence and tears was so fine that Butler's associates often despaired at predicting changes in his disposition. One minute he would bluster and his face would grow as bright

[2] Dave O. Thompson, unpublished memoirs, pp. 380-381.
[3] Julian C. Bentley, former associate of Butler, quoted in Thompson, p. 110.
[4] Jack Williams, personal interview, December 26, 1966.

as the orange rug under his desk as he pounded with his fists, while during the next minute he might cloud up and cry.

These were not the only sides to a man who was extremely complex, whose contradictory actions neutralize any conclusions that one might be inclined to draw about him and stood as testimony of the battle within him.

While he reserved the right to express his own widely fluctuating emotions, he was less tolerant of the right of others to express their emotions or threaten his viewpoints. If an argument got heated, he would shout, "I don't want to hear any more of it!" and kick the wastebasket against his desk. The safest response was, "Yes, Mr. Butler."

Despite his bullying, he exercised a type of respect for persons who stood up to him. The bully in Butler expected to be pampered. When he walked out of his office and tossed his car keys down the aisle, the junior employee was supposed to grab them before they stopped sliding.[5] Once in a dining room in Washington, D.C., Butler noticed words of several patriotic songs printed on the menu. Instead of reading the menu while the waiter stood waiting to take his order, Butler read the songs. Shortly he turned to the waiter, a Negro, and said, "Have you ever read any of these?" The waiter replied, "No, sir, I haven't." "Well, read them. That's the reason you're a waiter, because you never read anything like that," Butler announced. "Now stand up there and read this one to me."[6] The waiter did so.

Another time Butler and a friend were driving to a football game in Connecticut. As they passed through a small town they approached a large policeman standing in the middle of the road directing traffic. Butler stopped beside the surprised man and shouted, "You're too fat to be a policeman. You take up half the road yourself."[7]

On occasion, Butler also tried to bully employees into staying with his firm. He once stopped at the desk of a woman employee who was considering a move. Tapping his cane sharply on the floor, he announced in stentorian voice, "Young lady, I am leaving for

[5] Joe Bumgarner, quoted in Thompson, p. 226.
[6] Glenn Snyder, personal interview, June 15, 1967.
[7] John W. Holland, "Let's Start Something," undated, unpublished eulogy of Butler, p. 56.

KOY and *Arizona Farmer* this winter, and when I get back I expect to find you right here." [8] She left despite the command, but not without some trepidation.

Butler sometimes used his bullying tactics to test people, to see if they would stand up to him. At one meeting WLS executives were talking about the home talent shows the station was staging throughout the area. Butler, who inwardly was proud of them, turned to the director of the shows and said "You don't like that. That's show business. You've got no use for show business." The director replied, "Well, yes, Mr. Butler, I do. That's the hand that feeds me and I am not going to bite it," and from then on Butler had a high regard for the man. [9]

Butler was both generous and niggardly. The many thousands of dollars which he donated to various philanthropies testify to his generosity and bear fuller discussion in a later chapter. However, he left testimonies of pettiness in financial matters. Butler had a reputation for paying employees no more than he had to. His fellow farm publishers pursued the same policy, but Butler's wage scale seemed especially odd for a crusader who professed undying concern for the common man. At times a strong supporter of unions, Butler did not seem concerned that many of his employees were earning less than union wages. Even the widely known host of WLS Dinnerbell, Arthur C. Page, at one time earned less than the union man who turned records during Page's program. When confronted with this fact, Butler snorted, "Damn unions. They really squeeze you." Only moments before he had been praising unions for what they had done for working people. [10]

Butler gladly would foot the bill for sending a 90-man cast of the WLS National Barn Dance to perform at a benefit show hundreds of miles from Chicago, yet refuse to pay a $3 admission fee when his party forgot to bring complimentary tickets. The gatekeeper, a farmer, paid the fee out of his own pocket.

Even as a millionaire, Butler apparently thought nothing about letting a $50-a-week employee pay his taxi fare. His habit of never carrying money meant that whoever was with him paid the bill. Butler would fumble in his pocket as if searching for change, but associates soon learned that it was only an empty gesture.

[8] Viola Epperson, quoted in Thompson, pp. 257-258.
[9] Glenn Snyder, personal interview, June 15, 1967.
[10] John Strohm, personal interview, February 25, 1967.

Butler often imposed needlessly upon others, yet at times almost impulsively stepped in to help those being imposed upon. During one business trip to New York City, rain left him with a wet, wrinkled suit. He stepped into a dry cleaner's shop, walked into the back room, removed his trousers, and sat waiting while they were being pressed. A disgruntled customer entered and began a profane harangue. Butler emerged from his waiting room and said, "I don't care what the argument's about, but you're not going to talk like that in front of me. Out you go." [11] He hoisted the customer by the back of the neck and threw him into the street, then realized that he was in the street himself without pants.

The same Butler could ask a field editor to spend Thanksgiving Day driving Butler's car from Indianapolis to Chicago, then receive it without thanks.

Warm and sensitive in many respects, Butler also could be cold as a cobra. Children were most effective in exposing his soft side, for in their presence he was almost timidly gentle. Sometimes he surprised employees, too, with his personal warmth. One day Butler learned that a headache was bothering his secretary.

"I know just how to fix you up," Butler announced as he planted her on a chair at her desk in the open office area and began to rub her neck and back. Thoroughly embarrassed by this odd display within eyesight of her friends, she soon found her hairpins flying, hair falling, and shirt tail out.

"Now," he concluded, "isn't that better? Don't you feel better? Mrs. Butler feels wonderful when I do that. Now you just go in and lie down and relax for a few minutes." [12]

She retired to the lounge, but could not relax after this touch of Butler's concern.

Such incidents surprised employees all the more because they knew Butler's reputation as a hard businessman. Puffing at his big cigar, he could hold his own at any conference table, reacting venomously if he thought someone was double-dealing him.

Butler was critical of wealthy persons but impressed by being associated with them. Members of the Union League Club of Chicago often became objects of criticism by Butler, but he valued his membership in that club.

He was a confident grandstander, yet nursed feelings of in-

[11] Davenal W. Hardy, personal interview, April 28, 1967.
[12] Margaret Connell, personal interview, March 3, 1967.

adequacy. Some of Butler's acquaintances proposed that he should have been in show business because he seemed to plan his actions for maximum impact, often tossing verbal bombshells during meetings. At college commencement exercises, garbed in academic gown and doctor's hood, he seldom reached his seat on the platform with other trustees of Blackburn College. Anywhere along the march he might fall out of the procession, take a seat among the observers, and thereby create a new center of attention.[13] His action in this case may reflect both a desire for attention and a feeling of inadequacy, for Butler was sensitive to his lack of formal education.

At other times his grandstanding left companions cringing in embarrassment. In restaurants he was apt to refuse food which he had ordered or wander about in search of something while complaining loudly enough for all in the room to hear. If he spotted movie stars in public, he was known to point at them and fairly shout, "Look! Movie actors making a big show of it. Movie actors."[14]

At one baseball game he began to wave his cane over everyone's head, then exclaimed, "Look at them. They're Jewish, all Jewish."[15]

Among relatives he was an habitual tease and would cling to a family joke "like a puppy hanging onto a root."[16]

Associates concluded that there was plenty of ham in Butler and that he resorted to every trick in the book to attract attention, sometimes hiding behind the pretense that he did not want it.

Grandstanding played a smaller part in his relations with agricultural leaders and farm people. At banquets and similar farm affairs he seemed almost timid and if he spoke at a meeting of farmers (which he resisted), his remarks almost invariably were serious and intense. Perhaps he felt uneasy among farm people because they were too close to his emotions for him to be comfortable. Among agricultural dignitaries, however, he probably was quiet because he did not know the details of what they were doing and because they appealed to him less than his "common people."

Butler was an avidly independent man who incurably needed others depending upon him. He loved to break rules but resented

[13] Florence B. Hudson, "Happy Birthday, Mr. Butler!" *Blackburn College Alumni Bulletin,* 35 (February, 1941), 1.
[14] Glenn Snyder, personal interview, June 15, 1967.
[15] Glenn Snyder, personal interview, June 15, 1967.
[16] Harold Christopher, personal interview, March 22, 1967.

having others suspect that he might. At the same time he needed to feel the dependence of those around him—his wife, his employees, and indeed the entire midwest farm "family" that he claimed.

He was a dictator, but he liked to insist that employees feel independent. Butler's firm control left more than one employee wondering what kind of future a Butler-owned enterprise could offer. The same Butler could admonish an associate to put his feet up on his desk, even spit on it, because he would own the desk some day.

Such eccentricities gradually formed a kind of storybook which his employees enjoyed opening and sharing. Who but Burridge Butler would notice that his office girls were primping in the women's restroom a few minutes before quitting time and respond by barging in unannounced, banging on the stalls, and shouting, "I want everybody at their desks—now!"? Who but Burridge Butler would enter an employee's home for the first time and, without a word of greeting, march around the living room straightening every picture? Such oddities led some employees to conclude they would rather be Butler's mortal enemy than his pet because in the latter case "one might be sure that the wind would change in a day or so." [17]

Butler was at least partly aware of what he was doing, for he often referred to himself as cantankerous. Indeed, he saw strength in such a role. To one former employee he advised, ". . . as you find your backbone getting stiffer so that you can get mad and knock things over, at the same time let your heart get softer and more tender for other people who are less fortunate than you are." [18]

If Butler could exert some control over these elements which seemed to engage in a constant tug-of-war within him, it was only partial control. They descended at his birth with a strength beyond his command, originating with parents whose dissimilar personalities help explain the fluidity of his own.

The Butler Birthright

Thomas D. Butler, Burridge's father, was a stocky, brusque man who, despite the New Testament gospel which he preached, showed

[17] Thompson, p. 3.
[18] B. D. Butler to George Biggar, October 24, 1939.

signs of unusual self-esteem. The elder Butler was proud of his ancestry and religious heritage, having been born January 1, 1838, in Shrewsbury, England, to a family reportedly descended from one of that country's defenders of the Christian faith. His father was an elder in the church at Shrewsbury. The chief event in Thomas' boyhood had been a visit in 1847 by Alexander Campbell, a leader in the Disciples of Christ movement which Campbell's father had shaped. During a stay at Butler's home, Campbell suggested that Thomas should come to America, which he did in 1859.[19]

The boy stayed three months at Campbell's home in Bethany, West Virginia, before moving to Louisville, Kentucky, as the Civil War was about to erupt. There Thomas met his future wife, Marie Radcliffe, through their common membership in the Walnut Street Christian Church. They were married August 21, 1861.[20]

Records do not show when Butler began preaching, for he pursued assorted trades for some years after marriage, perhaps preaching part-time. During the war he worked with the U.S. Sanitary Commission, then as a carpenter with his step-father-in-law, John S. Christopher, in Louisville until about the time Burridge was born on February 5, 1868. One of the characteristics of Thomas Butler's career was his frequent moves which some observers imputed to offensive behavior and an overbearing manner that soon alienated him. Relatives were cool to him because he tended to be unbending and argumentative.

His wife was his opposite in disposition: quiet, gentle, highly sensitive. Their major meeting grounds seem to have been English ancestry and a shared religious zeal sufficient to over-ride differences in personality. Family history cites her as a great granddaughter of George Augustus Frederick (later George IV, King of Great Britain and Ireland, 1820-30) through a mistress. Marie was born at Jordan, New York, on February 15, 1839.[21] Her parents, Jonathan and Frances Radcliffe, soon moved to Ohio where she

[19] Nathaniel S. Haynes, *History of the Disciples of Christ in Illinois, 1819-1914* (Cincinnati: Standard Publishing Co., 1915), p. 489; Holland, pp. 1-2; *Christian Standard*, August 24, 1878, p. 270, and May 7, 1921, p. 30.

[20] Thomas D. Butler, ed., *Poetry and Prose of Marie Radcliffe Butler* (Cincinnati: Standard Publishing Co., 1884), p. ix, cites August 22. However, *Marriage Register*, 8, of Jefferson County, Kentucky, p. 66, lists August 21 as date of marriage.

[21] T. D. Butler, ed., *Poetry and Prose*, p. vii.

lived until she was 14 years old. In 1853 the family moved to
Wheeling, Virginia, where her father died during an epidemic of
cholera. Her mother then opened a school for instruction in music,
drawing, and embroidery. In about 1856 Fannie Radcliffe and her
daughter accepted positions as governess and assistant, respectively,
for a private boarding school at Brownsboro, Kentucky. Brownsboro
was a busy little center lodged among steep wooded hills near the
Peewee Valley area just northeast of Louisville. Farmers found it
a handy stopping point on their trips to and from the city, so
Brownsboro supported a hotel, woolen mill, seminary, harness
manufacturer, millinery store, two blacksmith shops, and two sa-
loons.[22]

One of the children at the boarding school belonged to a wid-
owed builder in Louisville who caught the eye of Marie's mother.
He was John S. Christopher, whose first wife, Frances, had died a
year earlier.[23] Christopher and Fannie Radcliffe were married in
January, 1857, he a man "so homely he was beautiful" and she a
tall and very straight woman with thick, wavy, dark hair.[24] They
moved to Louisville and thereby gave Marie an opportunity for
more schooling. Marie was one of nine graduates in the class of
1860 at Girls' High School, completing the four-year program in
two years.[25] Her graduation essay, "Woman and Dreams," gained
the attention of the editor of the *Louisville Journal*, and he commended its "maturity of thought very rare among young girls."[26]
However, he observed that the strong-mindedness in her essay was
objectionable and reminded her that a girl's business in life is to
brighten a fireside and not to discuss woman's rights.

Plagued by ill health from her youth, Marie seemed distant and
almost mystical at times. Her ponderings often took the form of
poems which she wrote by the dozens during her remaining years.
They tended to be sad and melancholy, almost always dealing
with the destiny of humans:

> Here in the twilight of weak indecision,
> Groping through mist of our gathering tears,

[22] Mrs. Clay Johnston, personal interview, June 7, 1967.

[23] Jefferson County, Kentucky, *Marriage Register,* 1, p. 116; tombstone, Lot
219, Section M, Cave Hill Cemetery, Louisville.

[24] Marriage license, Oldham County, Kentucky, recorded in Book 1857, p.
166.

[25] *Girls' High School 50th Anniversary* (Louisville: C. T. Dearing Printing
Co., 1958), p. 25; T. D. Butler, ed., *Poetry and Prose,* p. viii.

[26] T. D. Butler, ed., *Poetry and Prose,* p. viii.

We longingly strive for that purified vision
That comes with the sorrow and patience of years.[27]

This poetic emotion in Burridge Butler's mother was to become a part of him, bursting out sporadically to the surprise of those around him.

Butler's craving for a family seems to stem in part from the one-sidedness of family life during his own youth. His mother and grandmother raised the four children (two other children died in childhood); in fact, during Burridge's first seven years his father was away more than at home.

Thomas Butler moved alone to New York City before his son Burridge was born and became religious editor of the *New York Independent*.[28] He also served as New York correspondent of the *Christian Standard*, a publication in Cincinnati devoted to the "Restoration of Primitive Christianity." Burridge's father was a friend of the founder of the *Standard* and contributed regularly for years, starting in 1866. Marie, too, contributed prose and poetry, including a long poem on the first page of the first issue.

During his stay in New York, Thomas Butler railed against the "popular preachers" for preaching so much of the sensational "that Christianity—the Gospel and the Christ—are hardly mentioned."[29] Henry Ward Beecher drew Butler's special criticism for "mixing up the mud of his own fancies with the crystal stream of Gospel truth, so that wise men become honestly muddled, and the wayfaring and simpleminded men are often hopelessly befogged."[30]

Burridge's father apparently spent some time in Louisville between 1871 and 1874, for city directories identified him as an employee of a general insurance agency in Louisville, Slaughter and Company. The Slaughter family was active in the Walnut Street Christian Church to which the Butlers and Christophers belonged.

A visit to England took Thomas Butler away from his family for another year during 1874-75. Listed as foreign correspondent of the *Christian Standard*, he left for England in July, 1874, when

[27] T. D. Butler, ed., *Poetry and Prose*, p. 102. Three books of writings by Marie Radcliffe Butler have been published. In 1872 she published *Riverside* and *Grandma's Patience* (Cincinnati: Bosworth, Chase and Hall), two serials which had appeared in *Christian Standard*. Third was *Poetry and Prose*, cited earlier.

[28] *Christian Standard*, May 7, 1921, p. 30.

[29] *Christian Standard*, January 22, 1870, p. 27.

[30] *Christian Standard*, September 3, 1870, p. 282.

Burridge was six years old. The paper carried reports of his travels and observations throughout the year.

Meanwhile his wife became severely ill. Three months after he had arrived in England, she was lying "near the gate of death" in Louisville.[31] Her mother nursed her through the winter and into the next spring when she and the children moved to Maine Prairie, Minnesota, "on the quiet shore of whose 'Silver Lake' her only brother had been resting for many months."[32] Marie Butler weathered the illness, but the crisis may have had a profound influence upon a young son who later criticized his father for having left Marie in deprivation.

Thomas Butler's return to America and reunion with his family in Minnesota led to a major change in his career. He and his recovering wife decided that he should devote full time to the ministry, and they began an eight-year series of pastorates which carried the Butlers throughout the eastern half of America and into Canada.

In October, 1876, they moved to Detroit, Michigan, where Thomas became associated with Central Church and a mission in Del Ray, a suburb.[33] His wife shared this ministry, lecturing for the Women's Christian Temperance Union, preaching on occasion, and editing a weekly temperance paper called *Truth for the People.*

To an active nine-year-old boy, the rigors of being the son of a stern minister began to arouse conflicts and broadened the gap between Burridge Butler and his father. In time Burridge began to rebel against not only his father but also the religion that the boy felt his father was serving at the expense of his family. The impact was so strong that 70 years later Burridge Butler could recall the time his father spanked him for raising questions in Sunday School. A teacher had remarked that there is only one way to go to heaven, whereupon Burridge had asked if it were not true that the little Chinese boy unaware of Christianity or religion would go to the same heaven. When word got back to Pastor Butler, young Burridge got a spanking. The boy also became embittered by cases in which he felt his father failed to practice what he preached.

Early in 1878 the Butlers moved to western Michigan where

[31] T. D. Butler, ed., *Poetry and Prose,* p. xi.
[32] T. D. Butler, ed., *Poetry and Prose,* p. xi.
[33] *Christian Standard,* November 4, 1876, p. 349.

Thomas became pastor of the Lyon Street Church of Christ in downtown Grand Rapids.[34] During this stay, which lasted little more than a year, Marie served as preacher at Byron, Michigan, and evangelized at Bailey, north of Grand Rapids.

By April, 1880, the family was in Canada where Thomas served the Church of Christ at Bowmanville, Durham County, Ontario.[35] A year later, the Butlers were at Akron, Ohio.[36] And within another two years they were living in Johnstown, Pennsylvania.[37] His wife continued her temperance and mission efforts—once delivering 28 hour-long addresses in 25 days, not counting some shorter talks—but her strength was failing her. She preached her last sermon at a church in Troy, Pennsylvania, on February 10, 1884, and died in Johnstown on March 28. After funeral services there, her body was transported to Louisville for burial.

She left behind her a teen-age son who would always be inspired by his kind, yet zealous, mother. Lacking a similar respect for his father and now able to exercise his independence, Burridge parted company with his father soon after Marie died. The father traveled southward to a new pastorate in Tennessee; the son returned to Louisville, embodying an odd blend of forces which he could sense but never fully control.

"My father was a preacher who pulled wings off of flies—he was a sadist," Butler told a friend late in life. "And my mother was a poet. I am a combination of both."

[34] C. Muller of the Central Christian Church, Grand Rapids, to author, April 12, 1967; *Grand Rapids City Directory,* 1878-79 (Grand Rapids, Mich.: R. L. Polk and Co., 1879), p. 343; *Christian Standard,* April 13, 1878, p. 117.

[35] Reuben Butchart, *The Disciples of Christ in Canada Since 1830* (Toronto: Canadian Headquarters Publications, 1949), p. 435; *Christian Standard,* April 17, 1880, p. 127.

[36] T. D. Butler, ed., *Poetry and Prose,* p. xiv; *Christian Standard,* May 7, 1921, p. 30; *Christian Evangelist,* January 20, 1921, p. 87.

[37] *Christian Standard,* June 9, 1883, p. 225.

A Scripps Man

CHAPTER 2

The *Prairie Farmer* of Butler's era often surprised publishers of other farm papers. They were not accustomed to seeing a farm paper devote its front page to photographs of convicts, the getaway car, the villains' notebook with hand-sketched plans for crime, and smiling heroes who brought the rogues to justice.

Prairie Farmer did not do so regularly, for much of its content dealt with the normal life and activities of farm people. However, cops-and-robbers reporting was a specialty. Editors of *Prairie Farmer* knew how to go about it with a flair that sometimes gave readers the excitement of a detective novel.

Such reporting came from Butler whose background had uniquely prepared him to champion farm people vigorously. He had given the cue to his approach almost as soon as he arrived at *Prairie Farmer* in 1909 as its new owner: "No man on earth can beat one of my readers." [1] Shortly after that, Butler expressed his editorial philosophy and plans to a reporter:

I like the freedom of the farm. I hate the conventionalities of life. I need room.

[1] *Prairie Farmer*, 81 (December 1, 1909), 12.

18

I have studied the farmer and believe he will appreciate the same grasp of affairs in his line which is the life blood of a daily newspaper.

I don't look upon a paper as a product of ink and paper, but a psychological product of ideas.

I am making a business paper for the farmer, just as keen as the city daily. . . .

I believe that no publication has ever made a lasting and substantial success—except upon its editorial merit. . . .

I find that in the territory of the paper, Illinois and the states adjoining, there are the most satisfactory conditions for such a publication. . . . The people are free and independent and I know they appreciate my kind of a paper, and I propose to spend all the money necessary to give them a paper as high in character as the people for whom it is issued.[2]

A reader who wished to speculate about the paper's future could get at least three hints from those comments. First, they reflected the views of a man who seemed strong-willed and self-sufficient. Second, they signalled the arrival of a newspaper man who was about to impose a newspapering logic upon *Prairie Farmer*. Third, they echoed some of the editorial philosophy of E. W. Scripps, a notable figure in American newspapering at the turn of the century.

The First Taste of Newspapering

Newspapering first got into Butler's blood when he was about 17 years old. Butler spent several weeks without work after he moved to Louisville following his mother's death. He lived first with his grandparents, although they were in a poor position to support him, having lost most of their assets during the Civil War. Butler, who already stood six-feet-four and weighed 200 pounds, reportedly got a job shoveling coal on the docks. Two months later he got a better job in a foundry by concealing his age. It lasted until the superintendent learned he was only 16 years old.

Next, according to somewhat conflicting accounts that he gave to others in his later years, he decided to be a streetcar conductor.[3] The street car firm informed him that to get a conductor's job he

[2] *Prairie Farmer*, 82 (February 15, 1910), 17.

[3] Facts about Butler's work experience in Louisville and Cincinnati are from the following sources: Neil M. Clark, "I've Never Lost Money By Calling a Spade a Spade," *American Magazine*, 111 (June, 1931), 67ff.; *Prairie Farmer*, 82 (February 15, 1910), 17; John W. Holland, "Let's Start Something," unpublished eulogy of Butler, no date, pp. 6-9; Taylor Hay, manager, Union League Club of Chicago, personal interview, June 12, 1967; James E. Edwards, former associate of Butler, personal interview, December 12, 1966; Julian Bentley, former associate of Butler, personal interview, January 24, 1967.

must pay a $25 bond. He tried without success to get the money from a wealthy elder in his grandfather's church. (Butler never forgave this "confounded hypocrite.") Discouraged, he returned to his tiny attic room, flung himself on the bed, and cried. His land-lady heard him and offered money from her savings (a kindness which Butler also never forgot). Butler's work as a conductor ended abruptly, however, with his dismissal. By one account he was fired for striking a customer who was abusive. By another he broke company rules in paying the fare of an elderly lady who had forgotten her coin purse. As this version goes, Butler slammed out of the company office swearing, "If you run this line so that a man can't help a poor old woman, you can all go to hell."

Then, as Butler related the story, he sat on the curb at Fourth and Broadway. Noticing a newsboy, he asked how he might get a job with the newspaper. The newsboy pointed to the nearby Courier-Journal Building where Butler soon got his first job in newspapering as a reporter for the young *Louisville Evening Times*, earning $6 a week. The *Evening Times*, which first appeared on May 1, 1884, was proving successful under an editorial motto: "Publish all the news without fear or favor. Do justice to all men, especially those who most object to having justice done them." [4] It catered to sensationalism and devoted most of its local front-page features to court actions involving crime or sex.

Butler hardly had time to master this editorial style because a week after he began the editor reportedly called Butler in, an-nounced, "You're no writer," and fired the boy.

Temporarily giving up hopes of a career in newspapering, Butler joined Uncle Tom's Cabin Show, a barnstorming outfit which, as Butler recalled, never made expenses. In Bardstown, Kentucky, the proprietor vanished on payday and left his troupe moneyless and at loose ends. Butler returned to Louisville and worked at various jobs through the fall and winter of 1885. Then he moved to Cincinnati and used his experience with the *Evening Times* as a lever for getting his second job in newspapering. This one was with the *Cincinnati Enquirer* as a sports writer.

After only one or two months at that job, Butler "had a great

[4] J. Stoddard Johnston, *Memorial History of Louisville from its First Settle-ment to the Year 1896*, II (Chicago and New York: American Biographical Publishing Co., 1896), 72; *The Story of Your Newspaper*, booklet published by the *Louisville Courier-Journal*, undated, p. 33.

hunger for somebody who knew me, cared about me." His loneliness led him to recall a girl named Winnie Whitfield who had lived next door to him eight years earlier in Grand Rapids.

An inquiry about train fare to Grand Rapids showed Butler that he had only enough money to get within about 20 miles of the city.[5] He took the Grand Rapids and Indiana Railroad as far as his money allowed, then hitch-hiked the remaining distance and arrived early in 1886, broke and with a rip in his pants. However, he found a warm welcome from his former neighbors, the I. J. Whitfields.

Grand Rapids gave Burridge Butler his first taste of success. It was alive and restless, just as he was. Situated at the swift, gliding rapids of the Grand River, it had doubled in size between 1880 and 1886 to a population of more than 50,000.[6] Immense forests of nearby pines and hardwoods offered more than 44 billion feet of merchantable lumber and Grand Rapids was at their southern doorway. Furniture was easily the city's largest manufacturing industry; [7] Grand Rapids had more than 30 furniture factories.[8] Business was active in the downtown district, tucked between the river and the sharply rising slopes to the east which housed the city's more prosperous residents.

Butler's first job in the city was with its oldest furniture manufacturer, Berkey and Gay. He worked in the shipping department of the six-story brick building on the corner of Canal and Hastings Streets, putting in 10 hours a day, six days a week, at $1 a day. His home was a room at 125 Court Street on the industrial west side of the river. Too restless for such a steady job, Butler began to write articles and take them to the *Grand Rapids Morning Democrat* just across the river. An editorial opening in March, 1886, gave him the chance for more excitement, a raise to $7 a week, and a solid step toward his career in publishing.

Grand Rapids had an over-supply of daily newspapers in early 1886: *Grand Rapids Eagle, Evening Leader, Morning Telegram,*

[5] Recollections of a description by Butler to Samuel H. Ranck, librarian, Grand Rapids Public Library. Reported in a letter dated October 31, 1941, from Ranck to Laurence W. Smith, president, Grand Rapids Board of Library Commissioners.

[6] L. Lloyd Shaw, ed., *The Industries of Grand Rapids* (Grand Rapids: J. M. Elstner and Co., 1887), pp. 8, 15.

[7] Shaw, pp. 14, 33.

[8] Rob H. Baker, ed., *The City of Grand Rapids* (Grand Rapids: B. F. Conrad and Co., 1889), p. 68.

Times, and the *Morning Democrat.* The city's surge of population from 16,500 in 1870 to 50,000 in 1886 had seemed to justify more newspapers, but Butler saw many of them die or change hands during his eight years there.

The *Grand Rapids Eagle,* a Republican evening paper under the proprietorship of A. B. Turner and Company, published both daily and weekly issues. It was the city's second oldest paper, started as a morning daily in May, 1856.[9]

The *Evening Leader* had been started in 1879 as an organ of the Greenback party. When Butler came to Grand Rapids, W. B. Weston was its manager and editor with offices at 95 Pearl Street, next to the *Morning Democrat.*

The *Morning Telegram,* youngest of the group, began on September 30, 1884, then merged with *Brezee's Herald* only a month after Butler joined the *Democrat.* A new moderate Republican paper called the *Telegram-Herald* grew out of the merger with Lloyd Brezee as its editor.[10]

First fatality after Butler's arrival was the *Daily Times,* a 16-year-old morning paper considered to be "free-swinging politically with no firm party allegiances." [11] The *Democrat* absorbed it on July 21, 1886.[12]

As a new staff member of the *Morning Democrat,* Butler found himself working for the city's oldest paper, if one counted its ancestors. Formed in 1865, it was one name change removed from the first daily in Grand Rapids, the *Daily Herald,* which began in 1855.[13] Politicians viewed the *Democrat* as the party's leading paper in Michigan, outside of Detroit. It was an unswerving, straight-laced party supporter.[14] Frank W. Ball had owned it for about four years when Butler arrived.

News about organized labor commanded considerable space in the *Democrat* during 1886, as did news about the activities of courts, churches, commerce, and commodity markets. Human interest also enlivened the columns. For example, when Butler arrived, the *Democrat* was busy covering an inquest into the death

[9] Z. Z. Lydens, ed., *The Story of Grand Rapids* (Grand Rapids: Kregel Publications, 1966), p. 518; Arthur Scott White, ed., *Incidents in the Lives of Editors* (Grand Rapids: White Printing Co., 1920), p. 42.

[10] Lydens, p. 519; White, p. 42.   [11] Lydens, p. 519.

[12] Albert Baxter, *History of the City of Grand Rapids, Michigan* (New York: Munsell and Co., 1891), p. 267.

[13] Lydens, p. 517.   [14] Baxter, p. 263; Lydens, p. 518.

of a woman after a Doctor Aiken's abortion efforts. Advertising depended heavily upon venders of all kinds of cures and medicines, from Dr. Pierce's Pleasant Purgative Pellets to Tutt's Pills for torpid livers.

Whatever its limits as a means of literary uplift, the *Democrat* offered just what Butler wanted: excitement, challenge, lively associates, and a personal idol. Butler entered the paper's "kindergarten," a term used by managing editor Tom Fletcher to describe the city editor's cub reporters. Guidance by city editor Henry Wanty and William M. Hathaway, an editorial writer, helped Butler improve his writing style which—despite the effort—never earned strong acclaim. Hathaway, whose huge brush mustache dwarfed his other fragile features, more than once roasted Butler for using the editorial "we" in a reportorial story.[15]

Butler also learned about the presses, type-setting, and page make-up. He learned to do his own illustrating, and his chalk plate work brought him into contact with the stereotyper, whose art he studied. All of this gave the novice an appreciation of the complicated processes involved in making a newspaper.[16]

But while other associates taught methods to Butler, he was getting his inspiration from the *Democrat*'s managing editor. Tall and congenial-looking, Tom Fletcher proved to be Butler's oracle and model. He was one of the leading newspaper workers of the city. A fine judge of copy, he was understanding whenever his workers tried to do their best, however ineptly. He also could be "a wild Indian with tommiehawk and scalping knife when a fellow tried to spring a fake on him."[17] For years Butler was to quote the editorial ethics of Tom Fletcher to his own associates. Butler remarked 25 years after leaving Grand Rapids, "Tom Fletcher is one of the few men I have met whom I never knew to lie or deceive, and his rare influence will live after him in the best that is in the lives of many of his 'boys'."[18] Even later, at the age of 73, Butler observed that "Ed Scripps must have worked for Tom Fletcher to have gotten his inspiration and sense of rugged editorial honesty."[19]

Butler's loyalty to the *Morning Democrat* lapsed only once. That was in 1887 when he joined the *Eagle*, whose day-work schedule might allow him to go to school and "add to and adorn an eighth

[15] White, p. 73.   [16] White, p. 36.   [17] White, p. 19.   [18] White, p. 38.
[19] *Grand Rapids Press,* January 24, 1941, p. 26.

grade education." [20] In a few months he returned to night reporting on the *Democrat* after offending the editor of the *Eagle*, who looked askance at live news. One night in the editor's absence Butler gave front-page play to a local murder and suicide.[21] Summarily fired, he never felt apologetic about this effort to do "some realistic reporting."

Spurred by men he respected, Butler progressed at the *Democrat* from reporter and illustrator in 1886 and 1887 to sports editor in 1888. Family roots formed in Grand Rapids as his grandparents and step-uncle moved from Louisville during mid-1886. His grandfather Christopher died shortly thereafter on September 14, 1886.

On the evening of May 31, 1889, staff members learned that the Conemaugh Lake Reservoir dam 16 miles above Johnstown, Pennsylvania, had burst and sent a wall of watery destruction 40 feet high upon the unsuspecting city. This disaster gave Butler what he later considered to be his most noteworthy reporting assignment. The *Democrat* sent him to Johnstown, and from June 1 through June 11 it carried a series of reports from the site. Butler got no bylines for his accounts, which appeared in the *Democrat* and which the Associated Press released, but he went all out to describe the scenes of destruction. As a result, he earned a certain editorial fame which followed him throughout his career. He also earned a promotion to city editor by 1890.

His second major event of 1890 came three days before Christmas when he married the young woman who had prompted his move to Grand Rapids four years earlier. Winnie L. Whitfield was the 24-year-old daughter of a pioneer Grand Rapids physician, Dr. I. J. Whitfield, who had come to the city in 1871.[22] Born October 11, 1866, at Big Rapids, Michigan, she was the second of five children, including three sisters and a brother.[23] Her jolly, outgoing manner appealed to Butler and seemed to have a moderating influence. An attractive, big-framed, slightly plump brunette with blue eyes, she could flash a broad smile and smooth things when he was blustering.[24] She was the home-loving, motherly type to which Butler could turn for a steadying hand.

[20] *Grand Rapids Press,* January 24, 1941, p. 26.   [21] White, p. 35.
[22] *Grand Rapids Press,* May 7, 1932, p. 13; December 10, 1934, p. 16.
[23] Mrs. Marvin L. Germain to author, June 9, 1967; Davenal W. Hardy to author, April 16, 1967.
[24] Margaret Howard and Harold Christopher, personal interview, March 22, 1967.

They were married in a double wedding at the Church of Christ, along with Winnie's youngest sister, Myrtie, and George E. Hardy,[25] an employee of the Michigan Trust Company.[26] His serious, meticulous manner differed greatly from that of Butler, but their mutual respect later led them into several business ventures.

Soon after marriage, Butler became state editor of the *Democrat*. He and Winnie moved to 155 Crescent Avenue, a more prosperous residential area atop the city's bluff, facing westward over the river and business center.[27]

Reminiscing much later, Butler counted these as rewarding years. Grand Rapids newspapers of the era, however competitive, employed what became a coterie of journalists who knew each other well and had their special haunts. The Morton House was more like a club than a hotel, for in the course of a day practically anyone in town whom a newspaper man ought to see drifted in and out. They formed a fellowship so enduring that their reunions extended at least 40 years after Butler left Grand Rapids. Members proudly cited the careers of alumni such as Fletcher, Frank I. Cobb, and Butler.

His associates considered Butler a "born newspaper man, a tremendous worker and an intense partisan," and added that occasionally his "boyish enthusiasm was a little ruthless." [28] Not afraid of a scrap, Butler once got into an argument with another staff member who went after him with a cane. The skirmish ended with Butler's foe hanging around his neck in an effort to stop the fistwork.[29] In Grand Rapids Butler first displayed another tactic which became a personal trademark. One Saturday afternoon a reporter approached Butler and announced that he was quitting the *Democrat*. Butler's arms fell folded upon the desk and his head dropped upon them as he sobbed, "I never in my life liked a man and began to get acquainted with him that he did not quit." [30]

Butler tried his first personal publishing venture in 1893. Noting a wave of enthusiasm for cycles, he and several friends decided to capitalize on the market. Their *Michigan Cyclist* first appeared in

[25] Kent County, Michigan, *Marriage Record*, Book 10, p. 244.

[26] Davenal W. Hardy, personal interview, April 28, 1967; Samuel H. Ranck to Laurence W. Smith, October 31, 1941.

[27] *Grand Rapids City Directory*, 1890-91 (Grand Rapids: R. L. Polk and Co., 1891), p. 252.

[28] White, p. 19.   [29] White, p. 30.   [30] White, p. 69.

1893 as a weekly which sold for $1 a year. It continued until 1898.[31]
As one observer summarized results: "They squandered brain
storms, pocket savings and great expectations in its behalf" only
to see it sink "into the troughs of the journalistic sea as the amateur
exuberance dwindled into apathy."[32]

In a broader sense, more than the *Michigan Cyclist* was sinking
into the journalistic sea during the early 1890's. In 1891 Frank W.
Ball had sold an ailing *Morning Democrat* to I. M. Weston.[33] Weston was determined to give Grand Rapids a real metropolitian
paper, copied along the lines of Chicago's *Herald*. He imported a
number of Chicago newspaper men, employed an unusually large
staff, and "dissipated a small fortune" selling advertising at less than
production costs.[34] The strategy had at least two effects: it led the
other papers of Grand Rapids to a precarious existence,[35] and it
caused friction within the staff of the *Democrat*, now headed by
outsiders. The new managing editor was a militant named Moses
Almy Aldrich who, during his second day, called a meeting of the
whole office force. He ordered everyone to line up at attention,
then informed them that they would address him as Colonel Aldrich and salute him when entering his office.[36] It was the only dress
parade he called, but no man as independent as Burridge Butler
would fail to react. Apart from that, Butler could see the *Democrat*
being outstripped by a new local paper, the *Morning Press*. As he
recalled later, the *Morning Press* "introduced to Grand Rapids real
journalism with capital and modern methods."[37]

Commercialism had attracted his interest, so Butler resigned from
the *Democrat* during 1894 and accepted a job in St. Louis publiciz-
ing Majestic steel ranges.

Butler and the Scripps-McRae League

When Butler's contract expired in 1895, he left the stovemaker
and moved to Chicago. Records are unclear about his work shortly
after he arrived, but they imply that he rejected an editorial open-

[31] *Grand Rapids City Directory*, 1894-99; *N. W. Ayer and Son's American Newspaper Annual*, 1897 (Philadelphia: N. W. Ayer & Son, 1897), p. 377.
[32] White, pp. 48-49.   [33] Lydens, p. 518.
[34] White, pp. 20, 69; B. D. Butler, quoted in *Grand Rapids Press*, January 24, 1941, p. 26.
[35] Frank I. Cobb, quoted in White, p. 41.
[36] White, p. 67.
[37] *Grand Rapids Press*, January 24, 1941, p. 26.

ing with the *Chicago Journal* and negotiated unsuccessfully to sell advertising for that paper. Butler recalled, "That summer the pleasant parks on the lake front afforded ample walking space for another unemployed." [38] He could use the peace and quiet, for Butler was about to enter the 12 busiest years of his life.

F. W. Kellogg, advertising manager of the Scripps-McRae League, offered Butler a position on the Chicago sales staff.[39] At the time, Scripps-McRae was beginning what would be an explosive growth under its founder, Edward W. Scripps. Scripps had dreamed for years about such a newspaper empire. Five years earlier, in 1889-90, he had lost control of the *Cleveland Press* and *Detroit News* to his older half-brother, James E.[40] Left with the *Cincinnati Post* and *St. Louis Chronicle*, E. W. had withdrawn to "lick his wounds" for a year or so.[41] By 1892 he was ready to start building again. During Butler's year of selling ranges in St. Louis, Scripps was pooling his resources with another half-brother, George H. Scripps, and Milton A. McRae. Out of that nucleus grew a vast, amorphous system which came to include the largest number of daily newspapers that had ever been established by one man. Before he retired in 1908, Scripps and his associates founded 32 newspapers and acquired 15 others.[42]

From probably the latter part of 1896 until he left the Scripps-McRae League in 1899, Butler was assistant manager of the Chicago sales office at 140 Dearborn Street. The Butlers lived on the south side during their first year in Chicago, at 799 50th Street, then moved to the west side. Professionally, he was in a new type of operation. Where he had sat at the feet of kind and patient Tom Fletcher in Grand Rapids, now he was force-fed into the orbit of a man who claimed that "the habit of subordination, obedience, and discipline was fatal to the development of any sort of greatness," yet even more firmly insisted upon one-man power.[43] This is not to say that E. W. Scripps stifled initiative among his associates. On the contrary, his powerful incentives of shared ownership earned

[38] *Grand Rapids Press*, January 24, 1941, p. 26. However, *Prairie Farmer*, 82 (February 15, 1910), 17, reports an interview with Butler noting that he sold advertising for the *Journal* for six or eight months.
[39] *Grand Rapids Press*, January 24, 1941, p. 26.
[40] Oliver Knight, ed., *I Protest: Selected Disquisitions of E. W. Scripps* (Madison: University of Wisconsin Press, 1966), p. 72.
[41] Knight, p. 78. [42] Knight, p. 78.
[43] Knight, pp. 62, 67, 79, 152, 171, 192, 260, 290, 300.

accusations that Scripps papers "devoured the youth" of their men, most of whom were young. Even so, his organization—however unstructured—was under his control and employees knew it. This lesson had a powerful effect upon Butler in future years. In fact, the origin of Butler's entire publishing philosophy snaps into sharper focus under the light of comparison with the philosophy of his remote-control teacher, E. W. Scripps. The following is some of Scripps' philosophy which became a part of Butler's own:

1. The core of Scripps' journalism was his blasphemous prayer: "God damn the rich and God help the poor." This philosophy, as Oliver Knight has pointed out, gave Scripps' newspapers a spirit of protest and a brand of independence.[44] They championed the rights of the common people, fought for reform and justice, and cheered the underdog. Scripps believed that newspapers should be honest and impartial witnesses, which they could be only if independent. He wanted his papers to be *news*papers, not political mouthpieces. Such a platform had an added appeal for Scripps because he learned that he could get rich championing the poor, and wealth had been one of his early goals. He insisted, however, that wealth is a byproduct rather than an end.[45]

2. Editors run the paper; business managers simply sell the paper and advertising space. Scripps followed an inviolate rule that the editor is supreme, holding full control over the composing room, and that the editorial and business departments should be divided.

3. In making up a newspaper, use many short articles. Scripps adopted the rule that every issue of every paper should contain at least 400 or 450 stories.

4. Each newspaper should be independent of other enterprises in the chain.

5. As an editor, a man can be noble of purpose and broad of vision, but as a businessman he must be hard-boiled and cold-blooded. Scripps aimed for a net profit of at least 15 per cent.

6. A newspaper should rely on circulation for much of its income to avoid undue dependence upon advertisers. This is related to his principle that a Scripps paper should be the tool of no interest group.

7. Gimmicks have no part in building circulation. He wanted

[44] Knight, p. 80.
[45] For a fuller discussion of this philosophy, see Knight, pp. 34-35, 40, 60, 80, 185, 272.

circulation arising only from the reader's desire to read the paper.

8. Advertising, a necessary evil, should be local; it must be in good taste. Scripps became the first newspaper publisher deliberately to exclude patent medicine advertising on principle.[46]

9. Newspapers are more than products of paper or ink, or even institutions. To E. W. Scripps, his newspapers were living organisms, each with its own personality. He considered them "children of his spirit," with the *Cleveland Press* as his first-born.[47]

10. It is exciting to start things. Scripps thrived on ideas rather than details, and his enterprises bored him more and more as they aged.

11. Avoid contact with both the rich and the poor. Scripps followed this guideline and once vowed that he would die for the common man but he did not want to live with him.

12. A successful man should retire when he is 40 years old. This became a company policy after Scripps concluded that the secret of one-man rule is in a succession of supreme commanders at about five-year intervals.

No available records show the extent to which Butler worked personally with E. W. Scripps. They undoubtedly were acquainted, for Scripps reportedly offered Butler $200 a week in 1899 if Butler would stay with the Scripps-McRae League as its advertising manager.[48] The young man clearly respected Scripps. Soon after Butler left the League he described Scripps as "a man of wonderful mind and executive force, of rare creative ability." [49]

Scripps Formula Applied: Clover Leaf Partnership

Another man in the organization watched Butler's progress with interest. F. W. Kellogg, Butler's supervisor, had ideas for a business of his own, and he saw in Butler a promising associate. Kellogg was a self-confident young man who had grown up as a protégé of Scripps. He began as a delivery boy for Scripps' first major success, the *Cleveland Penny Press*. After finishing high school, Kellogg joined the circulation department of the *Press* and became an advertising salesman a year later.[50] The boy's ambition and alertness

[46] Knight, p. 206.   [47] Knight, p. 72.   [48] Holland, p. 12.
[49] *Omaha Daily News,* October 15, 1899, p. 2.
[50] Winfield S. Downs, ed., *Encyclopedia of American Biography* (New York: American Historical Co., 1941), p. 454.

led Scripps to take Kellogg with him to Detroit as advertising manager of the *Detroit Evening News.* During Kellogg's first year in Detroit, the paper's advertising rose $200,000. The *News* soon became one of the nation's leaders in advertising revenue. Kellogg stayed until 1894 when he joined the Scripps-McRae League as director of advertising. At the time, Butler had just left Grand Rapids.

Another Scripps man who soon entered Butler's career was an imposing salesman named Larry V. Ashbaugh. Little more than a year older than Butler, Ashbaugh was a native of Freeport, Pennsylvania.[51] His first newspapering experience was as a reporter on the *Youngstown Telegram* in Ohio about the time Butler was with Uncle Tom's Cabin road show.[52] In 1894 Ashbaugh became business manager of a new paper, the *Kansas City World,* which began January 11.[53] He automatically became involved with the Scripps-McRae League when it later bought the *World.* Available records do not show how closely Butler and Ashbaugh worked in their positions with Scripps-McRae.

As Kellogg and Ashbaugh watched Scripps adopt his pattern of low-priced, independent papers in small cities, they began to consider using the system themselves. Urged to do so by George H. Scripps, they formed a partnership in 1899. George Scripps provided financial help; E. W. Scripps and McRae offered their "good will and . . . assistance."[54]

Like Scripps, the two partners "determined to associate with us the best men we could get, not only by giving them employment, but by helping them to acquire stock holding in the different publications that might be established. . . ."[55] Their first choice was Butler, who accepted and almost immediately was assigned to help form a new daily in Omaha, Nebraska. Kellogg and Butler moved to Omaha—the former as president and manager, the latter as editor—and set up at 114 S. 14th Street.[56]

[51] Louis A. Duermyer, "Ashbaugh Outline," mimeographed account, dated November, 1939, p. 4; *Proceedings of the Fifty-Eighth Annual Convention of the Minnesota Editorial Association,* Minneapolis, February 15-16, 1924, p. 57; *Minneapolis Journal,* March 8, 1923, p. 19.

[52] *St. Paul Dispatch,* March 8, 1923, p. 1.

[53] Carrie W. Whitney, *Kansas City, Missouri—Its History and Its People 1808-1908,* I (Chicago: S. J. Clarke Publishing Co., 1908), 395.

[54] R. S. Thain, "The Farm League List of Papers," *Agricultural Advertising,* 19 (May, 1908), 51.   [55] Thain, p. 52.

[56] *Omaha City Directory for 1900,* 26 (Omaha: McAvoy Directory Co. and Omaha Directory Co., 1900), p. 574.

Omaha looked like a promising market for young publishers whose success would depend upon the city's viability. Between 1880 and 1890, the population of Douglas County (encompassing Omaha) had quadrupled, from 37,870 to 157,782.[57] Drouth and depression between 1891 and 1897 had contributed to a decline of about 17,000 residents by 1900.[58] However, between 1890 and 1900 the state's total wealth had continued to grow.[59]

Butler watched the first issue of the *Omaha Daily News* come off the press Monday, October 9, 1899. It sold for a penny and consisted of only four pages. He had used the right-hand third of his front page for advertisements, a policy which the paper continued for years. Advertisers paid $1 a column inch for space, prorated on the basis of 20,000 circulation. In that first issue, then, they paid only a fraction of the base rate because circulation was 6,445.

Kellogg and Scripps were the identified publishers; Butler was listed as editor. In his commencement editorial the new editor stressed his paper's independence. He promised that news of the day would be printed in fact, not diluted or colored with prejudices or politics. His aim for the *Daily News* was to "give the reader light from all sides" at a price all people could afford.[60]

Later issues during the first week included letters to the *Daily News* from E. W. Scripps, James E. Scripps, and A. M. Hopkins, editor of the *Kansas City World*. All exhorted the new Omaha paper to fearless independence and honesty.

At the end of its first week, the *Daily News* had a circulation of 7,524. Progress during the next two months convinced Kellogg and his associates that their project might succeed. On December 1 they incorporated the Daily News Publishing Company with a capital stock of $50,000 and a debt limit of $25,000. Incorporators were Kellogg (president), Butler (vice-president), Butler's friend, George E. Hardy (treasurer), Homer T. Ashbaugh (secretary), and Edward S. Kellogg.[61]

Two well-rooted morning dailies—*Omaha Morning World-Herald* and *Omaha Daily Bee*—watched the newcomer in editorial silence. The *World-Herald* had a circulation of slightly more than 30,000

[57] *Nebraska Blue Book,* 1899 and 1900 (Lincoln: State Journal Co., 1899), p. 163.
[58] *Nebraska Blue Book,* 1901 and 1902, p. 163.
[59] *Nebraska Blue Book,* 1920, p. 436.
[60] *Omaha Daily News,* October 9, 1899, p. 2.
[61] Douglas County, Nebraska, *Corporation Record,* Book K, pp. 56-58.

and sold for 2¢ a copy or $4 a year by mail subscription. The *Bee* averaged about 25,000 and was higher priced, selling for 5¢ a copy or $8 a year.

Strong partisanship had characterized the *World-Herald* in recent years because William Jennings Bryan had become chief of its editorial staff on September 1, 1894. His part-time responsibility gave him a daily platform for political discussion, and he continued in the capacity until July, 1896, when Democratic, National Silver, and Populist national conventions united in nominating him for the presidency.[62]

Political protest also played an important part in the 28-year-old *Omaha Bee.* A Jewish Bohemian immigrant named Edward Rosewater had founded it on June 19, 1871, to influence public opinion in favor of a bill then pending before the state legislature to create a board of education for Omaha. Rosewater, a fast and pungent writer, still edited the paper in 1899.[63]

Despite steady gains in circulation and advertising, Kellogg and Ashbaugh faced a severe financial crisis in 1900, a crisis which was to change Butler's role.

Encouraged by continuing good times and the healthy growth of their *Omaha Daily News,* Kellogg and Ashbaugh decided to expand more. On March 1, 1900—less than five months after their venture in Omaha began—they printed the first issue of a new sister paper, the *St. Paul Daily News,* under Ashbaugh's direction. Suddenly they found themselves without money at the death of George H. Scripps, the man on whom they had counted to back them. Their cash amounted to only $2,400, and that belonged to an employee. Scouting frantically for new funds, Butler travelled to Grand Rapids and managed to get a loan of $25,000. Kellogg, Ashbaugh, and Butler built their papers on that money. Personally, it was a turning point for Butler because it made him a full partner in what was to become a profitable venture.

[62] Federal Writers' Project, *Nebraska—A Guide to the Cornhusker State* (New York: Viking Press, 1939), p. 136; William Jennings Bryan, *The First Battle: A Story of the Campaign of 1896* (Chicago: W. B. Conkey Co., 1896), pp. 60, 168, 188, 238, 259, 621.

[63] Richard Hewitt, *A History of Omaha 1854 to 1954* (Omaha: P. C. Doss and Co., 1954), p. 84; John T. Bell, *Omaha and Omaha Men* (Omaha, Nebraska, n.p., July, 1917), p. 51; Federal Writers' Project, p. 136; Arthur C. Wakeley, ed., *Omaha: The Gate City and Douglas County, Nebraska* (Chicago: S. J. Clarke Publishing Co., 1917), p. 305.

Butler returned to Omaha after the crisis and settled briefly to the task of keeping his paper on the move editorially. By July 1 he had added a Sunday edition. His *Daily News,* which in later years became highly sensationalized, held to a restrained editorial policy. Butler used a clean-looking page make-up characterized by many short articles. Advertising columns of 1900 were free from patent medicine advertising and consisted instead of good quality local retail advertising.

In September Kellogg turned the business management over to a new associate named Mel Uhl and moved to Kansas City for work on the *Kansas City World.*[64] Butler in turn relinquished his editorial duties and left Omaha because of a pending family emergency—his wife had developed a tumor. In order to be closer to her family, the Butlers returned in late 1900 or early 1901 to Chicago, where he staffed the partnership's "foreign" advertising sales office with a new associate, C. D. Bertolet. Butler retained his title as vice-president of the *Omaha Daily News,* however.[65]

Kellogg and Butler left a robust young paper behind them in Omaha. The *Daily News* passed its first birthday with an average circulation of 20,000 and a special 16-page celebration issue. Already boasting more readers in Omaha and Douglas County than any other newspaper, it was proud to have "delivered Omaha from the reputation of having no journals except personal newspapers apparently published solely for the gratification of personal revenge and without thought as to how much the city was injured by this style of journalism."[66] The paper began to crusade in 1902, helping to close policy shops and gambling houses in Omaha, protecting public schools from the "grip of machine politics," agitating for street signs, and contributing to the success of various public enterprises.

Conversely, crusading helped the *Daily News* work its way into the Omaha market. On its third birthday, now with an average circulation of 33,895, the *Daily News* announced that it had become first in circulation among dailies of Nebraska. Advertising revenue had nearly tripled. Prosperity allowed it to invest $60,000 in a new Goss

[64] Downs, p. 454; *Omaha City Directory for 1901,* p. 426; *Omaha Daily News,* September 24, 1900, p. 2.

[65] *Omaha Daily News,* September 24, 1900, p. 2; *Lakeside Directory of Chicago,* 1901 (Chicago: Lakeside Press, 1901), p. 367.

[66] *Omaha Daily News,* October 9, 1900, p. 4.

press, "largest and fastest in Nebraska." [67] The paper moved into
expanded quarters during 1906. By 1908, Butler's last full year of
association with his partnership, the "People's Paper" stood at a
record circulation of 57,000. It was a loud crusader, hounding the
water and gas companies in a local fight for municipal ownership.
Front pages carried heavy doses of sensationalism, intrigue, and
violence. This editorial approach would continue through February 13, 1927, when the *Omaha Daily News* consolidated with the
Omaha Bee. William Randolph Hearst took over the new *Omaha
Bee-News* within a year. In 1937 Hearst, by then thoroughly frightened by the Gargantuan $126 million debt he had created, was
forced to liquidate many of his newspapers.[68] He sold his Omaha
paper to the *World-Herald* and thereby removed Butler's first newspaper from the Omaha scene.[69]

Some hectic years nagged Butler after he left Omaha. He became
a long-distance commuter as he and his failing wife agreed that
she would get better care at home in Grand Rapids among relatives.
Upon returning to Michigan, probably in 1901, Winnie stayed with
her older sister, Addie, throughout the ensuing illness.[70] Butler
boarded at the Lexington Hotel in Chicago, although his advertising work for the growing newspaper chain demanded constant
travel. He arranged his schedule to allow visiting his wife regularly.

Meanwhile, Kellogg, Ashbaugh, and Butler grew more confident
about the publishing formula they were applying. The Omaha
paper was progressing under its policy of low-priced issues, tight
financial control, and editorial championing of the common people.
So too was the *Daily News* in St. Paul, a city of nearly 200,000
"long well known as a graveyard of newspaper ventures." [71] Forecasts of failure had greeted Ashbaugh and his group when they
arrived and incorporated the Daily News Publishing Company of
St. Paul on July 16, 1900. The board of directors included Ashbaugh
as president; J. Harry Lewis and Nevill W. Reay as vice-president

[67] *Omaha Daily News,* November 9, 1902, p. 17; October 9, 1903, p. 1.

[68] W. A. Swanberg, *Citizen Hearst* (New York: Charles Scribner's Sons,
1961), pp. 484-485.

[69] Federal Writers' Project, p. 136; Hewitt, p. 86.

[70] Margaret Howard, personal interview, March 22, 1967; *Grand Rapids
Press,* May 7, 1932, p. 13; Davenal W. Hardy, personal interview, April 28,
1967.

[71] W. B. Hennessy, *Past and Present of St. Paul, Minnesota* (Chicago: S. J.
Clarke Publishing Co., 1906), p. 192.

and secretary, respectively; Butler; and Butler's silent partner–
friend, George Hardy of Grand Rapids.[72]

Observers had reasons for predicting an early death when they
learned that St. Paul would get a new *Daily News*. For one thing,
the city had watched two papers of that name die without ceremony
within the past 20 years. The first lasted only eight months during
1879-80; the second, which began in 1887, struggled for seven years
before payroll pressures killed it.[73] Also, St. Paul had three dailies
in 1900, two of them very well established. Oldest and second
largest was the *Pioneer-Press*, whose ancestry traced back to less
than two months after Congress organized the territory of Minnesota; it had absorbed some 30 rivals in the meantime. A loyal Republican paper, the *Pioneer-Press* listed an average circulation of
31,252 during February, 1900. Subscriptions sold for $4 a year by
carrier, half again that of the *Daily News*.

A second well-established competitor was the *Daily Dispatch*,
which had shown "remarkable progress" during the 10 years to
1900 and led the local field with a circulation of 44,300.[74] Like the
Pioneer-Press, it was no newcomer, for it had been established
before 1870. It sold for 10¢ a week by carrier or $3 a year by mail.[75]

Ashbaugh's other competitor, the *Daily Globe*, was the youngest
and most vulnerable of the group because of a parade of changes
in management and ownership after it was founded in January,
1878. The *Globe* also was St. Paul's most expensive paper at $6 a
year by carrier, $4 by mail—double the rates for Ashbaugh's *Daily
News*.[76]

A third source of skepticism by onlookers in St. Paul was the
fact that the *Daily News* began under modest conditions. It was
printed on an old-fashioned Potter press at 94-96 E. 4th Street.

Therefore, few had reason for enthusiasm when they saw the
first four-page edition on March 1, 1900. It looked puny compared
with the 10- to 20-page editions of its competitors. But it was
not puny-looking by accident; it was another pea in the Scripps
pod: four pages, many articles, advertisements on the front page,

[72] Ramsey County, Minnesota, *Book of Incorporations*, Book I, pp. 124-126.
[73] Hennessy, pp. 191-192; Henry A. Castle, *History of St. Paul and Vicinity*
(Chicago and New York: Lewis Publishing Co., 1912), p. 334.
[74] Hennessy, p. 189; *St. Paul Dispatch*, March 1, 1900, p. 6.
[75] *St. Paul City Directory*, 1900 (St. Paul: R. L. Polk and Co., 1900), p. 97.
[76] *St. Paul City Directory*, 1900, p. 97.

a one-cent price tag and that trademark banner—"The Independent Newspaper." Editor Ashbaugh even used in his introductory editorial much of the same copy that Butler had used to announce the first edition of the *Omaha Daily News*. However, Ashbaugh reached more readers than Butler had, judging by his average circulation for March of about 10,000.

Some proven associates helped Ashbaugh introduce his paper. F. E. Crawford, first city editor of the *St. Paul Daily News*, had spent his entire newspaper career in Minnesota, most recently as managing editor of the *Globe*.[77] Advertising manager was J. Harry Lewis who had worked with Ashbaugh in Kansas City, as had business manager Nevill W. Reay. Reay, in fact, had grown up working for papers which Scripps owned. As a 15-year-old boy he started collecting for the *Cincinnati Post*. His later work for the Scripps-McRae League led him to the *Kansas City World* where he earned Ashbaugh's respect as an auditor.[78]

Circulation of the St. Paul paper exceeded 20,000 at its first birthday. Editors concluded that their paper ". . . has made good the promise of a clean, condensed, impartial and honest newspaper."[79] They listed local accomplishments which the *Daily News* had helped make possible, including war on fake medical concerns, defeat of a franchise "grab," adoption of a new city charter, and a move to compel public service corporations to submit reports.

After two years, circulation of the St. Paul paper was nearly 30,000 and after three years, nearly 34,000.

A restlessness for more growth carried the partners into a three-paper scrap for existence in Des Moines, Iowa, by 1902. Kellogg became president of the Des Moines News Company, which had published the *Des Moines Daily News* since 1881.[80] Ashbaugh became vice-president and J. J. Hamilton retained his title as general manager. The *Daily News* and its evening competitor, the *Capital*, were competing on about an equal footing in terms of circulation. And both were hounding the morning *Register and*

[77] Hennessy, p. 193.

[78] See biographical facts about Lewis and Reay in Theodore Christianson, *Minnesota—The Land of Sky-Tinted Waters*, III (Chicago: American Historical Society, 1935), 85-86; Hennessy, pp. 192-193; *Minneapolis Journal*, December 26, 1933, p. 1; *St. Paul Dispatch*, December 26, 1933, p. 1; *St. Paul Daily News*, March 1, 1900, p. 2; Thain, pp. 52-53.

[79] *St. Paul Daily News*, March 1, 1901, p. 1.

[80] *Des Moines Directory*, 1902 (Des Moines: R. L. Polk and Co., 1902), pp. 100, 291, 1083.

Leader, which, while holding no advantage in circulation, was somewhat pre-eminent.[81]

During this same period, the partnership—beginning to identify itself as the Clover Leaf League—took part ownership in the Scripps-McRae paper which Ashbaugh had helped establish, the *Kansas City World.*[82] Kellogg had charge of this endeavor, which soon proved ill-fated.

The partners apparently held minor interest in both the *Des Moines Daily News* and the *World;* Scripps held control. Butler apparently never worked directly with either paper.

In mid-1903 Butler moved to Minneapolis to start another evening daily. This one, named the *Minneapolis Daily News,* was entirely his responsibility. He was its president and publisher from the day it incorporated, August 5, 1903, with a capital stock of $100,000.[83] Just as its stock was double that of Butler's paper in Omaha, so were its problems. For one thing, he was under the pressure of helpless responsibility to his dying wife. The 1904 Minneapolis City Directory listed him as a resident of Grand Rapids, which indicates that he must have spent considerable time with her there. He also maintained a business listing in Chicago. Winnie Butler died in Grand Rapids on July 26, 1904, at an age of less than 38 years.[84] At the time Butler's new paper was nearing its first anniversary in an extremely competitive market. Even though Minneapolis was a growing city, two papers were active in their domination. The *Tribune,* which published a morning and evening edition, averaged 85,558 in daily circulation for the first five months of 1904.[85] The *Minneapolis Journal,* an evening competitor, averaged more than 57,000.[86] Another paper, the *Times,* ran a poor third with a circulation of about 29,600.[87] Butler's *Daily*

[81] *N. W. Ayer and Son's American Newspaper Annual,* 1904, p. 252; Cyrenus Cole, *I Remember, I Remember* (Iowa City: State Historical Society of Iowa, 1936), pp. 251, 253.

[82] Whitney, p. 395, states that control passed to Clover Leaf. However, Kellogg maintained (Thain, p. 52) that Clover Leaf did not own the controlling stock.

[83] Hennepin County, Minnesota, *Miscellaneous Record,* 95, p. 134. Articles of incorporation of the Daily News Company of Minneapolis.

[84] Kent County, Michigan, *Death Record,* Book 6, p. 159.

[85] *Minneapolis City Directory,* 1904 (Minneapolis: Minneapolis Directory Co., 1904), p. 7.

[86] *N. W. Ayer and Son's American Newspaper Annual,* 1904, p. 434.

[87] *N. W. Ayer and Son's American Newspaper Annual,* 1904, p. 435.

News was hardly making a dent with a circulation of less than 15,000.

One of the possible reasons readers failed to respond quickly to the *Minneapolis Daily News* was that it did not enjoy the same price advantage as had the Omaha paper. The *Tribune, Times,* and *Daily News* all sold for 1¢ an issue; the *Journal* sold for slightly more. Competitors also were using some imaginative devices for building circulation. For example, the *Journal* aroused interest through its 12-passenger motor car which offered scenic 14-mile tours of the city for 25¢. Minneapolis had only about 500 autos at the time, which probably accounted for the novelty of this offer.[88] The *Tribune,* which "proudly wore its badge of Republican partisanship," also lacked little modesty in pursuit of circulation. Under W. J. Murphy, it was "not averse to attracting the reader with a regular quota of crime and sex sensationalism."[89] Editorially, the *Times* had operated as an independent since it was founded in 1889, but was suffering badly in 1904 from financial setbacks and management turnovers.[90]

In response to such competition, Butler borrowed F. E. Crawford from the sister paper in St. Paul. Crawford remained in Minneapolis as managing editor for more than a year, after which a Minnesotan named John Burgess stepped into the position. Burgess eventually became president of the company.[91]

While Butler was laboring in Minneapolis between 1903 and 1909, the Clover Leaf partnership continued its expansion. On December 28, 1904, Clover Leaf introduced the *Rural Weekly,* a "high-powered mail order paper" published in association with the *St. Paul Daily News.*[92] It sold for 25¢ a year, or 10¢ a year under

[88] Horace B. Hudson, *Hudson's Dictionary of Minneapolis and Vicinity,* 8 (Minneapolis: Hudson Printing Co., 1904), xvi, 8; *Minneapolis Journal,* "Fiftieth Birthday 1878-1928," 1928, p. 5.

[89] Bradley L. Morison, *Sunlight on Your Doorstep* (Minneapolis: Ross & Haines, 1966), p. 20.

[90] Horace B. Hudson, *A Half Century of Minneapolis* (Minneapolis: Hudson Publishing Co., 1908), p. 220; Willoughby M. Babcock, "The *Minneapolis Star,* the *Minneapolis Tribune* and their Predecessors," a manuscript prepared by the Curator of Newspapers, Minnesota Historical Society, March 18, 1955, p. 7.

[91] Lee Brothers Historical Collection of Portraits of Prominent Citizens of Minnesota of the Twentieth Century. Sketch of Burgess, dated November 22, 1917, in Galleries of the Minnesota Historical Society, St. Paul.

[92] *Rural Weekly,* December 28, 1904, p. 1; Harold Shugard, personal interview, June 26, 1967.

special offers. Advertisements featured patent medicine, real estate, investments, and beauty care while editorial material catered to an isolated rural reader suffering from boredom:

"Tale of Horrors in Electric Box"
"Woman Wears Men's Clothes"
"This Millionaire's Wife Earns $4 a week"
"Calls Her 'Ice,' But Still Loves Her" [93]

In July, 1906, the Clover Leaf sold its interest in the *Kansas City World* to Scripps-McRae, who killed it in 1908.[94] In turn, Clover Leaf acquired the *Rural World* of Kansas City. The year 1906 also saw Butler and his partners buy control of the *St. Joseph Star* (which had begun publication a year earlier) and found their fifth paper, the *Sioux City Daily News*. By bringing in new talent through stock incentives, they continued their rapid growth into 1907. They founded the *Daily Star* in Duluth, Minnesota, in June, 1907, and ended the year by buying control of the *Farm Magazine* of Omaha.

An apparent trend toward rural audiences and the accompanying low subscription prices suggest that the partners were trying to drive circulation deeper into the market of common readers. For example, the *Sioux City Daily News* sold for $1 a year against competitive dailies selling for as much as $4. Likewise, the *Duluth Daily Star* sold for $1 against dailies charging $5-6.

Continuing its rapid action, Clover Leaf sold its interest in the *Des Moines Daily News* during February, 1908, under competition from a potent new team at the *Register and Leader*: Gardner Cowles, Sr., and Harvey Ingham.[95] On May 15, 1908, Clover Leaf took over the ownership of *Prairie Farmer*, Chicago.

Three months later, it entered into an agreement with the St. Louis Republic Company, publisher of two St. Louis farm papers, *Farm Progress* and the *Twice-a-Week Republic*. Out of this agreement to share advertising sales efforts came an announcement during August that "one of the most important organizations of farm publications in America" had been formed.[96] Called the Farm League List, it consisted of *Prairie Farmer, Farm Progress, Twice-a-Week Republic, Farm Magazine,* and *Rural Weekly* of St. Paul. Its

[93] *Rural Weekly,* December 28, 1904, pp. 2, 8.
[94] Thain, p. 52; Knight, p. 766.
[95] William J. Peterson, *The Pageant of the Press* (Iowa City: State Historical Society of Iowa, 1962), p. 9; Cole, pp. 300-301.
[96] Thain, p. 50.

owners claimed a combined circulation of more than 700,000. By
this time, the Clover Leaf partners were declaring themselves to
be the first American publishers to give farmers on the rural routes
low priced daily papers, delivering "more daily rural route circulation . . . to the most prosperous people on earth than any other
publishers in America." [97] The *Rural World* of Kansas City, with
another 120,000 circulation, was not a part of this new Farm League
List, perhaps because it competed directly with the St. Louis farm
papers.

Despite—or perhaps because of—its frenzy of expansion, the
original Clover Leaf partnership was about to dissolve. Kellogg,
in fact, had moved to California two or three years earlier, about
the time Clover Leaf sold its interest in the *Kansas City World*.
In a professed retirement (for he had reached 40 years of age,
that magic mark for associates of E. W. Scripps), he spent several
months a year on business involving Clover Leaf.

Butler also passed the 40-year mark in early 1908, which may
have been one of his reasons for leaving the newspaper chain.
Butler told a reporter soon after buying *Prairie Farmer* that he
had left Clover Leaf because "things were running smoothly, money
was easy and plenty, but the business was established—fixed." [98]
This sounds like something he would conveniently say for public
consumption because the Clover Leaf operation in 1908 appears
to have been anything but fixed. A more compelling argument is
that Butler left because of disagreement among the partners. [99]
The nature of the disagreement remains unknown, but Butler's
silent partner and friend, George E. Hardy, interceded to protect
the financial interest of both. Some evidence suggests that Butler
became disenchanted with a trend by the partnership toward lower-
quality advertising and lower editorial standards. He may have
become discouraged in his efforts with the Minneapolis paper. And
he may have felt himself being squeezed out, for in 1908 he was
president of only one of the nine Clover Leaf papers.

[97] Thain, p. 52.

[98] *Prairie Farmer*, 82 (February 15, 1910), 17.

[99] Indications of support for this argument arise from recollections by per-
sons later associated with Butler: James Edwards, personal interview, Decem-
ber 12, 1966; Leslie Troeger, personal interview, January 8, 1967; George
Cook, personal interview, January 13, 1967; Herman Steen, personal interview,
January 25, 1967; Davenal W. Hardy, personal interview, April 28, 1967.
However, no documentary evidence has been located.

Whatever the combination of reasons, Butler sold his interest during the first half of 1909 and took ownership of *Prairie Farmer* as part of his settlement. As he left Clover Leaf, he could scan an operation which was still progressing. His original *Omaha Daily News* was at new highs in advertising and circulation. Ashbaugh's paper in St. Paul had nudged the *Pioneer-Press* out of second place with a record circulation of more than 40,000. The *Minneapolis Daily News* was up to nearly 30,000 circulation but still far behind the *Journal* (about 76,000) and the *Tribune* (about 103,000). The *Duluth Daily Star* was earning profit after one year, although its life would be short. *St. Joseph Star* was "growing faster . . . than any St. Joseph paper has ever grown before." [100] The *Sioux City Daily News* was progressing although it still was far behind competitors. The *Rural Weekly* of St. Paul, *Rural World* of Kansas City, and *Farm Magazine* of Omaha were attracting profitable patent medicine advertising as they forced circulation into the rural home.

Personally, Butler took nine years of publishing experience out of the Clover Leaf partnership. His total 24 years of newspapering had offered him a panorama of publishing which encompassed problems of the reporter, editor, advertising salesman, production man, artist, circulation director, publisher, and stockholder.

By then Butler knew the rigors of competition. He had played midwife to new papers trying to catch the breath of life amid the muffling efforts of established competitors. He knew how advertisers reasoned in deciding which publications would get their life-giving revenue. He had formed opinions about the audience a newspaper should serve, the part a paper should play in its community, and the editorial stance which such a role demands. Twenty-four years of experience had led him to feel confident in predicting how readers would react to a publisher's efforts.

In short, Butler left Clover Leaf and entered farm publishing with a formula for successful newspaper publishing, a formula which he inevitably applied to the farm publishing field. The methods which he used on *Prairie Farmer* to the surprise of his fellow farm publishers appear more understandable in the light of that formula.

[100] Thain, p. 51.

Out of the Middle Years

CHAPTER 3

Farm people of Illinois, who in mid-1909 were busy tending a crop which looked like it might break records, had no way of knowing that they were about to be claimed by a self-chosen guardian and champion. The notice came quietly on page three of the July 15th issue of *Prairie Farmer,* sandwiched among assorted articles and advertisements about cream separators, axle grease, hog dip, and Hood's Sarsaparilla. It read simply, "Burridge D. Butler, Publisher."

Very few saw this first announcement of change in control of the "Oldest Publication of its Class in America," for only one out of six farmers in Illinois subscribed to *Prairie Farmer.* For those who saw the notice, it meant nothing because they had not heard of Butler.

Like its readers, *Prairie Farmer* was looking for a good year in 1909; in fact, it needed a good year more than many of the farmers it sought to serve. Financial records show that Butler took over a paper which was long on tradition and short on vigor:

May 1, 1901—April 30, 1902	$ 355 profit [1]
May 1, 1902—April 30, 1903	7,846 loss

[1] From minutes of the annual meetings of Prairie Farmer Publishing Com-

May 1, 1903—April 30, 1904	18,211 loss
May 1, 1904—April 30, 1905	7,596 loss
May 1, 1905—April 30, 1906	10,515 loss
May 1, 1906—April 30, 1907	10,065 loss

Not even the Civil War or the Chicago fire of 1871 which swept away its office and equipment had confronted *Prairie Farmer* with a greater threat to its future.

The crisis did not arise overnight, or even within a 10-year period. In a larger sense, it appears to have accumulated during more than 50 years of uncertainty, error, and change arising from leadership which was sometimes inspired but often erratic.

Start of the Middle Years

Staff members of *Prairie Farmer* refer to the period of 1857-1909 as the middle years. Significantly, that period connects two strong personalities, John S. Wright and Burridge Butler. Lloyd Lewis has recorded, in *John S. Wright—Prophet of the Prairies*, the life of this vigorous reformer who founded the *Union Agriculturist and Western Prairie Farmer* in January, 1841.[2] The middle years began in September, 1857, when ownership of *Prairie Farmer* passed out of Wright's hands and into those of his printers, James C. and William H. Medill. He lost the paper because of a national financial panic, a crop failure, and vanished editorial prestige connected with his interest in a reaper which failed. The Medill brothers also found no success in their new enterprise and sold *Prairie Farmer* on October 1, 1858, to Emery and Company which, since January, had been publishing an agricultural weekly in Chicago, *Emery's Journal of Agriculture*. The new combination appeared as *Emery's Journal of Agriculture and Prairie Farmer* until December 22, 1859, when the title became simply *Prairie Farmer*.[3]

---

pany during the last six years of ownership by Rand, McNally and Company. Financial records are not available for 1908 through mid-1909 when *Prairie Farmer* was under the control of Clover Leaf Newspapers.

[2] Lloyd Lewis, *John S. Wright—Prophet of the Prairies* (Chicago: Prairie Farmer Publishing Co., 1941).

[3] *Emery's Journal of Agriculture and Prairie Farmer*, 19 (January 6, 1859), 8; *Prairie Farmer*, 20 (December 22, 1859), 1; 113 (January 11, 1941), 17; and Stephen C. Stuntz, "List of the Agricultural Periodicals of the United States and Canada Published During the Century July 1810 to July 1910," U.S. Department of Agriculture, Miscellaneous Publication No. 398 (Washington: U.S. Government Printing Office, 1941), p. 139.

Henry D. Emery edited the paper with Charles D. Bragdon, who had been on the staff for two years before Wright lost it. Bragdon's departure in May, 1861, created an opening for W. W. Corbett, former assistant editor who had been with the paper since Emery bought it.[4]

Issues printed on high-quality paper help indicate the prosperity of *Prairie Farmer* during the years of civil war. On February 21, 1863, it announced that it had bought the *Farmers' Advocate* from Jeriah Bonham, a commission merchant in Chicago who had controlled that paper for three years.[5] Shortly thereafter in December, 1864, the owners of *Prairie Farmer* also bought the *Illinois Farmer*, a seven-year-old paper published in Springfield and edited by M. L. Dunlap on his farm in Champaign County.[6]

Encouraged by profits and the end of the war, *Prairie Farmer* began a monthly edition in German during mid-December, 1865. Called *German Prairie Farmer*, it was intended to "meet the wants of the Germans of the West who comprise so large a portion of the inhabitants in many parts of the country."[7] The new venture lasted no more than two years, however.[8]

The prosperity of *Prairie Farmer* during and immediately after the Civil War led its editors to celebrate a 25th anniversary with this proclamation: "The time has come when western farmers need not feel dependent upon the east for an agricultural paper."[9] Three years earlier it had started printing a statement claiming the largest circulation of any paper in its class in the west and northwest.

With sights set for a circulation of 50,000 by 1868, *Prairie Farmer* broadened its base of ownership in early 1867. Prairie Farmer Company, which was incorporated on March 23, encompassed the old Emery and Company plus the labor and capital of other persons. Incorporators were Emery, Corbett, Henry T. Thomas, Albert T. Emery, and Joseph F. Bonfield.[10]

[4] *Prairie Farmer*, 23 (May 2, 1861), 288.
[5] *Prairie Farmer*, new series, 11 (February 21, 1863), 114; Richard Bardolph, *Agricultural Literature and the Early Illinois Farmer* (Urbana: University of Illinois Press, 1948), p. 100; Stuntz, p. 56.
[6] Stuntz, p. 81; Bardolph, p. 99.
[7] *Prairie Farmer*, new series, 16 (December 23, 1865), 460.
[8] Issues of the period did not report when the German edition ceased. Bardolph, p. 168, states that it proved a failure after a few issues. However, the Stuntz list, p. 139, indicates that it may have continued until 1868.
[9] *Prairie Farmer*, new series, 17 (January 6, 1866), 8.
[10] *Prairie Farmer*, new series, 19 (March 23, 1867), 188.

Henry D. Emery and Corbett continued as co-editors along with Thomas, whose name first appeared on the staff listing on January 4, 1868, a month before Burridge Butler was born near the Peewee Valley in Kentucky.[11]

Evidence suggests that some of this outward optimism was as much because of competitive pressure as of progress. A publication edited in Detroit and entitled the *Western Rural* was established during 1864. By 1868 it professed to have more subscribers in Illinois than *Prairie Farmer,* and the latter responded by changing its format to imitate the new competitor.[12] More significant than its change to a full-size, five-column newspaper format, however, was a shift in editorial emphasis which affected *Prairie Farmer* for many years.

Rejecting its former emphasis upon agricultural and horticultural information, the new *Prairie Farmer* added more "pleasant and instructive reading of a miscellaneous nature." [13] Under a new banner—*Prairie Farmer,* "A Weekly Journal for the Farm, Orchard and Fireside"—it began its new approach. Readers found themselves confronted with articles about laborers on the Nile, fossil horses in North America, "Cousin Jack's Courtship," and poems by Oliver Wendell Holmes. The resulting potpourri allowed editors to insist in early 1869, ". . . there is no agricultural paper in the United States that contains more reading material than *Prairie Farmer,* and none west of New York that contains anywhere near so much." [14] The paper added Rodney Welch to its editorial staff on January 2, 1869, and drew on special contributors from eight states in an effort to broaden its base of circulation geographically.[15] However, quantity and breadth could not solve the problems engulfing a paper which was trying to be all things to all people, especially on the eve of a destructive fire, another financial panic, and another error which would take away the prestige which *Prairie Farmer* had regained.

Chicago's great fire on October 8, 1871, left the company's office and equipment at 96 W. Randolph Street in ruin. However,

[11] *Prairie Farmer,* new series, 21 (January 4, 1868), 8.

[12] Roy V. Scott discusses the nature of this competition and later developments involving the *Western Rural* in *The Agrarian Movement in Illinois, 1880-1896* (Urbana: University of Illinois Press, 1962), pp. 22-36; also see Bardolph, footnotes on pp. 95, 103.

[13] *Prairie Farmer,* 39 (July 4, 1868), 4.

[14] *Prairie Farmer,* 40 (January 16, 1869), 20.

[15] *Prairie Farmer,* 40 (January 2, 1869), 4.

Emery managed to save his list of subscribers, account books, business papers, and a full set of past issues. A two-page issue went into the mail on schedule the following week, and *Prairie Farmer* retained its record of continuous publishing.

Two years later it weathered another threat, the panic of 1873.

A third problem arose within a year, ironically due to the paper's traditional interest in helping farmers cooperate. *Prairie Farmer* had been dedicated at birth to education and agricultural cooperation. In fact, it was established by the Union Agricultural Society, the state's first multi-county union of agricultural societies.[16] In 1867 *Prairie Farmer* adopted the cause of what became the Grange movement. American farmers by then were feeling grievances as the nation adjusted from an agrarian to an industralized economy. Hard money, high freight rates, monopoly, and loss of political power emerged as issues which dominated the rural scene until nearly 1900.

Heading this movement by farmers was a society called the Patrons of Husbandry, or Grange, which began in 1867. Within Illinois the first Grange meeting convened in the office of *Prairie Farmer* on April 23, 1868.[17] That particular Grange failed to develop, but Oliver Kelley—who founded the movement—continued to use *Prairie Farmer* for informing farmers about the movement.[18] In 1870, when the Illinois State Grange was organized at Chicago, "the list of officers chosen read almost like the roster of the *Prairie Farmer's* editorial staff."[19] Corbett was made General Deputy for the state; Emery became Overseer; Welch became Lecturer; and a special contributor, Edgar Sanders, was Gate Keeper.

Accordingly, the national and state Granges had ready access to readers of *Prairie Farmer* during the next four years. Unfortunately for the paper, some of its staff members got involved in more than publicity for the Grange. Corbett and two other employees of the paper, H. T. Thomas and John P. Reynolds, had formed a com-

[16] Alfred C. True, "A History of Agricultural Education in the United States, 1785-1925," U.S. Department of Agriculture, Miscellaneous Publication No. 36 (Washington: U.S. Government Printing Office, 1929), p. 84.

[17] Oliver H. Kelley, *Origin and Progress of the Order of the Patrons of Husbandry in the United States* (Philadelphia: J. A. Wagenseller, 1875), p. 97, cited in Scott, p. 56.

[18] Solon J. Buck, *The Granger Movement* (Lincoln: University of Nebraska Press, 1913), pp. 45-46.

[19] Bardolph, p. 162.

mission firm which the Grange helped finance. The bankruptcy of their firm came to light in late 1874 when a small notice signed by Corbett and Reynolds announced it, explaining: "Financial manager Thomas had been using the paper of the firm in his own private and profitless operations, crippling it beyond hope of continuance."[20]

This distasteful affair, mixed with the financial strain of a year earlier, undoubtedly damaged *Prairie Farmer* with respect to both finances and prestige. In fact, issues from 1875 through 1884 listed neither editors nor the publisher. City directories for that period show that H. D. Emery continued as president of Prairie Farmer Company until late 1877 or early 1878, after which his associate, Joseph Bonfield, replaced him for several years. Corbett remained as editor through 1878, after which a veteran staff member, Jonathan Periam, became editor.

A native of New York City, Periam had come to Illinois in 1838 and farmed from 1841 until 1849 when he began writing. First a correspondent for *Prairie Farmer,* then a special writer, he later served as associate editor before becoming editor.[21] Apparently he continued as editor from 1879 through 1884, but got no credit in the paper.

Meanwhile, the management of *Prairie Farmer* changed at least twice, first when J. B. Barton replaced Bonfield as president in 1881. Records do not show details of the next step, except that on February 17, 1882, Rand, McNally and Company of Chicago bought the paper from a man named Charles R. Williams for $20,000.[22]

Rand McNally chose to experiment with *Prairie Farmer,* which had been filled with standing-head columns, material borrowed from other periodicals, and little local information. In August, 1882, the board of directors changed its name to the *People's Illustrated Weekly and Prairie Farmer,* "A Journal for Everybody." Less than two months later the board voted instead to publish two weekly papers: *Prairie Farmer,* "A Weekly Journal for the Farm, Orchard and Fireside"; and the *People's Illustrated Weekly,* "A Journal for Everybody."

[20] *Prairie Farmer,* 45 (December 12, 1874), 396.
[21] *Prairie Farmer,* 84 (January 1, 1912), 10. For other biographical information, see *Prairie Farmer,* 60 (June 16, 1888), 390.
[22] Minutes of a meeting of the board of directors, Prairie Farmer Publishing Company, February 17, 1882.

People's Illustrated Weekly lasted less than four months. Stockholders voted on February 1, 1883, to discontinue it after they learned that the two publications operated at a loss of $6,522 during 1882. It lost another $2,246 in 1883 before stockholders killed it.

Effort by Orange Judd

Two years of losses convinced Rand McNally that the matter called for a major change. On April 18, 1884, it entered into a two-year contract with one of the nation's best-known agricultural editors, Orange Judd, who had earned a reputation on the *American Agriculturist*. Judd agreed to serve as editor and business manager for $30 a week and one-half of the company's net profits. He and his sons also got the right to buy up to 800 shares of the capital stock.[23]

Judd assured his readers in the first issue, "We have not come a thousand miles to take part in post-mortem games."[24] Drawing on 31 years of experience in farm publishing, he set out to make every page "clean, safe and trustworthy." Nearly all medical advertising was gone within a month. Then Judd improved the quality of paper and increased the number of subscribers seven-fold by the end of his first year in Chicago. His paper operated at a loss of $9,309 between March 1, 1884 and May 1, 1885.[25]

Continuing his drive for circulation, Judd distributed more than 150,000 "specimen editions" during August, 1885. Parallel stress on editorial work is implied by an expanding staff which soon included three associate editors (including his son, James), seven editors of special departments, and 39 special contributors. Gradually, Judd's efforts brought results as *Prairie Farmer* lost $3,869 in 1885-86, $1,771 in 1886-87, and earned a profit of $3,679 during 1887-88. However, on June 9, 1888, Judd announced that he was leaving because he and the proprietors differed about finances.

Lean Years

His successor as editor was Jonathan Periam, whom Judd had

[23] Minutes of a meeting of the board of directors, Prairie Farmer Publishing Company, April 18, 1884.

[24] *Prairie Farmer*, 56 (May 3, 1884), 280.

[25] Minutes of a meeting of the board of directors, Prairie Farmer Publishing Company, May 12, 1885.

replaced four years earlier. In the meantime, Periam had edited the *Farm, Field and Stockman.*[26]

Prairie Farmer changed little in style during the next five years, except that it showed its first color. Black ink on yellow stock greeted readers on the cover of their New Year's number in 1893. The paper's first color printing was another seven years away. However, *Prairie Farmer* was far from colorful editorially. Full-page advertisements promoted clubbing offers which promised readers almost anything for buying or selling subscriptions: watches, pocket knives, rifles, wall maps, mandolins, or books about bee culture.

The paper underwent another editorial blackout after Periam left in December, 1893, this time to retire because he was more than 70 years old. Issues listed no editor during the following 12 years, the first of which were among the darkest in its history. Issues between 1894 and 1902 were very light on advertising and heavy on promotion for *Prairie Farmer;* editorial matter was seasonal but not newsy.

According to city directories, Lewis C. Brown managed *Prairie Farmer* during this time. He came to the paper in 1894, remained about three years, left during 1898 and 1899, and returned as managing editor from 1900 through 1904. Records do not show who, if anyone, was editor until December 21, 1903, when a man named J. J. Edgerton assumed that position.[27] He remained until January 1, 1905.

Prairie Farmer Home Mazagine

Rand, McNally and Company decided to experiment again in 1902, and the September 25 issue carried a new monthly supplement called the *Prairie Farmer Home Magazine for Country Gentlewomen.* It was a 16-page magazine which accompanied the regular issue, and it differed in its high-quality, slick stock. Women wrote the articles, which covered a wide range of topics: school legislation, telephones for country homes, social life on the farm, styles, and recipes. It also contained love fiction and a youth page.

[26] *Prairie Farmer*, 60 (July 7, 1888), 438; *Lakeside Directory of Chicago,* 1886 (Chicago: Lakeside Press), p. 1167; *Lakeside Directory of Chicago,* 1887, p. 1225.

[27] Edward F. Dunne, *Illinois—The Heart of the Nation,* III (Chicago: Lewis Publishing Co., 1933), 49.

In general, the quality of this supplement was much higher than that of *Prairie Farmer*.

Prairie Farmer Home Magazine never carried much advertising, a lack which may have put an end to it. Beginning in May, 1903, it became a section of *Prairie Farmer* rather than a supplement, carrying its own cover page but no separate issue number. A year later—in June, 1904—the section became "The Prairie Farmer Magazine" and shifted away from features of interest to women. Rand McNally dropped the section entirely after December, 1904, ending what apparently had not been a profitable endeavor despite its commendable quality.

Some editorial vigor appeared in *Prairie Farmer* in 1905 after the arrival of a new editor on March 30. He was a 30-year-old former editor of *Drovers Journal* named Chauncey P. Reynolds, and he became the first identified editor of *Prairie Farmer* since late 1893. Under his guidance the paper began to get interested in matters of timely interest to farmers of Illinois. Items discussed hard roads for Illinois, politics, rural free delivery, and current farm events. He was a picture enthusiast who encouraged readers to send photographs, and he experimented with color. For the first time in many years, *Prairie Farmer* seemed to be directing its attention again to agriculture and farm life in Illinois rather than rural people at large.

Finances again crowded in, however, and the paper reverted to a more threadbare condition during 1906: fewer pictures, paper of poorer quality, more general serials, and less local coverage. It began requiring cash in advance for subscriptions after December, 1906, and obviously was in trouble financially.

"There is no begging for money, no statements that we are hardup, no suggestions that we should be favored if not to the subscriber's interest—nothing of the kind," it reported in March, 1907.

On January 1, 1908, *Prairie Farmer* changed from publishing weekly to semi-monthly (1st and 15th). Its rationale to readers was that the change would allow larger issues and paper stock of higher quality, but issues did not increase in size proportionately, and subscription prices remained the same as before. Another sign of financial strain was a full-page advertisement on the front cover of the issue for February 15, 1908, after which the paper sold most of its front covers. It even offered $1-a-year subscriptions for 35¢, or 10 issues for 10¢ on a trial basis.

This was the rather desperate state in which Butler and his Clover Leaf partners found *Prairie Farmer* in mid-1908. A year later, after pumping a high share of patent medicine advertising into the paper, Clover Leaf turned *Prairie Farmer* over to the man who would bring it out of its erratic middle years.

Backed by Agriculture's Prosperity

Butler had important factors working in his favor as he took control of *Prairie Farmer*. One was his newspapering experience which had given him a broad view of publishing. He also brought strong financial backing to the paper. Corporate records do not show what he paid for it, although associates believed that he bought it for only $20,000–$24,000, little more than Rand McNally had paid 27 years earlier.[28] By 1909 Butler had personal resources amounting to about $250,000, and he took special care to impress readers with the fiscal soundness of his *Prairie Farmer*.[29] Starting on December 1, 1909, the masthead of each issue contained the statement: "Paid-up-Capital $150,000.00." A nearby item assured readers that "$150,000 GUARANTEE Is Right Back of Every Prairie Farmer Advertisement." [30]

A third and vital element in Butler's favor was the fact that he bought *Prairie Farmer* during one of the most favorable periods in the history of American agriculture. The period between 1897 and the end of World War I is commonly known as agriculture's golden era. Most of the land immediately available for farming had been taken by 1900, the farm population had leveled off, and farming became intensive rather than extensive under pressure of increasing values of land and farm products.[31]

[28] An obituary in the *Chicago Daily News*, March 31, 1948, p. 1, stated that Butler bought *Prairie Farmer* for $20,000. One of Butler's early employees, Herman Steen, recalled during a personal interview with the author that Butler said he paid $22,000. Another associate, Dave O. Thompson, reported in his unpublished memoirs, p. 10, that the purchase price was $24,000.

[29] Neil M. Clark, "I've Never Lost Money by Calling a Spade a Spade," *American Magazine*, 111 (June, 1931), 130.

[30] *Prairie Farmer*, 81 (December 1, 1909), 12.

[31] Harold U. Faulkner, *American Economic History*, 6th ed. (New York: Harper and Brothers, 1949), p. 391.

Prices for farm commodities had risen through strong demand in Europe and at home and stood 89 per cent higher in 1910 than in 1899. Meanwhile, prices which farmers paid for production supplies and equipment were well in line with income. The cost of farm machines had dropped an average of 49 per cent between 1860 and 1900. A two-horse riding cultivator that had cost $45 in 1860 cost only $28 in 1900.[32] This decline in prices of farm machinery had stopped in about 1900 and prices remained steady for about 10 years. They were due to rise sharply under the influence of war between 1910 and 1920.

Rising prices for the commodities farmers sold and low prices for items they bought had given them a measure of prosperity and a buoyant optimism during the first decade. Average annual value of farm products in Illinois had risen from nearly $186 million in 1895-99 to more than $288 million in 1905-9.

Butler's first five years as publisher of *Prairie Farmer* found agriculture in what later became identified as the period of agriculture's most wholesome relationship with commerce and manufacturing. For about five years after 1910, agricultural prices varied around the general price level with relatively small fluctuations, and the 1910-14 period became agriculture's parity base period to which its leaders often looked wistfully during future decades.

The outbreak of war in Europe set up a wave of shocks throughout agriculture after 1914, driving prices sharply higher. Where corn growers of Illinois netted about $4 an acre during 1900-1904, the figure doubled by 1910-14, then doubled again to $16.21 an acre during 1915-17. A grower of winter wheat netted about $1.69 an acre during 1900-1904 and was getting $11.85 an acre profit by 1915-17.[33] In Illinois producers owned livestock valued at close to $194 million in 1900; by 1918 that figure had more than doubled to $444,682,000.[34]

Mortgage indebtedness increased to the point of concern during agriculture's golden era. However, the value of farm property in Illinois grew even faster, nearly doubling within 10 years.[35]

With this prosperity came the urge for a higher standard of

[32] Ernest L. Bogart and John M. Mathews, *The Modern Commonwealth, 1893-1918*, vol. V of *The Centennial History of Illinois* (Springfield: Illinois Centennial Commission, 1920), p. 60.
[33] Bogart and Mathews, p. 495.
[34] Bogart and Mathews, p. 498.
[35] Bogart and Mathews, p. 68.

living on the farm. A life that had required only food, shelter, clothing, and security now demanded more. New homes and barns appeared across the countryside between 1910 and 1920. By 1920 nearly three out of four farm homes in Illinois had telephones. More than half of them had electricity (either from a power line or home plant) and owned automobiles. One Illinois farm out of 10 owned a tractor by 1920.[36]

This new prosperity moved farm equipment, washing machines, pianos, and a wide range of other items onto the farm. Items which in former years farm families could only dream about while browsing through their "wishbooks" from Sears Roebuck and Montgomery Ward now came within reach.

Butler could not have anticipated all of this, but he gained from it. New demand on the farm meant new and larger advertisers for *Prairie Farmer* during the first 10 years that he owned it. The good times gave Butler a chance to put the paper on its feet financially, before farm prices and profits nose-dived during 1920.

Starting Fresh

Once he had moved from Minneapolis to Chicago, Butler seldom talked about his earlier work, which might imply that he was intent upon making a complete break. His ownership of *Prairie Farmer* promised him the independence he craved and perhaps a more reputable kind of enterprise than some of his earlier projects.[37] He told a reporter in Chicago soon after he arrived, "It gives me a chance to do the work which I like best, to deal in things which ring true. . . . It brings me in contact with just the kind of people I like, and enjoy doing business with. No politics, no schemers, just square-toed affairs. . . ."[38]

Perhaps Butler saw the promise, too, of a certain security with *Prairie Farmer* that he had not felt with the Clover Leaf. By then he could appreciate the effort involved in keeping a publication alive for 68 years.

Finally, this period marked the start of a new life for Butler in

[36] From summary figures for 1920, reported in U.S. Department of Commerce, *U.S. Census of Agriculture*, 1950, vol. I, part 5 (Illinois) (Washington: U.S. Government Printing Office, 1952), pp. 3, 6.
[37] Thompson, p. 15; James Edwards, personal interview, December 12, 1966.
[38] *Prairie Farmer*, 82 (February 15, 1910), 17.

the sense that he had gained a new wife. She was a strikingly attractive, petite easterner named Ina Hamilton Busey. Her family
in this country started with Henry Busey, who came from England
some time before the American Revolution and is said to have been
with his friend George Washington during the famous "Crossing
of the Delaware." [39] In honor of that friendship, he named his first
son (Ina's great-grandfather) George Washington Busey.

Ina Busey had been born in Baltimore on November 1, 1871, to
two Virginian cousins, Norval H. and Emma Busey, as the third
of four children.[40] Her father was a pleasant, easy-going commercial
photographer; her mother, a more powerful personality than he,
was a devout Episcopalian with a passion for opera. The Busey
family lived in "a kind of genteel poverty" while in Baltimore,
with the girls attending a girls' school.[41]

When she was about 20, Ina accompanied her parents to Europe
where her father studied painting, which he practiced with limited
success as long as he lived. The family remained in Europe—mostly
Paris—for about 10 years. After returning to America, the Buseys
lived in New York City with all four children doing something to
earn money. Ina shopped on commission for out-of-town buyers
and sold advertising art. For a time the parents, four children, and
a grandchild lived in a duplex studio apartment at 23 W. 67th
Street.

The most animated child in her family, Ina shared the good looks
of her parents. Gay, quick, impulsive, she often chattered at a great
rate, sometimes seeming almost scatter-brained. However, when
important matters arose, she almost always uncovered an ability
to handle them.[42]

Butler's first acquaintance with her remains unidentified. According to one version, he spotted Ina from a balcony overlooking
the dance floor at a function in New York City nearly two years
after Winnie died, then announced, "There's a very beautiful woman
and I'm going to marry her." [43] At the time, she reportedly was

[39] William W. Hinshaw, Jr., to George Cook, January 16, 1967.
[40] Chart 3, Thomas Henry Busey Branch, William W. Hinshaw, Jr., "The
Busey Family in America" (undated); certified extract from the Register of
Marriages, Church of the Transfiguration, New York, July 30, 1906.
[41] Hamilton Cottier to author, May 29, 1967.
[42] Hamilton Cottier to author, May 29, 1967.
[43] George Cook, personal interview, January 13, 1967.

going with or engaged to a tobacco magnate.[44] The courtship appears to have been relatively short. One of the first things that Butler did was to take his prospective bride to New Jersey for approval by his first wife's sister, Myrtie, and her husband George Hardy.[45] Soon afterwards, he reportedly gave Ina two alternatives; she could marry him either tomorrow or the next day.[46] The result was that on July 3, 1906, the couple exchanged vows before the Botticino marble altar and ornate carved oak reredos of the famous wedding chapel in the Little Church Around the Corner.

They were married not without some reservation on the part of Ina's parents, who hardly knew what to think of this large, exuberant midwesterner. Indeed, the couple which departed for a honeymoon to Europe in mid-1906 differed in several respects. Ina was attractive, refined, almost regal in bearing, and immaculate in garb. Butler, standing head and shoulders taller, could be gruff, uncouth, and most unconcerned about whether or not his socks got changed.[47] But the marriage between Butler and his "rose"—as he called her—would last until he died more than 40 years later.

The honeymoon trip abroad remains largely undocumented, except for the time he got arrested for stepping over the guard rail in one European hall, mounting the king's throne, and shouting, "Down ye varlets!" in a display of showmanship.[48]

Three years later, as he and Ina Butler moved to Chicago from Minneapolis in September, 1909, he had adjusted to his new marriage and set aside the grief which followed the death of his first wife.

Butler's Approach

Butler apparently reached several conclusions about the approach he would take in rejuvenating *Prairie Farmer*. Influenced by his background in newspapering, he envisioned *Prairie Farmer* as a business paper for the farmer, "just as keen as the city daily." [49]

[44] Margaret Howard, personal interview, March 22, 1967; Glenn Snyder, personal interview, August 31, 1967.

[45] Davenal W. Hardy, personal interview, April 28, 1967.

[46] Davenal W. Hardy, personal interview, April 28, 1967.

[47] George Cook, personal interview, January 13, 1967; Jack Williams, personal interview, December 26, 1966; Emmett McLoughlin, *People's Padre* (Boston: Beacon Press, 1954), p. 113.

[48] Harold Christopher, personal interview, March 22, 1967.

[49] *Prairie Farmer*, 82 (February 15, 1910), 17.

Such a paper required that every issue be "filled with original high-class editorial matter that challenges comparison among farm journals." [50] Looking at sources of funds to finance an active editorial program, he chose to reject the whole field of patent medicine advertising which had formed the basis for the farm papers in his Clover Leaf group. "I have no ambition to run a mail-order paper of immense circulation," Butler concluded, turning his back on the possibility of continuing *Prairie Farmer* as another *Rural World* or *Rural Weekly*.[51] To have done otherwise might have shaped a far different future for *Prairie Farmer* than the one it found.

Butler also elected to turn his back on the free-wheeling circulation methods that had characterized his farm papers in the Clover Leaf group, methods which encouraged advertisers to suspect everyone's claims of circulation.

Years later, Butler said that when he came to *Prairie Farmer* he studied the rules which the paper's founder had followed. Of these, Butler said he chose to keep five:

1. Put no half-truths in the paper.

2. Learn every new wrinkle in relation to agriculture.

3. Send reporters and subscription men into the field to get "hot news" from the farmers.

4. Strive to make the paper contribute to the whole of the farm family.

5. Determine to accept no advertising which would deceive the people, and put service to the farmers ahead of money-making for the paper.[52]

With these decisions as guidelines, Butler began to organize his nine-member group on the 12th floor of the Boyce Building at the northwest corner of Dearborn and Madison Streets. His editor, C. P. Reynolds, became a vice-president of the company as Butler applied some incentives which he had learned from Scripps.

Butler's younger brother, William Radcliffe Butler, became secretary and advertising manager. W. R. was not without credentials for the new position, for his career had always plowed along in the newspapering wake of his more aggressive brother, from Grand

[50] *Prairie Farmer*, 82 (February 15, 1910), 17.

[51] *Prairie Farmer*, 82 (February 15, 1910), 17.

[52] Thompson, p. 69; John W. Holland, "Let's Start Something," unpublished eulogy of Butler, no date, pp. 15-16.

Rapids to the Clover Leaf papers to *Prairie Farmer*.[53] However, his tenure as advertising manager of *Prairie Farmer* was relatively short because, favoring his mother, he much preferred reading ancient poetry or the history of Roman emperors to selling advertising.

New assistant advertising manager was Charles P. Dickson, a nephew of Ina Butler, who soon replaced W. R. and headed the advertising department until 1942.[54] Dickson had worked with Butler on the *Minneapolis Daily News*.

Butler's circulation manager was E. T. Wood, who had been on the staff before Butler took over.[55] For business matters, Butler relied on Gus A. Holt, a former auditor with Clover Leaf who had been transferred to *Prairie Farmer* from Clover Leaf headquarters in St. Paul during February, 1909.[56] Holt soon shifted from auditing to circulation where he became recognized nationally as an authority.

With the arrival of 1910, Butler made what some observers consider one of his wisest editorial moves, adding as new associate editor a farmer by the name of Frank I. Mann. Mann was an articulate farmer-scientist from Gilman who was decades ahead of his time in many respects. While the average farmer in Illinois was growing 16 bushels of winter wheat an acre, Mann had an eight-year average of 54 bushels an acre.[57] While the average yield for corn in Illinois was 35 bushels an acre, Mann was averaging 83 bushels and talking about growing 200-bushel yields.[58] His 500-acre farm became a focus point among farmers throughout the state partly because of the yields it produced and partly because of the methods Mann used to get them. He grew crops almost exclusively in a day of more diversified farming and used no livestock manure. Instead, he followed the Illinois system of permanent soil fertility, which drew on crop rotations, rock phosphate, and limestone. Mann's new position as soil fertility editor for *Prairie*

[53] *Grand Rapids City Directory*, 1891 through 1900 (Grand Rapids, Mich.: R. L. Polk and Co.); R. S. Thain, "The Farm League List of Papers," *Agricultural Advertising*, 19 (May, 1908), p. 53.

[54] Thompson, p. 57.

[55] *Agricultural Advertising*, 21 (August, 1909), 364.

[56] *Prairie Farmer-WLS Round-Up*, 1 (August, 1948), 3; Thompson, p. 417.

[57] Bogart and Mathews, p. 495; *Prairie Farmer*, 92 (October 9, 1920), 33.

[58] Bogart and Mathews, p. 495; *Prairie Farmer*, 92 (October 9, 1920), 33; 84 (October 15, 1912), 8.

Farmer gave him a platform for his evangelism; it also enhanced
the paper's prestige and effectiveness for many years.[59] He answered questions by the hundreds in his columns.

Seven other new associate editors and seven special contributors
began writing for *Prairie Farmer* in 1910, each as an expert in some
segment of farming or homemaking. Most were from the midwest
and several were widely known among farmers of Illinois. Not full-
time employees, they supplemented the efforts of Butler's small
staff in Chicago.

Editorially, *Prairie Farmer* began to change in September, 1909,
starting with higher quality paper. Cover pages formerly devoted
to quiet pastoral scenes and tables of contents gave way to news
articles and news pictures as Butler and Reynolds shifted to a
newspaper page make-up. *Prairie Farmer* took "a backward step
forward" in October by reintroducing the ornate masthead which
had been killed 20 years before. (Butler considered it one of the
most artistic heads that ever appeared in a farm publication.)[60]
Once again Reynolds got a chance to exercise his love of photographs, printing between 10 and 30 of them in each issue.

New columns began to appear, such as "Crops and Soil Treatment," "Destruction of Animal and Vegetable Pests," "Talks with
the Lawyer," and a "Land Department and Information Bureau
for the Benefit of Home Seekers." The major articles in each issue
usually featured events of local interest. For example, during the
growing season of 1910 *Prairie Farmer* published crop reports from
various parts of the state. Articles stressed news about fairs, farmers' institutes, corn (the state's major crop), and timely issues such
as farm roads in Illinois. It appeared that Butler aimed to get as
much mileage from local news as his readers expected from the
Ruthstein steel shoes they saw advertised in *Prairie Farmer* during
1910.

Also noticeable is the fact that in the same issue which Butler
used to extend his first welcome to "the new members of The
Prairie Farmer family," he took the first step toward protecting that
"family." That issue—December 1, 1909—contained the first in a
38-year chain of crusading articles by *Prairie Farmer* on behalf of
its readers. Under the front-page headline "Harpooned by the Milk

---

[59] For more complete biographical sketches of Frank I. Mann, see *Prairie
Farmer*, 90 (November 2, 1918), 11; 109 (October 23, 1937), 23-24.

[60] *Prairie Farmer*, 81 (October 15, 1909), 12.

Distributors," it aired grievances of dairymen in northern Illinois
against milk distributors in Chicago.[61]

Early Progress

Responding to Butler's efforts with little delay, the circulation
of *Prairie Farmer* rose from about 40,000 in 1908 to nearly 70,000
by late 1910, then exceeded 100,000 by early 1915. Total pages increased from 520 in 1909 to 796 in 1911. Never timid about promoting his work, Butler bought two pages in *Agricultural Advertising* to shout in April, 1910: "B. D. Butler turns the Searchlight on
the Reasons for the Tremendous Increase in the Pulling Power of
the Prairie Farmer. My phenomenal reconstruction of PRAIRIE
FARMER must get the attention of every advertiser." "I took an
old paper and made it sparkle with freshness," Butler explained.
"I have delighted in lavishing money on the upbuilding of this
great power in Illinois agricultural affairs." He closed the advertisement by assuring readers, "I back Prairie Farmer." [62]

His combination of results and audacity attracted new advertisers. By 1910 readers began to see offers to buy a new Hudson
Touring Car for $1,150 or a Sears, Roebuck and Company Model
"L" for $495. They hardly would have thought about buying an
automobile three years earlier. Cement companies began to adver-
tise in issues accompanied by editorial articles about the advantages of concrete for homes, farm posts, hog houses, and other uses.
Manufacturers of gasoline engines also bought space as the farmer
became interested in this new way to pump his water, saw his
wood, shell his corn, spray his orchards, shear his sheep, run his
cream separator, sausage grinder, feed and fanning mill, washing
machine, and grindstone and otherwise help him and his family do
more work with less time and trouble.

Progress of the paper was set back temporarily when Reynolds
died of typhoid fever on November 21, 1910, leaving only two full-
time members on the editorial staff: Frank M. Chase, associate
editor, and James E. Dorman, new dairy editor, who had joined
the staff only a week before Reynolds died.[63] Three months later—
on March 1, 1911—the name of Leslie Troeger first appeared on

[61] *Prairie Farmer,* 81 (December 1, 1909), 1.
[62] *Agricultural Advertising,* 21 (April, 1910), 370-371.
[63] *Prairie Farmer,* 82 (December 1, 1910), 16.

the staff listing. Troeger, who brought experience from the *Iowa Homestead*, became livestock editor and general field reporter under Butler's instruction to "get next to the real farm people of Illinois." [64]

In the meantime Butler continued searching for an editor to replace Reynolds. He talked about hiring Dr. Cyril Hopkins, a well-known agronomist from the University of Illinois, but friends discouraged the idea because it might result in a *Prairie Farmer* with too little stress on livestock. Arthur J. Bill of the *Farmers Voice* expressed interest in the position. However, Butler's interest converged upon a bulletin editor for the Iowa Experiment Station. Clifford V. Gregory, a 27-year-old graduate of Iowa State College, had written Butler about the editorship in early December.

Gregory had been raised on a farm near Mason City, Iowa. As boys, he and a brother had handled much of the farm work because their father preferred carpentry to farming. Gregory earned money for college by farming and writing articles about college activities on assignment from newspapers. By the time he had completed his degree in animal husbandry in 1910, Gregory had sold articles to *Country Life* and written a bulletin, "Pure Seed Investigations," which earned praise as a concise piece of writing.[65] He continued on the staff for one year as an editor and instructor of journalism.

A pleasant, outgoing man, Gregory had a frame five feet nine inches tall, crowned with a prematurely shiny bald head which became a source of comment from those he met. When his sons traveled with Gregory in later years, people joked constantly about their having more thair than their father. The follow-up remark almost invariably was, "But if you have as many brains in that head as your father has, you'll be a great man." [66]

Gregory had an incisive mind aided by an excellent memory. He loved to get at the crux of issues, to analyze and reduce them to their simplest form. The same love created a strong personal pride in clear and simple writing.

Butler offered Gregory the editorship with these remarks: "I ask you to come largely on account of your personal character and the feeling that we could work together harmoniously and effectively.

[64] L. E. Troeger, personal interview, January 8, 1967.

[65] C. V. Gregory, "Pure Seed Investigations," Iowa Agricultural Experiment Station, Bulletin 99 (popular edition, 1908), Ames, Iowa, 14 pp.

[66] Merrill Gregory, personal interview, January 14, 1967.

Your actual qualifications I can only at best guess at and I say this meaning to be only complimentary. You must be the judge of this in making your decision, and it will be up to you to demonstrate by your work that you have in you the ideals and ability to make a great editor."[67]

Two days later Gregory returned word of his acceptance to begin a relationship which extended more than 26 years. Dorman's name disappeared from *Prairie Farmer* on May 15, 1911, and in the next issue (June 1) Butler introduced his new editor as coming to the paper "better equipped than any man in this country for the great work before him. . . ."[68] Butler's words probably reflected more confidence than he felt, but they contained some prophecy. Soon he was getting enthusiastic reports from agricultural leaders in Illinois and other states commending Gregory and his work. H. A. McKeene, secretary of the Illinois State Farmers' Institute, wrote Butler that "Mr. Gregory is a very strong man, and I congratulate you upon securing him as an editor of your great paper."[69] Cyril Hopkins told Butler that "Greogry is already the peer of any agricultural editor in the country and he is fast placing the *Prairie Farmer* on the plane that you talked to me about some two years ago."[70]

Butler now had a cluster of associates capable of helping revitalize *Prairie Farmer* to cope with the competitors which had bested it in recent years.

[67] Butler to Gregory, March 20, 1911.
[68] *Prairie Farmer*, 83 (June 1, 1911), 12.
[69] Undated copy of a letter from H. A. McKeene to Butler.
[70] Undated copy of a letter from Cyril Hopkins to Butler.

Prairie Farmer
and the
Farm Press

CHAPTER 4

Fifty farm publications were headquartered in Illinois when Butler arrived, far more than in any other state. New York ranked second with 37.[1] Rich agricultural resources and the state's centralized location had made Illinois a natural hub for expansion during the late 1800's. Where the state housed only 19 farm publications in 1881, that figure grew to 33 in 1890, then to 50 in 1900, after which the number remained about steady.[2]

Many of these publications served specialized audiences related to agriculture. Among them, the *Breeder's Gazette*, a journal for the purebred livestock trade, enjoyed the most respect within farm circles when Butler bought *Prairie Farmer*.[3]

[1] *N. W. Ayer and Son's American Newspaper Annual*, 1908 (Philadelphia: N. W. Ayer and Son), pp. 1075-1076.

[2] Trends in the number of agricultural journals published, by state, between 1881 and 1930 are shown in Allen D. Wilson, "Agricultural Periodicals in the United States," unpublished master's thesis, University of Illinois, Urbana, 1930, Appendix Table II.

[3] William E. Ogilvie outlines the work of James H. and Alvin H. Sanders in *Pioneer Agricultural Journalists* (Chicago: Arthur G. Leonard, 1927), pp. 67-81. See also brief biographical sketches of other *Breeder's Gazette* staff members, William R. Goodwin and Joseph E. Wing, in Ogilvie, pp. 83-93.

Of the Illinois-based farm publications directed toward a general farm audience at the time, four were major competitors for *Prairie Farmer* because they depended heavily upon circulation in Illinois: *Farmer's Call, Farmers Voice and Rural Outlook, Farmer's Review,* and *Orange Judd Farmer.* Table 1 shows that *Prairie Farmer* ranked fourth in total circulation and third in circulation within Illinois.

TABLE 1. CIRCULATION FIGURES FOR MAJOR GENERAL FARM PUBLICATIONS OF ILLINOIS, 1908

Publication	Total Circulation	Circulation in Illinois
Farmer's Call	62,628[a]	37,577[b]
Farmer's Review	33,875[c]	15,244[b]
Farmers Voice and Rural Outlook	54,318[c]	35,760[d]
Orange Judd Farmer	94,691[e]	18,938[b]
Prairie Farmer	39,877[f]	30,000[g]

[a] 1908 Ayer, p. 191.
[b] Estimate based on a listing of percentages of total circulation of agricultural papers, by states, in *Agricultural Advertising,* 20 (April, 1909), 560.
[c] Ayer, p. 152. [d] Ayer, p. 1263. [e] Ayer, p. 157. [f] Ayer, p. 158. [g] Ayer, p. 1266.

Orange Judd Farmer, largest of the group in 1908, was headquartered in Chicago and published as one of three Orange Judd farm weeklies. Although it professed to be edited primarily for Illinois farmers, only about one of five readers was in Illinois. A weekly service whereby farmers submitted crop reports in exchange for free subscriptions gave *Orange Judd Farmer* some editorial advantage over *Prairie Farmer* in 1909. Accurate records of its circulation methods are not available before 1914, but at that time it was using premiums extensively. The books, magazines, and other articles which it offered ranged in retail value from 25¢ to 40¢.[4] *Orange Judd Farmer* employed canvassers in the country, paying them either salary or commission.

Farmer's Review of Chicago, a veteran weekly which had passed its peak of prestige with the turn of the century, changed hands during the year Butler took over *Prairie Farmer.* The National Stockman and Farmer Company of Pittsburgh and Chicago bought

[4] Audit Bureau of Circulations, Auditor's Report for *Orange Judd Farmer* for 12 months ending December 31, 1914.

it from H. H. Chandler, who had owned it since 1883.[5] *Farmer's Review* employed about 10 traveling canvassers on a commission basis in 1914 and offered special clubbing rates to subscribers, but no contests. Two years later, half of its subscriptions were in arrears, signalling a death which was soon to come.

Farmers Voice and Rural Outlook of Chicago was growing fast in 1909 but would leave the scene first among the five. It celebrated its 50th anniversary that year by hiring a new editor, A. J. Bill, who formerly was agricultural editor of the *Bloomington Pantagraph* and press bureau editor for the Illinois Farmers' Institute.[6]

Farmer's Call of Quincy, which had been a weekly for more than 20 years, consolidated with the *Illinois Farmer* of Chicago just before Butler became publisher of *Prairie Farmer*. On July 1, 1909, they formed a twice-monthly paper called *Illinois Farmer and Farmer's Call*. Illinois Farmer Company of Chicago had been publishing its monthly as an official organ of the Farmers' Mutual Fire and Windstorm Insurance Companies of Illinois. At the time, Illinois had 229 such companies with a membership of almost 200,000 farm owners.[7]

At least one out-of-state paper was reaching more Illinois farmers than any farm publication published within the state. *Successful Farming* of Des Moines, Iowa, a magazine yet to celebrate its 10th birthday, was advertising a paid circulation of 400,000 monthly, including 44,295 subscribers in Illinois.[8]

Farm Journal of Philadelphia professed in mid-1909 to have the largest circulation of any farm paper in the world.[9] Perhaps 30,000 of its total 600,000 paid subscribers lived in Illinois.[10] Editorially, the *Farm Journal* was having trouble getting "out of the rut of

[5] *N. W. Ayer and Son's American Newspaper Annual*, 1908, p. 152; James L. Regan, *The Story of Chicago in Connection with the Printing Business* (Chicago: Regan Printing House, 1912), pp. 170-171.

[6] *Agricultural Advertising*, 21 (October, 1909), 580.

[7] *Agricultural Advertising*, 21 (May, 1909), 9.

[8] Stephen C. Stuntz, "List of the Agricultural Periodicals of the United States and Canada Published During the Century July 1810 to July 1910," U.S. Department of Agriculture, Miscellaneous Publication No. 398 (Washington: U.S. Government Printing Office, 1941), p. 165; *Agricultural Advertising*, 21 (May, 1909), 89, and 21 (June, 1909), 196.

[9] *Agricultural Advertising*, 21 (June, 1909), 120.

[10] The circulation figure for Illinois is based on a projection from the ratio of Illinois-to-total circulation of *Farm Journal* shown in earliest (1914) auditor's reports of the Audit Bureau of Circulations.

nineteenth-century thinking" under its aging founder, Wilmer Atkinson.[11]

Two other out-of-state farm periodicals—*Farm and Home* of Springfield, Massachusetts, and *Farm and Fireside* of Springfield, Ohio—also commanded significant readership in Illinois. *Farm and Home* put out a western edition which carried a Chicago dateline, but Phelps Publishing Company edited and printed the paper in Massachusetts.

Dozens of other more nondescript papers fought for a place on the reading tables of farm homes in Illinois. Their scramble for the limited income from advertising and subscriptions placed a financial pressure upon them that leaves little wonder about why many were (as one observer put it) as amateurish as a country weekly and dry as an experiment station bulletin. It helps explain why cries of plagiarism resounded throughout the field of farm publishing and why farmers hooted in scorn at much of what farm papers were giving them as editorial content. What kind of editor would explain methods for drying broomcorn to readers who had never seen broomcorn, much less raised it? And an editor needed but little expertise to conclude that "A fowl that will not fatten when heavily fed on corn is not in good physical condition." [12]

The bargain-basement editorial methods which many farm papers with low budgets were using aggravated another problem which they had throughout the country: making readers out of farm people. Social pressures still worked against reading during the early 1900's. Any farmer who took to reading earned a reputation among neighbors as being lazy. Worthless content of farm papers fed the ardent opinions of those who disclaimed any value from reading.

Editorial Strategy

The Butler-Gregory combination which proved powerful enough for *Prairie Farmer* to absorb all of its competitors based in Illinois within 22 years got much of its strength from editorial alertness. Butler's newspapering experience had convinced him that publica-

[11] See a discussion of *Farm Journal's* editorial policy during this period in Nora Cruz Quebral's "*Farm Journal* and American Agriculture, 1877-1965," unpublished doctoral dissertation, University of Illinois, Urbana, 1966, pp. 83-90.

[12] Incident reported in *Hoard's Dairyman*, 51 (March 3, 1916), 244.

tions without strong editorial foundations were doomed, and he brought to the team a love for championing the underdog and a degree of emotionalism. Perhaps even more significantly, Butler brought some of the Scrippsian philosophy that an editor should have control of his paper. Butler may not have been able to remain as detached as Scripps in this respect, but he subscribed to the idea that the editor should be independent of pressures from both inside and out. This was exactly the kind of setting in which Gregory needed to work, and it explains why Gregory loomed so large in the editorial strategy of *Prairie Farmer* while Butler remained in the background. The two men, who differed greatly in many personal respects, worked smoothly for many years under this arrangement.

As C. V. Gregory looked at his readers, his paper, and the other farm papers of his day, he decided that a change was in order. Too many farmers were satisfied with their own wisdom, he concluded. They lacked the enthusiasm to learn new things or to practice the old. "They are as wise as owls, and their wisdom does them about as much good," in Gregory's opinion.[13] The farmer must always move ahead and change, Gregory believed, for that was what he saw agriculture doing.

Farm papers, he felt, were guilty of the same complacency. Gregory saw two fairly distinct classes of agricultural papers. One consisted of those which saw a rather standardized agriculture and assumed that their main duty was to "keep dishing up standard information for its readers." By this same viewpoint, an April issue would look about the same from year to year. Instead, Gregory sided with what he considered a second class of papers which viewed new problems arising daily and crying for new solutions. He insisted in 1914, as the new movement toward farm unity was gathering momentum, that "the change of farm practice from the mere art to the science of agriculture is taking place so rapidly that a good many men who pose as agricultural leaders do not realize that it has yet begun."[14] Gregory said he intended for *Prairie Farmer* to be at the front of that change. He aimed to edit a farmers' paper rather than simply a manual of farm practice, a paper "real and human and practical all the way through."

[13] *Prairie Farmer*, 84 (January 15, 1912), 10.
[14] *Prairie Farmer*, 86 (January 15, 1914), 10.

Gregory did not insist that *Prairie Farmer* would be an oracle or preacher. Rather, it would be "only a friend" that has "a little better chance than the farmer to keep in touch with changes in agriculture."

In that spirit Gregory resurrected a philosophy upon which *Prairie Farmer* had been founded: "Farmers, Write For Your Paper." He did not literally adopt the slogan, by now dusty with disuse. Rather, he revived the philosophy through his notion that a farm paper should be a clearing house for farming experiences. He rejected Butler's earlier approach of relying heavily upon articles from contributing experts. One of the main jobs of a good farm paper, he felt, is to provide a place where farm people can get together and exchange ideas.

Butler grew to concur with this philosophy. *Prairie Farmer* could be a type of community meeting place, Butler observed in 1919, and he encouraged readers to "talk it over in *Prairie Farmer*." [15]

From 1911 until Gregory left *Prairie Farmer* in 1937, issues bristled with questions and comments from readers. Response from readers became a source of great pride for him, even a standard of excellence. Gregory announced in one issue of 1915 that it contained 117 letters, questions, and opinions from readers. "That's what makes a real farm paper," he added.[16] He expressed similar pride in mid-1919 when he announced that *Prairie Farmer* had printed 1,486 letters from readers so far that year. One issue had contained 150 items from readers.

Small cash prizes for the most interesting letters about various topics added incentive for readers to take part in these periodic "meetings." Gregory was at the height of his pleasure when the editorial department was getting 40,000 to 50,000 letters a year because he felt sure that if people were bothering to write *Prairie Farmer* they also were talking about it in their homes and neighborhoods.

Neither Butler nor Gregory balked at investing in editorial staff or the expenses associated with it. Gregory felt that a farm paper could not be edited successfully from a city office. "A large and capable editorial staff, traveling through the country collecting news, studying farm problems, and keeping in close touch with farm conditions, is necessary to any farm paper that hopes to give

[15] *Prairie Farmer*, 91 (October 4, 1919), 13.
[16] *Prairie Farmer*, 87 (January 2, 1915), 10.

its readers real service," he maintained.[17] As a result, the editorial
staff of three men in 1911 grew to nine members who traveled
more than 100,000 miles in 1927. *Prairie Farmer* described itself
in early 1928 as having the largest editorial staff of any farm paper
in the country.

Under Butler's insistence that *Prairie Farmer* was a newspaper
rather than a magazine (he was extremely sensitive about the dif-
ference), the paper placed unusual stress upon timeliness. On occasion, traveling staff members telegraphed their articles to Chicago
when they saw a chance to meet a close deadline. However, the
paper was working at a competitive disadvantage for about 10
years after Butler bought it because *Orange Judd Farmer* and
Farmer's Review were weeklies. *Prairie Farmer* had changed on
January 1, 1908, from weekly to semi-monthly.[18] On January 2,
1915, it had changed to every other Saturday.[19] However, the prosperity of the late 1910's and new competitive threats raised when
Orange Judd Farmer bought the *Farmer's Review* on June 1, 1918,
forced another change. Beginning October 4, 1919, *Prairie Farmer*
published every Saturday, a schedule it maintained (except for
July-September, 1921) until May 30, 1931, a few months after
Prairie Farmer absorbed its last rival, *Illinois Farmer* (called *Orange
Judd Farmer* until 1924).[20]

Perhaps the most flamboyant device that *Prairie Farmer* used to
gain an upper hand in coverage and timeliness was its staff airplane. During the summer of 1928, the editors of *Prairie Farmer*
became celebrities as they whizzed across the countryside at 70
miles an hour flying 500 to 1,000 feet high in their open-cockpit
Waco biplane. Cow pastures marked by white bedsheets served
as landing strips for their white plane carrying big letters, "*Prairie
Farmer*," on the fuselage and wings. When the project ended in
October, editors had touched down in nearly every county in Illinois at least two or three times, logged more than 20,000 miles,
and stirred up public awareness of *Prairie Farmer* throughout the
area.

Fictitious characters became another means by which *Prairie
Farmer* captured the fascination of readers. Gregory was adept at

[17] *Prairie Farmer,* 99 (November 26, 1927), 8.
[18] *Prairie Farmer,* 80 (January 1, 1908), 2.
[19] *Prairie Farmer,* 86 (December 15, 1914), 3.
[20] *Prairie Farmer,* 103 (May 16, 1931), 8.

creating characters whose views tickled the fancy of rural people. He liked the device because it tied in with his belief that farm people enjoyed stories and straightforward, simple writing; it also allowed him to make his points through humor.

Gregory began to experiment only a few months after he joined Butler. Perhaps taking a cue from the Peter Tumbledown character in *Farm Journal,* he published his first "Song of the Lazy Farmer" as "an experiment of good cheer" in February, 1912.[21] The Lazy Farmer became a favorite for 25 years, drawing chuckles and preaching lessons every issue through his ineptness. Objecting to the use of silos, for example, the Lazy Farmer concluded:

> I'll husk my corn the good old way,
> In spite of what my neighbors say.
> Then when the snow is two feet deep,
> I'll turn my cows in, and my sheep.
> My stock don't need their fodder canned,
> For they have come to understand
> The only thing that makes them grow
> Is hunting fodder in the snow!

One auctioneer in Indiana memorized more than 200 songs of the Lazy Farmer and used them to get his crowds into a mood for buying. Whenever a lull came in the bidding, he would start a series of songs which soon had buyers laughing and ready to raise their bids.[22] The Lazy Farmer gained even more fame from the hundreds of impersonations that he inspired throughout the midwest. At all kinds of social functions, farm people loved to dress like him and his wife, Mirandy, then act out his laughable errors.

One subscription salesman worked up an act which he performed at meetings, to the delight of his audiences. By 1922 the Lazy Farmer was appearing at the Illinois State Fair, in later years accompanied by his wife. Two years later, Homestead Films Company produced a comedy which featured the Lazy Farmer trying to farm with the aid of his new radio, and *Prairie Farmer* used the film for years as a laugh-getter in circulation meetings.

In 1920 Gregory added to his "laughing staff" a pair of hired men in a cartoon named "Adventures of Slim and Spud."[23] They were a barnyard parallel of Mutt and Jeff and got into an assortment of predicaments working for Farmer Penny Pincher. Car-

---

[21] Tumbledown first appeared in April, 1884. See Quebral, pp. 38-40.
[22] Dave O. Thompson, unpublished memoirs, p. 25.
[23] First appearance was in the issue of January 3, 1920, p. 12.

toonist P. R. Carmack became their creator in January, 1921, and later was replaced by Ray Inman.

Gregory's most lovable character was his star dirt farmer and reporter, John Turnipseed, a man "who can write entertainingly on any subject under the sun, whether he knows anything about it or not." [24] Turnipseed was a back-40-acres philosopher who admitted that his name was funny but insisted it was the only one he had, "and it's good on the bottom of a check, which is more'n some folks can say." Fairly heavyset with bushy eyebrows and smiling eyes that twinkled with dry wit, he came to readers decked out in his vest, plaid shirt, crinkled hat, and the smelly pipe about which his wife kept scolding him.

Turnipseed "worked on assignment" for Gregory after his debut on November 4, 1922. He not only covered meetings but invariably imposed his own interpretations upon outcomes. His interests ranged from politics (he favored Will Rogers on the Anti-Bunk Party platform in 1928) to religion (he insisted that falling asleep in church is a sign of clean conscience). He might speculate about the next president of the American Farm Bureau Federation or the problems of unmarried women. A fast-moving world did not frighten John Turnipseed, but he questioned whether or not the commotion was causing much progress: "We know too much now, and that's what all the worryin' is about. A man used to have brains or not and that was all there was to it. Now he's got an inferiority complex or an emotional ego, and that's why he forgets to bring back your cross-cut saw. Life is gettin' too complicated for me. I'd like to go back to the days of suspenders and chillblains [*sic*]." [25]

Gregory often used Turnipseed to analyze current issues from a farmer's viewpoint. The "elevator man" became a natural antagonist because he represented the middlemen whom farmers often blamed for widening gaps between farm and consumer prices. Turnipseed remained a regular feature in *Prairie Farmer* until Gregory left in 1937. More than 10 years later, editor Paul C. Johnson revived the character, who still greets readers with his homespun humor and philosophy.

Among Gregory's other fictitious characters was Senator Hiram Cornborer, who wrote weekly letters to his "old farmer friend

[24] *Prairie Farmer,* 96 (November 22, 1924), 8.
[25] *Prairie Farmer,* 96 (November 1, 1924), 23.

John Huckleberry" while the Illinois legislature was in session each year. This strategy allowed the staff of *Prairie Farmer* to move well beyond the limits of straight reporting.

Two other effective devices helped *Prairie Farmer* gain an editorial advantage. One—well-worn—was that of hiring the competitor's editor. On Christmas Day, 1926, the paper announced that it had employed Arthur C. Page, the 14-year veteran editor of its only remaining competitor, *Orange Judd Farmer*. Page was a tall, gangly Missourian with the demeanor of Abraham Lincoln. He had graduated from the University of Missouri with a major in dairying, a career interest which he abandoned after getting some editorial experience during college. His "we folks" approach on *Orange Judd Farmer* had tended to parallel that of *Prairie Farmer*, and it is not surprising that Page appealed to Butler, for his expressed motto was: "To stand four-square as a champion and defender of agriculture against all who would go against it." [26] Furthermore, Butler could not be taking a good editor from any publication whose loss would please him more, competitively.

Another editorial strategy which *Prairie Farmer* used was localization of content for subscribers outside of Illinois. The paper got its first foothold in Indiana during 1919 when its circulation in that state increased to nearly 19,000 from a level in 1918 of only 4,000. Determined to strengthen that footing, Butler and Gregory began a special edition for subscribers of Indiana in May, 1923. They employed Floyd Keepers, former assistant farm adviser from Grundy County, Illinois, as Indiana editor and set up an editorial office in Indianapolis. From then on readers in Indiana received editions containing pages devoted to local news. Later (January 3, 1931) the Indiana edition began to offer special advertising as well as editorial matter.[27]

A new general edition of *Prairie Farmer*, which began during June, 1939, was aimed largely at readers in Wisconsin. Gregory arranged for editorial coverage by a staff member, Della Loui, headquartered in Wisconsin. The third expansion outside of Illinois was a Michigan edition, begun in June, 1944.

These editorial efforts, plus the crusading for which *Prairie Farmer* became known, resulted in a publication that readers came to prefer amid the many farm papers being stuffed into their mail-

[26] *Prairie Farmer*, 98 (December 25, 1926), 9.
[27] Prairie Farmer's *Half Acre*, 12 (December 27, 1930), 4.

boxes during the early 1900's. *Prairie Farmer* became what one reader termed a "hummer."

Circulation Strategy, 1909-30

Burridge Butler had no fondness for the newspapering methods of William Randolph Hearst, but the two publishers shared a healthy respect for circulation. Circulation was Hearst's god, as one of his biographers put it; news became only the commodity that made circulation.[28] Butler was not prepared to follow the dictates of circulation so far along the paths that led Hearst to editorial sensationalism. However, Butler's test for editorial work was its effect upon circulation.[29]

He pursued growth of circulation for *Prairie Farmer* in two stages of about 20 years each: an absorption stage and an expansion stage. Between 1909 and 1931, the paper gained a major but unmeasurable share of its circulation growth at the expense of competitors. Table 2 traces this steady absorption which began with *Farmers Voice and Rural Outlook* in 1913 and ended with *Illinois Farmer* in 1931, after which *Prairie Farmer* was the state's only general farm paper.

Butler and Gus Holt, his circulation manager, appear to have relied on three main strategies during that period. The first was to help bring some order to the chaos which *Prairie Farmer* faced in trying to convince advertisers of its worth. Circulation figures for farm papers were unreliable, often wildly so, because of the circumstances under which subscription lists arose. As one viewer put it, "A circulation manager was commonly called a 'circulation liar,' and, to be a good and effective circulation manager, you needed to be a skillful liar with an imagination developed to the nth degree."[30]

Circulation figures stripped of meaning left conscientious publishers with no means of expressing their advantage. Therefore, Butler helped found what became a new national movement to get a referee into the circulation game. Publishers' sworn statements of circulation had proved futile, and efforts by advertisers

[28] John Tebbel, *The Life and Good Times of William Randolph Hearst* (New York: E. P. Dutton and Co., 1952), p. 78.
[29] Butler to Dave Thompson, October 1, 1936.
[30] Fred W. Stone, quoted in Charles O. Bennett, *Facts Without Opinion* (Chicago: Audit Bureau of Circulations, 1965), pp. 54-55.

to conduct independent audits under an Association of American Advertisers enjoyed only modest support through 1913.[31] The movement in which Butler took part grew out of a reorganization of the Association of American Advertisers into a new auditing bureau called the Advertising Audit Association. Butler was one of four members of the original organization committee and when the members first met on January 5, 1914, Butler was named to a membership soliciting subcommittee.[32] Several months later, the new group united with an equally new eastern unit called the Bureau of Verified Circulations to form the Audit Bureau of Circulations on May 20, 1914. Butler became a member of the 16-man combined organization committee and on May 20 was elected to the board of directors, a position which he held until June 2, 1916.[33] Between the end of May and the middle of July he met more than 30 times as a member of the committee on standard forms and audits. When Butler left the board of directors, membership in ABC had reached 1,165 publications and the Bureau had made 1,123 field audits.[34] His pleasure with this progress could be heightened by the knowledge that farm papers which refused to join the Bureau became suspect, and those who joined were required to report not only their circulation but also the methods they used to get it.

Prairie Farmer, Orange Judd Farmer, and *Farmer's Review* each underwent audits during 1914, the first year of activity by ABC. From then on, *Prairie Farmer* could compete for advertising under more standardized ground rules.

Direct selling was the second major strategy which *Prairie Farmer* used for circulation. Almost from Butler's arrival, the paper relied heavily upon its own sales force. It hired subscription salesmen on a salary plus 15 per cent commission. Holt, a meticulous worker, supervised his staff "with an iron hand," coached it carefully about how to sell, and insisted that each salesman report weekly. Periodic contests among salesmen helped stimulate interest and effort.

The reliance which Butler and Holt placed upon personal selling explains why the paper was so adamant about sheetwriters and other fly-by-night subscription salesmen. In its editorial columns *Prairie Farmer* presented major articles exposing selling schemes

[31] Bennett, p. 17.
[33] Bennett, pp. 42, 51, 261, 274.
[32] Bennett, p. 36.
[34] Bennett, p. 63.

TABLE 2. CONSOLIDATION OF ILLINOIS GENERAL FARM PUBLICATIONS, 1900-1950

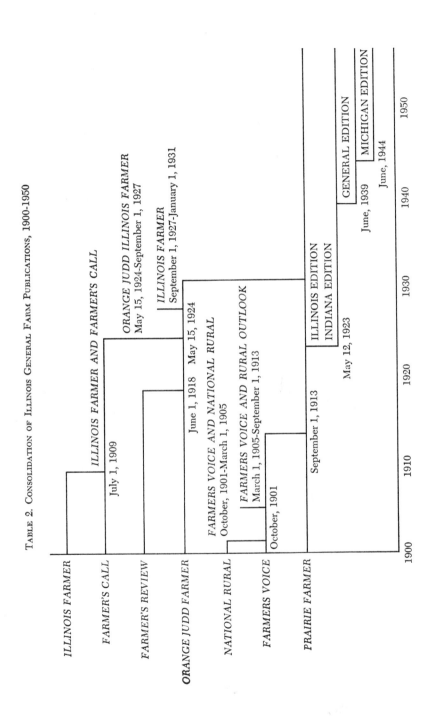

and offered $100 rewards to those responsible for the arrest and conviction of anyone who misrepresented it. Editors also scolded readers who let offers of cheap premiums induce them to buy farm papers which they would not buy otherwise. "Our readers can get their dishpans at the hardware store," *Prairie Farmer* insisted.

This did not mean that *Prairie Farmer* sent its sales people on the road empty-handed. Until 1917, they too could offer premiums in the form of books such as *Frank Mann's Soil Book*. The paper then replaced premiums with assorted items which a customer could buy in addition to paying the regular subscription price. One of the most popular of these was a county farm directory. Records do not show for how many counties *Prairie Farmer* produced such directories, but it offered more than 20 different directories between 1917 and 1919. These were hard cover books that often ran to more than 250 pages and were entitled *Prairie Farmer's Reliable Directory of Farmers and Breeders—(county name) County*. Very thorough, they listed all farmers in the county (name, address, family size, acreage, ownership status, tenure in the county), all breeders of purebred livestock, all business houses, all automobile owners on farms, numbers of tractors by make, county officers, county census data, and other facts of interest to farmers. *Prairie Farmer* sold the directories for $2.50 plus three- and five-year subscriptions at regular rates.

A canvasser could get double duty from the directories because he approached a prospective customer as a semi-official gatherer of facts as well as a salesman. From the standpoint of the paper, this project stimulated salesmen to visit all farmers in each county. During 1919, for example, solicitors for *Prairie Farmer* called on 66,454 farms to get 41,779 prepaid subscriptions plus data for county directories.[35]

In later years, other types of books became available. One of the most popular in the 1920's was *The Adventures of Slim and Spud*, copies of which *Prairie Farmer* sold to 15,000 subscribers. The paper also offered automobiles, tractors, pianos, phonographs, fur coats, and other prizes in a form of popularity contest whereby subscriptions afforded votes.

Prairie Farmer's advertising guarantee provided subscription

[35] Audit Bureau of Circulations, *Blue Book (Periodicals)*, publisher's statement for *Prairie Farmer* for six months ending December 31, 1919.

salesmen with another talking point. Just before Christmas, 1909, Butler had proclaimed his "square deal" advertising guarantee:

I believe in the square deal—man to man—and I want you all to feel that I am publishing *Prairie Farmer* that way.

No man on earth can beat one of my readers. I will protest and fight any advertiser who don't [*sic*] play "square"—the way I run my own business.

The *Prairie Farmer* has $150,000.00 paid up capital, and every cent of it is back of every ad in this paper.

THERE ARE NO CONDITIONS in this guarantee—no tail to the kite. All I require is to know that you are a regular subscriber, and that you mentioned *Prairie Farmer* when you answered the ad, and you must write me within 30 days of the date of the transaction.

And I ask you please mention *Prairie Farmer* when you write advertisers.

Your friend,
Burridge D. Butler [36]

Prairie Farmer was not the first to publish such an advertising guarantee, even among farm papers in Illinois, but it appears to have been more militant than its competitors in promoting the guarantee.[37] In fact, *Prairie Farmer* seldom missed an opportunity to impress readers with its intent to place readers ahead of advertisers. Another example was its well-publicized policy of refusing cigarette advertising, a policy which Butler set aside only briefly when *Prairie Farmer* was losing money during the early 1930's. To readers, the policy meant a "good, clean paper"; however, to Butler it was a way of exercising his active dislike for cigarettes. As far as he was concerned, cigarettes (which he variously termed "coffin nails" and other less complimentary names) were only for "lounge lizards."

The third and possibly strongest device which *Prairie Farmer* used to build circulation during the absorption stage was the Prairie Farmer Protective Union. Certainly the Protective Union

---

[36] *Prairie Farmer*, 81 (December 1, 1909), 12.

[37] As early as 1850, *Moore's Rural New Yorker* had announced that it would exclude "patent medicines and other quackery—including deceptive advertisements of all classes." (See Albert L. Demaree, *The American Agricultural Press, 1819-1860* (New York: Columbia University Press, 1941), pp. 148-149.) *Farm Journal* holds claim to having led all other farm magazines in guaranteeing its advertisements as early as October, 1880 (Quebral, p. 16). Within Illinois most of the major competitors had guarantees before Butler arrived. *Orange Judd Farmer* first mentioned its guarantee on May 5, 1900, *Farmers Voice and Rural Outlook* in June, 1905, and *Farmer's Review* in October, 1908.

was the most visible symbol of the influence of *Prairie Farmer* throughout Illinois and adjoining states. By 1922 nearly one out of every two farms in Illinois had a black and yellow "tin sign" posted at its front entrance announcing that it was protected by the Prairie Farmer Protective Union. This share rose even higher in future years as the Protective Union became the farmer's business adviser, complaint adjuster, bill collector, and corruption fighter.

It grew out of the prosperity between 1910 and 1920 when farmers had more money than ever before. Many were naive about investments outside their home communities and no effective "blue sky" laws existed, so peddlers of speculative or fraudulent issues of stock found a new happy hunting ground. Farmers soon began to write *Prairie Farmer* with questions about the soundness of certain investments. When the paper printed some of the questions and replied to them, a flood of new inquiries arrived. Reports of deceptive mail order operations also drew vigorous reaction from readers.

Drawing on an idea which the *Orange Judd Farmer* was using, Holt established the Protective Union, an informational bureau through which readers could seek solutions to such problems.[38] Holt and Gregory began the project rather modestly on January 26, 1918, with a small article about regulations in selling vinegar. Seven months later, a full page in each issue was devoted to the Protective Union. The volume of questions and problems swamped Gregory, who at first tried to handle them himself, and he assigned the department to a full-time manager.

As a means of increasing circulation, the Protective Union documented its value within five months after it was formed. An article exposing a fraudulent cooperative meat-packing operation reported that farmers in the Mississippi Valley had lost $3 million in four

[38] As early as 1913, a reader had written asking why *Prairie Farmer* did not have a department like the *Rural New Yorker* to warn farmers against shady manufacturers, commission men, and gold brick schemes. Orange Judd of the *American Agriculturist* had maintained for many years a popular column in which he exposed fake claims, "humbugs," and get-something-for-nothing lures (Quebral, p. 15). *Orange Judd Farmer* of Chicago had begun printing a column entitled "Our Service Bureau" on April 5, 1913, and offered readers free "answers to questions about business matters, financial advice or other helps in commercial affairs." It soon expanded to a one-half page department called "Orange Judd's Service Bureau," which appeared regularly through 1930.

years, while promoters got returns of 12 to 35 per cent. It closed
with the advice, "Set the Dog on Salesmen from Ottawa and Rockford." Sales of the stock nosedived and the paper later said that
it had saved readers "a good many thousand dollars." [39] Immediately
the cooperative sued *Prairie Farmer* for $250,000 in a libel suit
which never came to trial. Holt in turn sent his subscription salesmen into the field with the libel suit as evidence that *Prairie Farmer*
really worked for the best interest of farmers.[40]

By 1928 the Protective Union offered to perform the following
services for its reader-members:

1. Advise about legal matters, marketing, investment, insurance,
or "any subject."

2. Handle claims against advertisers in *Prairie Farmer*.

3. Handle claims against transportation companies, mail order
houses, commission firms, and all other claims except (a) those
against other individuals or businessmen in the same community,
(b) those more than six months old, and (c) those in which the
claimant said he answered advertisement in some other publication unless the advertiser was also using *Prairie Farmer*.

It considered itself the first such service by a farm publication to
undertake the collection of claims for readers.[41]

Within five years the Protective Union had collected $316,324.65,
furnished legal information to thousands about topics ranging from
line fence disputes to game laws, and interceded with hundreds
of firms on behalf of readers. Table 3 shows that during 1929, a
peak year, it helped settle more than 2,500 claims, collected $100,000
in adjustments for its readers, and answered more than 35,000
letters.[42] At times the work required three professional staff members.

"We tackle every job that comes up with deadly earnestness—
whether it seems important or relatively trivial," *Prairie Farmer*
promised. A request from a high school girl to help force her
former boyfriend to return her class ring got the same attention as
an extended campaign against fake eye doctors. Multiplied by tens
of thousands each year, the requests helped build circulation as
it strengthened loyalty toward *Prairie Farmer* among farm people.

[39] *Prairie Farmer*, 90 (June 29, 1918), 4.
[40] Herman Steen, personal interview, January 25, 1967.
[41] *Prairie Farmer*, 99 (November 26, 1927), 10.
[42] *Prairie Farmer*, 102 (January 4, 1930), 21.

Circulation Strategy, 1931-48

Circulation for *Prairie Farmer* entered a new phase soon after it bought its last competitor, *Illinois Farmer,* early in 1931. By then Butler's paper had a paid circulation of 170,000 in a state with only 214,500 farms.[43] If he confined his future efforts to Illinois, as in the past, expansion of the paper would be limited. In the meantime, a new kind of competitor seemed to be a growing threat: the regional and national farm magazine.

TABLE 3. AVAILABLE RECORDS OF PRAIRIE FARMER PROTECTIVE UNION ACTIVITIES, 1920 THROUGH 1929[a]

Year	Letters Received	Claims Adjusted	Value of Collections
1920[b]	15,718	1,568	$41,195
1921[c]	19,140	1,652	N/A
1922[d]	32,285	2,609	68,698
1923[e]	39,860	3,640	96,721
1924[f]	23,445	1,871	N/A
1925	N/A	N/A	N/A
1926[g]	25,000	N/A	N/A
1927	N/A	N/A	N/A
1928[h]	32,000	2,253	80,000
1929[i]	35,000	2,516	100,000

[a] The only remaining records showing Protective Union activity summaries between 1918 and 1950 are the following which were published in *Prairie Farmer.* Activity is reported to have continued at more than 20,000 letters per year, but details are not available.
[b] *Prairie Farmer,* 93 (January 8, 1921), 8.
[c] *Prairie Farmer,* 97 (June 6, 1925), 29.
[d] *Prairie Farmer,* 95 (January 13, 1923), 8; 97 (June 6, 1925), 29.
[e] *Prairie Farmer,* 96 (January 19, 1924), 8; 97 (June 6, 1925), 29.
[f] *Prairie Farmer,* 97 (June 6, 1925), 29.
[g] *Prairie Farmer,* 99 (January 1, 1927), 12.
[h] *Prairie Farmer,* 100 (December 29, 1928), 10.
[i] *Prairie Farmer,* 102 (January 4, 1930), 21.

Table 4 shows that *Successful Farming, Farm Journal, Country Gentleman, Farm and Fireside* (later *Country Home*), and *Capper's Farmer* had grown in Illinois right along with *Prairie Farmer* between 1909 and 1930. During the 1930's they pulled close enough to cause Butler serious concern. For instance, by 1939, when *Prairie Farmer* was holding steady at a circulation in Illinois of about 171,000, all five regional-nationals had increased to more

[43] Summary for 1930, reported in U.S. Department of Commerce, *U.S. Census of Agriculture,* 1950, p. 3.

TABLE 4. NET PAID CIRCULATION OF DOMINANT AUDITED GENERAL FARM PUBLICATIONS IN ILLINOIS, 1914–50

Year	Prairie Farmer	Orange Judd Farmer	Farmer's Review	Farm Journal	Successful Farming	Country Gentleman	Capper's Farmer	Farm and Fireside
1914	68,591	40,048	62,231	43,564	51,855	—	—	19,530
1915	—	67,576	—	49,828	52,597	—	—	—
1916	—	—	71,466	50,427	—	—	—	43,351
1917	84,105	69,961	—	—	63,613	22,709	—	50,151
1918	93,232	81,136		49,252	68,214	27,368	—	45,963
1919	108,827	87,036		52,424	72,124	23,470	51,675	62,213
1920	123,416	85,638		55,317	73,662	41,239	58,215	60,575
1921	123,648	86,472		65,626	72,462	55,996	56,389	59,818
1922	126,470	90,209		70,473	76,350	55,241	42,414	42,364
1923	131,438	96,734		67,223	77,610	46,477	31,141	42,542
1924	132,025	99,131		65,028	76,121	40,725	35,012	50,469
1925	133,914	97,158		73,697	80,202	51,339	48,153	48,945
1926	141,031	110,837		78,869	78,561	62,298	33,891	55,880
1927	148,283	142,211		78,937	88,551	69,142	47,529	59,013
1928	154,536	146,212		75,266	89,928	71,296	48,333	71,481
1929	163,078	145,555		81,400	93,821	75,293	53,408	89,176
1930	169,452			81,970	92,440	100,890	54,102	—
1931	182,621			81,382	95,656	95,402	55,135	100,209
1932	174,336			80,751	95,116	92,694	56,399	95,580

TABLE 4. (CONCLUDED)

Year	Prairie Farmer	Orange Judd Farmer	Farmer's Review	Farm Journal	Successful Farming	Country Gentleman	Capper's Farmer	Farm and Fireside
1933	172,836			76,550	102,339	88,259	57,369	90,159
1934	170,438			76,945	103,324	76,134	70,154	93,518
1935	172,366			82,511	104,335	74,188	80,096	94,690
1936	169,134			87,043	97,516	83,849	82,150	88,770
1937	168,347			90,332	92,965	94,588	88,818	94,919
1938	172,054			88,576	105,554	109,588	102,768	103,176
1939	171,312			161,094	106,084	112,592	105,403	106,438
1940	170,986			161,973	107,641	114,884	105,548	
1941	171,828			166,082	106,327	117,994	108,180	
1942	169,293			173,579	108,826	113,989	103,986	
1943	168,621			177,106	108,100	107,718	100,105	
1944	168,532			171,384	103,149	114,656	110,751	
1945	172,144			170,794	104,577	120,412	120,232	
1946	175,990			165,685	108,487	123,590	138,918	
1947	177,918			171,265	112,416	136,624	132,603	
1948	180,214			170,281	110,787	137,228	133,784	
1949	184,136			178,404	112,336	137,804	138,410	
1950	188,329			180,727	110,475	136,641	138,990	

SOURCE: Audit Bureau of Circulations, *Blue Book (Periodicals)*, publishers' statements for the final six months of each year.

than 105,000. *Farm Journal* was within 10,000 subscribers of matching *Prairie Farmer* in Illinois after it bought the subscription list
of *The Farmer's Wife* in April, 1939.[44]

The regional-national farm magazines made some dramatic moves
during the decade after 1928. Rebelling against the "by cracky"
days of farm publishing, they began to use coated stock, four-color
covers, and a brand of editorial vigor that frightened publishers
of state farm papers. The trade paper idea has worn itself out in
the farm field, this new school said; the old idea of the "family
farm" is dead.

Successful Farming, a regional which concentrated on the "heart
states" from Canada south to Oklahoma and east around Michigan
and Ohio, used more how-to-do-it information than the nationals.
Its gross revenue from advertising in 1937 was comparable to that
of nationals and its subscription rate was higher than that of
Country Gentleman, Farm Journal, or *Country Home.*

The other regional magazine popular in Illinois was *Capper's
Farmer* of Topeka, Kansas. Senator Arthur Capper of Kansas had
converted a local farm paper into *Capper's Farmer* during 1919,
after which it grew steadily. The magazine circulated largely in
the agricultural midwest and southwest and relied heavily on
practical farming experience in its editorial columns.

Most prestigious among national farm magazines of the 1930's
was *Country Gentleman,* a Curtis publication. It was about comparable with *Farm Journal* in circulation throughout Illinois, but
ahead nationally. In 1937 its gross advertising revenue surpassed
that of its nearest farm competitor by $1 million and exceeded even
Fortune, New Yorker, or *Redbook.*[45] Under editor Philip S. Rose,
Country Gentleman kept its agricultural flavor but ranged far and
wide and often drew upon well-known writers in the best tradition
of George H. Lorimer. Its approach attracted a larger share of circulation among nonfarmers than other farm magazines. Competitively, it caused a disturbance in 1938 by cutting its subscription price in half.

Country Home—a sister publication to *Collier's, American,* and
Woman's Home Companion—was almost out of the picture as a

[44] Audit Bureau of Circulations, *Blue Book (Periodicals),* publisher's statement for *Farm Journal* for six months to December 31, 1939.

[45] Harland Manchester, "The Farm Magazines," *Scribner's Magazine,* 104
(October, 1938), 26-27.

farm magazine by the late 1930's. When the Crowell publishers took over *Farm and Fireside* after its financial crisis in 1929, they decided that farmers no longer had firesides and changed its name to *Country Home*.[46] They also changed it from an agricultural magazine to a general magazine slanted for farm readers. After a circulation error, Crowell killed the publication in 1939.[47]

The other major national, *Farm Journal*, went into receivership in 1935 after its advertising revenue plunged from $1,903,052 in 1926 to only $322,096.[48] On the eve of its public sale it entered the hands of the Pew family, of the Sun Oil Company and other interests. Under a new publisher, Graham Patterson—"short, beaming and as dynamic as Billy Sunday"—*Farm Journal* became a news magazine for farmers. Its slogan was "four days from writer to reader," a feat which it achieved by abandoning its printing plant and sending its work to a press in Chicago which could turn out 300 76-page issues a minute. A newly organized field staff of 15 men began to inject fresh material into its pages. By the end of 1937, the magazine was grossing three times its advertising revenue of 1935 and had added 338,000 subscribers.[49]

Despite their color and slick stock, these farm magazines all were priced to compete with the more homely state farm papers. A farmer could subscribe to any of the five for no more than 50¢ a year.

Publishers of state farm papers feared for their future, and with reason, because advertisers were praising the "new look" in farm magazines. Word got around in publishing circles that eventually the nationals were going to squeeze others out completely.

Prairie Farmer now found itself on the defensive against interests which were more powerful than others it had faced. Smarting under the pressure, Gregory retorted in 1935:

We could spend a lot more money for more expensive paper and four-color printing. We could easily spend so much time and money on those things that we wouldn't have much time left to worry about what goes into the paper. . . . We could spend so much time printing a pretty paper that the information it contains would be weeks old when it reaches our readers.

[46] For discussion of the early *Farm and Fireside*, see Theodore Peterson, *Magazines in the Twentieth Century* (Urbana: University of Illinois Press, 1964), pp. 133, 135.
[47] Wheeler McMillen, cited in Thompson, p. 265; Peterson, p. 136.
[48] Publishers Information Bureau Report, figures cited in Quebral, p. 114.
[49] Manchester, p. 29.

That isn't being 'modern' to our way of thinking. Being modern (*Prairie Farmer* style) is giving our readers each issue in concise, understandable form, all the information there is about anything that will help them to make more money and live more happily.[50]

Even so, Butler and Gregory began calling in experts to study their paper and suggest ways to improve it. During the experimenting that followed, page layouts and type faces changed to extremes which became almost shrill, and the office mails were full of staff memos devoted to soul-searching, finger-pointing, and plans for change. Everyone got interested in the appearance of *Prairie Farmer*, to which few had paid so much attention earlier. Members of the staff disagreed about the image the paper portrayed (mainly to advertisers) when it pictured a farmer wearing work clothes and boots covered with manure. Gregory and his editors contended that this is farm life in its reality; others were quick to reply that *Country Gentleman* did not do it.

The old masthead which Butler had resurrected disappeared again, and stark, modern type replaced the ornate letters, the pastoral scenes, and the vines which wound among the letters. An eight-page rotogravure section began in late 1935, filled with colorful but nonlocal material stressing human interest. Readers were likely to find anything in the section, from a picture of Alaskan children holding a walrus by his tusks to a pin-up picture of a movie star. The Slim and Spud cartoon appeared in color and expanded to one-half page in early 1937, joined by a new syndicated comic strip called the Wilksies which occupied another half-page.

Several years of financial deficits added to the unrest at 1230 Washington Boulevard in the mid-1930's. Advertising had dropped more than 60 per cent, from 517,322 lines in 1928 to only 192,515 lines in 1933, before it began to rise during 1934.[51] Linage figures do not reflect the full financial effect, however, because the rate per line also declined. An advertising income of $738,437 in 1928 fell to only $182,639 in 1933. Income from subscriptions dropped by nearly two-thirds, from $178,431 in 1928 to $62,507 in 1933.[52] Table 5 summarizes net income during that period when employees sometimes were paid in quarters that readers and listeners had sent in exchange for jig-saw puzzles which *Prairie Farmer* and WLS

[50] *Prairie Farmer*, 107 (January 19, 1935), 22.
[51] Memorandum from Gregory to Butler, May 27, 1935.
[52] Statement by F. G. Paddock and J. J. Kaberna to the First National Bank of Chicago, July 12, 1934.

offered. On occasion those quarters were the only money at hand
for payroll and postage.

TABLE 5. NET INCOME FOR PRAIRIE FARMER PUBLISHING COMPANY, 1928-33

Year	Net Income or (Deficit)
1928	$97,051
1929	61,229
1930	38,957
1931	(43,417)
1932	(48,417)
1933	(36,725)

SOURCE: Statement by F. G. Paddock and J. J. Kaberna to First National Bank of Chicago, July 12, 1934.

It was in this setting of burgeoning competition and financial
strain—plus ownership of a radio station whose signal knew no
state lines—that *Prairie Farmer* shifted its circulation strategy to
one of expansion after 1930. Butler's hired consultants had suggested that he embrace circulation within small towns as a means
of expanding, but this would have changed the general nature of
his audience. Rather, he turned to a geographic expansion among
farm readers. A publisher who at one time thought 100,000 might
be a maximum in circulation for *Prairie Farmer* now began to talk
quietly with his associates about his dream of one million subscribers.

Butler's immediate "Lincoln Land Market" became 236 agricultural counties: 100 in Illinois, 87 in Indiana, 36 in Wisconsin, and
13 in Michigan. It conformed roughly to the primary signal of
WLS and served as the center of growth for *Prairie Farmer* as
long as Butler lived.

WLS gave Butler a unique tool for building the circulation of
his farm paper. The popularity of the station among farm people
helped increase awareness of *Prairie Farmer*, for Butler insisted
that the two institutions be welded as one. His weld did not always
hold, as later discussion will show, but the two worked closely in
many ways. For instance, *Prairie Farmer* aired its own farm program each noon and Gregory presented a weekly show called
Parade of the Week. WLS often announced the dates and places
of meetings designed to sell subscriptions to *Prairie Farmer* and
musicians from WLS took part in them. These were elaborate

affairs which the circulation staff reported to be extremely effective.

In Indiana, for example, the circulation manager ran three sales crews on a county-by-county plan. Each crew opened its campaign in a given county by setting up a big entertainment show in the county seat or other centrally located town. Admission to the show was by ticket only and residents got their tickets free from members of the crew, with or without buying a subscription. Merchants often gave door prizes in exchange for publicity at the show. One part of the show consisted of entertainment films and publicity films for the merchants. A second part involved live entertainment by some of the stars from WLS. Each show closed with a goodwill talk by the circulation manager who also introduced salesmen who would be calling on residents during the campaign.[53]

The home talent shows which began in 1933 offered another type of joint action. They were designed to encourage local talent, arouse community spirit, discover entertainers for WLS, and sell subscriptions to *Prairie Farmer*.

Radio was of special value to *Prairie Farmer* during World War II, when help was scarce and rationing of tires and gasoline restricted the work of subscription salesmen. Under those conditions WLS announced rates and urged farmers to renew their subscriptions by mail.[54]

In general, WLS gave salesmen for *Prairie Farmer* the advantage of calling on people who were accustomed to hearing about the paper on a day-to-day basis. The radio station helped serve as a congenial door-opener.

Indiana responded first and most forcefully to the paper's efforts to expand, partly because of its nearness to Chicago and partly because it lacked a strong state farm paper. Circulation in Indiana grew from 4,000 in 1918 to a maximum of 110,000 by 1937. Then, until Butler died, Indiana provided between 100,000 and 108,000 paid subscribers, or nearly one-third of the paper's total. *Prairie Farmer* had more readers in Indiana by 1941 than the state's own farm paper, *Indiana Farmer's Guide*.[55]

[53] Thompson, pp. 196-197; memorandum from Gregory to Butler, May 27, 1935.

[54] Memoranda from Ralph Ammon to Butler, January 6, 1943, and January 11, 1943.

[55] Audit Bureau of Circulations, *Blue Book (Periodicals)*, publishers' statements for *Prairie Farmer* and *Indiana Farmer's Guide*, 1918 through 1948.

Circulation in Michigan never reached major proportions and amounted to only 22,000 when Butler died.

Wisconsin and Iowa offered an entirely different case, one which pitted Butler against a farm publisher who was as aggressive as he —Dante M. Pierce. Pierce published the *Wisconsin Farmer* and *Iowa Homestead* after his father, James M., died on November 1, 1920. A solidly built man who stood about five feet ten inches tall, Dante Pierce had a voice so loud that his employees were confident he would not really have had to use the telephone for long-distance conversations. On-lookers sometimes thought he was trying to run his businesses by verbal violence alone, and an editor reportedly could learn more profanity during three months with him than during two years with the military. Never one to delegate responsibility, Pierce held close control over advertising, circulation, and editing in the Des Moines office where he headquartered.

Tension increased between Butler and Pierce in 1929 when Pierce showed signs of doing what Butler had in mind—expanding. His *Wisconsin Farmer* bought its 52-year-old competitor, *Wisconsin Agriculturist,* and he consolidated them into *Wisconsin Agriculturist and Farmer* beginning June 1, 1929.[56] However, less than four months later Pierce announced his decision to give up farm publishing interests in Iowa after John P. Wallace, of arch-rival *Wallaces' Farmer,* offered $2 million for the *Iowa Homestead.*[57] A new combination, *Wallaces' Farmer and Iowa Homestead,* appeared October 26, 1929, with a circulation of 250,000.[58] Pierce's absence from Iowa proved temporary, however, because he was forced to repossess the newly combined paper in 1932.

Pierce's next move brought him into direct competition with Butler. The July 1, 1930, issue of *Illinois Farmer* announced that Dante Pierce was its new publisher. This came as a surprise to men in the Prairie Farmer Building and Pierce seemingly intended it to be so. His negotiations with Arthur C. Haubold, publisher of the *Illinois Farmer,* appear like something out of a detective novel. The two would arrange to meet in a certain hotel in Chicago. At the appointed time, Pierce would take an elevator from his room to perhaps two floors above the chosen room, then walk the rest of

[56] *Wisconsin Agriculturist and Farmer,* 58 (June 1, 1929), 8.
[57] Edward L. and Frederick H. Schapsmeier, "The Wallaces and Their Farm Paper: A Story of Agrarian Leadership," *Journalism Quarterly,* 44 (Summer, 1967), 292.
[58] *Wallaces' Farmer and Iowa Homestead,* 54 (October 26, 1929), 3.

the way. Meanwhile, his conferee would take an elevator up to
within two floors, then walk to the meeting room.[59]

No one knows exactly why Pierce chose to buy *Illinois Farmer*.
Some say he bought it for protection or nuisance value, for leverage
in Illinois to force Butler to stay out of Wisconsin. He may have
wanted to compete in the Illinois market, although this is unlikely
because the *Illinois Farmer* was in debt and the fiscal outlook was
not favorable. Another possible explanation is that he viewed the
purchase as a promising short-term business venture.

Butler's first reaction was a full-page article in the issue of
August 23 "exposing" an abortion remedy which the *Wisconsin
Agriculturist and Farmer* had advertised and later defended editorially. The article in *Prairie Farmer* drew on authorities showing
that the remedy consisted essentially of wheat shorts and brown
sugar and that the Wisconsin paper was in error.[60]

Butler's next action was to ignore the depression, with the losses
it was forcing upon *Prairie Farmer,* and offer to buy *Illinois Farmer*
from Pierce. On December 19, 1930, *Prairie Farmer* contracted to
buy *Illinois Farmer* for no more than $278,000. Only $18,500 was
cash and *Prairie Farmer* agreed to pay the remainder in monthly
installments equal to seven and one-half cents a line on all commercial advertising that *Prairie Farmer* carried the previous month.
Also, *Prairie Farmer* would pay interest at 3 per cent.[61]

A second contract signed that same day gave Pierce what he
hoped would be relief from future pressure by Butler for circulation in Wisconsin. *Prairie Farmer* consented not to solicit subscriptions in Wisconsin beyond the territory it presently occupied or
increase subscriptions in Wisconsin beyond 25,000 for 10 years
after January 1, 1931. In turn, Pierce agreed not to: (1) solicit subscriptions in Illinois beyond 10,000 for 10 years, (2) solicit subscriptions in Indiana beyond its present territory or increase subscriptions within 10 years, or (3) publish for circulation in Illinois or
Indiana within 10 years.[62]

[59] Richard Pierce, personal interview, March 24, 1967.

[60] *Prairie Farmer,* 102 (August 23, 1930), 5.

[61] From the contract signed on December 19, 1930, by Dante Pierce for
Orange Judd Publishing Company and C. V. Gregory for Prairie Farmer Publishing Company. Later correspondence (Fred Orlemann to Butler, December
31, 1941) stated that the actual price was $277,250 and that monthly pay-
ments were $.062475 a line rather than $.075 as stated in the contract.

[62] From a contract signed on December 19, 1930, by Dante Pierce and
C. V. Gregory.

For the third time in its history, *Prairie Farmer* had absorbed a publication carrying the name *Illinois Farmer*.[63] Butler lost some pride along with his money in this transaction, for both parties agreed that Pierce got the better end of the bargain. Later, however, Pierce was not pleased with the way he felt Butler had abused the agreements. *Prairie Farmer* met all payments through the depression years, but in the 1940's Butler's anxiety to settle up led to asking Pierce to accept less than the contract price in a lump sum.

TABLE 6. *Prairie Farmer* AVERAGE TOTAL PAID CIRCULATION, BY YEAR, 1908-48

Year	Circulation	Year	Circulation
1908	39,877[a]	1929	265,076
1909	52,532[b]	1930	293,676
1910	69,847[b]	1931	317,359
1911	70,000[c]	1932	306,561
1912	83,821[d]	1933	299,807
1913	85,694[e]	1934	296,583
1914	99,602[f]	1935	303,504
1915	101,321[g]	1936	310,945
1916	101,321[h]	1937	323,869
1917	102,379[i]	1938	342,047
1918	107,298	1939	328,251
1919	134,004	1940	330,265
1920	155,397	1941	340,293
1921	156,080	1942	347,547
1922	156,888	1943	342,015
1923	168,228	1944	339,951
1924	170,032	1945	347,617
1925	172,258	1946	360,791
1926	183,223	1947	365,388
1927	226,137	1948	368,098
1928	249,306		

[a] 1908 Ayer, p. 158.
[b] Average of circulation figures published in *Prairie Farmer* during the last six months of the year.
[c] 1911 Ayer, p. 183. [d] 1912 Ayer, p. 178. [e] 1913 Ayer, p. 181.
[f] Audit Bureau of Circulations, Auditor's Report for 12 months ending December 31, 1914.
[g] 1915 Ayer, p. 190. [h] 1916 Ayer, p. 191.
[i] Circulation figures for 1917 through 1950 are from Audit Bureau of Circulations publisher's statements, called *Farm Publishers' Semi-Annual Statement (Periodicals)* until December 31, 1924, after which they were called *A.B.C. Blue Book—Periodical Publishers' Statements.*

[63] Richard Bardolph, *Agricultural Literature and the Early Illinois Farmer* (Urbana: University of Illinois Press, 1948), pp. 98-99, reports the first two cases.

Pierce resented the request, but on January 15, 1948, authorized a discount of $4,865 if the remaining $115,000 were paid within five days.[64] Four days later—shortly before Butler died—*Prairie Farmer* made its last payment on the old *Orange Judd Farmer* that had bothered Butler since he arrived in Chicago almost 39 years earlier.

The other source of irritation for Pierce was Butler's abuse of the circulation agreement. Circulation of *Prairie Farmer* in Wisconsin passed the 25,000 mark in 1937, when it averaged 33,106. It then climbed to 37,326 during 1938 and closed out the 10-year contract period with 34,312.[65] Pierce had less trouble with *Prairie Farmer* in Iowa where Butler's paper usually had fewer than 3,000 subscribers between 1920 and 1948.

Butler never lived to see *Prairie Farmer* reach his goal of one million subscribers. Yet, as Table 6 indicates, he did see circulation exceed 365,000, more than half of which was outside Illinois, and the expansion which he began continued for many years after him.

Advertising Sales Strategy

The most distinctive feature of the approach which *Prairie Farmer* used to sell space to advertisers under Butler was its co-operation with other state farm papers. This strategy began for *Prairie Farmer* in January, 1914, when it was elected to join the Standard Farm Paper Association.[66] By that time the association consisted of 13 other farm papers throughout the country, most of them general state papers: *Wallaces' Farmer* (Iowa), *Ohio Farmer* (Ohio), *Indiana Farmer* (Indiana), *Wisconsin Agriculturist* (Wisconsin), *The Farmer* (Minnesota), *Oklahoma Farm Journal* (Oklahoma), *Missouri Farmer* (Missouri), *Hoard's Dairyman* (class paper), *Breeder's Gazette* (class paper), *Progressive Farmer* (regional paper), *Michigan Farmer* (Michigan), *Kansas Farmer* (Kansas), and *Pennsylvania Farmer* (Pennsylvania). The group had grown from 10 papers in the original association formed December 2-3, 1908. Before then the papers were represented individually by an eastern and a western representative, George W. Herbert of Chicago and Wallace C. Richardson of New York City. The papers joined forces to standardize width of columns, adver-

---

[64] Dante Pierce to Fred Orlemann, January 15, 1948.

[65] Audit Bureau of Circulations, *Blue Book (Periodicals)*, publisher's statements for *Prairie Farmer* for the years cited.

[66] *Prairie Farmer*, 86 (January 1, 1914), 2.

tising rate cards, advertiser relations, and "other actions that may be of value to advertisers and publications alike." [67]

Prairie Farmer got perhaps two-thirds to three-fourths of its advertising through the Standard Farm Paper Association after joining.[68] As a member it offered group rates to advertisers and helped support a sizable sales staff. For example, eight or nine sales representatives operated from the Chicago office of the Association by 1925.[69]

The Association continued until December, 1930, when the depression forced its dissolution. Convinced that cooperation was as important in adversity as in prosperity, Butler and several farm publishers in neighboring states formed a new group, the Midwest Farm Paper Unit, Inc., in January, 1931. Members of this group consisted of the *Nebraska Farmer, Wallaces' Farmer and Iowa Homestead, The Farmer, Wisconsin Agriculturist and Farmer,* and *Prairie Farmer.* They set a group rate and staffed offices in Chicago and New York with salesmen from each paper, which meant that each paper kept its men on the payroll but offered their services to the Unit. The system did not work smoothly, so after two or three years members pooled budgets rather than salesmen and the Unit hired a separate sales staff.

Membership in the Unit brought Butler into a unique group of farm publishers which included Dante Pierce, Horace C. Klein, and Samuel McKelvie. Horace Klein of *The Farmer* was a short, dapper outspoken man to whom Butler snortingly referred as the Little Peacock. To Dante Pierce, Klein was Little Napoleon. His paper had led all other Standard Farm Papers in circulation until 1922, when *Prairie Farmer* overtook it, so some intramural rivalry existed.

Samuel McKelvie of the *Nebraska Farmer* was a quieter, more diplomatic man but he, too, was experienced at publishing. He had bought the *Nebraska Farmer* in 1908 when he was only 27 years old and stayed with it until he retired in 1935, except for four years when he was governor of Nebraska.[70]

Meetings of this group became legendary among staff members

[67] *Agricultural Advertising,* 20 (January, 1909), 226.
[68] Herman Steen, personal interview, January 25, 1967.
[69] Vernon Anderson, personal interview, April 7, 1967.
[70] For a discussion of McKelvie's activities in farm publishing, see Bruce H. Nicoll and Ken R. Keller, *Sam McKelvie—Son of the Soil* (Lincoln: Johnsen Publishing Co., 1954), pp. 33-37, 111-126.

because, judging by the shouting inside, listeners could easily fear that the participants would slay each other before the meeting adjourned. None of the four men came to meetings of the Unit with orders from home, for they were the order-makers. They made decisions as they went, each seeking his own ends, sometimes in competition with other members. However, the financial forces uniting them proved stronger than their personal differences, and the Midwest Farm Paper Unit remained active even during years of extremely serious financial problems. The depression caused total advertising in U.S. farm periodicals to drop until linage in 1932 was only 40 per cent of what it had been in 1928. Among members of the Unit, *Nebraska Farmer* and *Prairie Farmer* lost 66 per cent of their advertising business during that period. *Wallaces' Farmer and Iowa Homestead* lost 59 per cent, while *Wisconsin Agriculturist and Farmer* lost 57 per cent.[71]

One of their competitors was feeling the pinch even more and directed a legal suit against the Unit in 1933. *Indiana Farmer's Guide* had lost more than 70 per cent of its advertising revenue between 1928 and 1932. In its suit *Indiana Farmer's Guide* charged that it was losing advertising revenue because of the combination rates which the Unit offered to advertisers. Members of the Unit had set combination rates below the total of the separate rates in order to compete more strongly with national farm magazines.

The suit came under Sections 1, 2, and 7 of the Sherman Act dealing with combinations to restrain or monopolize a business in interstate commerce. It moved through the courts for more than three years and went twice to the United States Supreme Court before a final judgment came in favor of *Prairie Farmer* and its fellow members. The Circuit Court of Appeals, Seventh Circuit, concluded on March 23, 1937, that there was not sufficient evidence to sustain a verdict of unlawful restraint.[72]

Prairie Farmer continued to sell cooperatively after Butler died. By then the paper was regaining confidence that it could hold a place for itself even in a market with strong national farm publications.

[71] *Federal Reporter,* 70 (2nd series), 5.
[72] Court actions in this case are cited in: *Federal Reporter,* 70 (2nd series), 3, 5; *United States Reports,* 293, p. 268; *Federal Reporter,* 82 (2nd series), 704; *United States Reports,* 299, pp. 156-157; *Federal Reporter,* 88 (2nd series), 979-982; *United States Reports,* 301, p. 696; and *United States Reports,* 302, p. 773.

A Crusading Paper

CHAPTER 5

Working at his desk one day, Dave Thompson, who was then an associate editor of *Prairie Farmer*, looked up and saw Butler rushing toward him waving a letter. It proved to be one of those hand-written letters on tablet paper, this time from the wife of a hired man in Iroquois County. The couple had three children and within the last year the husband had begun to spend not only his money but also a good deal of his time with a woman who lived at the edge of a nearby town. The situation was intolerable for his wife and she wanted advice from *Prairie Farmer* about what she could do.

Enraged by such an abuse, Butler instructed Thompson to go to Iroquois County, investigate the matter, and give the wife any legal or other help that she needed. "And," Butler concluded, "if there is nothing else you can do, just take this fellow out back of the strawstack and kick the hell out of him. No reader of *Prairie Farmer* can treat his wife like this and get away with it." [1]

Thompson knew better than to entertain such a demand lightly, yet he also knew that this was a personal matter in which *Prairie*

---

[1] Dave O. Thompson, unpublished memoirs, p. 377.

Farmer had a definite rule not to take part. Gus Holt and Thomas Murphy, the corporation's lawyer, advised Thompson against going to see the woman and suggested that he instead write her a letter, which he did. In it he told her that he could come to see her on a given date if she liked, added that it would be best not to have her husband along at that first meeting, and asked her to confirm a time and place to meet.

Months later, Butler stopped at Thompson's desk and asked what had happened to that woman whose husband was abusing her. Thompson replied that he had sent the letter and got no reply, whereupon Butler stiffened, doubled up his fist, and said sternly, "I don't know how you can sleep nights. You don't know whether this woman has been killed, whether he has beaten her up with an ax. You don't know anything about it and still you can sit there at work, eat your meals, write your story, without knowing whether or not this woman is still abused.

"Now, I tell you again. You go down there and find out about it. And if you can't do anything else, you just kick the hell out of him."

Under Butler's order and despite another warning from Holt that he might be shot for interfering, Thompson drove down to Iroquois County and found that the family had moved. He spent a day tracing them before he arrived at a small, well-kept tenant home in another county. Thompson turned into the driveway, a woman came out to the car, and he introduced himself. His name did not register so he reminded her about the letter. She turned to the children who had followed her, sent them into the house, and then told Thompson that when his letter came she showed it to her husband and he had behaved himself ever since.

Butler was a little set back by this report; he probably would have been happier to hear that Thompson had taken the husband behind a strawstack. First Butler walked away from Thompson's desk, then he returned and said he guessed that he had been too emotional. "But you know that is the way I am. I get concerned about a thing like this and I have to see it through."

Such incidents seemed to call out the fatherly instinct in Burridge Butler. He could never get that emotional about the productivity of agriculture or a presidential veto of the McNary-Haugen Bill. Butler's feeling was for people, especially common people, and as long as he lived his main concern embraced the little farmer on

80 acres out in the hill country with a wife, three or four children,
a few cows, hens, and pigs. His editors often heard his advice to
"reach the fellow out there at the end of the road." [2] If a man introduced himself as "only a farmer," Butler immediately preached a
sermon about how George Washington, Thomas Jefferson, and
others were proud of being farmers. "You have the first and best
vocation in the world," Butler would scold. "You keep the rest of
us from starving." [3]

Into this picture of the downtrodden farmer, Butler projected
himself as defender and spokesman. Butler's experience in newspapering had told him that a successful newspaper is a crusading
thing which gives a voice to the people, defends them from evil
and destroys it. A natural way to perform such functions was
through campaigns, so they were fundamental to Butler's view of
publishing. As long as Butler owned *Prairie Farmer*, the paper
moved from campaign to campaign, sometimes juggling two or
more at a time. Crusading was one characteristic which dominated
his paper, regardless of who edited it.

Butler used three main criteria in judging whether or not to
enter a campaign: [4]

1. Whatever service the paper undertook should pay for itself
in some way. For example, a $50 reward demanded outlays of cash,
but its value in helping sell subscriptions and advertising could
exceed the expense.

2. A good campaign should not close out too quickly. Butler
felt that a campaign which closed out after one or two issues was
of little value. He liked to begin with an editorial, follow with a
major illustrated story, then use double-column articles reporting
progress, run another hot editorial, and end with a major feature
story which stressed accomplishments.

3. He entered only those campaigns which he felt quite sure
he could win. Butler's usual rule was, "Never start a fight in the
other fellow's alley." He intensely disliked having *Prairie Farmer*
or WLS embarrassed, so he carefully calculated the risk when deciding whether or not they should begin a campaign.

Between 1909 and 1948, *Prairie Farmer* engaged in more than 50
editorial campaigns on behalf of its readers. Nearly half might be

[2] Verlo Butz, personal interview, January 14, 1967.
[3] John W. Holland, "Let's Start Something," undated, unpublished eulogy
of Butler, p. 53.
[4] Thompson, pp. 107-108.

classed as campaigns against crime and deception, and these were specialties of Butler because they best served his self-chosen role as protector of the underdog. Other campaigns—which stressed farm production, marketing, legislation, education, and community betterment—chiefly bore the mark of Clifford Gregory, who also was an avid campaigner but of a different sort.

Campaigns Against Crime and Deception

Probably the longest running campaign of this type was one directed against phony investments. It started informally in 1911 when *Prairie Farmer* began to warn farmers (many of whom now had some savings) about stock salesmen who were swarming into the countryside.[5] In mid-1916 the paper started printing the names of bogus stock issues and reporting cases in which farmers had been swindled. *Prairie Farmer* seldom was without a law suit during 1918 and 1919 as it concentrated upon helping drive promoters of fraudulent stock issues out of the state or into receivership. At one time, Butler's paper had suits aggregating half a million dollars outstanding against it, but none came to trial.[6] *Prairie Farmer* in turn claimed to have saved its readers millions of dollars within only two years and helped bring about a change in the state's Blue Sky Law during 1919.[7] Table 7 shows some of the firms which *Prairie Farmer* exposed during the peak of this campaign.

Whenever oldtimers talk about the crusading *Prairie Farmer,* they almost invariably refer to the paper's chicken thief campaign which enlivened the farm scene from 1926 into 1931. It portrayed Butler's spirit at its brightest and was full of cops-and-robbers excitement quite foreign to a staid farm press.

For years farm people had been well acquainted with chicken thievery, but it assumed the more treacherous form of an organized business as more automobiles and more miles of all-weather roads allowed thieves to work their trade. Syndicates operated out of Chicago, Milwaukee, St. Louis, Quincy, and other towns along the western side of the state.[8] The paper estimated in 1926 that organized and lone-wolf thievery was costing poultry raisers in Illinois

[5] *Prairie Farmer,* 83 (August 1, 1911), 12.
[6] *Prairie Farmer,* 93 (August 6, 1921), 8; Edward F. Dunne, *Illinois—The Heart of the Nation,* III (Chicago: Lewis Publishing Co., 1933), 50.
[7] *Prairie Farmer,* 93 (August 6, 1921), 8.
[8] *Prairie Farmer,* 95 (July 21, 1923), 8; Thompson, pp. 97-98.

TABLE 7. RECORDS OF SOME OF THE BUSINESS CONCERNS EXPOSED BY *Prairie Farmer*, 1918 THROUGH EARLY 1920

Name of Firm and Date Exposed in *Prairie Farmer*	Date of Failure	Capitalization
Consumers' Service Supply Co.[a] May 18, 1918	January, 1921	$ 600,000
Guarantee Mortgage & Trust Co. June 1, 1918	January, 1919	400,000
Riley-Schubert-Grossman Co.[a] August 20, 1918	October, 1919	3,000,000
Industrial Securities Co. October 19, 1918	January, 1920	12,000,000
United Owners Supply Co. November 16, 1918	February, 1921	500,000
Moore Motor Vehicle Co.[a] December 14, 1918	May, 1921	1,600,000
Consumers' Packing Co.[a] December 14, 1918	February, 1919	2,000,000
Pan Motor Co.[a] February 8, 1919	November, 1919	3,000,000
American Co-operative Association March 18, 1919	October, 1920	1,000,000
B. M. Way Stores Co. March 22, 1919	May, 1921	100,000
Daniel Hayes Land Co. March 22, 1919	February, 1920	3,500,000
Little Motor Kar Co. August 9, 1919	May, 1920	500,000
General Oil Co. January 17, 1920	November, 1920	2,000,000

[a] Promoters of these companies were prosecuted for using the mails to defraud.
SOURCE: Gregory to Prof. F. W. Beckman, Ames, Iowa; undated.

$1.5 million a year and those in Indiana about $1 million a year.[9] It appears that Butler gave *Prairie Farmer* at least part of its impetus for a campaign against chicken thievery after 200 laying hens were stolen from his Burr Ridge Farm south of Hinsdale. With an editorial headed "Let's Stop Chicken Stealing," the paper initiated its most frenzied campaign on January 30, 1926.[10] Two weeks later the Prairie Farmer Protective Union announced that it would

[9] *Prairie Farmer*, 98 (June 19, 1926), 8.
[10] *Prairie Farmer*, 98 (January 30, 1926), 10.

pay $100 each for the capture and conviction of poultry thieves. *Prairie Farmer* became a swapping center for ideas about how to catch chicken thieves. "Tell him to halt," advised the Protective Union, "and shoot him in the legs if he doesn't." The columnist balked, however, at one reader's idea of charging the fence around his poultry house with 3,300 volts of electricity. Other suggestions from readers, if not so straightforward, often were ingenious. One reader reported success with a mounted camera aimed at the door of the chicken house. The thief released the shutter when he touched a wire across the door. Another farmer used the same idea, except with a shotgun instead of a camera.

A farmer in Indiana wrote that he built two doors to his poultry house, one which led into the poultry house and the other into a tiny room which closed with a spring and had a lock that the thief could not reach. Some farmers tried to identify their birds by punching holes through the web of the birds' feet or by clipping wings. Another reader suggested simply staying home more at night.

The thieves, in turn, lacked nothing for imagination. Some used sulfur fumes to keep chickens from squawking and brought meat to pacify the farmer's dog. One thief stole two hogs while the owner was helping a neighbor chase chicken thieves. Perhaps most resourceful of all was a thief in Wisconsin who went out on cold nights, warmed a rod, and eased it into poultry houses among the roosting birds. When the birds stepped onto the warm rod, he gently drew them out and slipped them into a waiting sack.

Anxious to do more than publicize this problem, *Prairie Farmer* introduced its own poultry marker in September, 1927, a marker which tattooed a number in the web of each bird's wing. Each buyer got a personal number which was certified to him and registered with the Protective Union. The Protective Union then sent lists of these numbers, names, and addresss to law officers in Illinois, Indiana, Wisconsin, and eastern Iowa. In little more than two years *Prairie Farmer* sold nearly 84,000 markers, which meant that many millions of birds carried the tattoo.

Part of the paper's emotionalism during this campaign was due to a new manager of the Protective Union who had a flair for on-the-run reporting. He was Dave Thompson, a tall, likable man with what friends called a "million-dollar smile." Thompson joined *Prairie Farmer* in April, 1926, after having been the first county agent in Marathon County, Wisconsin, the first animal husbandry specialist in extension at Purdue University, the first farm adviser for McLean County, Illinois, the first executive secretary of the Illinois Agricultural Association, and an organizer of the American Farm Bureau Federation.[11] Most recently, he had formed a rural motion picture firm which he abandoned as unprofitable.

Thompson could get mightily indignant about abuses to farmers, so the violence of thievery—including occasional killings—offered material for editions which reverberated with the best of thrill-hungry dailies. Headlines and copy often rang with terms such as notorious gangs, confessions, orgies, and blood. At times, the pages of *Prairie Farmer* looked like a rogues' gallery because editors often prevailed upon prisoners to pose for pictures.

By May, 1928, *Prairie Farmer* had paid more than $11,000 in rewards covering more than 220 cases and probably 500 to 600 convicted thieves. The sum nearly doubled to $20,350 by late 1930, "a greater sum than has been paid out by any other agency for the suppression of rural crime." [12] A few months later in March, 1931, the paper announced the end of its rewards, which by then had been reduced from $100 to $25 each. Even so, the paper had paid $21,300 for the conviction of captured thieves. It had obtained the passage of laws in Illinois and Wisconsin requiring all poultry buyers to be licensed and to keep records of the birds they bought. It also obtained passage of a law in Indiana which increased the penalties for stealing from farmers and helped prevent the passage of a bill in Illinois which would have outlawed farm protective associations.[13] Outside of Illinois, nearly a dozen other farm papers had followed the lead of *Prairie Farmer* by starting anti-thief campaigns.

Chicken thievery became front-page material at times after 1931, but *Prairie Farmer* broadened its battle to include thievery in general. It conducted a half-dozen campaigns against other types of crime and deception during the 1930's.

One of these was against traveling "eye doctors" who preyed mostly upon older people who were isolated. They often introduced

[11] *Prairie Farmer*, 98 (April 17, 1926), 10; "A Resume of the Life of Dave O. Thompson, Sr.," undated mimeo; *Prairie Farmer*, 87 (February 13, 1915), 3; John J. Lacey, *Farm Bureau in Illinois* (Bloomington: Illinois Agricultural Association, 1965), pp. 55-56, 65.
[12] *Prairie Farmer*, 102 (November 8, 1930), 8.
[13] *Prairie Farmer*, 101 (December 28, 1929), 8.

themselves as salesmen of eyeglasses and if the contact man saw
major eye trouble, he would announce that a well-known eye surgeon from Chicago happened to be with him in the car. If the
victim fell for this story, the "surgeon" appeared to inspect, then
apply magic potions. Next he placed a patch over the treated eye,
collected a healthy fee, and left. When the patch came off at an
appointed time, the victim found himself far from cured and far
from the money he had invested.

Publicity in *Prairie Farmer* helped lead to the arrest of two members of such gangs, one of whom reportedly vowed, "Believe me,
if I get out of here I won't be caught in *Prairie Farmer*'s territory
again." [14]

Somewhat akin to this was a campaign against gypsies which
began after Thompson assumed editorial control in 1937, although
the paper had warned readers against gypsies as early as 1923.
Each summer carloads of the nomads moved northward into the
midwest and lived (as Thompson put it) "on the land" as they
traveled. The indignant editor warned readers to "have nothing
at all—strictly nothing at all—to do with these gypsies. They are
not picturesque. They are dirty, and greasy, and bad." [15]

One of their methods, Thompson explained to readers, was to
reconnoiter an area and find an elderly couple who seemed fairly
prosperous and lived alone. Usually a man and two women approached the home, and one of the women would enter the house.
She would explain to the couple that she had healing powers and
if they would cooperate she would cure any aches, pains, or diseases. Money played a vital part in this cure, so she asked the
victims to place cash in bills within an envelope and seal it. Then
she attached it to a place on the body nearest the ailment and departed with instructions to leave the envelope in place for several
days; otherwise, the cure could not come about and the ailment
might even worsen. At the end of the appointed period, victims
would find only their ailment and an envelope filled with blank
paper. Losses often ran from $100 to more than $1,000.

Prairie Farmer tried to help readers avoid such losses by reporting cases which it heard about and alerting readers to methods
which itinerants employed to defraud.

The paper also decided that the rural trespass laws needed teeth,

[14] *Prairie Farmer,* 100 (January 7, 1928), 6.
[15] *Prairie Farmer,* 112 (June 15, 1940), 6.

so in March, 1938, it proposed seven changes.[16] Basically, the proposals called for fines of $5 to $50 or jail sentences of up to six months for trespass upon a posted farm or farm home. By May, 1939, *Prairie Farmer* could report that Indiana had passed a law as the paper had proposed, and less than two months later a similar rural trespassing law went into effect in Illinois.[17] Despite editorial pressure in Wisconsin, a state Senate judiciary committee killed the paper's trespassing proposal after the bill had passed the Assembly.[18]

The result of this campaign was that the front gate of a farm became its legal entrance and a "no trespassing" sign carried some legal force.

Even slot machines, marijuana, and strip-tease acts became the objects of campaigns in *Prairie Farmer* during the 1930's. Staff members of the paper helped write and promote the passage of a law against slot machines for Indiana. Illinois officially recognized slot machine gambling as illegal, so the role of the paper in Illinois was one of pointing out violations. Editors would photograph slot machines in use throughout the area and print the picture asking residents of that area to crack down.

Prairie Farmer called for readers to rid the area of marijuana plants during 1938, a year in which more than 16,500 tons of the plant were destroyed within the paper's circulation zone. Editors rallied support by dramatizing the effect of marijuana—two boys who went insane, a girl who had been molested, and a man who attempted murder.

A brief campaign during late 1939 decried strip-tease acts at the Illinois State Fair and called for officials to make the fair "more nearly serve the purposes for which it was founded."[19]

During the 1940's *Prairie Farmer* stirred up some of the crusading spirit by protesting against bingo, roadhouses, and liquor. An appeal to "Clean Up the Roadhouse Mess" struck a responsive note among readers, and when Indiana drafted legislation involving alcoholic beverages, it included a suggestion from *Prairie Farmer* that no license would be issued to the owner of a place outside of corporate limits, beyond police protection.[20]

[16] *Prairie Farmer,* 110 (March 26, 1938), 1.
[17] *Prairie Farmer,* 111 (May 20, 1939), 14; 111 (June 17, 1939), 1.
[18] *Prairie Farmer,* 111 (July 15, 1939), 6; 111 (October 7, 1939), 18.
[19] *Prairie Farmer,* 111 (August 26, 1939), 2.
[20] Thompson, p. 106.

Such campaigns, although still unique among farm papers, by now were only a thin shadow of earlier campaigns in *Prairie Farmer*. Its days of fighting crime were ending; the heyday of its detective-type reporting was past.

Campaigns in Farm Production

One of the paper's main campaigns dealing with farm production actually began before Gregory arrived. Under the influence of Prof. Cyril Hopkins and his Illinois system of permanent soil fertility, Butler assigned a reporter in 1910 to campaign for increased use of limestone and more facilities for crushing limestone in the state. He intensified this campaign in 1911 by printing chapters from Hopkins' book, *The Story of the Soil*, plus case histories of farmers who used ground limestone. *Prairie Farmer* chose a live issue in advocating the Illinois system of soil fertility, which largely ignored livestock manure as a means of enriching soil. In 1915 it professed to have been the first—"and still almost the only"—farm paper "to admit that the grain farmer has any business on earth": "For years it was the only farm paper honest enough to admit that man cannot live by meat alone, and that raising grain to sell is just as legitimate a business as raising livestock. It was the first and for years the only paper to tell the grain farmer how he could maintain the fertility of his soil without livestock. For years it has been popular to berate the grain farmer as a soil robber, and to tell him that the only way to salvation is to feed his crops to stock. *Prairie Farmer* has not joined in this clamor." [21]

Editor Gregory hastened to assure the livestock industry that he did not belittle it, but he insisted that if a man's conditions promise more income from selling grain than feeding it, the man should do so. In Gregory's opinion, the cry that livestock is the basis of permanent soil fertility only helped meat packers hold an advantage over farmers.

"As long as farmers are taught that they must feed their crops to livestock, regardless of profit, or be classed with the soil robbers, just so long will the packers be able to continue their present policy." [22]

Farmers who tried the Illinois system were not only pronounced

[21] *Prairie Farmer*, 87 (January 30, 1915), 12.
[22] *Prairie Farmer*, 87 (May 8, 1915), 8.

soil robbers; they also heard dire predictions. Some critics warned that a farmer who applied rock phosphate was in danger of cementing his land. Another story charged Hopkins with holding financial interest in a fertilizer company. In the face of such charges *Prairie Farmer* defended the system and the man who promoted it. Future years treated its stand kindly, for the rich Illinois prairies proved well suited to specialized grain farming.

However, the paper was less consistent in its judgment about commercial mixed fertilizers. *Prairie Farmer*—and the state as a whole—was relatively slow to adopt them. Gregory concluded in 1912 that commercial fertilizers were not suited to conditions in the middle west. "It would be unfortunate indeed," he added, "if middle western farmers should ever come to the point where they would find it necessary to depend on commercial fertilizers for every crop they raise, as is done in the East." [23]

As a result, he accused the Middle West Soil Improvement Committee of appearing to be educational while really promoting the sale of commercial fertilizer for the National Fertilizer Association. Fertilizer men are trying to fill the country papers with free "boiler plate," he complained. He challenged the commercial fertilizer interests to buy 500 acres near the farm of Frank Mann and then compare results. As far as he was concerned, mixed fertilizer could not build up a soil's fertility except at prohibitive expense. "Their system tends ultimately to ruin the land and decrease profits." [24] Instead, *Prairie Farmer* favored the "mixed fertilizer" recommended by one farm adviser, eight-five-one: eight loads of manure, five tons of limestone, and one ton of raw rock phosphate.

This stance began to change by late 1918, however, when *Prairie Farmer* ran a full-page advertisement by the National Fertilizer Association. Improvements in quality and breadth of choice led Gregory to conclude by 1929 that it was not only possible but also advisable to give commercial fertilizers a place in the Illinois system of improvement. What had begun as a campaign against commercial mixed fertilizers ended as an endorsement.

Another production-oriented campaign in which *Prairie Farmer* took a major part was the adoption of soybeans in Illinois. The crop was hardly known in the state before 1920, although as early as 1912 *Prairie Farmer* had begun to discuss its possibilities as a

[23] *Prairie Farmer*, 84 (April 15, 1912), 11.
[24] *Prairie Farmer*, 86 (August 1, 1914), 8.

valuable crop for the middle west.[25] Most of that early interest
was in soybeans as a forage crop to be interplanted with corn and
"hogged down," but this new plant from the Orient was not to
have such a modest role. From a crop in 1919 of only about 16,000
acres in Illinois and almost nothing in Indiana, it grew to more
than 300,000 acres in the two states by 1922. It soon replaced many
acres of oats and challenged even corn and wheat as a cash crop.

Early in 1922 *Prairie Farmer* called soybeans the Corn Belt's
new hired man and added a plank in its editorial platform, "Grow
more soybeans." During the next two years it ran more than 100
columns of news about soybeans. This confidence arose from a new
commercial use for soybeans, as an oil for soap and paint. Before
the growing season of 1922, one firm in Illinois assured growers
that it would provide a cash market for all the beans available for
seed that season, and farmers of Illinois responded by boosting the
acreage of soybeans five-fold over 1921. In 1922 North Carolina
kept its hold on first place as a soybean-producing state, but by
1923 Illinois was an easy first, producing nearly twice as many
beans as second-ranked Missouri or third-ranked North Carolina.[26]

Livestock feeders also found in 1923 that soybean oilmeal served
as an excellent protein supplement. It was not new to dairymen
and hog raisers in the southern and western parts of the country,
but 1923 was its first season as a feed for livestock in Illinois and
Indiana. Continuing strong demand brought another increase of
70 per cent in the acreage of soybeans grown in Illinois and Indiana
during 1924. Table 8 shows the rapid climb in acreage through
1937. *Prairie Farmer* later expressed pleasure with the part it had
played in speeding the adoption of this new crop. It felt that it
had helped account for an adoption rate which was faster in Illinois
than in neighboring states.[27]

Farm tractors became the objects of campaigning in *Prairie
Farmer* soon after Gregory joined the paper. Discussions about
tractors did not really amount to much in *Prairie Farmer* until
about 1913, after which tractors became light enough for the
paper to start talking about how to select one for use in the mid-

[25] See, for example, *Prairie Farmer*, 84 (March 15, 1912), 5; 85 (March 15,
1913), 7; 86 (February 15, 1914), 11; 89 (February 10, 1917), 14.
[26] U.S. Department of Agriculture, *Agriculture Yearbook*, 1923 (Washington:
U.S. Government Printing Office, 1924), p. 792.
[27] Dunne, III, p. 50; *Prairie Farmer*, 95 (September 29, 1923), 6; undated
letter from Gregory to Prof. F. W. Beckman; Thompson, p. 21.

TABLE 8. ACRES OF SOYBEANS GROWN ALONE IN ILLINOIS, NIEGHBORING
STATES, AND THE UNITED STATES, 1924-37

Year	Illinois	Indiana	Iowa	Wisconsin	Missouri	U.S.
1924	315,000	204,000	23,000	38,000	165,000	1,567,000
1925	290,000	148,000	18,000	20,000	157,000	1,539,000
1926	350,000	189,000	24,000	19,000	220,000	1,871,000
1927	429,000	210,000	48,000	14,000	252,000	2,057,000
1928	463,000	289,000	63,000	22,000	281,000	2,154,000
1929	514,000	326,000	80,000	16,000	317,000	2,429,000
1930	720,000	443,000	124,000	14,000	442,000	3,072,000
1931	969,000	585,000	159,000	21,000	536,000	3,835,000
1932	776,000	563,000	217,000	89,000	616,000	3,704,000
1933	786,000	428,000	248,000	115,000	530,000	3,537,000
1934	1,715,000	621,000	853,000	251,000	720,000	5,764,000
1935	2,431,000	850,000	1,200,000	181,000	450,000	6,966,000
1936	2,043,000	748,000	586,000	101,000	360,000	6,127,000
1937	2,241,000	812,000	753,000	160,000	200,000	6,332,000

SOURCE: U.S. Department of Agriculture, "Soybeans, Cowpeas, and Velvetbeans, By
States, 1924-53," Statistical Bulletin 211 (Washington, June, 1957), pp. 2, 3, 4, 10.

west. It printed its first special Farm Power and Machinery Issue
in February, 1914. In the issue experts debated the value of horses
against tractors, discussed facts to consider in buying tractors, and
offered pointers for maintenance. More and more articles from
farmers about their tractors began to appear, encouraged by prizes
for the best letters. Farmers liked the way tractors outworked
horses, required no attention after the day's work, made better seed-
beds, and never came down with colic or corn stalk disease.

That fall, when Gregory traveled the country looking for a tractor which might suit his own farm west of Chicago, he began to
wonder why Illinois could not stage a big tractor demonstration
where farmers could see all the major makes at one time. Out of
that idea grew an Illinois Tractor Demonstration at Champaign
on August 3-6, 1915. Cooperating sponsors were *Prairie Farmer,
Orange Judd Farmer, Farm and Home,* the Champaign Chamber
of Commerce, the Champaign County Agricultural Improvement
Association, and the University of Illinois. It was publicized as
the first big demonstration of its kind east of the Missouri River.[28]
Roughly 20,000 farmers watched 78 tractors at work during the
three days. When Gregory returned to Chicago he predicted:

[28] *Prairie Farmer,* 87 (June 19, 1915), 8.

"When the complete history of agriculture shall be written, the decade from 1910 to 1920 will be marked as the era of the development of farm power. The invention of the grain binder was revolutionary. The binder has been supplemented by a line of planting, harvesting and tillage machinery that has made twentieth century farming possible. But machinery without power to operate it is valueless. . . . So the present decade is witnessing the perfection of a machine more wonderful and more far-reaching in its possibilities than the self-binder—the gas tractor. . . ." [29]

Soon a new column, "Farm Mechanics," appeared with answers to hundreds of questions which farmers faced in adjusting to a new type of power.

Sometimes *Prairie Farmer* initiated its own incentives for increasing the quantity or quality of output by farmers. For example, during World War I the nation called its farmers to all-out production with a slogan, "Food will win the war." *Prairie Farmer* responded to the call by setting up an award system which recognized wheat growers who produced the highest yields. Any farmer who raised at least 10 acres of wheat yielding 50 bushels an acre or more earned a place on the list of Illinois Master Wheat Growers which *Prairie Farmer* published beginning in 1918. This program brought congratulations from officials across the country, including Herbert Hoover, who was U.S. Food Administrator, and Clarence Ousley, acting U.S. Secretary of Agriculture.

During World War II the paper clustered its call for production around a crusade called "Food for Humanity." It asked readers to fill out and return a coupon stating: "You can count on me and my family to do our best in producing, saving, and sharing Food for Humanity." [30] *Prairie Farmer* then mailed a red, white, and blue window card to each respondent. Within 30 days after it started the campaign in March, 1943, it got 124,200 letters.

Prairie Farmer also tried to boost wartime efficiency in a lighter vein by waging a campaign against "gillygimpers." These were gremlins which always seemed to toss monkey wrenches into whatever the farmer was doing. The paper offered $1 for ideas about how to beat the gillygimper. Readers who sent in ideas automatically became members of the Battalion of Gillygimper Battlers, whose membership card was sealed with the imprint of a grinding

[29] *Prairie Farmer,* 87 (August 28, 1915), 8.
[30] *Prairie Farmer,* 115 (May 1, 1943), 4.

heel. Readers had great fun with this campaign which even inspired some cobhouse poetry:

> Old Gillygimper stands a 'peekin'
> Around the corner slyly sneakin'
> And if your watchfulness should weaken
> He'll steal the can that stops the squeakin'.[31]

Another incentive was the Master Farmer Award Program which Gregory founded in 1925. Gregory liked men who farmed "from the nose up." Early in the year he produced a Prairie Farmer Score Card for Farmers, by which a farmer could evaluate himself. The card encouraged the farmer to think about his farm operation, business methods and ability, general farm appearance and upkeep, home life, and citizenship. Five months later, in June, Gregory announced that *Prairie Farmer* was going to award a Master Farmer degree to farmers who scored highest on the card.

The editor liked this idea because it saluted real farmers. He conceded that farmers' halls of fame had been set up and biographical sketches of famous farmers had been published, but he argued that "the men who get the recognition are not farmers, but professors or scientists or inventors or something else. . . ."[32]

Anyone could nominate a farmer, and a three-man selection committee chose winners on the basis of the score card. *Prairie Farmer* honored its first 23 Master Farmers at a dinner in Chicago on December 2, 1925. Frank O. Lowden, former governor of Illinois, was the main speaker, and Butler presented gold medals to the honored farmers. Throughout the following year the paper printed a feature article about each Master Farmer.

Local communities quickly adopted the program and honored their own candidates. Farm papers in neighboring states also began to use this program, and by 1926 the Standard Farm Papers in six other states were sponsoring Master Farmer awards. Seventeen states offered awards in 1928, a growth which led to the organization of a Master Farmers' Club of America that year. The movement expanded to more than 25 states in 1929, then went international in 1930 when the *Nor'West Farmer* of Winnipeg, Canada, asked permission. By 1936 about 1,400 Master Farmers had been named in 28 states and four western provinces of Canada, although many farm papers temporarily stopped the program during the

[31] *Prairie Farmer,* 115 (May 15, 1943), 2.
[32] *Prairie Farmer,* 97 (June 20, 1925), 3.

depression.[33] *Prairie Farmer* discontinued it after Gregory left in
1937, but he was extremely pleased with the program and felt that
it had contributed to the creation of a real national consciousness
of the need for soil conservation. He also felt that it helped give
farm people more sense of pride and permanence.

A campaign to promote calfhood vaccination against brucellosis
was one of the editorial efforts which staff members considered
most noteworthy under Dave Thompson. The paper's decision to
recommend a new vaccine—Strain 19—was based on an investigation which took Verlo Butz, a field editor, 4,000 miles as he checked
on results throughout the dairying states. Authorities at the University of Illinois opposed endorsement at the time, but *Prairie
Farmer's* advocacy proved to be well-founded because calfhood
vaccination with Strain 19 soon became part of the official USDA
brucellosis control program.[34]

Campaign for Fair Prices

From time to time *Prairie Farmer* felt compelled to help readers
adjust unfair prices which it felt farmers were getting. One of the
earliest and most dramatic of these campaigns was in 1918 against
the price of wheat. The paper announced in August that Illinois
farmers were not getting a high enough price for wheat at local
elevators. Pressures of war had caused the federal legislature to
pass the Lever Act in 1917, setting a minimum price of $2 a bushel
for the 1918 crop of wheat.[35] In Illinois country elevators were to
pay official Chicago and St. Louis prices, less freight and 8¢ a bushel
for handling.

Prairie Farmer began to get complaints soon after the threshing
season started. At that time the Grain Corporation of the Food
Administration advised dissatisfied farmers to get adjustments
through their county food administrators. However, the county
food administrators almost unanimously passed the buck to the
Grain Corporation. Gregory—getting interested at this point—assigned an associate, Herman Steen, to look into the matter. Steen

[33] C. V. Gregory, "The Master Farmer Movement," *Agricultural History*, 10
(April, 1936), 50.
[34] U.S. Department of Agriculture, *Yearbook of Agriculture*, 1956 (Washington: U.S. Government Printing Office, 1956), p. 206.
[35] James H. Shideler, *Farm Crisis, 1919-1923* (Berkeley: University of California Press, 1957), pp. 12-13.

had joined *Prairie Farmer* in July, 1916, as assistant editor after having conducted a farm page in the *Des Moines Register and Leader,* and his investigation was an early effort in a career devoted largely to the grain trade.[36]

Steen learned that farmers were getting 2¢ to 15¢ a bushel too little for at least half of their wheat crop. Starting with the announcement on August 10, *Prairie Farmer* began to print one or more articles about the subject in every issue. It cited examples of unfair dealings by elevators and millers and explained how farmers could get fair prices.

Illinois was not alone in the problem of its wheat prices, but publicity by *Prairie Farmer* resulted in 10 times more protests to the Grain Corporation from Illinois than from any other state.[37] The paper believed that it had been the first to print anything about this problem and the first to register a protest with the Grain Corporation. A resulting investigation by the Grain Corporation caused it to issue a ruling on October 7 that country elevators must make proper refunds to all customers. Farmers in Illinois thereby recovered an estimated $600,000 in refunds on their wheat crop, and *Prairie Farmer* gained some friends among readers.[38]

In later years the paper initiated similar campaigns to correct errors, misunderstandings, or abuses involving prices of milk, livestock, and eggs. Chapter 6 will deal more specifically with efforts by *Prairie Farmer* to help farmers increase farm prices through legislation and marketing cooperatives.

Campaigns in Education

If *Prairie Farmer* showed more than usual concern for the education of its readers, it came honestly by that concern. John S. Wright had been as much interested in education as in agriculture. In fact, when preparing the first edition of his *Union Agriculturist* (forerunner of *Prairie Farmer*), he devoted the paper's most controversial article to schools instead of agriculture.[39] Wright was inclined to spend more time in Springfield lobbying for his school

[36] *Prairie Farmer,* 88 (July 29, 1916), 10.
[37] *Prairie Farmer,* 90 (October 19, 1918), 6.
[38] *Prairie Farmer,* 91 (April 19, 1919), 9.
[39] The *Union Agriculturist* first appeared on October, 1840, as forerunner of *Union Agriculturist and Western Prairie Farmer,* which began the following January as a regularly published journal.

bills than in Chicago editing the farm paper.[40] His interest was not
unfounded, for even in 1840 one of every 17 white residents of
Illinois over the age of 20 could not read or write.

By Butler's day the common schools, normal schools, high schools,
and colleges for which Wright had fought were functioning. Public
schools dotted the countryside of Illinois. In fact, in 1909 Illinois
had 10,638 one-room school houses, an average of more than 100
in each county.[41] Consolidated schools were almost unknown in
the state; by 1911 it had only 13 of them.[42] The little white schoolhouse held full control, even though some observers were beginning to point out that it cast a faint shadow of its former glory.
"What the unobserving, unthinking farmer of today recalls as the
country school of his boyhood no longer exists. The wide-awake
scholarly young man he remembers as the country teacher has long
ago attained his desired ambition in the law or the ministry, and
has been replaced by an inexperienced, untrained slip of a girl
from city high school or neighboring community. The comfortable,
convenient building he remembers is now aged and dilapidated,
while the troop of hearty boys and girls his imagination sees have
turned cityward in search of a more extended training than the old
system can maintain, and left but a handful of unfortunate strag-
glers." [43]

Many schools which once handled 40 to 50 pupils now worked
with fewer than 10. Indeed, almost 30 per cent of all country
schools of Illinois in 1912 had fewer than 15 pupils.[44] The level
of quality was also of growing concern. For example, in 1909 the
Illinois Department of Public Instruction began offering diplomas
to schools which met a set of standard requirements dealing with
the yard and outbuildings, school house, furnishings and supplies,
teacher, and organization. Only 700 of 10,632 country schools had
met the standards by 1912 and of those 700 no more than one-fifth
had been up to standard when first inspected.[45] Many buildings

[40] Lloyd Lewis, *John S. Wright—Prophet of the Prairies* (Chicago: Prairie
Farmer Publishing Co., 1941), p. 85.

[41] Illinois Department of Public Instruction, "The One-Room Country Schools
in Illinois," Circular 51 (Springfield: Illinois State Journal Co., 1910), p. 9.

[42] Mabel Carney, *Country Life and the Country School* (Chicago: Row,
Peterson and Co., 1912), p. 160.

[43] Carney, p. 142.

[44] *Prairie Farmer*, 84 (May 15, 1912), 9.

[45] Illinois Department of Public Instruction, "The One-Room Country Schools
and Village Schools," Circular 65 (Springfield: Illinois State Journal Co.,
1912), pp. 5, 7.

stood stark and barren, disclaiming the "family circle" warmth which one-room schools professed to capture. Too often the schoolrooms were dark and forbidding. Unjacketed stoves placed in the middle of rooms forced children to use their books as much for heat shields as for enlightenment. School seasons sometimes ran only five or six months, and teachers paid less than $350 a year were expected to be as good at chopping wood as at teaching physiology.

What had once been a center of neighborhood life—housing spelling bees, literary societies, singing schools, and debating clubs—was being bypassed as a result of industrial changes, educational specialization, migration to the city, and a host of other causes. In turn, parents looked at that small enrollment and began to think about hiring a lower-cost teacher because "anyone can handle so small a school."

A favorite story of the period reported that farmers in one district had joined forces and bought a stallion for $3,500 to upgrade the quality of their work horses. Then they hired a man for $75 a month to care for him. At about the same time these farmers needed a new school teacher. After much bickering and hair-splitting they hired a frivolous young woman from town because they could get her for $30 a month and she would board herself. Educators insisted that the joke was not on the teacher.

Perhaps the most serious indictment came, however, from the Commission on Country Life, which had held hearings throughout the country during late 1908 at the request of President Theodore Roosevelt. In its report the Commission concluded: "The schools are held largely responsible for ineffective farming, lack of ideals, and the drift to town. This is not because the rural schools, as a whole, are declining, but because they are in a state of arrested development and have not yet put themselves in consonance with all the recently changed conditions of life." [46]

Support for the one-room country school came partly from its easy access. The usual size of the school district was four sections of land, encompassing about 16 families. Children could walk to school, a vital factor in a day when unimproved roads made travel seasonal. A second point of argument was that consolidated schools would cost more, although few facts undergirded most discussions

[46] U.S. Commission on Country Life, *Report of the Commission on Country Life* (New York: Sturgis & Walton Co., 1911), pp. 121-122.

about cost. Another virtue which spokesmen saw in the country school was its similarity to the farm home. People generally believed that the farm home was the best place to rear children and the country school was much like a big farm family. Younger children learned from listening to and being with the older youths, defenders argued, while older youths gained from the presence of smaller children.

Prairie Farmer stood as an unwavering proponent of the country school, not only in 1911 but until 1945—and perhaps contributed to the fact that Illinois was one of the last states in the country to give up rural schools. Gregory saw some value in consolidating schools in the country, but he felt that it would be a mistake to send country children to town schools because of the long bus rides and crowded conditions. Town schools are dominated by town viewpoints, Gregory wrote in 1923, and he felt that farm youths exposed to those viewpoints may "soon come to regard farm life as a life of hardship, and their ambition will be to live in town and have a good time." [47]

Sentiment also entered into Gregory's support of country schools. "Many of us got our first schooling in a one-room school. That training, we believe, was good training and for that reason we are not anxious to see these schools dispensed with." [48]

In 1911 *Prairie Farmer* tried to approach the problem by urging neighborhoods to take more part and more pride in their schools. Articles encouraged readers to plant trees and shrubs around their schools, give each pupil a drinking cup, and simply commend the teacher for her work. However, the problem ran deeper than that, and in 1912 the paper began to discuss low enrollments, poorly qualified teachers, and low salaries. It observed that pupils were dropping out of school "as though from a pestilence."

During the next 30 years *Prairie Farmer* continued to stress ways in which country schools could improve, but to little avail because they were an intense problem by the 1940's. In Illinois enrollment in one-room country schools had dropped 69 per cent between 1880 and 1942, from 437,220 to 135,524. Nearly three-fourths of the existing schools had fewer than 15 pupils. [49] Mechanization of agriculture had greatly reduced the number of people needed to

[47] *Prairie Farmer*, 95 (February 10, 1923), 8.
[48] *Prairie Farmer*, 105 (January 7, 1933), 3.
[49] Illinois Agricultural Association, *Report of the Illinois Agricultural Association School Committee*, November, 1944, p. 19.

farm the land, farm couples were having fewer children, the
average age of farmers had risen (reducing the share who were
most likely to have children in elementary school), and farm parents who had young children were sending them to school in
town.

A survey in 1945 by the Illinois Chamber of Commerce showed
that the state still had 9,405 one-teacher school districts. Of them,
4,100 enrolled fewer than 10 pupils.[50] Teachers were so scarce that
2,355 emergency teaching certificates were issued during 1943.[51]
Rural teachers were getting less than half the wages of urban teachers.[52] Even at that, local school districts were paying between $90
and $225 a year for each pupil and getting a limited teaching pro-
gram for their money.[53]

Aroused by a White House Conference on Rural Education,
Prairie Farmer in 1944 joined the call for immediate action. Consolidation was its solution this time, and it did not rebel at the idea
of bus rides and town influence. The paper reported favorably
during the mid-1940's as counties reduced the numbers of school
districts. By 1948 it could observe that nearly every community was
coming to grips with its school problem, adding: "Reports show
that there is more opposition in towns and villages to school reorganization than in the country." [54]

In other matters involving formal education, *Prairie Farmer* took
an active part in community high school legislation between 1920
and 1923, prompted relief efforts in 1939 for parents who could
not afford textbooks for their children, and helped conduct a drive
starting in 1944 to found a College of Veterinary Medicine at the
University of Illinois.

The paper's interest in informal education was as keen as its
interest in formal education, partly because the country was alive
with educational activity for adults as well as youths soon after
Butler and Gregory arrived. Land-grant agricultural colleges had
been established for nearly 50 years and the federally subsidized
state experiment stations at these colleges for more than 20 years.

[50] Dwight H. Green, "The State's Interest in Rural Education," in *Proceedings of the Governor's Conference on Rural Education*, Springfield, Illinois,
January 18-19, 1946, p. 13.

[51] *Prairie Farmer*, 116 (September 16, 1944), 1.

[52] *Prairie Farmer*, 116 (October 28, 1944), 16.

[53] L. H. Simerl, "Finance," in *Proceedings of the Governor's Conference on
Rural Education*, p. 28.

[54] *Prairie Farmer*, 120 (March 13, 1948), 8.

Farm leaders began to feel in the early 1900's that available knowledge about farming far outstripped actual farming methods. Research was producing chemical fertilizers, the Babcock milk test, sprays to control plant diseases, serums for treating livestock diseases, new kinds of machines, new types of cropping systems, and new approaches to marketing and farm management.

Now, leaders felt, the country needed a nation-wide extension program. The Country Life Commission explained in its report of 1909: "The first or original work of the agricultural branches of the land-grant colleges was academic in the old sense; later there was added the great field of experiment and research; there now should be added the third coordinate branch, comprising extension work, without which no college of agriculture can adequately serve its state." [55]

Farmers' institutes had helped perform this task since at least 1863.[56] However, by 1900 they had begun to change and farmers were asking for more specific types of knowledge. The institutes suffered because they usually reached farmers only once a year in any community and had no way to follow up whatever ardor they might have created among those who attended. After 1914 many lost their identity and were absorbed into other extension-type meetings.

Their replacement appeared first through new departments of extension within the agricultural colleges and land-grant institutions. Rutgers College reported extension work beginning in 1891. By 1907, 39 state agricultural colleges—including the University of Illinois—were carrying on some kind of extension effort.[57] "The Professor deserted his classroom . . . and started out to spread the gospel of good farming." [58]

The next idea was that of placing a farm expert in a single county

[55] U.S. Commission on Country Life, p. 127.

[56] The itinerant lecture system for the instruction of farmers had been used for years, but the first farmers' institute may have been at Springfield, Massachusetts, in 1863. See Clarence B. Smith and Meredith C. Wilson, *The Agricultural Extension System of the United States* (New York: John Wiley and Sons, 1930), pp. 28-29; Orville M. Kile, *The Farm Bureau Movement* (New York: Macmillan Co., 1921), p. 64; A. C. True, "A History of Agricultural Extension Work in the United States, 1785-1923," U.S. Department of Agriculture, Miscellaneous Publication No. 15 (Washington: U.S. Government Printing Office, October, 1928), pp. 5-8.

[57] Smith and Wilson, p. 31; True, "History of Agricultural Extension Work," pp. 45-46.

[58] Kile, *Farm Bureau Movement*, p. 67.

to live with farmers on a day-to-day basis and help them improve their farming methods. Originated in 1904 by Dr. S. A. Knapp, this idea touched off widespread demonstration work in the south. Smith County, Texas, hired the first single-county agent in 1906 and by 1911 the southern states had more than 580 county agents. Northern states did not have county agents until March, 1911.

DeKalb County was the starting point for county agent work in Illinois, and *Prairie Farmer* claimed to have printed the first public announcement of this movement.[59] The issue of January 15, 1912, reported a meeting 10 days earlier at which a group of farmers and businessmen of DeKalb County had "come to the conclusion that they can not wait for the federal government to provide them with money to hire an expert. They are willing to put up the money to get one at once." [60] Three sponsoring groups in the county—farmers' institute, newspapermen's association, and bankers' association—approved formation of the DeKalb County Soil Improvement Association at a meeting on January 20. By June 1 the county had a new soil expert on the job, William G. Eckhardt.

Prairie Farmer commended the appointment, cautioning that the whole success of such a movement depended on the man who did the work. From then on, the paper became a kind of tempering influence during the sometimes mad scramble of counties to get on the "crop doctor" bandwagon. Make haste slowly, Gregory suggested, as he warned that a program which starts and fails will not recover for a long time. It will take time to develop men especially fitted for this work, he argued. His comments reflected a prevailing view that only an extremely well-grounded agriculturist could meet all standards which the Illinois system of permanent agriculture imposed.

Through feature articles and a new column, "With the County Advisors," *Prairie Farmer* followed the activities of this new movement in rural education. However, its major contribution was on the editorial page where Gregory in turn praised and reproved the program. He thought the county agent movement opened a new era in agriculture but wanted it to have firm guidance. Gregory knew all of the county advisers and often felt compelled to offer

[59] *Prairie Farmer*, 87 (February 13, 1915), 12. Articles from *Prairie Farmer* were the only references cited in a description of the development of the county agent movement in Illinois by True, "History of Agricultural Extension Work," pp. 89-91.

[60] *Prairie Farmer*, 84 (January 15, 1912), 6.

suggestions in print. If advisers seemed inclined to run their job from the office, *Prairie Farmer* urged them to get out into the country. When rumors spread that the Illinois Farmers' Institute was opposing the movement, Gregory promptly squelched them. When overly enthusiastic observers said that county advisers were increasing the wealth of single counties by $500,000 to $600,000 a year, he rejected it as "bunk." All were doing notable work, he maintained, but he was sure that advisers themselves would be the last to make any such "absurd claims." [61] When an Illinois legislator proposed in 1917 that state funds for the adviser be channeled through the Department of Agriculture rather than through the state university, *Prairie Farmer* raised objections. Why divide the responsibility, Gregory asked, and run the risk of putting the county adviser into politics? [62]

In moments of praise, the paper urged readers to take their hats off to county advisers, most of whom are "filling their jobs so well that the county wouldn't seem like home without them." [63] In moments of concern during the mid-1920's *Prairie Farmer* called for a plan of "county agent relief" because it believed the adviser's real job had got pushed aside.

He is supposed to be a marketing expert, and to aid in the organization and management of cooperative marketing enterprises. He must keep up the morale of his membership by holding meetings and picnics, arranging for speakers and showing motion pictures. Frequently he must do a large part of the work in organizing and managing membership campaigns. Often he must be responsible for the sale of auto insurance, gasoline, fertilizer, apples, and salt. In his spare time he manages the county baseball team, puts on a few hog-calling and corn-husking contests, gets out his farm bureau paper and organizes and leads the boys' and girls' clubs.

He is surely an all-around man. But where is all of this getting us? How many counties have a definite county farm program as a result of eight or 10 years of county agent work, and can show progress year by year toward the realization of that program? [64]

Despite his general support of the county adviser movement, Gregory parted from it in two respects. First, he counselled against hiring county home advisers. The editor acknowledged that in time they would be desirable but argued in 1914 that the primary purpose of the whole movement was to help the farmer make more

[61] *Prairie Farmer*, 85 (September 15, 1913), 10.
[62] *Prairie Farmer*, 89 (April 21, 1917), 10.
[63] *Prairie Farmer*, 97 (August 22, 1925), 8.
[64] *Prairie Farmer*, 99 (August 20, 1927), 8.

money. In his opinion, the work of a women adviser would necessarily deal more with spending money than making it.[65]

Second, Gregory protested during World War I when the federal government encouraged putting a farm adviser into every county of the country to increase food output. As far as Gregory was concerned, the plan would do little immediate good in boosting food production and would do a great deal of harm through the hasty employment of unqualified men by counties which were not deeply interested in such a program.

Prairie Farmer devoted less of its attention to the county adviser movement after 1918, partly because of Gregory's growing interest in newly emerging farm groups.

Campaigns for Community Betterment

Another series of campaigns in *Prairie Farmer* came under what might be described as efforts to stimulate community action and improve the condition of communities. The "Prairie Farmer Community Book," a loose-leaf, leather-bound guide for community clubs became one of the early efforts. Planners could turn to this guide for organizing their clubs and arranging programs of activity: for example, dime socials, hog-calling contests, mock trials, or radio banquets. Fifty community clubs used the "Community Book" during its first year, 1925.

The second such campaign began in March, 1926, when the paper announced a Community Club contest. Organizations competed for a trophy and cash on the basis of numbers of meetings during the year, membership, neighborliness, and accomplishments. *Prairie Farmer* then featured winning clubs in its pages to encourage action by others. The paper continued this contest for three years.

A new type of community activity took its place in 1933 when *Prairie Farmer*–WLS began to sponsor home talent barn dance shows in local communities.[66] These shows were miniature barn dances and drew largely on local talent. Six hundred communities staged these home talent shows through *Prairie Farmer*–WLS Community Service, Inc., during the first three years. More than 60,000 persons performed before a combined audience of nearly 660,000, and the shows left more than $60,000 in profits to local community

[65] *Prairie Farmer*, 86 (August 15, 1914), 8.
[66] Memorandum from Arthur C. Page to Butler, August 7, 1934.

chests.[67] For its part *Prairie Farmer* did not consider the shows an important source of income, for they contributed only about $5,000 a year.[68] When war ended the project after eight years, 2.5 million persons had seen more than 200,000 performers in these shows, and *Prairie Farmer*–WLS Community Service needed a staff of 15 full- and part-time workers to handle it.[69]

A less entertaining project—but one close to the hearts of farm people—was *Prairie Farmer's* campaign for better roads. Butler and Gregory arrived in Illinois about the time that farm opinion began seriously to favor improved roads in Illinois. The state had been somewhat slow in improving its roads because first waterways and then railways had offered ready transportation. Even as late as 1894 these channels had remained almost unchanged from 50 years earlier.[70] Farmers had balked at road projects because of their cost, so although Granges, farmers' institutes, and other groups often discussed such projects, no one took action. Many residents thought the new electric interurban railroads would replace hard roads in the major rural areas and farmers thought dirt roads could be improved enough for their needs.

A good roads commission was appointed in 1903 to study road improvement in the state and it found that only 26.5 miles of macadam roads had been built in 22 years under the hard roads law of 1883.[71]

A growing use of automobiles convinced farm people by about 1910 that they must build more roads, regardless of cost. A Farmers' Good Roads League of Illinois, formed in 1907, favored building permanent hard roads by federal and state aid. By 1910 the Illinois Farmers' Institute endorsed bond issues for road improvement. The Illinois Grange in turn called for a complete system of improved roads for the state, to be built by federal, state, and county aid plus proceeds from an automobile tax.[72] The farmer who once thought any good-road campaign was a part of city autoists' plot to kill his dog and frighten his wife's driving horses into the ditch now began to buy his own car and value good roads.

[67] *WLS Family Album*, 1937 (Chicago: Prairie Farmer Publishing Co., 1936), p. 42; *Prairie Farmer*, 109 (December 19, 1936), 24.

[68] Memorandum from Gregory to Butler, December 27, 1935.

[69] *WLS Family Album*, 1942, p. 29.

[70] Ernest L. Bogart and John M. Mathews, *The Modern Commonwealth, 1893-1918*, vol. V of *The Centennial History of Illinois* (Springfield: Illinois Centennial Commission, 1920), p. 147.

[71] Bogart and Mathews, p. 148.   [72] Bogart and Mathews, p. 148.

The change in philosophy came none too soon, in the opinion of
many. In 1909, 90 per cent of the public roads in Illinois were unimproved.[73] American farmers paid an estimated annual "mud tax"
—that is, the financial loss due to transporting crops over bad
roads—of $250 million.[74] Poor roads cost farmers in Illinois an
estimated $5,200,000 on the corn and wheat crops of 1910 alone,
according to Homer C. Tice, an Illinois legislator, in a speech to
the Illinois Farmers' Institute.[75] He charged that farmers were
losing more money each year on bad roads than they would pay
for their share of a sound program of improvement.

By 1912 *Prairie Farmer* was among those who concluded that
road improvement was no longer a local matter. The time had come,
it reported, for the state to take a more active hand in the matter of
road improvement.[76] However, it rejected the idea of federal aid.

Road construction increased sharply in Illinois starting in 1916,
but spiralling costs during and after World War I placed new
limits upon mileage. *Prairie Farmer* began a campaign in 1920 to
make the money stretch by using gravel. It called for farm-to-
market roads instead of through-route boulevards. "The issue is
clearly drawn," Gregory announced in a front-page editorial of
March, 1921. The issue was ". . . a large mileage of common-sense,
low-cost roads, kept in first-class condition by patrolmen, versus
a few boulevards built at almost prohibitive expense."[77] His rule
of thumb was: one-third of the state's road-building funds for pav-
ing, the rest for what he called a "common sense" policy of grading,
draining, oiling, graveling, and patrolling.[78]

Prairie Farmer and the Illinois Agricultural Association lost that
contest in 1921 as the state continued its trend toward concrete and
postponed construction of gravel roads. From then until 1924,
Prairie Farmer was a firm critic of the approach which the State
Highway Department was taking in building roads for Illinois.

Another segment of community life in which *Prairie Farmer*
inevitably got involved was the changing country church. At least
10,000 country churches across the nation were standing idle by
1910—doors asag and windows broken or boarded, some serving

[73] American Highway Association, *Good Roads Yearbook,* 1912 (Washington,
D.C., 1912), p. 229.
[74] Carney, p. 109.
[75] *Prairie Farmer,* 84 (March 15, 1912), 7.
[76] *Prairie Farmer,* 84 (October 15, 1912), 7.
[77] *Prairie Farmer,* 93 (March 19, 1921), 1.
[78] *Prairie Farmer,* 93 (November 19, 1921), 2.

as horse stables or hog houses. Thousands of others were deathly ill, suffering from a revolution in rural life. Communities were trying to support too many churches of too many sects, many fighting bitterly among themselves. As a result, often all were weak. Most churches lacked funds to carry out a vigorous program, so many hired only part-time pastors or pastors lacking proper education.

A growing trend toward tenant farming made neighborhoods more unstable and less united in their social actions. Furthermore— as one reader noted in *Prairie Farmer* in 1911—the discovery of artificial ice and dry farming methods had spoiled the terrors of hell for most people. "The odor of brimstone can no longer frighten people to church." [79] Also, those new autos were stimulating dances on Saturday nights, outings on Sundays, and many other diversions.

Such were the types of problems which led the Country Life Commission to suggest in 1909 that ". . . as a whole the country church needs new direction and to assume new responsibilities." [80] It offered only general guidance for this new direction: (1) more church federation, (2) more work of the Young Men's Christian Association in rural areas, and (3) a "complete conception" of the country pastorate.

Likewise, *Prairie Farmer* side-stepped a strong crusade to overhaul the country church. It elected in this case to serve as a debating center. In Gregory's first years as editor, the paper carried charges and counter-charges from readers. Some called for church union. Some argued that the church should take more interest in agriculture, ". . . teaching the people how to live and make a living rather than devoting all their time in teaching them how to die." [81] Others denied that "corn in the pulpit, oats in the choir loft or any other tomfoolery will ever reach, convert, or draw a poor lost soul to God." [82] Some commended farm people as deeply religious; others charged that farmers would rather hear a hog grunt than pray for a lost soul.

In later years readers debated for months about whether or not farm people should play baseball on Sunday. The major issues often went untouched, however, and *Prairie Farmer* chose to leave

[79] *Prairie Farmer*, 83 (December 15, 1911), 3.
[80] U.S. Commission on Country Life, pp. 139-140.
[81] *Prairie Farmer*, 84 (June 1, 1912), 5.
[82] *Prairie Farmer*, 84 (February 1, 1912), 11.

Burridge D. Butler in 1941, the year that *Prairie Farmer* celebrated 100 years of continuous publication. This was Butler's favorite photograph of himself.

Butler as a salesman for the Scripps-McRae League of newspapers just before the turn of the century.

Emblem of Clover Leaf Newspapers in 1905. The emblem became unwieldy as the chain embellished it to accommodate as many as 10 papers in 1914.

Crusading by *Prairie Farmer* began soon after Butler became owner. This cover article introduced the first of more than 50 editorial campaigns between 1909 and 1948.

Staff members became celebrities during the summer of 1928 because of this airplane. It touched down in cow pastures of nearly every county to help the staff cover agricultural events.

Editor Clifford V. Gregory (seated at center) and his staff in 1933: (left to right) Orpha Han, Arthur C. Page, Dave O. Thompson, Lois Schenck, Virginia Seeds, Floyd Keepers, and Ray Inman.

As many as 95,000 persons attended Illinois State Corn Husking Contests sponsored annually by *Prairie Farmer* between 1924 and 1941. The paper also sponsored state contests in Indiana and hosted several national meets.

This spirited call for action reflects the temper of depression-ridden farmers in 1932. Under Clifford Gregory, *Prairie Farmer* urged farmers to unite in support of cooperatives and farm legislation.

The PRAIRIE FARMER

Since 1841

Illinois   OCTOBER 10,   1936

Why *We Are for the Roosevelt*
Farm Program

by CLIFFORD V. GREGORY

A few days ago Mr. Butler, our publisher, said to me:

"Our readers have so much at stake in this campaign that I believe we should present the issues to them with absolute frankness in the next issue of Prairie Farmer."

I agreed with him, and this plain statement of the issues as we see them is the result.

Neither Mr. Butler nor I owe allegiance to any political party. We have voted for Republicans as often as for Democrats. Our views now are not partisan. Our only allegiance is to our readers. Our only interest is in the welfare of American agriculture, which underlies the welfare of the entire nation.

THERE is a knock at the door. Mrs. John Smith of Boston or Mrs. William McAllister of Philadelphia or Mrs. Levi Straus of New York City opens the door.

"I have nothing to sell," the visitor hastily assures her. He has a market basket of typical food products on his arm. Each package is marked with its price today, and in the spring of 1933. "See how the cost of your food is going up," he says. "That is what the pig-killing and plowing-under programs of the Roosevelt administration have done to you."

Many big city dailies are telling and retelling the same story.

A Chicago newspaper bluntly tells its city readers that —"Mr. Roosevelt's hog program has deprived 50,000 men and women of the chance to earn a decent living." and adds: "Pork chops which sold for 17 cents a pound when Mr. Roosevelt took office now cost the housewife 35 cents a pound."

That is the city end of the Republican farm campaign. It can mean only one thing. It means that the powers that control the Republican party are in favor of unrestricted farm production so that there will be more jobs and profits in the business of transporting and handling and processing farm products.

It means that the Republican party is in favor of $3 hogs and 15-cent corn so that housewives can again buy pork chops for 17 cents a pound.

"Back to 1932 farm prices" is the plain meaning of the Republican cheap food campaign in the cities.

There is nothing in their announced farm policies to prevent this. Gov. Landon says that farm production must not be restricted. He assails the Roosevelt "program of scarcity"; says that the real function of government is "to help the farmer to produce and to finance carry-over crops."

That is what the Hoover farm board did. There was no program of scarcity then— (To page 24)

Readers long recalled this unprecedented political endorsement by *Prairie Farmer* just prior to national elections in 1936. Editor Gregory helped develop the farm program for Roosevelt's New Deal.

"This Is WLS Unlimited." The words and the sound of a train whistle helped the Solemn Old Judge, George D. Hay, create a nationwide trademark for WLS.

Ford and Glenn served as the Lullaby Twins on WLS soon after it began broadcasting in 1924. Their bedtime program for children featured a mythical Woodshed Theater.

Gene Autry came to the WLS Barn Dance in 1930 as the Oklahoma Yodeling Cowboy. His song, "Silver Haired Daddy of Mine," was a favorite among listeners by 1933.

George Gobel (originally Goebel) got his early experience in show business as the Little Cowboy on WLS. In 1933 he was a regular on the Barn Dance as a 13-year-old singer.

Pat Buttram brought his tall tales and on-stage chicanery to the Barn Dance in 1934 from Winston County, Alabama. *WLS Family Albums* show him at WLS until 1942.

Red Foley played with the Cumberland Ridge Runners and performed as Burrhead, the bashful beau of Lulu Belle, early in the 1930's. He returned to the Barn Dance in 1940.

More than 2,600,000 persons paid to see the WLS National Barn Dance during its 25-year-run in the Eighth Street Theatre. Crowds filled the 1,200-seat theatre twice every Saturday night.

National Barn Dance performers in the Old Hayloft. Between 70 and 100 performers appeared on each program after 1933. From 1933 until 1946 the Barn Dance was sponsored nationally over NBC.

The Hoosier Hot Shots produced laughs and unique musical sounds for about 13 years on the Barn Dance using their odd assortment of instruments.

Lulu Belle and Scotty began a sweetheart routine on WLS that lasted for a quarter-century. In 1936 Lulu Belle was voted National Radio Queen.

Burridge Butler presents medals to two WLS staff members who became "radio's greatest heroes" in 1937. Herbert Morrison (receiving medal) and Charles Nehlsen recorded an historic eye-witness account of the Hindenburg disaster.

Agricultural leaders appeared regularly on WLS programs such as noontime Dinnerbell. Shown here are Eugene Davenport, dean of the University of Illinois College of Agriculture, Dinnerbell host Arthur C. Page, Butler, and station manager Glenn Snyder.

THE WLS CREED

"*To me radio is far more than a mere medium of entertainment. It is a God-given instrument which makes possible vital economic, educational and inspirational service to the home-loving men, women, and children of America. As long as it is our privilege to direct the destinies of WLS, we will hold sacred this trust that has been placed in our hands. No medium developed by mankind is doing more to broaden the lives of rich and poor alike than radio.*

"*When you step up to the microphone never forget this responsibility and that you are walking as a guest into all those homes beyond the microphone.*"

Burridge D. Butler

November 12, 1938

Blackburn College of Carlinville, Illinois, presented an honorary doctorate to Butler in 1932. The self-help concept at Blackburn attracted Butler's respect and active support.

Burridge D. Butler Boys' Club of Phoenix reflects Butler's role in starting a program in that city during the 1940's. Earlier he had helped form a Boys' Club program in Chicago.

Eightieth birthday celebration for Butler in the studios of KOY, Phoenix.
Program director Jack Williams (later governor of Arizona) is holding the
microphone. WLS staff pastor John Holland is at right.

Almost until he died, Butler enjoyed roughing it in the southwest. He is
shown with Mrs. E. B. Sayles, wife of the assistant director of the Point of
Pines Archaeological Field School which he helped finance.

Burridge and Ina Butler at Casa Davenal.

them so. The paper's relative quietness did not reflect religious apathy in its publisher and editor. Gregory was a steady church worker in Wheaton, where his family lived during his editorship. Butler often was rabidly critical of orthodox religion (as he put it, "phony religion") due to the encounters of his boyhood. Some people claimed that Butler's father cured him of religion. He could shower abuse upon ministers and their religion, convincing them that he was the devil beclothed, yet he was incurably religious. Emmett McLoughlin aptly described Butler as "a deeply religious soul who vociferously hated all religions." [83] Good works were the religion which Butler saw in the Jesus whom he admired but whose divinity he questioned. John Holland, pastor for *Prairie Farmer–WLS*, quoted Butler as saying that he (Butler) had a calling and that he and the priests and ministers were really working on the same great job.[84] Therefore, religion played a part in Butler's enterprises, but on a nonsectarian basis. He contracted with Dr. Holland to write a regular religious column beginning Febuary 18, 1922, and later employed the pastor on a full-time basis.

Butler's actions suggest that *Prairie Farmer* may have avoided a firm stand on the issue of country churches because of his desire to avoid sectarian affairs and to promote religious welfare in his own manner.

These and other campaigns meant a great deal to Butler and Gregory. They helped assure Butler that he was providing the fatherly leadership which he envisioned, and they helped Gregory feel that he was carrying out one of his early pledges to the readers of *Prairie Farmer*: "(We) want to help you to make more money by keeping you in touch with the most successful methods of farmers and experimenters. We want to inspire you to greater efforts by telling you of the success of others. We want the roads and schools and churches and homes of our readers to be the best that can be found anywhere." [85]

Chicken thieves, slot machines, gypsies, rock phosphate, gillygimpers, muddy roads, crop doctors, wheat prices: these and dozens of other items like them gradually combined to help give the *Prairie Farmer* its most striking feature under Butler—a crusading spirit.

[83] Emmett McLoughlin, *People's Padre* (Boston: Beacon Press, 1954), p. 113.

[84] Holland, p. 47.

[85] *Prairie Farmer*, 83 (June 15, 1911), 12.

Prairie Farmer
and the
New Farm Equality Movement

CHAPTER 6

About 40 years had passed since Illinois had seen a farm movement
as vigorous as the one which began to form between 1915 and 1920.
In the early 1870's Illinois farmers, disheartened by a slump in farm
prices after the Civil War, had turned to a new group—the Patrons
of Husbandry, or Grange. They felt it would help them oppose
the bankers, railroads, legislature, tariffs, monopolies, and other
forces which they blamed for debts and low prices. The Granger
movement spread quickly in Illinois after gaining a foothold in
1869.[1] It agitated to bring railroads under control, organized independent parties to resist domination by capitalists, and started cooperative agencies for buying and selling in order to restore the
farmer's economic independence.

First of this country's large agricultural orders, the Grange col-
lapsed as rapidly as it had begun. Lack of control over an un-
wieldly membership, the failure of Grange-sponsored legislation
against railroads, unwise business ventures, and other factors caused
its rapid decline between 1875 and 1880.

[1] Solon J. Buck, *The Granger Movement* (Lincoln: University of Nebraska
Press, 1913), p. 47.

A second movement in agrarian reform had taken shape in 1880 to embrace the Grange and enlarge upon it. New and more aggressive farm groups formed to enact class laws which would protect farmers against wealthy interests. In Illinois these took the form of five groups: (1) Patrons of Industry, which held a small loyalty in extreme northern Illinois, (2) Patrons of Husbandry, which continued strong in west-north-central parts of the state, (3) National Farmers' Alliance, active in east-central Illinois, (4) National Farmers' Alliance and Industrial Union, with a cluster of members in west-central Illinois, and (5) Farmers' Mutual Benefit Association, which was a force in the southern half of Illinois.[2]

The five groups competed for membership but held one common objective. All agreed that the domination of wealthy interests was causing their distress and that farmers could protect themselves only by joining forces just as their antagonists had. Their approach differed from that of the Grange in openly espousing the use of political organization. Working through existing parties, they pressed for the election of candidates with rural sympathies and acted through petitions at all levels of government between 1880 and 1890. They set up cooperative units for buying and selling and even proposed a farmers' agricultural implement manufacturing company.

Their brush with politics proved unsuccessful, however, and after the state senatorial election of 1891, most farmers decided that farm groups had no business in politics and should limit their political role to stressing informed voting. The alliance movement ground to a halt by 1894, at which time only the Grange remained as an active statewide body in Illinois. A Populist party which had started in Illinois during the early 1890's and hoped for success through the backing of farm groups instead found only a hollow shell. Farmers of Illinois had returned to their old parties, apathetic and disgusted with politics in general.

Farmers knew by then that they could not drive America back to the simplicity of the early 1800's. Instead, they turned with renewed interest toward agricultural education and progress through which farmers might compete in an industrial society. This was not a direct and concerted effort at first. In fact, Orville M. Kile has termed the period of 1896 to 1910 as one of "agricultural dis-

[2] Roy V. Scott, *The Agrarian Movement in Illinois, 1880-1896* (Urbana: University of Illinois Press, 1962), p. 62.

organization."[3] Farmers were bitter about recent failures of farm groups, and many concluded that farmers were by nature simply too independent to cooperate. Two other developments helped account for relative quietness among farmers between 1896 and 1915. One was a welcomed rise in prices of farm products after the price panic of 1893. Except for a few years, prices were normal or above normal through World War I.

Another quieting development was the enactment of reforms for which farmers had pressed. These included public regulation of railroads, popular election of U.S. senators, rural free delivery of mail, parcel post, postal savings banks, anti-trust laws, a federal land bank system, and greater flexibility of the currency.

The agrarian movement did not die out, but it had little nationwide character and it stressed economic rather than political cooperation. Typical of the farm groups formed after 1894 were the American Society of Equity and the Farmers' Union. The American Society of Equity was founded in Indiana in 1902 with cooperative efforts as its central feature.[4] It boasted nearly 200,000 members by 1906, but probably had only half of that total, even at its peak. Membership dwindled drastically by 1914.[5] Illinois had an Equity unit, but the unit was not among the group's strongest.

Farmers' Educational and Cooperative Union of America (called Farmers' Union) began in 1902, "built upon the ruins of the Farmers' Alliance." [6] By 1914 it was established in 20 states of the south and midwest and stressed cooperative rather than social features. Again, Illinois was not among the stronger states in this movement.

Clifford Gregory came to *Prairie Farmer* when farm leaders were beginning to deplore the lack of cooperative spirit among farmers. President Roosevelt's Commission on Country Life had concluded recently that many so-called cooperative groups really were not cooperative, but rather served personal interests. Nor were the many agricultural societies and clubs truly cooperative, the Com-

[3] Orville M. Kile, *The Farm Bureau Movement* (New York: Macmillan Co., 1921), p. 52.

[4] Everett E. Edwards, "American Agriculture—The First 300 Years," in *Yearbook of Agriculture, 1940* (Washington: U.S. Government Printing Office, 1940), pp. 245-246; Theodore Saloutos and John D. Hicks, *Agricultural Discontent in the Middle West 1900-1939* (Madison: University of Wisconsin Press, 1951), p. 113.

[5] Saloutos and Hicks, p. 118; Kile, *Farm Bureau Movement*, p. 39.

[6] Kile, *Farm Bureau Movement*, p. 30.

mission felt. It said: "While there are very many excellent agricultural cooperative organizations of many kinds, the farmers nearly everywhere complain that there is still a great dearth of association that really helps them in buying and selling and developing their communities. . . . The need is not so much for a greater number of societies as for a more complete organization within them and for a more continuous active work." [7]

Gregory was well suited for abetting this idea because he believed in it strongly. Even when he was writing for *Prairie Farmer* on a trial basis, Gregory hit first and hardest at cooperation. A month before he became editor, he wrote: "A good many things are due to happen in this country in the next ten years. There will be clubs and granges and cow-testing associations organized." [8]

"The one thing that farmers in most communities need more than anything else is more of the get together spirit," Gregory wrote in the following issue. He even offered to send rules and pointers to help readers organize local clubs.

His first word of greeting as editor of *Prairie Farmer* stressed the same idea. "There is going to be more community spirit, more getting together for the advantage of all concerned," he insisted.[9] He came to the paper already convinced that the idea of cooperative buying and selling was correct in principle.

Some of his early efforts featured local farmers' clubs. "Why not start a club in your community this winter?" he asked. Articles in *Prairie Farmer* reported how such clubs helped farmers through mail-order buying, reduced threshing prices, anti-hunting rules, savings on mill-feed, egg marketing, cow testing, and winter amusement.

Gradually, Gregory's interest focused more and more upon the new county agent movement and the farm bureaus which grew out of it. Chapter 5 outlined his part in the origin and educational phase of this movement which began in Illinois in 1912. The organization side also merits attention, for it gave birth to the country's newest farm group.

County agents worked within many types of local systems in those early days. One common feature throughout the northern states, however, was that the agent always had a body of local

[7] U.S. Commission on Country Life, *Report of the Commission on Country Life* (New York: Sturgis & Walton Co., 1911), pp. 130-131.
[8] *Prairie Farmer*, 83 (May 1, 1911), 16.
[9] *Prairie Farmer*, 83 (June 15, 1911), 12.

farmers behind him—for advice and moral support as much as for financial help. By 1913 a number of states were requiring that a county organization of farmers (called farm bureau in northern states) had to exist before a county agent could be assigned. Members had to pay dues, help the agent plan his work, and support him in general.

Enthusiasm mounted as farmers got involved, for more members meant more funds. County farm bureaus gained importance during World War I when a government keenly aware of needs for food "found ready made and in perfect working order county farm bureaus, each with its technically trained leader and advisor." [10] Emergency funds helped expand the system rapidly between 1918 and 1919.

County farm bureaus soon took two natural, if uncertain steps. One was to begin buying and selling cooperatively. This was work which county agents could not perform because they were public employees to a large extent, so many farm bureaus handled this new phase of their programs separately. Before long, such non-educational activities became a bigger part of the work of farm bureaus than of the county agent segment, at which point *Prairie Farmer* shifted its main interest from the county agent side toward the business side.

A second step was the clustering of county farm bureaus into state groups which promised to be useful in lobbying for state funds or special legislation to serve farmers.

Gregory and Illinois Agricultural Association

Illinois became the fourth state with county agricultural groups organized statewide. [11] As early as December, 1913, county advisers had organized an Illinois Association of County Agriculturists which met regularly twice a year. At their invitation, a number of farmers from organized counties appeared in Urbana on January 26, 1916, for a meeting to consider forming a state federation of county agricultural associations. [12] Illinois Agricultural Association (IAA) got

[10] Orville M. Kile, *The Farm Bureau Through Three Decades* (Baltimore: Waverly Press, 1948), p. 42.

[11] Kile, *Farm Bureau Through Three Decades*, pp. 45-46.

[12] John J. Lacey, *Farm Bureau in Illinois* (Bloomington: Illinois Agricultural Association, 1965), p. 42.

its start that day as the farmers adopted the name, set dues of $100
a year for each county, and elected officers with orders to perfect
the new group. Thirteen county groups signed as members under
a constitution and bylaws adopted seven weeks later.

Gregory was excited about this association which he felt "promises to take a decisive part in the development of agriculture in
Illinois. . . ." [13] He liked the idea because "hard-headed, practical
farmers" had formed it, and it echoed his deep-seated faith that
farmers "can accomplish almost anything by working together. . . .
Let's all work together to make the Illinois Agricultural Association
the greatest constructive force in the state," he concluded.

Records do not show how Gregory got involved personally with
the Illinois Agricultural Association, although it seems likely that
he did so through his close friend William Eckhardt of the DeKalb
County Soil Improvement Association. The new statewide group
elected Gregory third vice-president on April 15, 1918, by which
time it had 23 member counties and was doing some cooperative
buying.

Among others watching this movement was Charles Adkins, Director of Agriculture for Illinois, who suggested in late 1918 that
both the Farmers' Institute and the Illinois Agricultural Association
should become divisions of the state Department of Agriculture.[14]
Adkins believed that the two groups could get more done from a
single office in Springfield. Gregory disagreed strongly and in doing
so expressed his idea of what the IAA should be:

No real farmers' organization can be maintained at state expense. . . .
Such an organization, to tackle big problems fearlessly and work for the
farmers' interests in every line, must be financed and controlled wholly
by the farmers themselves. . . .

The Illinois Agricultural Association is founded upon the county farm
bureaus because they are the best existing basis on which to form such
an organization. But the purpose of the Illinois Agricultural Association
is not primarily educational. In fact, our most successful farm bureaus
and county advisors are finding that their duties are far from being
wholly educational, and that their broader field of usefulness lies in
serving their members in every possible way.

The Illinois Agricultural Association will deal with the big problems
of agriculture—the business, economic, social and legislative problems—
and leave educational work to the university and law administration to

[13] *Prairie Farmer*, 88 (February 12, 1916), 5.
[14] *Prairie Farmer*, 90 (December 28, 1918), 3.

the Illinois Department of Agriculture. This association cannot accomplish its purpose if it is supported by state funds.[15]

Obviously, however, IAA could not deal with the big problems of agriculture on a budget of $100 a county from about 20 counties. It could hardly hire a part-time secretary with that. Therefore, Gregory and Eckhardt spearheaded a new plan for financing at the annual meeting of 1919. It called for annual dues of $5 for each member, creating a budget which might surpass $100,000 a year. Many delegates came to the historic meeting in Peoria on January 21 instructed to vote against high membership fees. "It was nip and tuck for hours," according to Lacey.[16] However, leaders exerted enough persuasion to get approval of the new plan. Delegates also approved a statewide drive for membership and hired a full-time executive secretary, Dave Thompson.

To Gregory, this was the most important meeting ever held in Illinois. "As a result of this meeting, organized agriculture takes its place beside organized labor and organized business," he assured readers.[17] Undoubtedly, the action took IAA out of the class of farm groups which simply met once or twice a year to hear reports. Its motto became "Organized for Business," and it had finances to conduct business because a membership drive resulted in dues from more than 50,000 members during the first year. Furthermore, the action assured that IAA would be not merely a federation of county farm bureaus but an association in which the farmer paid for and held his own membership.

Most issues of *Prairie Farmer* during 1918 and 1919 carried items about actions of IAA. "*Prairie Farmer* is giving its heartiest support to the work of the Illinois Agricultural Association because we believe that it is absolutely necessary for Illinois farmers to organize," Gregory wrote in 1919, "and we believe that the Illinois Agricultural Association is the best sort of an organization for our conditions."[18]

Gregory's formal part in the group ended January 24, 1920, when he was replaced as a member of the executive committee. This too was part of his doing because he backed a new constitutional provision that all members of the board must be men whose main interest was farming. Gregory had long criticized farm groups run by nonfarmers and he did not want the IAA to be in that category.

[15] *Prairie Farmer*, 90 (December 28, 1918), 3.
[16] Lacey, p. 55.
[17] *Prairie Farmer*, 91 (February 8, 1919), 5.
[18] *Prairie Farmer*, 91 (May 17, 1919), 11.

Forming a National Farm Bureau

One of the noteworthy features of the farm bureau was that it did not arise as a child of poverty. Unlike agrarian movements between 1870 and 1895, the farm bureau did not grow out of the discontent of low prices and heavy debts. Indeed, it gained its early growth in one of agriculture's great boom periods. Clothed in conservatism, it looked askance at more radical farm groups such as the Nonpartisan League and Farmers' Union. It prided itself in being sane and stable and attracted wide support because it was built upon the respected base of the county agent system. Basic goals of the farm bureaus differed regionally, however, and these conflicts came to light when state farm bureaus met to discuss a national federation.

Illinois was one of 12 states represented at the first meeting on February 12-13, 1919, at Ithaca, New York. Gregory was one of the Prairie State's three delegates and was among the speakers at this session, out of which came a committee to outline plans for organization.[19] The American Farm Bureau Federation staged its organizational meeting in Chicago on November 12-14, 1919, to the rumble of conflict. Midwestern leaders with whom *Prairie Farmer* was aligned meant for the new group to help solve marketing problems under a nationwide cooperative plan. They saw it as a business tool for farmers. However, educational groups and farmers of the eastern, southern, and western states believed that it should be mainly educational. Agricultural colleges feared that "in the hands of necessarily inexperienced men the great powers created might in the end be the means of wrecking all their carefully built-up work of years."[20]

Sounds of debate filled the Red Room of the LaSalle Hotel and Gregory helped kindle it. *Prairie Farmer* published a daily report of proceedings and after the first day—which the pro-education forces had dominated—Gregory inserted an editorial. It said, in effect, that if the educator "pests" from afar would only get some idea of what the midwest was advocating, a worthwhile association might arise. But, Gregory concluded, it looked as though these "pests" were about to handcuff the midwestern delegates.

Vigorous protests to the editorial came from educators long be-

[19] *Prairie Farmer*, 91 (February 22, 1919), 76; Kile, *Farm Bureau Through Three Decades*, p. 48.
[20] Kile, *Farm Bureau Through Three Decades*, p. 48.

fore the second day's session began, while equally vigorous support came from delegates of the midwest. When the session opened, some of the attacked parties presented a resolution denouncing Gregory's editorial as inaccurate and destructive and demanding that he apologize personally. Gregory refused and business proceeded in a very tense setting.

Butler came to the hotel at lunchtime, unaware of the discord which his editor had brought into the open. Gregory described the matter to Butler, then added that they had asked him to apologize at the full session and retract his statements.

"Apologize, hell!" Butler is reported to have said. "Give them both barrels in the morning." [21]

Gregory did, but he and his associates from the midwest were hardly satisfied with the final outcome of the Federation's first major meeting. They had preferred that the group be named the National Farmers' Association, but it became the American Farm Bureau Federation. They wanted representation based on numbers of members, but settled for a compromise. They favored a budget big enough to handle active business operations, but ran into the opposition of those who felt that educational goals did not require heavy fees. Some of the compromise came only after delegates from Illinois threatened to withdraw and form a midwestern association.[22]

Gregory's first reaction to readers after the meeting in November was one of disappointment: "The American Farm Bureau Federation was launched at Chicago Nov. 12-14, but it took the water with its hull stove in and its engines hitting on two cylinders. Instead of being born of the enthusiastic vision of big service to the business of American agriculture with which many of the delegates were inspired, it was born of the suspicion and conservatism which others brought to the meeting." [23]

He deplored the idea that no program of action had come out of the three-day meeting and found solace only in two facts: (1) a nationwide group of farmers had taken shape and (2) some problems might be ironed out at the upcoming organizational meeting.

His faith in the new federation was so weakened that in December he suggested forming four subsidiary groups, one for each section of the country. These district groups would handle business

[21] Dave O. Thompson, unpublished memoirs, pp. 28-29.
[22] Kile, *Farm Bureau Movement*, p. 120.
[23] *Prairie Farmer*, 91 (November 22, 1919), 5.

work of the Federation, which in effect would give the midwest its own head.

Such an action did not prove necessary because the midwestern groups gained impressive triumphs at the ratification meeting on March 3, 1920. Other factions had shifted since November to a more broad-minded view about what the American Farm Bureau Federation should do. They felt more kindly toward efforts in cooperative marketing and agreed that each state should pay 50¢ a member, which meant a theoretical fund of $200,000 a year. Furthermore, the Federation's first president and secretary were midwesterners and Chicago became the national headquarters. The influence of the midwest plainly dominated what soon became the nation's largest farm group. Twenty-eight states ratified the original constitution. Fifteen months later, 43 states belonged to the Federation and membership was 1,052,114.[24] Iowa and Illinois headed the list in numbers of members and *Prairie Farmer* had helped play midwife to another farm organization.

Promoting Cooperative Marketing

Among the keenest expectations which farmers held for the American Farm Bureau Federation was the hope that it would help them reduce what they felt were exorbitant profits for middlemen. It seemed perfectly natural to form a central agency large enough to control the flow of grain to the market. The farmer could control his own marketing and no longer be at the mercy of his bogeymen—the grain dealers, brokers, and speculators—who, he was sure, profited at his expense.

Gregory felt he same way. If he had had his way, the wheat pit on the Chicago Board of Trade would never have reopened in July, 1920, after its wartime hiatus. He became even more certain in the following months of plunging farm prices which marked the first real crisis for farmers in more than 20 years. By November, as prices plummeted below costs of production, Gregory was adamant about the grain speculation system. Gossip fixes grain prices, he insisted, then illustrated:

When John Smith of Assumption, Ill., hitched up his team to haul a load of wheat to town the Chicago price was $2.05. Before he could load his wagon some trader heard that there had been a heavy dew in Timbuctoo, and the price went down to $1.98. While John was on the

[24] Saloutos and Hicks, p. 272.

way to town a new variety of chinch bug was discovered in Kamchatka, sending the price back to $2.06. Before he reached town, however, a couple of freight handlers in Marseilles, France, fell off the dock, reducing the French demand for wheat and sending the Chicago price down to $2.03. While John was driving off the scales the King of Madagascar died, and the bottom went out of the market entirely.

Small wonder that John and several million other farmers have decided that it is time to junk the speculative method of fixing grain prices! [25]

Gregory recoiled at the thought that the wheat crop of 1920 had been sold more than a half-dozen times within three months while "grain gamblers and foreign buyers have hammered down the market until the producers have lost something like $900,000. The consumer has received no benefit yet." [26]

Gregory's interest in "delousing the grain trade" made him a logical prospect among 150 whom J. R. Howard, president of the American Farm Bureau Federation, considered in choosing a 17-man committee to study grain marketing and form plans for a cooperative effort. This was the Federation's first big project and its first big test.

In September, 1920, Gregory was announced as a member of the new Committee of Seventeen and it began work in early October. Members visited cooperatives in Canada, California, and other places where the cooperative system had met with success. They heard statements from experts holding diverse views, then agreed upon a marketing plan which they presented in February, 1921, and which delegates ratified in April. It called for a central, nonprofit, nonstock sales agency whose members would be grain growers only. Each would pay $10 to enter and would sign a contract to sell his grain for five years through specified channels, all of which funneled through the national agency.

Prairie Farmer greeted this new plan warmly as a farmer's declaration of independence. "Delegates from every corner of the United States . . . were on their feet shouting approval and pledging allegiance to the new plan. The vote was unanimous; there was not a dissenting voice to the universal pledge of support." [27]

The success of U.S. Grain Growers, Inc., depended upon sign-up by members, so grain farmers soon became the object of intense persuasive efforts. Many thousands of dollars' worth of literature

[25] *Prairie Farmer*, 92 (November 6, 1920), 10.
[26] *Prairie Farmer*, 92 (October 23, 1920), 1.
[27] *Prairie Farmer*, 93 (April 16, 1921), 5.

reached farmers through the mail, and agents called in person to argue for and against sign-up as the hostile grain trade poured money into a campaign against the new plan. For its part, *Prairie Farmer* argued in favor of sign-up and belittled the efforts of the grain trade. On one cover page it said: "The board of trade has men working in various parts of Illinois, at $25 a day and expenses, urging farmers to cancel their farm bureau dues. Do you think they are doing this because they love you, because they want to make you more prosperous and help you get more money for your grain? Or is it because they are afraid the plans of farmers to market their own grain will give the farmer more money and the trader less? Think this over." [28]

Gregory was doubly upset that summer of 1921 because the same interests had killed bills which would have regulated practices of grain exchanges in Illinois. The Board of Trade had plowed $600,000 into this fight, Gregory charged. "Its noble work of relieving the farmer of the responsibility and the profits of marketing his grain can go on unhampered. . . . No matter how hot it may be in the harvest field, it is comforting to know that it is hotter still in the pits, where the farmer's true friends are panting and sweating and scalping solely because they love him so. . . ." [29]

Gregory was so disgusted that he decided to get away from it all and headed for his farm in DuPage County to work off steam by pitching hay.

In the meantime, sign-up in U.S. Grain Growers was so slow that it had reached 10,000 only after four months of hard work. "All set for a million members this year," Gregory had predicted confidently in April, but the membership of 26,000 in December was far short of his goal. Cries of bolshevism and other fears kept farmers from joining.

A year after its debut, U.S. Grain Growers had spent more than half a million dollars but was yet to handle its first bushel of grain. Membership stood at a meager 50,000, many of the larger groups had abandoned it, and officers were—as Gregory described them— quarreling and fiddling while Rome burned.

He had termed the start of U.S. Grain Growers as a new declaration of independence for farmers, but after the first year he concluded that farmers of the grain belt were instead standing at Val-

[28] *Prairie Farmer*, 93 (June 25, 1921), 1.
[29] *Prairie Farmer*, 93 (June 25, 1921), 6.

ley Forge, their ranks shot to pieces. This was the blackest spot on
the record of organized agriculture, as far as Gregory was concerned.[30]

His advice was to organize by state rather than within a single
national unit and he called for such a reorganization (which never
came about).

A reorganization in August failed to help U.S. Grain Growers,
although it limped along for another two years. The Chicago Board
of Trade denied it a seat on the exchange, but perhaps more important were the internal strife and heavy debts which sapped its
strength and robbed it of whatever confidence farmers might have
had in the most ambitious project ever devised for marketing grain.
As early as October, 1923, *Prairie Farmer* observed that the revival
effort had failed and the organization was practically dead, although
it was moving some grain through the Minneapolis exchange. By
April, 1924, the American Farm Bureau Federation decided to give
up the project and soon closed the office of U.S. Grain Growers.
Prairie Farmer announced the action with a short, inconspicuous
item which contained a germ of Gregory's final verdict: "The failure
of this ambitious grain marketing program is not due to defects of
the plan of the Committee of 17, as that plan was never tried." [31]

By now Gregory knew that all of those success stories which
Prairie Farmer had printed about cooperatives for specialty crops
in California could not guarantee success for the widely spread
wheat regions. He had now had his first taste of failure in farm
cooperatives and while he told readers that his faith in them was
unshaken, his attitude toward them began to shift.

As soon as he saw that U.S. Grain Growers was beyond repair,
Gregory became involved in the Wheat Growers Advisory Committee whose purpose was to help set up cooperative associations
for marketing wheat in all leading wheat states. This group formed
in October, 1923, under Frank O. Lowden, who had been directing
his attention to agriculture after losing his bid in 1920 for the presidential nomination. Herman Steen, Gregory's managing editor, took
a leave of absence to become secretary of the new committee, and
Aaron Sapiro, who had built a reputation in California as an expert
in cooperative marketing, became main field agent.

[30] *Prairie Farmer*, 94 (April 1, 1922), 7.
[31] *Prairie Farmer*, 96 (April 19, 1924), 6.

The approach of the Wheat Growers Advisory Committee appealed to Gregory because it used the state as the basic unit for organizing. A statewide, nonprofit association would serve as sales agent for each wheat grower who signed the standard marketing contract and paid the entrance fee of $10. The Committee hoped thereby to coordinate efforts of the 3,000 local cooperative wheat elevators in the Mississippi Valley and draw them into a confederation covering 16 states.[32]

Bickering among rival groups became one of the stumbling blocks in this new drive as some accused Lowden of using the Committee to further his own political nest. Sapiro's bluntness, excitability, occasional arrogance, high fees, and Jewish background also caused opposition and doubt.[33] The work of the Wheat Growers Advisory Committee ended during the summer of 1924.

Gregory, one of the most vocal supporters of the American Farm Bureau Federation at its start, had cooled to it by 1924. A power struggle between Sapiro and other executives nearly split the group before matters came to a head at the convention of December, 1923. Sapiro resigned and officers decided that the Federation should abandon efforts to actively direct cooperative marketing organizations.[34] The editor of *Prairie Farmer* interpreted this as a sign that the American Farm Bureau Federation "is not likely to do anything that will help its members get a better price for their products."[35] He therefore shifted his interest to the National Council of Cooperative Marketing Associations as "a most promising movement for the economic relief of agriculture." He was not prepared to abandon cooperative marketing.

Nor was he prepared to support the Federation's next step in trying to provide grain storage for farmers. The Federation got an offer to buy out four grain companies which offered enough capacity to store 65-70 per cent of the nation's commercial grain crop. Sellers wanted $26 million for the facilities.

Gregory quickly expressed doubt about this proposed venture. As John Turnipseed explained, "I don't know enough about it to be suspicious. . . . But I've traded horses some in my life, and I

[32] William T. Hutchinson, *Lowden of Illinois*, II (Chicago: University of Chicago Press, 1957), 523.
[33] Hutchinson, p. 524.
[34] Kile, *Farm Bureau Through Three Decades*, p. 119.
[35] *Prairie Farmer*, 96 (January 5, 1924), 8.

don't never trade sight unseen. I want to look at the critter's teeth and his ringbones." [36]

How strange it is, Gregory wondered in print, that the men most in favor of the deal are those who opposed past efforts by growers to market cooperatively. *Prairie Farmer* had announced the offer in late June, 1924, and by early August it was citing evidence that the proposed deal was "the biggest piece of blue-sky bunk ever attempted." One grain auditor reported to the paper that the American Farm Bureau Federation could reproduce better and larger facilities for one-fifth of the proposed sale price.

Gregory concluded by August 30 that the proposed merger "is neither fish, flesh nor fowl. It is a hard-boiled egg." [37] He considered *Prairie Farmer* to be somewhat alone in this stand and observed later that other farm papers in the territory were either silent or favorable toward the deal. The Illinois Agricultural Association and the Indiana Farm Bureau Federation soon took the same stand as *Prairie Farmer,* and together they helped prevent the Grain Marketing Company from selling much stock in Illinois and Indiana.

By July, 1925, *Prairie Farmer* could report that the Grain Marketing Company had reached the end of its trail. Farmers had not bought enough stock to meet the terms and Gregory concluded: "Out in the country the Grain Marketing Company will die 'unwept, unhonored and unsung.' Its passing will cause hardly a ripple. Farmers never accepted it as a bonafide farmers' company." [38]

He was partly wrong, for the company did not die unnoticed. Later investigation showed that the properties had been appraised at a figure far in excess of their value and the grain inventory in some elevators had been overstated. The string of frauds which came to light shocked and embittered farmers as it extended beyond 1927.

By then Gregory had changed his views about the role of co-operatives. He confessed in November, 1927: "The plain and disagreeable facts of the situation are that experience with cooperative marketing in this country indicates that the hope that we can quickly build up cooperatives in our staple crops powerful enough to handle surpluses and affect prices is a dream. We do not yet know how to sell cooperatively in a big way."

[36] *Prairie Farmer,* 96 (July 19, 1924), 5.
[37] *Prairie Farmer,* 96 (August 30, 1924), 8.
[38] *Prairie Farmer,* 97 (July 18, 1925), 3.

John Turnipseed put it even more lucidly:

Us farmers know all about cooperative marketing. We organized the U.S. Grain Growers and all kinds of wheat associations, to say nothing of havin' the Grain Marketing Company almost sold to us for three times what it was worth.

Some of the cooperatives have worked pretty well, especially the little ones that was close enough home so's we could keep an eye on 'em. They've made us some money, but they ain't raised the price up to where it ought to be, and they ain't goin' to. They ain't made us rich, and there ain't no prospect that they will.

Every time we've tried to organize a co-op big enough to be a trust and git us the price we ought to have, it went busted on account that job costs money and the members git tired of payin' the bill and havin' the outsiders git just as much good out of it without payin' a cent.[39]

Only after cooperative marketing came under sponsorship by the government through the Agricultural Marketing Act of 1929 did Gregory conclude that cooperative marketing of grain had become a reality. His painful experience with cooperatives between 1920 and 1929 sounded much like the experience of *Prairie Farmer* 50 years earlier when the Grange began its business ventures, for both started with high hopes and ended in disappointment. Fortunately, this time no staff members of *Prairie Farmer* got involved in fraud.

Legislated Relief for Farmers

After 1923 *Prairie Farmer* shifted its main attention from cooperatives to legislation, partly because the cooperative movement was floundering and partly because a new "farm bloc" was having some success in Washington. The price panic which began in late 1920 had again turned the eyes of farmers toward Washington, and they directed a new tide of protest toward legislators. Farm groups, including the new American Farm Bureau Federation, quickly activated offices in Washington as prices continued to slide during 1921 in the most crushing decline of prices that American agriculture had yet undergone. By May, 1921, prices of 10 leading crops were only one-third of what they had been a year earlier. Debt-ridden farmers looked to the government, convinced that if government policy could change agricultural conditions in wartime, it could also help in an economic emergency. Their experience with guaranteed prices and production standards during World War I

[39] *Prairie Farmer*, 100 (July 30, 1928), 6.

had confirmed their long-time argument that the welfare of agriculture was a public issue.

American Farm Bureau Federation furnished leadership in forming a bipartisan group of farm-oriented legislators in both houses during 1921. It became known as the farm bloc and its first year of efforts resulted in a long-sought Packer Control Act, the Futures Trading Act (soon declared unconstitutional and replaced by the Grain Futures Act of 1922), and other measures to help farmers get credit and find markets abroad. The farm bloc helped pass the Capper-Volstead Act of 1922 which legalized cooperative marketing associations and otherwise left an impressive record before it disbanded after 1923.[40]

Gregory's first personal crusade in farm legislation was for the McNary-Haugen Bill which came into the national limelight during early 1924 to begin an impetuous journey. Basically, it sought "equality for agriculture" through a device which would allow dumping farm surpluses over a tariff wall at world prices while holding higher prices at home. Thus, it was a two-price system aimed at raising the general level of prices. One unique feature was an equalization fee through which growers would finance the operation themselves. The plan called for an export corporation chartered by the government to buy surplus farm products at a fair-exchange, or parity, level. Fair-exchange level was defined as that which bore "the same ratio to the current general price index as a 10-year, pre-war average crop price bears to the average general price index, for the same period." It thereby sought to keep farm prices in line with prices in general and to give farmers a measure of equality compared with other segments of the economy.

If the corporation had to sell abroad at prices below parity level, it would recapture losses by charging an equalization fee against products benefited by the plan. Gains would more than cover losses, theoretically, because the export surplus comprised only a small share of most basic commodities.

This plan had been suggested two years earlier by two men in the farm machinery business, George N. Peek and Hugh S. Johnson. It was clearly a price-fixing scheme and aroused both fear and criticism on that account. However, three years of crisis had put farmers into a mood for action, and the plan gradually gained

[40] See a summary of these activities in Arthur Capper, *The Agricultural Bloc* (New York: Harcourt, Brace and Co., 1922), pp. 153-161.

support from Henry C. Wallace, Secretary of Agriculture. Congress received it on January 16, 1924, as a new bill sponsored by Senator Charles L. McNary and Representative Gilbert N. Haugen.

Gregory endorsed the new plan immediately and is credited with having brought about its approval by the Illinois Agricultural Association.[41] He reasoned that farmers could not make money selling their products on the level of world prices and buying supplies at levels of domestic prices heightened by a labor-protecting immigration law and industry-protecting tariffs. Supporters of the bill suffered defeat, but Gregory felt that the fight did IAA a great deal of good if for no more reason than building up its red corpuscle count. "It seems like old times to see our leaders breathing fire and issuing statements one after another, each one more exciting than the last." [42] He was impressed with the spirit of Samuel Thompson, who had become president of the IAA in early 1923 and was a vigorous advocate of farm relief.

Defeat and administrative inertia did not discourage those who saw in this new bill the biggest step yet toward farm relief. The proposal appeared again in revised form during 1925 but did not come to vote. By early 1926 *Prairie Farmer* claimed to have been the only farm paper in its territory to support McNary-Haugen. "We have never been discouraged," it assured. "For a time we stood almost alone in fighting for a change in policy in the American Farm Bureau Federation. That change has come." [43] It came as members elected Samuel Thompson new president of the Federation with a charge to fight for legislation which would help dispose of surpluses. A month later the IAA elected as new president Earl C. Smith, who became one of Gregory's closest colleagues in agitation for farm equality.

The strength of the movement was clear when supporters failed to buckle in mid-1926 after both the Senate and House rejected another version of the McNary-Haugen Bill. It came up again in February, 1927, and passed both houses of Congress only to be vetoed by President Coolidge. A fired-up Gregory responded with a full-page, signed, open letter to the President, assuring that the battle had not yet ended. He also took the occasion to promote

[41] James H. Shideler, *Farm Crisis, 1919-1923* (Berkeley: University of California Press, 1957), p. 276.

[42] *Prairie Farmer,* 96 (April 19, 1924), 8.

[43] *Prairie Farmer,* 98 (January 9, 1926), 36.

Frank Lowden (a supporter of the McNary-Haugen Bill) for president. Tempers ran hotter than the 160,000-volt electric plow that one inventor was testing in Illinois to kill weeds and insects.

A final round for the bill came in early 1928 when it passed both houses and again got a veto by Coolidge. Farmers of the midwest concluded that industry still controlled the country politically and economically and intended to keep that control.

Gregory, by now disenchanted with both cooperatives and farm legislation, decided temporarily that the greatest opportunity for agriculture in Illinois rested in doing a better job of farming.

Noting that "the road to legislative success is long and filled with disappointment," he predicted that agriculture would get more attention in Washington in the future, regardless of the party in power.[44] It was a well-founded certainty, for while midwestern farmers never won the McNary-Haugen fight, their efforts made the entire society much more aware of agriculture's problems. After McNary-Haugen, the basic question was not whether farmers should have legislated relief, but rather what form it should take. That form became more clear when the Hoover administration offered its new farm program in 1929. As far as Gregory was concerned, two-thirds of it was the same as the 1928 version of the McNary-Haugen Bill. It differed in omitting the equalization fee and putting greater stress upon cooperative marketing. He therefore favored the bill which became the Agricultural Marketing Act of 1929. "It marks the awakening of the nation to its responsibility toward agriculture," Gregory wrote. "It makes a beginning in the establishment of a national farm policy, something which this great agricultural nation has never had."[45] His only grave fear was that "professional promotors" might get their hands into the government's pocket through the new law.

Another effect of the McNary-Haugen sequence was that it brought together a cluster of men who soon became national leaders in agriculture. Gregory was in this group which included George Peek, Chester Davis, Edward O'Neal, Earl Smith, and Henry A. Wallace. Peek and his assistant, Davis, had been among the most avid spokesmen for the ill-fated bill. O'Neal was vice-president of the American Farm Bureau Federation under Samuel Thompson until May, 1931, when O'Neal became president. Smith was presi-

[44] *Prairie Farmer*, 100 (July 14, 1928), 3.
[45] *Prairie Farmer*, 101 (June 29, 1929), 8.

dent of the Illinois Agricultural Association, and Wallace, a former classmate of Gregory and son of the late Secretary of Agriculture, was editing *Wallaces' Farmer* in Des Moines. Together they were among the most active leaders in Franklin Roosevelt's farm program.

Supporter of the New Deal

Prairie Farmer was not greatly disturbed about the break in the stock market during late 1929. The farmer's stock moves on four legs under its own power, the paper observed, and the farmer is more interested in news from the Chicago stockyards than in ticker quotations from Wall Street. "The farmers of America are milking their cows and slopping their pigs as usual, while mother gets the breakfast and dresses the children for school. Farm conditions are steadily improving, and the deflation of stock speculation will help to give farmers more adequate and cheaper credit, and to teach the nation that the stockyards are more important than the stock market." [46]

Such optimism was encouraging if ill-based. Even after prices of wheat dropped six cents in one day on the Chicago grain exchange, Gregory interpreted the drop as proof that the Board of Trade was a speculative institution and not a farmer's market. By January the paper began to back away from its recent optimism, and the market editor talked about a "period of hesitation" in 1930 with net returns about the same as in past years.

Suddenly in 1930 the world came crashing down around *Prairie Farmer* as around millions of others. The new farm relief program was not working, prices were falling, and the worst drouth in nearly 30 years burned pastures of the midwest to a crisp and cut yields of corn drastically. By January, 1931, *Prairie Farmer* was admitting that its pessimism had not been enthusiastic enough, judging by the fact that aggregate farm income in 1930 dropped 15 per cent or more instead of holding about steady as the paper had predicted. Gregory too was getting excited; he always worked best and was at his sharpest when the pressure upon him was greatest. Prices for crops and livestock during 1931 were little more than half of what they had been two years earlier, and Gregory felt sure that he could aid farmers most by stressing legislative action. At first sympathetic

[46] *Prairie Farmer,* 101 (November 9, 1929), 21.

to President Hoover's efforts, Gregory grew more and more impatient, until in May, 1932, he wrote the President an open letter which ended with an emotional challenge, "Suffering millions are crying to you for help. Have you the courage to place your great ability and the power of your great office on their side? God grant that you will not fail the people in this hour of stress." [47]

Eagerness turned to disgust as Gregory watched the Republican Congress in mid-1932 kill several measures on which he had pinned hopes for raising prices. He was ready for the new deal which Governor Franklin Roosevelt was promising America's "forgotten" men and women. Readers had no trouble reading between the lines, although *Prairie Farmer* did not openly recommend voting for Roosevelt. After the election, Gregory told readers that they were facing the best opportunity in years to win their long fight.

He had met Roosevelt during the campaign when Wallace, Henry Morgenthau, Jr. (publisher of the *American Agriculturist*), Gregory, and some others met with the candidate to arrange articles about farm policy for their farm papers.[48] They conferred at other times that fall. Gregory later said that O'Neal, Smith, and he met with Roosevelt in the fall of 1932 in Chicago.[49] A biographer of George Peek reported that Gregory was among a group of five men (including O'Neal, Peek, Smith, and Davis) who met with Roosevelt and Morgenthau in early October.[50] Some of these mentions may have referred to the same meeting, but Gregory clearly was involved in early meetings of farm leaders with the presidential candidate. He said Roosevelt assured them: "One of the first things I am going to do is to take steps to restore farm prices. I am going to call farmers' leaders together, lock them in a room, and tell them not to come out until they have agreed on a plan." [51]

Staff members of *Prairie Farmer* state that from then on, Gregory spent as much time in Washington and in the offices of farm organ-

[47] *Prairie Farmer*, 104 (May 14, 1932), 3.
[48] Thompson, p. 176; Kile, *Farm Bureau Through Three Decades*, p. 186.
[49] Clifford V. Gregory, "The American Farm Bureau Federation and the A.A.A.," in Harwood L. Childs, ed., *Pressure Groups and Propaganda*, Annals of the American Academy of Political and Social Science, 179 (May, 1935), p. 152.
[50] Gilbert C. Fite, *George N. Peek and the Fight for Farm Parity* (Norman: University of Oklahoma Press, 1954), p. 239, cited in Christiana McFayden Campbell, *The Farm Bureau and the New Deal* (Urbana: University of Illinois Press, 1962), p. 51.
[51] Childs, p. 152.

izations as at his desk. He took part in the series of pre-inaugural
meetings during which farm groups ironed out their differences in
an effort to take advantage of the go-ahead which Roosevelt had
given them.[52] Gregory even became a rumored candidate for appointment as Secretary of Agriculture, along with Morgenthau,
Cully A. Cobb, Davis, Peek, and Wallace. Some observers believed that Roosevelt favored his friend Morgenthau but bowed to
demands by the Farm Bureau for a midwesterner and chose Wallace in a tossup over Gregory. Others believed that Roosevelt had
his eye on Wallace all along.[53] Gregory's wife said that her husband told Wallace he was not a candidate for the position and did
not wish to be.[54] Instead, Gregory backed his former classmate who
became Secretary of Agriculture on March 4, 1933, while Morgenthau became governor of the Farm Credit Administration.

It was almost like the days of the McNary-Haugen Bill as Wallace formed his circle of close advisers. He got his strongest political support from the Farm Bureau with Edward O'Neal as its
hearty, dominating mediator and business-like Earl Smith as what
many described "the real power behind the throne." [55] George Peek
was new administrator of the Agricultural Adjustment Act which
passed in 1933. With him as leaders of the Agricultural Adjustment Administration (AAA) were Charles J. Brand, who drafted
the first McNary-Haugen Bill, and Chester Davis, who had been
one of its ardent spokesmen.

Gregory, as a party not bound formally to either the Roosevelt
administration or the Farm Bureau, became a mediator. He could
influence Smith (which few people reportedly could) and O'Neal.
O'Neal acknowledged that he seldom made a major move without
consulting Gregory. Apart from his own active mind and knack for
incisive expression, Gregory was ideally suited for high pressure,
smoke-filled rooms. An editorial in *Wallaces' Farmer* described this
ability:

He liked people. He laughed easily. He could go into a meeting with
men whose ideas were contrary to his ideas and to each other's, and
come out with unanimous agreement on a compromise plan.
. . . Often and often, when a conference would be in a tangle, someone

[52] See, for example, *Prairie Farmer*, 104 (December 24, 1932), 4; Campbell, p. 52.
[53] Kile, *Farm Bureau Through Three Decades*, p. 194; Campbell, p. 62.
[54] Mrs. C. V. Gregory, personal interview, March 25, 1967.
[55] Kile, *Farm Bureau Through Three Decades*, pp. 172-173, 313; Campbell, pp. 57-61; Saloutos and Hicks, p. 548.

would say: "Wire Gregory and get him to come down." Or, in another
dogfight in a committee-room, some one would come panting out and
ask: "Where's Cliff? We need him bad!"

He could see the fair-minded part of a man, even tho it was buried
under rough language, short temper and hasty argument. And presently
the calm, reasonable friendly soul that was in Cliff appealed to what was
calm, reasonable and friendly in the other man.[56]

The result of this close contact was that *Prairie Farmer* soon
came squarely into the camp of the New Deal. Gregory was "tre-
mendously impressed with the intelligence and sincerity of purpose" with which the new administration met the farm problem.
He described the Agricultural Adjustment Act of 1933 as the best
farm relief bill that had ever been written and was proud of having
helped write it.[57] Even the Lazy Farmer chimed in with a happy
tune:

> By gum, it seems that better times has come
> The government has learned, gee whiz,
> How valuable us farmers is.
> No longer will we toil and sweat
> And be foreclosed because of debt,
> For now a kindly government
> Is offering our land to rent. . . .[58]

Gregory's confidence in the new plan grew as he saw farmers
getting more for their products than a year earlier and paying
about the same for things they bought. The IAA and American
Farm Bureau also evangelized for the new farm program during
its honeymoon and assured members that they should not heed
talk about a regimented agriculture.

However, some pressure against the AAA appeared to grow by
late 1934, and readers of *Prairie Farmer* began to express sentiment
against the program and *Prairie Farmer*'s support of it. In November Gregory assured readers that the paper was not interested in
any political party as such, but rather in the welfare of farm
people. It had backed the Farm Board under the Republican administration, he argued. "We are supporting Henry Wallace and
Chester Davis and Bill Myers and Henry Morgenthau now, because we know they are working sincerely to raise farm prices and

[56] *Wallaces' Farmer and Iowa Homestead,* 66 (November 29, 1941), 6.

[57] Walter T. Borg, "Clifford V. Gregory and His Writings," *Agricultural
History,* 16 (1952), 117; *Wallaces' Farmer and Iowa Homestead,* 62 (July 17,
1937), 1; Childs, p. 152, 155-157.

[58] *Prairie Farmer,* 105 (April 15, 1933), 4.

refund farm debts and give us an honest monetary system." [59]
However, criticism from readers increased during 1935, for example:

It's too bad there is not some way to stop such buzzards as you. You cause trouble by making lots of people believe they can get something for nothing. . . . The whole program is a fake. Kill pigs, control production, everything is sure out of gear. . . . You are causing trouble for the unborn and plenty of it. No more *Prairie Farmer* for me. [60]

If Mr. Gregory really believes his doctrine of destruction, he should bury his ostrich egg in the sand and let it mature a few years before he writes editorials again. He has prolonged the depression and made many enemies with his old Democratic bunk. If he had had given (*sic*) Hoover one-half the support he has already given Roosevelt and the AAA, this depression would never have gotten out of control. [61]

Your paper . . . is nothing but a Wall Street news and we do not want you to send it to us any more. We are disgusted with it. You can't make the farmers believe such as you print. We are sick and tired, disgusted and mad at the AAA program that H. Wallace is trying harder than ever to push down the farmers' throat. [62]

Rumors spread that Gregory was on the payroll of the AAA. Any questions which readers might have had about *Prairie Farmer's* allegiance got a crystal-clear answer when readers picked up their copies on October 10, 1936, and saw the headline on the front page: "Why We Are for the Roosevelt Farm Program." It was a startling move for a farm paper which carefully had avoided partisan politics. In the article Gregory denied partisan motives. He argued that farmers had been welcomed in Washington since 1932 and if Roosevelt's farm policies were unsound, farm folks had only themselves to blame. Moreover, he pointed to improved conditions for farmers.

A commotion followed as readers responded, some in agreement and others in scorn. They accused Gregory of being a wire-whiskered theorist, a rock-ribbed Democrat, and a string of other invectives. However, the circulation of *Prairie Farmer* continued to climb in 1937 and 1938, despite some adverse response reported by circulation salesmen in Indiana. [63]

[59] *Prairie Farmer*, 106 (November 10, 1934), 6. By that time, Davis had become administrator of AAA, Myers governor of the Farm Credit Administration, and Morgenthau Secretary of the Treasury.
[60] *Prairie Farmer*, 107 (January 19, 1935), 17-18.
[61] *Prairie Farmer*, 107 (February 2, 1935), 30.
[62] *Prairie Farmer*, 107 (July 6, 1935), 2.
[63] William Renshaw, circulation manager in Indiana at the time, reported in

Prairie Farmer tried to regain its image of nonpartisanship during the election of 1940, but a reputation as spokesman for the New Deal stayed with it for many years. Gregory's personal loyalty to the New Deal remained strong as long as he was at *Prairie Farmer.* He backed the plan for ever-normal granaries and was one of the group which in May, 1937, wrote what became the Agricultural Adjustment Act of 1938.[64] Butler also supported the New Deal, but the two men were finding less and less upon which to agree in other matters.

Rift between Butler and Gregory

Members of the staff watched with concern between 1930 and 1937 as they saw their publisher and editor grow further and further apart. The split may have been inevitable, a built-in outcome of the you-take-this-part-I'll-take-that agreement which they adopted at the outset. Evidence suggests that they worked harmoniously for at least a dozen years. Some members of the staff sensed a conflict as early as 1926, although the problem began to burst out in discernible shapes only in the late 1920's, after Butler started spending his winters in Arizona. Conflict between the two men grew more tense after 1934.

By and large, onlookers were sympathetic to Gregory in the matter. Many explained the conflict in terms of Butler's growing jealousy toward his widely heralded editor. They pointed out that probably not 10 out of 100 farm people in Illinois knew the name Burridge Butler, but nearly all knew the name Clifford Gregory. Many farmers assumed that Gregory owned and published the paper.

However, any real explanation of this phase of the Butler era cannot be stated so simply, for not all showed on the surface of this conflict. Butler may have had several reasons for concern about his editor. Undoubtedly, one was the realization he was being overshadowed. Butler's unusually strong sense of history probably dictated that he react against threats to his role as a modern-day John S. Wright. In so doing, he faced a dilemma because he could not outwrite Gregory, nor could he come close to Gregory in in-

Thompson, p. 41, that more than 10,000 farmers cancelled their subscriptions in protest, and Thompson observed that some salesmen could not earn a living selling subscriptions to *Prairie Farmer* after the endorsement.

[64] Kile, *Farm Bureau Through Three Decades,* p. 238.

fluence among agricultural—or other—national leaders. Gregory was the man who got invitations from Presidents Coolidge, Hoover, and Roosevelt for dinners and meetings at the White House. Gregory was the one who knew the inside story because highest level planning sessions were open to him. Gregory was the man from *Prairie Farmer* flooded with requests for speaking and whose poised and witty stage presence brought generous praise and calls for more. In fact, Butler found himself upstaged at every turn when it came to public awareness, not because Gregory was spiteful but because Gregory was a dynamic editor who had spent 20 years earning his place in the agricultural scene. Butler's showmanship flourished in the meeting room and the office, for he worked best in the shadows as a power behind the scenes among associates who would carry out his ideas. Frustration may have set in as his need for public appreciation became buried more deeply under layers of gruffness and outward scorn for personal display. One also needs to keep in mind that Butler was 62 years old in 1930; Gregory was only 47.

A second major concern of Butler's seems to have centered around the editorial and financial vigor of *Prairie Farmer* in the early 1930's. At times Butler expressed a fear that the paper suffered when Gregory was gone so much. In his tactless if well-meant manner, Butler occasionally told Gregory that the paper would benefit if Gregory would stay home and worry about his editorial responsibilities. Gregory envisioned himself as serving his readers best by working on legislation, but from Butler's standpoint the editorial office was vacant a great deal and assistant editors were not getting as much direction as he would have liked. This bothered Butler even more because of the new competitive pressures from national farm magazines.

Another source of uneasiness appears to have been Butler's fear that *Prairie Farmer* was becoming tied too closely to the Farm Bureau. Butler backed the political stand which Gregory espoused, but he was uneasy about the prestige which the paper created for the IAA and Earl Smith.[65] *Prairie Farmer* was consistently more favorable to the Farm Bureau than critical of it.[66]

[65] Thompson, p. 29.

[66] For exceptions to Gregory's support and endorsement of actions of the Farm Bureau, see *Prairie Farmer*, 93 (December 3, 1921), 8; 96 (January 5, 1924), 8; 97 (July 25, 1925), 8; 97 (August 15, 1925), 8; 102 (February 15, 1930), 10.

Finances entered the picture because the depression had eroded part of Gregory's autonomy and prestige within the organization. Not only was *Prairie Farmer* losing money, but it was having to lean on that rambunctious youngster, WLS. WLS bought space and put some of the paper's employees on its payrolls to help *Prairie Farmer* during the early 1930's, which psychologically shifted WLS from an image of handmaiden for *Prairie Farmer* to that of benefactor. Its staff members got paid more and enjoyed more prestige than staff members on the paper. It operated under a different set of standards, with entertainment as a major function. In response, editorial associates clustered even more firmly around their embattled editor and other staff members began to take sides, all of which only drove Butler and Gregory further apart.

The two men apparently were not able to settle the matter between them. Butler began criticizing Gregory to other members of the staff, a practice against which Gregory pleaded in vain. "Why not take up with me direct any criticism you may have?" Gregory asked Butler in a memorandum in June, 1935. "It may be based on misinformation or misunderstanding. If not, any needed change can be made quietly and without the necessity of any of us getting mad about it." [67]

Butler, in turn, felt that Gregory was inflexible in many dealings with him. "What have I done to deserve a stubborn editor?" Butler would implore after arguments. In 1935 Butler wrote, "You are about as positive a man as I have ever met and the people who work in your department are under pressure to carry out your ideas and policies and quit thinking for themselves." [68] Gregory's editors indicated little pressure of the type which Butler feared, although some felt that Gregory should have deferred more to Butler and tried to build him up in the minds of readers. Gregory realized the danger and said that he had begged Butler to keep at least a publisher's column in the paper to maintain a personal image. [69] The only such column which Butler wrote during his long tenure was in 1913 and lasted but four issues. [70]

A two-pronged climax brought matters to a head between 1935

[67] Memorandum from Gregory to Butler, June, 1935.
[68] Butler to Gregory, December 19, 1935.
[69] C. L. Mast, personal interview, June 12, 1967.
[70] See *Prairie Farmer*, 85 (October 15, 1913), 3; 85 (November 1, 1913), 3; 85 (November 15, 1913), 2; 86 (January 1, 1914), 2. Other articles appeared occasionally with his byline.

and 1937. One part began when Butler brought a new general manager to *Prairie Farmer*–WLS during August, 1935. He was Conklin Mann, who came to the paper from New York with experience in advertising and sales. Available accounts differ in their description of how Butler first met Mann, but they agree that Butler was impressed by Mann's editorial views. Mann was of the new school which maintained that farm publications needed style if they were to attract advertising. State farm papers were making an especially poor impression on both readers and advertisers, he argued in his initial proposal to Butler.

The present editorial policy of the *Prairie Farmer* is a definite interpretation of the living habits of the so-called average dirt farmer. Pictures are selected to show farmers and their children in overalls, farmers' wives in aprons at cook stoves or at other household work. There seems to be a carefully planned policy to visualize farm life in terms of chores, work, news and social interests which touch the average farm family. . . . My personal belief is that such editorial and pictorial treatment, regardless of its intellectual integrity, cannot win worth while advertising support. Furthermore, we have the circulation department's testimony that it is not winning the reading support of the younger farm families.[71]

As far as he was concerned, *Country Gentlemen, Country Home,* and *Successful Farming* were taking the cream, leaving *Prairie Farmer* only the skimmed milk. Actually, those magazines were facing the same depression-based problems as *Prairie Farmer* (see Chapter 4), but Mann's views threw into question the editorial side of *Prairie Farmer*; until then executives of the firm had largely blamed its financial woes upon limited advertising. Now Gregory was on the defensive and he did not like it: "If we happen to publish a story occasionally that is not up to par I never hear the last of it."[72] Neither then nor later would Gregory concede that the big problem of *Prairie Farmer* was anything other than lack of sales effort. "The paper itself has always been better than its salesmanship," Gregory stated flatly (and assumed some of the blame for that weakness). Furthermore, he cited cases in which he felt Butler was sawing the limb off behind him in editorial efforts aimed at attracting young readers.

The problem was complicated by Butler's departure for Arizona, for he left Mann with only a half-established authority as general manager. Staff members responded to Mann largely by department. Those with WLS hardly knew Mann because he did not bother

[71] Report from Conklin Mann to Butler, June 24, 1935.
[72] Memorandum from Gregory to Butler, June 19, 1935.

them. Those who worked with *Prairie Farmer* in production, circulation, and advertising were impressed with his outspoken call
for "styling up." Those on the editorial side opposed Mann because
they felt sure he was serving as Butler's "hatchet man" to get rid
of Gregory. A fairly congenial appearance hid the sparks which
flew as Gregory and Mann—neither with enough authority to control the other—competed in Butler's self-made sparring ring. Their
only meeting ground was a desire to help their paper survive
against the national farm magazines, and on that basis they experimented with new layout, type, and editorial approaches.

Mann did not precipitate the final parting between Butler and
Gregory. Maneuvers with wages and stock finally convinced Gregory that he had had enough of Butler's brand of paternalism. Along
with other employees, Gregory had taken a severe cut in salary
during the early 1930's. When business began to return to normal,
especially with WLS, Gregory did not share proportionately in the
rising scale of salaries for officers of the company. Another point
of contention was that Butler ceased all dividends on common
stock during the depression, yet got $12,000 a year himself on the
preferred stock (which he alone held).[73] Gregory owned 30 per
cent of the common shares outstanding during that period, Butler
and his wife 35 per cent, Dickson 15 per cent, Holt 10 per cent,
Orlemann and Edwards each 5 per cent.[74]

In the third and final maneuver which alienated Gregory, Butler
and the corporation's lawyer worked out a new stock plan while
Gregory was in Europe on a study tour of cooperatives during
1936. Corporate records show no details (Butler was famed for
his doctored minutes) except that in October, 1936, all board members except Gregory concurred in a plan to change the structure
of shares from 1,000 preferred and 1,000 common no par to 5,000
shares no par.[75] Gregory's close friends and family members felt
that Gregory convinced Butler of the merit of broadening the company's base of ownership and allowing more employees to hold
stock, but that Butler wanted to do so without watering down his
share.

After that power play which left Gregory stranded, he and Butler

[73] Financial report of Prairie Farmer Publishing Company by First National
Bank of Chicago, July 12, 1934.
[74] Minutes of annual meetings, Prairie Farmer Publishing Company.
[75] Minutes, Prairie Farmer Publishing Company, October 31, 1936.

bargained about a settlement through which Gregory would get *Prairie Farmer* and Butler would keep WLS. Bargaining continued into mid-1937 and Gregory thought that Butler was amenable to the idea because *Prairie Farmer* was not extremely profitable at the time and WLS looked like a real growth investment. Negotiations fell through, however, as Butler refused to give up the paper. The two men were on the edge of litigation at that point, for when they agreed that Gregory would sell out, he got only one-third to one-half of what he felt he should for his stock.

Gregory resigned on July 1, 1937, in an atmosphere rather incompatible with the tone of the corporate minutes, which read: "Mr. Gregory stated that he was leaving with the kindliest feelings toward everybody, and wished the *Prairie Farmer* success." [76]

Immediately, members of Gregory's editorial staff began to look for work elsewhere because they were indignant, they felt they would be discriminated against if they stayed, and they feared the paper would collapse after Gregory left. Soon after the staff scattered, Gregory approached his former employees about forming a new farm paper to compete with *Prairie Farmer* in Illinois. He was excited about the idea and set up a temporary office at 309 W. Jackson. [77] The group met several times to discuss the proposed publication and even chose a name for it—*Land*. None of his former associates had money to invest, but Gregory had some and was sure he could raise funds through an issue of stock. Excitement waned, though, as they faced the cold prospects of risking a half-million dollar investment in competition with both a well-established state farm paper and the national farm magazines which they feared might take over everything. They decided it was not worth the risk, especially to Gregory who was older and who had the most to lose.

Various offers came to Gregory, some in government and farm organizations, but he chose to join Dante Pierce as associate publisher of *Wallaces' Farmer and Iowa Homestead,* Des Moines, and *Wisconsin Agriculturist,* Racine. Part of Pierce's appeal to Gregory was that in a few years the two planned to start a new farm paper in Illinois to supplant *Prairie Farmer,* which Gregory felt was becoming as much a radio magazine as a farm paper. The idea never materialized, perhaps was never meant to, for Pierce—like Butler—

[76] Minutes, Prairie Farmer Publishing Company, July 1, 1937.
[77] Gregory to Governor Henry Horner, August 2, 1937.

often made ambitious promises. Pierce wanted Gregory to become
a spokesman for agriculture and to represent Pierce's farm papers
and others in farm councils and on the national level.[78] Gregory's
family felt that he was never his old self after leaving the editor's
chair at *Prairie Farmer*. He died unexpectedly on November 18,
1941, from complications after a successful operation for appendi-
citis.[79]

Nor was *Prairie Farmer* quite the same after Gregory left it.
Butler tore down the walls to Gregory's office, determined never to
allow an editor so much independence, and blacked out his former
editor to the extent of allowing almost no mention of his name in
the paper's centennial issue. Gregory's name appeared only once
in the account of *Prairie Farmer*'s history between 1909 and 1941,
and that was a passing mention. Butler had completely written
off this man who had seemingly challenged his coveted seat at the
head of the family table.

[78] Richard Pierce, personal interview, March 24, 1967.
[79] *Wallaces' Farmer and Iowa Homestead,* 66 (November 29, 1941), 6;
Prairie Farmer, 113 (November 29, 1941), 8; Merrill Gregory, personal interview, January 14, 1967.

Early Radio
and the
Illinois Farm

CHAPTER 7

Just imagine, the editors of farm papers began speculating to their readers in 1922. You may be able to stop at the end of the corn row in the middle of the afternoon, walk to a nearby post where there is a little box, slip a pair of phones over your head, and listen to the final official report about the corn market that day. You may hear how the big league baseball game is going or learn about a heavy rain that is on its way from the west.

Radio will be your "Aladdin's Magic Lantern"—just rub it and you will be transported wherever you choose. You will be able to sit by the cozy fire and be transported to the farthermost parts of the earth to listen to the great artists for whom you have hungered. Scientists will tell the secrets of nature and you can even hear the wise counsel of the President's voice at the White House.

This marvelous invention will keep both youngsters and older folks in the family circle. Why should the farmer of Illinois emigrate to California when the world at large can be brought to him? It sounds like a fairy tale or some wild dream, but it is true. Radio is worth its weight in gold because it will make the farm home attractive and interesting to both the young and old. It will keep the youngsters away from doubtful pleasures. You homemakers can patch and darn socks to the tune of your favorite orchestra.

Now farm people will have all the advantages of country life plus all the education and entertainment of the city. You will have something to cheer you up after a hard day's work outside. When wintry blasts sweep across barren fields to sigh and whistle under the eaves, radio alone can dispel the bleak isolation. No matter how deep the snowdrifts or how muddy the roads, you can travel to any playground of the world with a twirl of a small dial. Even in good weather, you will not have to go to town so much.

For once you will be on parity with the dealer who buys your grain and livestock. He pays telegraph tolls to keep you in touch with the markets; you will have a free source of up-to-the-minute information to help you plan shipments to take best advantage of market conditions.

It seemed that America was headed toward an era of radio farming. Indeed, the editors were largely correct, because even after radio passed out of the stage of being a fad, it was as important a part of the farm as the plow, silo, or cream separator. The farmer was truly one of radio's favorite children. No one talked much about radio programs for accountants or carpenters, but the value of radio for the farmer was clear from the beginning. Not only could it help banish the loneliness of farm life, but its fun and frolic could help take some of the bitterness and grief out of the farm crisis of 1920-23 with its heavy debts and foreclosures.

In their excitement about this new magic lantern, farm people who could afford radio receiving sets accepted programming uncritically. They did not care if programs were made up of offerings by volunteer musicians "whose ability did not always classify them as artists" and whose work sometimes should have been outcast rather than broadcast.[1] Poor acoustics and the buzz of background voices from studios which had no reception rooms also failed to bother farm listeners. In fact, the sound itself was exciting—a sliding chair, rustling skirts, a banged microphone. It was an age of sounds, an age during which radio fed listeners any sound it could find. Radio receiving sets in those early and mid-1920's vibrated with sounds of sea lions at dinner, prize fights, court trials,

[1] *Country Gentleman,* 92 (February, 1927), 143.

weddings, Chinese opera, circuses, fashion shows, songs of birds, and even the love song of the beetle.

But perhaps the most persistent sound of radio in Illinois was that of classical music, for radio in Chicago was born on opera. Chicago became a new dot on the nation's radio map November 11, 1921, when Westinghouse Electric and Manufacturing Company introduced KYW with the sound of Mary Garden, soprano of the Chicago Civic Opera.[2] Unlike pioneer Westinghouse stations KDKA, Pittsburgh (which began by broadcasting election returns), and WJZ, Newark (which made its "big splash" five weeks before KYW with a broadcast of the World Series), the Chicago station decided on opera.[3] Opera made up the entire schedule of KYW during the first season. The station broadcast all performances of the Chicago Civic Opera, afternoon and evening, six days a week— and nothing else.[4]

Of special interest to farm listeners beginning in 1921 were reports of grain and livestock prices.[5] Three stations in the country were broadcasting market reports by radio telephone during 1921. In late January, 1922, the Department of Agriculture began airing market reports from Chicago by radiophone. Reports at 2:15, 4:15, 6, and 7:30 P.M. kept listeners informed about trade in livestock, grain, dairy products, fruits, and vegetables. At about the same time, farmers in southern Illinois gained access to similar reports from St. Louis University's WEW, a 100-watt station which engineers on its faculty designed and built.[6]

The growth of weather reporting by radio stations paralleled that of market news reporting because both originated with agencies of the U.S. government.[7] A station owned by the University of

[2] Ann Lord, "Chicago Broadcasts," *Wireless Age*, 12 (April, 1925), 40.

[3] Erik Barnouw, *A Tower in Babel—A History of Broadcasting in the United States*, I (New York: Oxford University Press, 1966), 69, 84.

[4] Barnouw, p. 88.

[5] For discussions about early broadcasting of market and weather reports, see: W. A. Wheeler, "Down on the Farm in 1923," *Radio Broadcast*, 2 (January, 1923), 212-214; S. R. Winters, "What Does He Hear?" *Wireless Age*, 10 (February, 1923), 35-36; F. C. Gilbert, "Rural Life Modernized," *Wireless Age*, 12 (March, 1925), 24ff.; *Prairie Farmer*, 93 (April 30, 1921), 2; 93 (July 9, 1921), 7; *Orange Judd Farmer*, 70 (February 1, 1922), 4; Ward Seeley, "The Farm Moves Nearer the City," *Wireless Age*, 10 (January, 1923), 24ff.

[6] Winters, "What Does He Hear?" p. 36.

[7] Gilbert, p. 25.

Wisconsin began radiophone reports in January, 1921, using facts
from the U.S. Weather Bureau. Three months later, farmers of
Illinois could hear official weather reports from WEW, St. Louis.
Twelve stations had permission to broadcast official reports daily
by July, 1921, and that number grew to 140 by January, 1923.[8]

At the same time, the number of radio stations in the United
States mushroomed from only five in November, 1921, to 458 by
the end of July, 1922.[9] By April, 1924, *Orange Judd Farmer* could
inform its readers that they were located in the heart of the radio
world, with 131 broadcasting stations within 380 miles of central
Illinois.[10] The state itself had 37 radio stations by April, 1925.

Getting the Programs to Farmers

All of this growth in numbers of stations and types of programming did not deceive those who realized that signals in the air
often remained only that. Ownership of radio receiving sets by
farmers doubled between early 1924 and early 1925, yet even then
only about two of every 100 farms in the U.S. had sets.[11] The figure
for Illinois was somewhat higher. In early 1924 between 7 and 10
per cent of the farms in Illinois had receiving sets, according to
a survey of 73 county farm bureaus by the Illinois Agricultural
Association.[12] The 1925 Census showed 27,436 Illinois farms reporting radio sets, or 12 per cent.[13]

At this point the county agents, local banks, telephone companies, and other interested agencies combined efforts to help get
radio programs to farmers. Country banks began to look like miniature stock exchanges as bankers took market prices from radio
reports and posted them on blackboards where local farmers could
see current price levels. Several banks in Illinois entertained groups
every evening that popular stations aired musical programs.

[8] Gilbert, p. 25.
[9] Hiram L. Jome, *Economics of the Radio Industry* (Chicago: A. W. Shaw,
1925), p. 70, cited in Barnouw, p. 91.
[10] *Orange Judd Farmer*, 72 (April 15, 1924), 4.
[11] J. Farrell, "Farm Radio Making Rapid Progress," *Radio News*, 6 (January,
1925), 1143; William A. Hurd, "Harvest Time on the Air," *Wireless Age*, 12
(November, 1924), 19.
[12] *Prairie Farmer*, 96 (March 8, 1924), 6.
[13] U.S. Department of Commerce, *Census of Agriculture*, 1925, Part I, Northern States (Illinois) (Washington: U.S. Government Printing Office, 1927), p.
504.

By 1924 many community clubs, country churches, schools, and county farm bureaus were installing radio receiving sets. In fact, radio often served as the program for farm meetings during that era when most farmers did not have radio sets. Farmers who owned sets often did a great deal of entertaining until their neighbors were able to afford radios. One telephone company in eastern Illinois received market information through its set, then telephoned the facts regularly to its subscribers. Before long any farm bureau office or cooperative marketing group which did not use radio to keep in touch with current agricultural conditions was considered behind the times.

County agents were important in the effort to bring radio to farm families. They soon learned that one of the big reasons that farmers did not own radio sets was that the mechanics of them frightened prospective buyers. Terms such as "neutrodyne" and "heterodyne" confused people and led them to conclude that radio was too technical for them. Some county agents began giving radio demonstrations for farmers. They carried kits which allowed them to rig up an antenna in the farmer's front yard and get sets back into working order. They also helped form radio clubs through which farm boys and girls showed others how to install and service radio sets.

Antennas stretching from the farm home to perhaps the peak of a barn or windmill became more and more common as the popularity of radio grew and farmers moved out of their financial crisis. In 1922 wireless sets cost between $15 and $250.[14] Farmers were paying an average of about $110 in mid-1923, depending upon whether they bought or made their sets. Roughly equal numbers were buying and building sets. Farmers were paying about $175 for manufactured sets or building their own for an average cost of $83.[15] Nearly two-thirds of the sets were equipped with three or more tubes, indicating that farmers were going in for distance; very few bought crystal sets.

The radios were powered by storage "A" and "B" batteries and most of the listening was done through headsets, since horn-type ("morning glory") loudspeakers gave an inferior quality of sound.

[14] *Prairie Farmer,* 94 (March 11, 1922), 2.
[15] Survey by the Radio Market News Service of the U.S. Department of Agriculture, cited in *Printer's Ink,* 126 (January 24, 1924), 73-74; Gilbert, p. 27.

All-electric plug-in receivers with improved built-in speakers became available only about 1927.[16] Even then, most farm homes did
not have electric power from utility companies. Some had homemade electrical equipment with generators run by windmills, tractor power take-offs, or stationary gas engines. Reliance on battery
power meant that farmers often had to take their batteries to a
service station for recharging, which in turn meant that homes often
went without radio for long periods. This was especially true in
summer when farm people had little time to listen and static was
likely to be bad.

The value of radio steadily overcame its problems, however. A
survey by *Prairie Farmer* in 1930 showed that more than half of
the farms in Illinois were equipped with radio receivers.[17] By that
time, factory-built sets were the common rule.

Radio and Sears-Roebuck Agricultural Foundation

Meanwhile, the future of radio programming for farmers in Illinois was becoming blended with Sears, Roebuck and Company.[18]
For years Sears had periodically sent a season of wishful browsing
into farm homes by mail. In 1924 it added the radio dimension to
its contact with farm families. An advertising agency in Chicago,
Hayes-Loeb and Company, approached Sears in 1922 or 1923 with
the idea of building goodwill while rendering service to rural people.[19] This suggestion to E. H. Powell, advertising manager of
Sears, called for forming an agricultural foundation which would
help farmers with their economic problems.

Service to agriculture was not new to Sears, which had helped
invigorate the agricultural extension movement in 1911 by offering
$1,000 to each of 100 counties that first organized and hired an
agent.[20] The idea of a foundation also seemed worthwhile, so in

[16] George C. Biggar, "Forty Years in the Right Business," speech to the
South Dakota Broadcasters Association, Huron, South Dakota, May 22, 1964.
[17] *Prairie Farmer*, 102 (August 2, 1930), 4.
[18] This and later sections about the Sears-Roebuck Agricultural Foundation
draw heavily upon a memorandum, "Early History of Sears-Roebuck Agricultural Foundation and WLS," from George C. Biggar to Edward J. Condon,
June 28, 1960, and an undated manuscript entitled "How WLS Originated"
by Biggar.
[19] Grace E. Cassidy to author, March 9, 1967.
[20] Clarence B. Smith and Meredith C. Wilson, *The Agricultural Extension
System of the United States* (New York: John Wiley and Sons, 1930), pp. 39-
40; Alfred C. True, "A History of Agricultural Extension Work in the United

November, 1923, Julius Rosenwald, president of Sears, announced plans for forming a Sears-Roebuck Agricultural Foundation with headquarters at the west-side store in Chicago. He stated that the new Foundation would gather facts about farm economics and the condition of agriculture. Its stress would be upon agricultural research.[21] Rosenwald said he felt that the farmer needed most help in economics, ". . . in marketing his products. The foundation will deal exclusively with the economic problems of the farm."[22]

In practice, the work of the Foundation involved extension more than research. Its first secretary was Samuel R. Guard, former head of publicity for the American Farm Bureau Federation, who organized his new Foundation into four departments:

1. Farm Service Department. Edward B. Heaton, pioneer farm adviser in DuPage County and former director of dairy marketing for the American Farm Bureau Federation, became director of this department. His job was to answer all farm-related questions which customers sent to Sears. The company promoted this personalized answering service through special sections of the regular mail order catalogs. Catalogs contained blanks upon which customers could write questions, thousands of which came to the Foundation each year. Sears felt that the answering service not only helped customers but also helped build its mail order volume.

2. Home Service Department, directed by Mrs. Mary Puncke. She worked in a capacity similar to that of Heaton, answering questions related to the home.

3. Agricultural Research Department, directed by Perry Ewing. Its purpose was to build the Foundation as a primary source of farm information presented in a style that farm men and women could grasp. It prepared charts and graphs which showed trends in farm output, prices, and marketing and sent them in mat form to newspapers throughout the nation. All such releases included a credit line such as, "Prepared by the Research Department, Sears-Roebuck Agricultural Foundation." Officials of Sears were pleased with the wide usage of this material by newspapers which, in previous years, had mentioned Sears only in disparaging terms because it competed with local advertisers.

States, 1785-1923," U.S. Department of Agriculture, Miscellaneous Publication No. 15 (Washington: U.S. Government Printing Office, 1928), p. 75.

[21] *Prairie Farmer*, 95 (December 1, 1923), 10.
[22] *Prairie Farmer*, 95 (December 22, 1923), 9.

4. Boys' and Girls' Department. Director Ben Darrow, former secretary of a Young Men's Christian Association chapter in Ohio, started a short-lived plan to set up rural youth workers in midwestern counties. This plan is believed to have gone no further than one pilot county in Indiana.

Start of WLS

Work of the Foundation changed dramatically after March 1, 1924, when Edgar L. Bill joined the staff. Bill left the information department of Illinois Agricultural Association to become director of a new 500-watt (870 kilocycle) radio station for which Sears had been granted a license in 1923.[23] Widespread talk about the potential value of radio for farm people led Sears to house the new station in its Agricultural Foundation and devote most programming to agriculture.

Bill formed a small staff and arranged for a little drape-lined studio next to the office of the Foundation atop the Sears Tower at Homan and Arthington. The company's drafting department served as a control room while the transmitter was at Crete, about 30 miles south of the Loop. Sears also built what was considered the main studio on the mezzanine floor in the southeast corner of the Sherman Hotel in downtown Chicago.

Beginning on March 21, the Sears station—using its first assigned call letters, WBBX—broadcast a regular farm program from WMAQ from noon to 1 P.M. Monday through Friday.[24] Its first test program from the Tower studio was on Wednesday evening, April 9, 1924, under newly assigned call letters—WES (World's Economy Store). Director Bill explained to listeners that Sears was starting the new station as a service to agriculture. Other features of the first test program included a singer named Grace Wilson (whose favorite song, "Bringing Home the Bacon," would become a 35-year tradition at the station) and a musical comedy team known as Big Ford and Little Glenn.[25] Although this was only a test program for the new station, the Kedzie exchange switchboard "lit up like a Christmas tree" as listeners called in. All night long, men throughout the huge Sears Building were answering phones.

[23] Memorandum from George Biggar to Edward J. Condon, June 28, 1960; *Prairie Farmer*, 96 (March 15, 1924), 10.
[24] *Prairie Farmer*, 96 (April 5, 1924), 6.
[25] Grace E. Cassidy to author, March 9, 1967.

The new station aired test programs during the next two evenings, and then on the eve of formal dedication it changed its call letters to the set which it kept—WLS—World's Largest Store. The grand opening for WLS was April 12, 1924. George C. Biggar reports that the officials of Sears entertained numerous guests of the commercial, civic, press, and show worlds at a banquet in the Sherman Hotel that evening. The *Chicago Herald-Examiner,* with which WLS had tied in for cross-promotion, helped schedule a number of dignitaries: Ed Wynn, William S. Hart, Ethel Barrymore, and Arthur Brisbane of the Hearst newspapers.

Members of the staff long recalled that first program which began at 6 P.M. in the small Sherman studio with velvet velour curtains. Glenn Rowell of the Ford and Glenn team wrote later: "How well I remember that opening night with Ethel Barrymore and William S. Hart! How I worried about what Bill Hart could do on radio without seeing that long horse-face of his! How I felt confident that Ethel Barrymore would 'carry' the show with her tremendous dramatic experience! Then I'll never forget Miss Barrymore, after her flowery introduction, freezing and staring into the little round mike and finally saying those never-to-be-forgotten words: 'Turn the damned thing off!'—and how we hurried William Hart to the mike, with misgivings, and his excellent reading of Invictus in that rich voice—'I am the Master of my Soul.'"[26]

Another version by Samuel Guard explained that when Miss Barrymore ". . . raised her eyes and saw that insensate, merciless microphone, she fainted dead away and had to be carried out feet first."[27]

In any case, the engineer, cramped in a little cubbyhole which had been a clothes closet, knew he was taking part in an eventful evening. Part of the program came from New York by special wire. Well-known farmers and farm leaders who also appeared included Mr. and Mrs. Frank I. Mann of Gilman; E. T. Meredith, former Secretary of Agriculture; Walton Peteet of the National Council of Cooperatives; and W. H. Settle of the Indiana Farm Bureau Federation.[28]

[26] Letter by Glenn Rowell for the 40th WLS Anniversary Dinner Program at Sherman Hotel, April 12, 1964.

[27] Samuel R. Guard, "Experiences of a Broadcaster," *Prairie Farmer,* 97 (July 11, 1925), 7.

[28] *Prairie Farmer,* 96 (April 19, 1924), 6.

Early Programming on WLS

Perhaps staff members of WLS could find a special chuckle in the experience of Ethel Barrymore because famous actresses and opera singers were not the backbone of programming on WLS. As one of the radio trade papers observed in 1925, "WLS, Chicago, belongs to the farmer." [29] Its policy under Edgar Bill was to be a friendly station with clean, wholesome, and helpful programs. He insisted that each announcer have "a handshake and a smile" in his voice.

Such an approach was unique because American radio was in the middle of what Erik Barnouw termed the "potted palm" era. *Radio Digest* described the atmosphere in 1923 when it visited WMAQ, Chicago: "A visit to station WMAQ is like entering a music conservatory. You enter a reception room . . . then on into the studio . . . artistically furnished in brown tones . . . here and there, a large fern . . . and a Mason and Hamlin grand piano." [30] Some stations even referred to their studios as conservatories. Potted palm music often was recital music played by orchestras which hotels employed.

Within Chicago, WMAQ was considered highbrow by many because Miss Judith C. Waller, manager of the station, believed firmly in educational features.

The Westinghouse station, KYW, had grown to a staff of more than 30 by mid-1925 and still devoted much of its time to classical programs, drawing on talent from Europe as well as America. One exception was the popular dance music of Coon-Saunder's Night Hawks, who broadcast nightly from the Congress Hotel.

Other stations in Chicago had their own specialties. At the *Chicago Tribune*'s station, WGN, an announcer named Quin A. Ryan was the main attraction, ". . . as much a fixture in Chicago as the Chicago River or the Wrigley Building." [31] He helped radio usher in a new part of the day's routine—the bedtime story—as WGN's Uncle Walt. Another station, WBBM, specialized in jazz, to the horror of some listeners.[32] As station after station began broad-

[29] Lord, "Chicago Broadcasts," p. 56.
[30] *Radio Digest,* February 17, 1923, cited in Barnouw, p. 125.
[31] Lord, "Chicago Broadcasts," p. 41.
[32] Bruce A. Linton, "A History of Chicago Radio Station Programming, 1921-1931, with Emphasis on Stations WMAQ and WGN," unpublished doctoral dissertation, Northwestern University, Evanston, 1953, p. 60.

casting in Chicago, they formed a general pattern of evening programming: remote pickups of hotel orchestras, recitals by itinerant talent and "song pluggers" paid by music publishers, bedtime programs, and liberal doses of lectures.

The Sears station was not immune to this pattern. It had its Isham Jones Orchestra broadcasting dance music from the College Inn of the Sherman Hotel. For children it had Ford Rush and Glenn Rowell as the Lullaby Twins at 7 p.m. Glenn was the first musical director of WLS. Short, chubby, and cheerful, he provided piano backing and a tenor voice to harmonize with the baritone voice of a taller and more reserved Ford. Their repartee was quick and clever. One of their early projects was a mythical Woodshed Theater in which children (called actots) produced plays. Listeners could get "reserved seats" by sending two pins to WLS, an offer which resulted in thousands of pins.

In 1925 WLS also had the nation's most popular radio announcer, George D. Hay. Known to listeners as the Solemn Old Judge, Hay had come to WLS from WMC, Memphis, soon after the station began. His late evening programs, and especially his work on the National Barn Dance, became so popular that he won a gold cup award valued at $5,000 as the result of a popular nationwide radio vote.[33] The sound of a railroad whistle and the phrase "WLS Unlimited" became his trademark, and listeners long remembered his station breaks, "WLS, the Sears-Roebuck Station, Chi-CAW-go."

WLS was a pioneer Chicago station in the production of plays, including the Little Home Theatre on Homemakers' Hour and regular night-time dramas. Searching for something new and different, Edgar Bill introduced a Waukegan salesman, Tony Wons, to WLS with weekly programs of readings from Shakespeare's plays. The response in mail was so satisfactory that Wons became a staff member and he later started a 10-minute evening "Scrap Book" of poetry, humor, and epigrams. Organist Ralph Waldo Emerson frequently accompanied Wons's dramatic renditions. Emerson, who became one of the station's most popular performers, later married one of his students, Elsie Mae Look, in a ceremony broadcast by WLS.

But the core of programming on WLS was farm service, set at a pace which soon surpassed its rivals. Within the Chicago area, KYW was perhaps the most active in farm programming before

[33] Lord, "Chicago Broadcasts," p. 57; Guard, p. 7.

WLS began. As early as March, 1922, it had aired a farm service program daily at 6:30 P.M. in connection with the American Farm Bureau Federation, National Livestock Producers Association, Illinois Agricultural Association, and U.S. Grain Growers, Inc.[34] KYW also broadcast a regular weekly program for the American Farm Bureau Federation called Voice of the Farmer which began in September, 1923.[35] Only three nights after the formal debut of WLS, the Westinghouse station had staged "the biggest farm community meeting ever held in the world and the first one to be held by radio."[36] KYW had sent advance word about this meeting to farm leaders in 20 to 30 states, encouraging them to organize groups of listeners. President Coolidge telegraphed congratulations and said he hoped to listen; Secretary of Agriculture Henry C. Wallace tuned in the program which featured about 24 farm people at the KYW studio.

Among the other stations in Chicago which programmed for farmers before WLS was WDAP, a station which the Chicago Board of Trade purchased in June, 1923. WDAP broadcast grain prices at half-hour intervals each day for less than one year.[37]

WAAF, Chicago, had stressed livestock prices after it began in 1922 under the ownership of the Union Stock Yards and Transit Company.[38] By 1924 it was owned and operated by the *Daily Drovers Journal* as one of three radio stations under the Corn Belt Farm Dailies.

Soon after WLS signed on, Edgar Bill employed George Biggar, a former assistant at the Illinois Agricultural Association. Biggar, who had graduated in agriculture from South Dakota State College, joined WLS on May 1, 1924. His first job was handling fan mail, but within a few weeks he was named farm and market editor whose job was to build a schedule of farm weather and market reports in cooperation with the U.S. Weather Bureau and the U.S. Department of Agriculture. He also got in touch with agricultural leaders, offered the use of the new facilities of WLS, and arranged for guest appearances. Sears paid the expenses of well-known

[34] Vera Brady Shipman, "Behind the Microphone at KYW," *Country Gentleman*, 90 (March 21, 1925), 12.

[35] *Orange Judd Farmer*, 71 (September 15, 1923), 7; C. L. Burlingham, "Our Own Radio Service," *Breeder's Gazette*, 93 (June, 1928), 16.

[36] *Orange Judd Farmer*, 72 (April 15, 1924), 3.

[37] *Literary Digest*, 77 (June 30, 1923), 25; Linton, p. 62.

[38] Seeley, p. 26; Linton, p. 31.

farmers and specialists from agricultural colleges who came to Chicago for guest appearances on the station. Comments by these guests served as news material which the Agricultural Foundation could release to other media.

Actually, the daily broadcasting schedule of WLS was modest at first.

9:00- 9:30 A.M. Weather, market reports, homemaker chats.
12:00- 1:00 P.M. RFD Dinnerbell program (RFD meant "Radio Farmers Democracy," a name chosen in a contest among listeners).
3:45- 4:45 P.M. Homemakers Hour, with music and talks.
6:00-11:00 P.M. Evening entertainment by Ford and Glenn, Emerson, Isham Jones Orchestra, and Tony Wons; evening farm programs several times a week.

Sears did not use WLS for advertising the company's products during the first three or four years. On entertainment programs the station identified itself as "WLS—The Sears-Roebuck Station, Chicago." Farm programs were presented by "The Sears-Roebuck Agricultural Foundation." Advertising on radio was uncommon in the early and middle 1920's, partly because many leaders looked with disfavor upon "ether advertising" and partly because owners had not yet seen its possibilities.

It was a period of pioneering in radio and WLS took part in the innovations. One week after its debut, WLS aired its first Barn Dance, a feature destined to become the country's longest running continuous radio program. The station claimed to be the first to build an audience theater when it moved from the mezzanine floor of the Sherman Hotel to larger quarters on the sixth floor on November 1, 1925. The theater seated 100 people and was separated from the largest studio by a full-width plate glass window. On that same date WLS joined the ranks of "super-power" stations, for it boosted its power from 500 to 5,000 watts.

The station also pioneered in programming for in-school listening. In February, 1925, WLS began the Little Red Schoolhouse, an hour-long program which began at 2 P.M. during school days and was later cited as Chicago's first such school program.[39]

One year after WLS began, *Prairie Farmer* reported that replies from its readers showed WLS to be the most popular station among farm listeners of Illinois. Perhaps most important, however, was

[39] Grace E. Cassidy to author, March 9, 1967.

that 1925 became the year that WLS (like the Tin Woodman in *Wizard of Oz*) really got a heart.

Tornado in Southern Illinois

On Wednesday evening, March 18, Big Ford, Little Glenn, and the Solemn Old Judge had helped put the little ones to bed with Lullaby Time. The studio telephone rang and a staff member of the *Herald-Examiner* asked WLS to ask listeners for an X-ray machine to send to southern Illinois where a tornado had just struck. Soon the phone rang again and a man asked if WLS would take $5 for the relief of those who suffered from the tornado.

That is how the WLS Storm Relief Fund began. The Solemn Old Judge told listeners that humanity was on trial and that every listener should contribute something to help allay the suffering in the stricken area. Instead of signing off at 11 P.M., the station started a marathon. At 3 A.M. the telephone operators reported that more than $6,000 had been pledged. Singing and talking, playing and telling jokes, the announcing staff still was on the job at daybreak. Ford and Glenn came up with a new verse to "What Do You Say, Boys?"

> We've received a lot of checks and money orders, too,
> For the storm sufferers in Illinois,
> But we haven't heard from you.
> What do you say, boys?

By 8 A.M. the total was $11,000 a figure which nearly doubled when Sears pledged $10,000 more. At 11 A.M. Thursday, Edgar Bill and George Biggar took over the microphone while Hay, Ford, and Glenn slept on the settees in the studio. Meanwhile, Edward Condon of the Foundation was on his way to Carbondale to set up the first WLS relief station and Samuel Guard was travelling to Princeton, Indiana, to help establish the Indiana Farm Bureau relief depot. Donations soon were being used for blankets and clothing, food and medical supplies.

Five telephone operators at the Hotel Sherman were busy taking down names, addresses, and amounts as the marathon continued with banter, songs, and checks. "Here's another $75, this time from the Health Commissioner of Chicago. Put it on the right hand side, under the flatiron." A report from the scene revealed that no houses were left at Griffin, Indiana, so the Judge asked listeners for tents and stoves. Within five minutes tornado victims were promised tents, stoves, blankets, and clothing. A call from Carbondale reported a lack of X-ray machines. The announcement hardly had been made when a physician called to say he was ready with a machine. The Chicago Motor Club volunteered a car and within an hour the physician and the machine were on the road toward Carbondale.

Telephone operators had been on duty for 28 hours without sleep as Thursday passed, but they and others at the station had hopes of reaching a goal of $50,000. By 6 A.M. on Saturday, WLS reached that goal and a tired staff signed off for some needed rest.

However, the contributors did not sign off, for checks and money came in all day Saturday. Men, women, and children stopped at the hotel to deposit money and clothing. WLS was back on the air Saturday evening and the WLS Relief Fund was past $70,000. Some optimist saw a chance for $100,000 worth of relief, so that became a new goal. The total was $93,000 Sunday evening when Samuel Guard—just returned from work in the disaster area—conducted what became the first Little Brown Church of the Air on WLS. It was an emotional report about an overturned bus filled with children—seven dead—about a farmer who went in search of his child after the storm and found the dead baby partly buried in the mud of a newly plowed field, about widespread grief and suffering in communities in Illinois, Indiana, Tennessee, Missouri, and Kentucky.

By Monday noon the fund passed $100,000 and was still active. Tuesday night it reached $145,000 and by 10 P.M. Wednesday, one week after the marathon began, donations totalled $158,000. Final total for the fund was $216,905.

This experience galvanized the staff members of WLS as perhaps nothing else could. It convinced them of the power of radio and the responsibility of a radio station. It gave them an overwhelming feeling of warmth toward their listeners, a warmth which saturated WLS under the ownership of both Sears and Burridge Butler. After that experience, WLS could not be cold, aloof, or prissy. Its part was with the common people, not the potted palm. Its staff members knew they were in touch with a reservoir of personal warmth, feeling, and generosity, not with a faceless mass. The station with "a handshake and a smile" now had a heart to match.

Sears Decides to Sell WLS

Successful use of radio by Sears in Chicago brought calls within the company for similar arrangements in other cities. In the summer of 1925 the Agricultural Foundation opened a new office in Dallas and arranged for farm and homemaking programs on WFAA. WFAA offered the time free, while the Foundation produced and presented programs.

In August, 1926, a new Sears store in Atlanta called for radio and the Foundation arranged a program schedule on WSB (again without charge for time). Two new arrangements began during 1928, one with WMC, Memphis, Tennessee, and one with KMBC, Kansas City, Missouri.

In the case of KMBC, Sears paid $1,500 a month for "all the time needed, within reason." Programs mentioned many products which Sears sold, a policy which Sears had avoided earlier.

Soon the medium that had helped Sears shift from a mail order system to a retail store system began to cause problems for management. The firm could not provide such extensive radio support in every city with a Sears store. Broadcasting stations were beginning to capitalize on the demand for their time, which closed the door on goodwill broadcasting upon which the Agricultural Foundation had depended. Furthermore, officials at Sears felt they could not keep a commercial station such as WLS because Sears competed with almost any advertiser who might buy time on the station.

As a result, Sears decided in 1928 that the company would be better off to sell WLS to someone who had a keen interest in agriculture and then use advertising money to buy time on radio stations. *Prairie Farmer* entered the picture at this point.

Prairie Farmer and Radio to 1928

Butler, Gregory, and their associates had watched radio closely from its start. As early as April, 1921, when the U.S. Department of Agriculture telegraphed its first market reports from post office wireless stations, *Prairie Farmer* offered instructions to readers who wanted to erect receiving sets.[40] The buried offer brought more than 200 requests. Two months later, staff members of the paper were writing brief market summaries for a daily broadcast at 6:45

[40] *Prairie Farmer*, 93 (April 30, 1921), 2.

P.M. in code over the naval radio station in the Transportation Building six blocks away. High interest in radio encouraged Gregory to begin printing a regular column entitled "The Wireless Man," which first appeared in late 1921 and which answered questions from readers about receiving sets. Wireless telephony appealed to Gregory as having unlimited possibilities for farmers. No longer will it be possible to get lonesome on the farm, he wrote in an editorial during March, 1922. "Weather forecasts and market reports can be picked out of the air several times a day. At 7:30 a bedtime story will send the children off to bed happy. Then for an hour or two the rest of the family can listen to songs, music, speeches and more news. On Sunday father can sit on the porch in his old shirt and listen to the sermon." [41]

Early in 1924 Gregory cited radio as one of the past year's biggest accomplishments affecting the farm home. This respect for the medium induced *Prairie Farmer* to become the first midwestern farm paper employing an experienced radio editor.[42] The first column by the new staff member, S. L. Booth, appeared February 16, 1924.[43] A highly popular feature, it continued for three and a half years.

Part of the apparent excitement at *Prairie Farmer* over radio in mid-1924 undoubtedly was related to the start of WLS. The paper covered this new project thoroughly, from the announcement by Sears that it would form a new agricultural foundation through and beyond the debut on April 12. High interest was natural, for WLS promised to be a farmer's station. Even John Turnipseed got so excited about radio that he bet "they'll get it so you can order shoes or bananas or whatever you want by radio, and there it'll be hangin' on your aerial." However, he feared that he did not know all the tricks of that contraption yet and was afraid "they might take a collection right off me by radio." [44] Also, he was less convinced than some people that the farmer lacked entertainment. "That feller wan't talkin' about my farm. Them agents furnish me all the entertainment I need. . . ." [45]

As noted earlier, associate editors Mr. and Mrs. Frank Mann took part in the first formal program over WLS. Within a week,

[41] *Prairie Farmer*, 94 (March 18, 1922), 8.
[42] *Prairie Farmer*, 96 (May 10, 1924), 1.
[43] *Prairie Farmer*, 96 (February 16, 1924), 6; 96 (April 12, 1924), 3.
[44] *Prairie Farmer*, 96 (April 19, 1924), 15.
[45] *Prairie Farmer*, 97 (July 25, 1925), 6.

John Turnipseed was on WLS telling listeners how he had got a bad case of the radio fever. *Prairie Farmer* used its lead space on April 26, 1924, to report "Our Farm Editors Broadcast Over WLS."[46] In mid-May, Turnipseed and the Lazy Farmer began regular programs on Friday evenings and soon became one of the station's most popular features. Issues of *Prairie Farmer* listed upcoming programs on WLS and after the WLS relief drive of 1925, the paper hailed it as "an epic in radio history."[47]

However, *Prairie Farmer* was anxious to try farm radio itself, so in early 1926 it approached WMAQ about buying time for a program.[48] The new 15-minute program at noon went on the air May 31 with Gregory, Thompson, and Floyd Keepers at the microphone. *Prairie Farmer* explained to readers that this new show "will put us in daily touch with the farmers of our territory. It will be particularly valuable to Dave Thompson in his Protective Union work."[49] Timeliness probably was on the minds of staff members because the chicken thief campaign was just getting under way.

As the new program unfolded, *Prairie Farmer* stressed market reports, women's news, notices of meetings, and items about the Protective Union. One innovation was a system of 140 correspondents who provided crop reports in season. The staff also prided itself in avoiding prepared lectures by guests and using interviews instead. The Lazy Farmer appeared on WMAQ, but John Turnipseed remained at WLS.

Radio came even closer to *Prairie Farmer* after the paper moved into its new home at 1230 W. Washington Boulevard during January, 1927. Butler allocated one small room for a radio studio and issued a general order to the staff that during the 15-minute program "no misguided carpenter is to start hammering, or the man in the basement must not drop heavy rolls of paper which jar the building."[50] Despite Butler's order, listeners at times complained of programs that sounded as though *Prairie Farmer* were broadcasting in com-

---

[46] *Prairie Farmer,* 96 (April 26, 1924), 3.

[47] *Prairie Farmer,* 97 (March 28, 1925), 8.

[48] Agricultural Broadcasting Company, "Testimony and Exhibits of Agricultural Broadcasting Company, Radio Station WLS, Chicago, Illinois, before the Federal Communications Commission Clear Channel Hearings," Docket No. 6741, 1946, Book I, Section 5, p. 3.

[49] *Prairie Farmer,* 98 (May 29, 1926), 9.

[50] *Prairie Farmer,* 99 (October 15, 1927), 2.

petition with a boiler factory. Furthermore, as one editor explained, the studio was cozy in winter but like a Turkish bath in the summertime.

Staff members of the paper apparently felt a growing concern about whether or not people were listening. On June 1, 1928, when WMAQ installed a new 5,000-watt transmitter, *Prairie Farmer* confided that it had not been certain that *Prairie Farmer's* broadcast was within reach of every reader.[51] Six months earlier, Thompson had remarked that he was wondering if farmers really were listening and if the program was worth continuing.

Still another possible source of unrest was the entry into radio by the *Breeder's Gazette* during May, 1928. Several months earlier Westinghouse had moved radio station KFKX (570 kc) from Hastings, Nebraska, to Chicago where it became a sister station to KYW. Meanwhile, Samuel Guard (former director of Sears-Roebuck Agricultural Foundation) and Lloyd Burlingham had bought an ailing *Breeder's Gazette* in mid-1927. Guard's experience in radio and an interest by Westinghouse in farm programming led to a lease by which the *Gazette* took over part of the time of KFKX and built a substation at the Union Stock Yards. It began its farm programs on May 14 with four shows a day totalling more than two hours.[52] The *Gazette* contended that it had the most complete farm and market service on the air.

By mid-1928 *Prairie Farmer,* with two years of experience in radio, was somewhat restless about its arrangement, while Sears, Roebuck and Company was looking for someone who could buy WLS and continue its strong agricultural flavor.

Purchase of WLS by *Prairie Farmer*

Details of the first stages of bargaining are not well documented. Thompson reported that the management of Sears told Edgar Bill to look for a buyer. According to Thompson, Bill approached his former employer, Illinois Agricultural Association, which decided against taking on ownership of a radio station. Other parties (including International Harvester Company) reportedly were interested in buying WLS.[53] However, Sears turned to *Prairie Farmer,*

[51] *Prairie Farmer,* 100 (July 28, 1928), 10.
[52] *Breeder's Gazette,* 93 (June, 1928), 16.
[53] Mrs. C. V. Gregory, personal interview, March 25, 1967.

probably because the paper had worked closely with WLS, had
some experience in radio, and had a long-time record of farm
service.

The purchase price of $250,000 was high enough to encourage
caution at 1230 W. Washington Boulevard. Butler regularly had
put more money into *Prairie Farmer* than he got from it until 1918.
Only since 1922 had the paper shown consistent financial gain
(see Table 9). An investment of $250,000 looked especially risky
to a newspaper man because radio produced no income from sub-

TABLE 9. PROFIT AND LOSS FOR PRAIRIE FARMER PUBLISHING COMPANY,
1918-29

Statement for the Year Ending December 31	Surplus or (Deficit)	Statement for the Year Ending December 31	Surplus or (Deficit)
1918	$21,953	1924	(2,065)
1919	N/A	1925	11,777
1920	(17,300)	1926	2,796
1921	(37,480)	1927	48,213
1922	30,052	1928	97,195
1923	20,555	1929	90,557

SOURCE: Minutes, Prairie Farmer Publishing Company. Operating statement figures were
not recorded between 1909 and 1918. However, several sources (including Butler) stated
that the paper operated at a deficit during Butler's early years of building its editorial
and circulation strength.

scriptions, and no Scripps man—as a champion of editorial independence—cherished the thought of relying completely upon advertisers. Even the assurance of support from advertisers was not
strong in 1928. Butler's age was another factor, for he had passed
60 years, a stage at which most men would resist a new venture
of such risk.

After Sears approached *Prairie Farmer* with the offer to sell
WLS, Butler took two steps to help him judge the value of the
station. First, he assigned one of his long-time associates, James
Edwards, to get the feeling of advertisers about the future of radio.
Edwards had joined *Prairie Farmer* in 1913 from *Kimball's Dairy
Farmer* as a bookkeeper and was associate advertising manager
by 1928. His interviews showed that advertisers were optimistic
about radio.

Butler's second step was to use his subscription sales force to interview farmers about their use of radio. Sixty fieldmen worked for eight weeks (July 30 to September 22) asking farm people in Illinois, Indiana, and southern Wisconsin to rank their favorite radio stations. Of about 16,000 people interviewed, 25 per cent said they had radios. Nearly 60 per cent of those named WLS as their first choice (Table 10), a result which told Butler he would be buying a station already well accepted among farm people.

TABLE 10. RESULTS OF A SURVEY BY *Prairie Farmer* OF RADIO STATION PREFERENCES AMONG FARMERS OF ILLINOIS, INDIANA, AND SOUTHERN WISCONSIN IN 1928

Station	Number of Times Named as "First Choice"	Share
WLS, Chicago	2,330	59%
WGN, Chicago	365	10
WOC, Davenport	265	6
KMOX, St. Louis	149	4
WLW, Cincinnati	147	4
WMAQ, Chicago	89	2
KYW, Chicago	57	1
WENR, Chicago	28	1
WJJD, Chicago	14	—
WHO, Des Moines	6	—
WEBH, Chicago	3	—
Others	485	13
Total	3,938	100%

SOURCE: *Presentation of WLS*, Agricultural Broadcasting Company, 1928, p. 16.

Butler also called for opinions from associates who owned stock in *Prairie Farmer* at the time: Gregory, Dickson, Edwards, Holt, and F. W. Orlemann. Orlemann was a buoyant business manager who had joined *Prairie Farmer* in 1919 after 17 years of experience in newspaper production and management.[54] In the early 1920's he had played a major part in forming *Prairie Farmer*'s printing plant.

Each stockholder wrote a statement of his views about buying WLS, including his vote in the matter and the reasons behind it.

[54] Herb Horn, "The Fred Orlemann Story," *Prairie Farmer–WLS Round-Up*, 8 (December, 1955), 2-4; F. W. Orlemann, personal interview, June 19, 1967.

The final decision, however, remained with Butler and he decided to buy the station.

On September 15 *Prairie Farmer* contracted to buy 51 per cent of a new Illinois corporation known as Agricultural Broadcasting Company with capital stock of 2,500 shares, par value $100. The paper agreed to buy 1,275 shares for $125,000, payable as follows:

   1. $25,000 at the execution of the contract;

   2. Balance payable at $10,000 a year beginning October 1, 1931, with 6 per cent interest on deferred payments. All profits remaining after operating expenses were to be declared as dividends and divided as follows: 49 per cent to Sears as its own property and 51 per cent to Sears to be credited toward the purchase price. If receipts did not cover expenses, Sears agreed to contribute up to $12,000 a month for one year and *Prairie Farmer* up to $1,000 a month.

Sears kept the right to repurchase the 1,275 shares within 13 months after the transfer, if, in its opinion, "the station is not and cannot become self-supporting."[55] If Sears did not repurchase, *Prairie Farmer* could buy all remaining shares after settling the first note.

Terms also granted Sears the right to broadcast for 12 hours a week over WLS without charge as long as *Prairie Farmer* was indebted under the original note. Furthermore, WLS could broadcast no mail order or chain store advertising during that time without written consent from Sears.

The advantage of this agreement to *Prairie Farmer* was that the company could make a relatively small down payment and then have the station pay for itself out of hoped-for earnings. *Prairie Farmer* also enjoyed the assurance that Sears would share the risk of losses during the first year.

Officers of the new corporation were Butler, Gregory, Holt, and Dickson of *Prairie Farmer*; Edgar Bill, who came to *Prairie Farmer* with WLS; and Edward Condon and E. H. Powell, who represented the interests of Sears.

Readers of *Prairie Farmer* learned about the transaction on September 29 when the paper announced "Our Own Radio Station." Residents of Chicago learned about it from a full-page advertise-

[55] Contract between Sears, Roebuck and Company and Prairie Farmer Publishing Company, September 15, 1928.

ment in the *Chicago Daily News* on October 1. It was in the old Butler style, headed: "Why I Bought WLS." In the advertisement Butler said, "It is a settled conviction in my mind that no enterprise can expect to keep going ahead full speed without Radio." He expressed the feeling that *"Prairie Farmer's* station will be a living, breathing, human influence in the million farm homes of those states surrounding Chicago." He added that "WLS will be a vibrating power working for better cooperation and understanding between Chicago and the cities and towns and rural communities of the great Mid-west." Another purpose of this advertisement was to thank WMAQ publicly for its courtesy during the past two years.

October 1, 1928, was the formal date for change of ownership. In a special program at 7 P.M., E. H. Powell of Sears turned WLS over to the management of *Prairie Farmer*. Perhaps the most revealing remarks of the evening were Butler's closing sentences to listeners: ". . . I pledge you my utmost endeavor. And that carries with it the pledge of the utmost endeavor on the part of the whole *Prairie Farmer* family, to which we are now adding the members of the WLS family." [56]

Obviously, Butler was still building a family.

[56] *Prairie Farmer*, 100 (October 13, 1928), 6.

WLS:
The *Prairie Farmer* Station

CHAPTER 8

The $250,000 seemed like a great deal of money, but WLS was a sizable addition to Butler's enterprise. From a staff of about six people in 1924 it had grown to employ 35 people full-time and another 133 part-time by late 1928. Its main studios remained at the Sherman Hotel, but it had seven others throughout the city: farm and home studios on the third floor of the Prairie Farmer Building (with the poultry marker department); concert studio at 218 S. Wabash; livestock market studio, Union Stock Yards; Associated Press studios for news and sports; Sears, Roebuck and Company studio; Swift and Company studio; and a University of Chicago studio.

From a little 500-watt station tucked away on the ninth floor of the west-side Sears store, WLS had become powerful enough to attract more than 200,000 letters a year from listeners all over the country and as far away as New Zealand. In little more than four years its microphones had faced thousands—from President Coolidge to Sophie Tucker, Ted Lewis, and the Lazy Farmer's wife, Mirandy. It had broadcast everything from the wit of Will Rogers to the sermons of Ralph Sockman, from the charity of Jane

Addams to the hilarity of Pie Plant Pete. It had broadcast an air-to-ground report of the 1925 Military Tournament and Chicago's reception of Colonel Lindbergh. As host to 58 different bands, it had devoted more attention to band music than any other midwestern station. More than 130 farm groups had used the microphone of WLS without charge. A "farmers' station" known for its fiddlers' contests and barn dances, it also had presented more than 500 radio dramas by the time Butler bought it. On March 19, 1927, it had broadcast Beethoven's Ninth Symphony, ". . . the only complete performance of the work ever given on the air in the U.S."[1]

Butler's Guidelines for Radio

It is likely that Sears could have found no successor which would have taken the responsibility for WLS as seriously as *Prairie Farmer*. As a business man, Butler saw in WLS an opportunity for profit, if not directly, at least through broadened circulation for *Prairie Farmer*. However, as a patriarch Butler saw the station as a new voice for the family spirit which became more and more important to him through the years.

"This is a family station," he stressed. "All our ideals center around the firesides of our listeners."[2] Twenty-five years earlier in Omaha and Minneapolis he had championed "The People's Paper"; now, in the same spirit, he saw WLS as the "Station of the Common People." He did not know the intricacies of radio when he bought WLS and probably never did, yet he brought to the station some strong feeling about what it should be and do. Butler recognized, at least in public statements, that he did not own the signal of WLS. "No one can own a radio station any more than he can own a church. We can only consider it a stewardship, for which we are responsible to the people."[3] He felt that radio by its very nature "gets under the skin—it goes through the veneer of modern life. The false rings false and the true rings true, always."[4] His goal then was to ring true, to make WLS a part of the listening life of every family.

[1] "Presentation of WLS," scrapbook prepared by WLS, Chicago, 1928, p. 30.

[2] *WLS Family Album*, 1937 (Chicago: Prairie Farmer Publishing Co., 1936), p. 7.

[3] *Broadcasting Magazine*, April 5, 1948, 56.

[4] *Prairie Farmer*, 104 (October 15, 1932), 20.

"If I could meet you personally and you would say to me—
I consider WLS a next door neighbor of mine making friendly calls
every day extending a helpful hand at all times—I would know
that my dream of radio had come true." [5]

For his employees this goal took the shape of a constant ad-
monition: "When you step up to that WLS microphone, remember
that you are a guest in somebody's home. Act accordingly." [6] Employees learned that Butler would sternly reprimand any staff member who tried unseeming conduct or blue stories, either on the air
or in public appearances. A second offense would take the violator
off the air.

He formalized his views in 1938 through a brief "WLS Creed"
which had a marked and lasting effect upon members of the staff.
Almost 30 years later, former employees of WLS invariably referred
to that creed as their on-air guideline and could recall the essence
of the last sentence: "When you step up to the microphone never
forget this responsibility and that you are walking as a guest into
all those homes beyond the microphone."

Part of the impact of this philosophy might be attributed to
Glenn Snyder, who replaced Edgar Bill as station manager in 1931
and headed WLS for nearly 30 years. Snyder, a short and peppery,
fast-balding executive who had begun his career as a shoe cutter in
St. Joseph, Missouri, came to *Prairie Farmer* from a background in
farm publishing. He had worked for Samuel McKelvie on the
Nebraska Farmer as advertising manager from 1923 to 1927, boosting its linage markedly. Then he went to the *Wisconsin Agriculturist* as advertising manager, later general manager, from which
post he was fired. When Butler heard that Snyder was available,
he insisted on hiring the energetic Missourian as a salesman for
Prairie Farmer in August, 1929. [7]

Butler shifted Snyder to the position of commercial manager for
WLS in June, 1930, and asked Snyder if he would like to manage
the station when Edgar Bill left in 1931. Snyder said he was a farm
paper man and would rather stay that way, but he consented to
take charge until Butler found a replacement—which he never did.
Snyder remained as manager until 1960. [8]

[5] *Prairie Farmer,* 109 (April 10, 1937), 41.
[6] Dave O. Thompson, unpublished memoirs, p. 114.
[7] *Prairie Farmer*-WLS *Round-Up,* 3 (August, 1950), 2.
[8] Glenn Snyder, personal interview, June 15, 1967.

He subscribed fully to the idea of WLS as a station for the home. For example, testimony of WLS during clear channel hearings before the Federal Communications Commission in 1946 explained: "It is our conception that when our listeners have a problem, and they write in to discuss it with us, it becomes *our* problem. . . . Through the years this policy has developed what we like to think of as a *family spirit* between us and our listeners, and also between listeners themselves in different sections of our territory." [9]

Advertising Policies

Butler took several pages from his experience with *Prairie Farmer* in formulating advertising policies for WLS. First, on July 1, 1929, was an announcement of a guarantee by WLS: "WLS, the *Prairie Farmer* station, refuses to broadcast dishonest advertising and positively guarantees its listeners fair and honest treatment in dealing with its advertisers." [10] In so doing, it professed to be the first radio station to use a guarantee of the type common among publications. No evidence suggests that this guarantee played a vital role among either listeners or advertisers, but it was a useful talking point.

A second adaptation from publishing was a strong insistence that the program department do all that it could to avoid accepting unscrupulous advertising with exaggerated claims. His assignment of the task to the program department may have reflected a philosophy dating back to his days with Scripps-McRae. Butler did not get personally involved with advertising or advertisers for WLS, but on occasion he backed his manager in refusing to accept a debatable advertising account.

Another carry-over from Butler's publishing philosophy was his refusal to air commercials for cigarettes or alcoholic beverages. WLS ran its first cigarette commercial only after Butler died; until 1953 it refused to carry such commercials on either local or network programs.

Two of his policies influenced the nature of programs on WLS. One was a refusal to allow newscasts to be sponsored. Spot announcements could precede or follow newscasts (and sometimes

[9] Agricultural Broadcasting Co., "FCC Clear Channel Hearings," 1946, Book IV, Section 1, p. 2.

[10] *Prairie Farmer*, 101 (July 13, 1929), 4; *WLS Family Album*, 1930, p. 38.

be scheduled within 15-minute newscasts), but no news program could carry sponsorship. The Dinnerbell program at noon was another program which WLS would not sell, even though it was in prime time for farm listening. Advertisers made regular efforts to change the policy. One especially difficult refusal was during Henry A. Wallace's campaign for the vice-presidency. The managers of *Prairie Farmer* and WLS favored Wallace and knew him as personal friends, yet refused his request for commercial time on Dinnerbell.[11]

The WLS Signal, 1928-48

Prairie Farmer had hardly become accustomed to managing a radio station when it bumped solidly into the realities of radio as a part of the public domain. In earlier years WLS had never made a point of mentioning that it shared the 870 channel with a small station located about 40 miles north of downtown Chicago, WCBD, owned and operated by Wilbur Glenn Voliva of Zion, Illinois. WCBD had operated under federal license since 1924 and used about two-sevenths of the daily time schedule for programs of the Christian Catholic Church.

On November 11, 1928, a general reallocation of radio stations went into effect by order of the Federal Radio Commission. WLS was reassigned its five-sevenths time on 870, one of a limited number of clear channels. WCBD was changed to one-half time on 1080 kilocycles and replaced on 870 by WENR, Chicago. WENR was owned and operated by the Great Lakes Broadcasting Company, an association of public utility corporations controlled by Samuel Insull. It had started in 1925 and was broadcasting at 1040 kilocycles with 500 watts nighttime, 5,000 watts daytime, and 50,000 watts after midnight. In August, 1928, it had installed a new $450,000 transmitter for power of 50,000 watts.

WLS accepted the reallocation without protest, but WENR asked for a change which would give it full time on 870 or at least half-time. In response, WLS filed a request for full-time use of the same channel. WCBD also asked the Commission to return it to 870. Commissioners heard the three requests in mid-November, agreed that WLS should not have full time (for it had not been using all

[11] Glenn Snyder, "Original Policies Built WLS," unpublished manuscript, July, 1966.

of its five-sevenths time), disagreed about the the other two requests, and ended by denying all.

The three applicants then appealed to the Circuit Court of Appeals of the District of Columbia, which heard the cases on October 10, 1929, and announced its decision on January 6, 1930. It held that:

1. WCBD's request for change back to 870 was rightly denied by the Commission.

2. WENR should get one-half of the time on 870 rather than two-sevenths. Reasons cited were excellent service, large outlays for equipment and facilities, popularity, large transmitter, and strong financial backing.

3. WLS should get half-time use of the channel, not full-time or even five-sevenths. The court said it felt that the farming community would not be prejudiced by a 50-50 division inasmuch as WENR likewise broadcast agricultural news (15 minutes a day, *Prairie Farmer* scoffed). The court also held that WLS had no prior right to the time which it had held, "for neither station has any fixed right to the frequency as against the reasonable regulatory power of the United States." [12]

The *Prairie Farmer* station immediately asked for a rehearing of the case but received a denial on February 8 and grudgingly cut to half-time operation on February 15. Its next move was to ask the U.S. Supreme Court to consider the facts, but this petition was denied on June 2.[13] Feeling both indignant and somewhat helpless before the powerful interests of Samuel Insull, *Prairie Farmer* asked readers while the matter was being debated in court: "Is there a place on the air for the voice of the country—for the songs of the prairies and the hills, for the barn dance fiddlers, for the homely virtues of the everyday folks who have made America? We believe that there should be. We are fighting for that place. It is not our fight, but the fight of agriculture." [14]

WENR added insult to injury, WLS felt, by dictating the terms of a time split. The first instructions by the Federal Radio Com-

[12] *Federal Reporter*, 37 (2nd series), March-April, 1930, 995. Pages 993-995 outline details of this case, as do *Prairie Farmer*, 100 (November 24, 1928), 8; 102 (February 1, 1930), 8; 102 (February 15, 1930), 3, 41; 102 (February 22, 1930), 6, 29.

[13] *United States Reports*, 281, p. 706.

[14] *Prairie Farmer*, 102 (February 15, 1930), 41.

mission (prompted by WENR, according to WLS) called for a grossly unworkable system of alternate hours. WLS was to commence at 6 A.M. on odd-numbered days and WENR on even-numbered days, then alternate hours throughout the day. Within one week the stations agreed to scrap that system, and WLS accepted a schedule which allowed it to keep its morning and noontime farm programs plus the Barn Dance on Saturday nights.[15]

Even after the matter was seemingly settled, *Prairie Farmer* and WLS continued to rally public support for their stand. The paper published pages and pages of comments by readers throughout March and April, 1930, under the belief that public sentiment might restore time to WLS. "Politicians will listen to that," Gregory said. "In the long run, it is more powerful than the power and influence of the public utilities."[16]

Illinois Farmers' Institute passed a resolution deploring the loss of time, as did the Pure Milk Association, Indiana Farm Bureau Cooperative Association, and many other groups. Petitions soon were being sent to congressmen by the hundreds and letters by the thousands. One congressman from Illinois introduced a bill forbidding public utility corporations from owning radio stations, and Frank O. Lowden wrote on behalf of WLS.[17]

WLS even arranged in May, 1930, to use the WJJD transmitter (1130 kc) for an additional two and a half hours a day.[18] The station formed a Down the Dial Club and urged listeners to follow WLS between 870 and 1130. It also formed an Agricultural Radio Association of 11 midwestern farm leaders who were to help direct the policies of WLS and "assure agriculture a permanent and unrestricted voice on the air."[19] No evidence suggests that the Association ever played an active role in program policies of WLS.

The station had not recovered from its cut to half-time when a second threat arose, this time from a station in Milwaukee—WTMJ —which asked the Federal Radio Commission for full use of the 870 channel. WLS and WENR cooperated in defending themselves successfully during a hearing in October, 1930.[20]

[15] *Prairie Farmer*, 102 (February 22, 1930), 6.

[16] *Prairie Farmer*, 102 (March 8, 1930), 8.

[17] For example, see letter from Lowden to E. O. Sykes, Federal Radio Commissioner, November 30, 1928.

[18] *Prairie Farmer*, 102 (May 17, 1930), 4.

[19] *Prairie Farmer*, 102 (October 11, 1930), 4.

[20] *Prairie Farmer*, 102 (October 25, 1930), 16.

These challenges had convinced the management of WLS that only a big station would be able to defend itself on the clear channels, so WLS requested and received in 1929 permission to build a 50,000-watt transmitter. The station had no quarter-million dollars for such a transmitter—especially carrying only a half-time schedule—but the permit might give it some footing for protecting its channel.

The problem began to unravel in late 1930 and early 1931 when the National Broadcasting Company took over the control of WENR. On February 24, 1931, stockholders of WLS approved an agreement to trade the use of WENR's 50,000-watt transmitter for network programs. WLS got free access to a power of 50,000 watts in return for carrying 10 free evening hours a week of NBC programs plus certain other programs at specified times and rates. The two parties renegotiated from time to time, but the agreement was continued until Butler's 70th birthday—February 5, 1938—when WLS contracted with RCA to build a new 586-foot transmitter 25 miles southwest of Chicago. NBC bought a half interest in the transmitter shortly before it was dedicated on November 12.

WLS continued with 50,000 watts and its own transmitter through and beyond the time *Prairie Farmer* sold the station to American Broadcasting–Paramount Theatres on March 20, 1960. The only other change was one in frequency, from 870 to 890 kilocycles, on March 29, 1941.

Farm Programming

Butler and his associates prided themselves in owning a half-time station doing a full-time job of agricultural service. Roughly 15 per cent of its air time concerned farm news, analysis, and markets. Dave Thompson shifted from the Protective Union to become the first farm program director of WLS under the management of *Prairie Farmer*. One of his early projects was a three-week radio short course in early 1929. He invited 18 farmers from Illinois, Indiana, and Wisconsin to prepare talks about their farming methods, then aired these each noon and invited listeners to take notes. About 1,000 listeners received certificates for sending in evidence that they had listened. Another project in 1929 was a "radio party" in which the Pure Milk Association used WLS as the program for meetings throughout the listening area. A tabulation of telegrams and telephone calls showed that nearly 12,000 members were listening at 40 locations.

Under Thompson, WLS also pioneered in broadcasting during the early morning. Before 1929, radio stations seldom started broadcasting before 8 A.M. and WLS was practically alone in 1929 when it began programming at 6 A.M.[21] In May, 1931, it moved sign-on to 5 A.M. and became "one of the first stations in the Middle West on the air."[22] It had found that the choring habits of farm people resulted in big audiences during the early hours. Live programs reflected a feeling at WLS that it should start each day as a farmer starts it—in person.

Of all farm programs on WLS, none characterized the family spirit better than the Dinnerbell, a noontime program which by 1946 WLS believed to be the nation's oldest continuous farm program.[23] The station had aired its first Dinnerbell program on April 28, 1924, and the program was a daily ritual in the midwest by the time Butler died. This was largely due to Arthur Page, the man who took charge of it after about 1930 and became a nationally known farm broadcaster who helped found the National Association of Radio Farm Directors. Page was more evangelist than agriculturist. His writing was what Thompson described as "highly emotional and sometimes quite impractical," and it overflowed with superlatives.[24] He could face a five-minute segment with only a brief postcard in hand and fill the time without a pause, especially a card that "thrills me to the heels." His narrative bubbled with references to "unconquerable souls," "tenacious faith," "heroic effort," and praise for those "who never give up, never let loose, on a thing they knew was right." For Page, bad things should not happen and listeners responded to his eternal philosophy of optimism: "There are golden days ahead, waiting for the people of America. Waiting until we are fit, in our hearts, to reach out and grasp them. There is beauty, and peace, and progress in overflowing measure to be had just for the taking, when our eyes are opened."[25]

Some were critical of Page for invariably using 20 words to say

[21] "Brief History of Radio Station WLS," anonymous, unpublished manuscript dated August, 1951.
[22] *Prairie Farmer,* 103 (June 13, 1931), 4.
[23] Agricultural Broadcasting Co., "FCC Clear Channel Hearings," Book III, Section 3, p. 2.
[24] Thompson, p. 211.
[25] *Prairie Farmer,* 118 (August 3, 1946), 38.

what could be said in 10. For example, Gregory—who would just as invariably try to cut 10 words to five—often chafed at Page's approach, but as Butler expressed it, Page "put the heartbeat into Dinnerbell" and to a large measure into WLS. He developed the ritual to a point that people came to the studios just to watch Art Page conduct his Dinnerbell program.

Each day's program began with the ringing of between one and five dinnerbells. (The station had 17 bells which listeners contributed.) Then a live orchestra of 12 to 18 musicians played the national anthem, after which Page expressed his welcome and began the program. Page once said that he always tried to conduct his work in the spirit of a pastor. In that spirit he wanted programs which could "belong to the family" in every rural community of the midwest. People of all kinds paraded before his microphone during the more than 20 years of his direction. He reportedly never wrote a script for the program but relied instead on a manila folder into which he dropped items that he wished to use on certain days. In interviews with farm leaders Page showed some tendency to answer the questions that he was asking. He was most effective on items of human interest such as his custom of interviewing newlyweds. Hundreds of couples came to or through Chicago on honeymoons so they might appear on WLS to be greeted by a wedding march and Page's congratulations (or as he put it, "to tell them we love them, to wish them Godspeed").

Reports of good neighbor deeds were another specialty of the Dinnerbell which aired hundreds of reports about neighbors who helped families who were behind schedule because of sickness, injury, or other trouble. Rural safety also received special stress, and in 1944 and 1945 WLS received the National Gold Medal Award from the National Board of Fire Underwriters for the best fire prevention campaign of any radio station in America.

Bell-ringing, the national anthem, march tunes, country music, a closing sermonette, and a hymn were standard elements in the Dinnerbell ritual, but other parts of the program remained flexible. Dinnerbell went to state fairs, corn husking contests, and other farm-related events for live broadcasts. Before modern blood bank facilities were available, it often broadcast emergency calls for blood donors. It helped listeners find baling wire, stolen trucks, church bells, and a broad assortment of other items.

One morning's mail brought a letter from a doctor in downstate

Illinois who told about a farm girl who had had her left leg ampu-
tated and was in very low spirits. She listened to Dinnerbell on a
bedside radio in the hospital and the doctor asked Page to dedi-
cate a song to her. Page obliged with a dedication and "a message
of hope and cheer," followed several months later by a personal
visit. The girl went on to earn statewide honors in music, and her
mother credited WLS with doing more to bring her back and to
build her up for a successful life than anything the doctors could
have done.[26] The family spirit of WLS fed on such incidents.

Dinnerbell even helped name a pair of twin girls. The parents
asked the program to name them, so Page in turn asked listeners
to offer suggestions. After studying nearly 2,000 letters he and the
parents settled upon two names, Martha Lou and Margaret Sue,
taken after those of Martha Crane and Margaret Morton McKay
of the WLS staff. Page conducted a christening ceremony on
Dinnerbell with fitting dignity.

Such matters seemed natural to WLS because "these are our
people and the 'Dinnerbell' program is a part of their life." [27]
Dinnerbell operated on the basis that it owned part of every farm,
every steer, and every chicken within its signal. If someone lost
something, Dinnerbell helped find it; if someone found something,
Dinnerbell helped locate the owner. If a listener wanted information, Dinnerbell went to its audience and got it; if a listener discovered something, Dinnerbell helped him tell others about it.
"Dinnerbell Time is all things to all farm listeners. You will hear
a profound and learned discussion about a topic of great agricultural importance and you will often hear in the next few minutes
an interview with a pair of farm newlyweds . . . in town for a few
hours, part of them spent at WLS. When there is tragedy or joy
it is our tragedy and joy, we share it and become part of it." [28]

Dinnerbell helped WLS earn many awards, including the 1936
Variety Farm Service Citation and the 1940 George Foster Peabody
Award for meritorious service to agriculture.

In the process, WLS absorbed an unusually heavy expense for
farm programming. The Dinnerbell orchestra alone cost the station

[26] Agricultural Broadcasting Co., "FCC Clear Channel Hearings," Book III,
Section 2, p. 7.

[27] Agricultural Broadcasting Co., "FCC Clear Channel Hearings," Book III,
Section 3, p. 3.

[28] "Farm Programming at WLS," anonymous, unpublished, undated manuscript.

more than $100,000 a year by the time Butler died. Remote broadcasts, some for a week at a time, meant thousands of dollars for line charges, travel, and other extra expenses. It was a heavy load, especially for a program which accepted no advertising, but the Dinnerbell program held a special place among executives of the company as well as among its listeners.

Women's Programming

Programs for homemakers on WLS had a history which extended even beyond that of Dinnerbell. Elizabeth Weirick, a merchandise analyst for Sears, broadcast the station's first homemaking program on April 21, 1924, nine days after the station signed on. Soon a food authority named Ellen Rose Dickey took over the program, aided by a well-known Illinois clubwoman, Grace Viall Gray. Station director Edgar Bill believed that WLS could best inspire and serve farm women by featuring women who had distinguished themselves.

In 1925 two employees of Sears, Anne Williams and Sue Roberts, began to contribute news about styles, home decorations, cooking, and child care on a program called Tower Topics Time. *Prairie Farmer* added an afternoon women's program when it took over the station in 1928. Lois Schenck, women's editor of the paper, handled Homemaker's Hour at first with help from Martha Crane, a young former student at Northwestern University. Miss Crane had come to *Prairie Farmer* on October 15, 1928, as a mail sorter, but within a few weeks the station decided it wanted a women's program and she soon took over as Lois Schenck chose to stay with writing for the farm paper. Martha Crane thereby began the longest association of any staff member of WLS—from 1928 through the present time. She conducted Homemaker's Hour through 1934, then teamed up with a new staff member, Helen Joyce, to present a program called Feature Foods.

As in the case of farm programs, the Homemaker's Hour stressed service projects. During 1928-30, nearly 300 speakers appeared on the program in connection with many projects: dental clinics for school children, running water in homes, hot school lunches for rural children, rural recreation, good books, baby care, and others. WLS honored outstanding farm women in one series and backed a Master Farm Homemaker movement which paralleled the Master Farmer program. A series in 1939 featured Little Dramas from Life, brief plays about problems of love and marriage which listeners asked about. Homemaker's Hour continued until 1943 when a program devoted to homemaking in wartime replaced it.

Feature Foods limited its sponsors to food and grocery advertisers, all of whom allowed Martha Crane and Helen Joyce to write commercials for the program. One of its special projects was a 16-month series of reports from a homemaker in London explaining what life was like during the blitzes of 1944-45. In February, 1946, *Billboard Magazine* cited Feature Foods as an outstanding service program, the only women's program so designated by radio editors in the nationwide poll.[29]

Women's programs on WLS seldom had access to 15-man live orchestras, but a four-member staff during the 1940's denoted strong support from management. Butler actively backed homemaking programs within bounds of his built-in prejudice against businesswomen. He always was convinced that women had no business sense and should stay out of the business world. "No woman anywhere is worth more than $40 a week," he once said flatly. That meant modest wages (in fact, lowest of any major station in Chicago), but Butler offset them somewhat by giving staff members unusual freedom in trying out their own programming ideas.

News Programming

The news department made up for all of the emotionalism of Arthur Page or Dave Thompson. Carl Sandburg perhaps described it best in a column in the *Chicago Daily Times*: "No strain—no punch—no gee whiz—no lookit here now—no ponderifous opinions—just plain, straightway reading of dispatches picked from all the main news agencies—no attempt at rewriting and fixing over the news written where it is happening on the spot by men hired for their ability to see and hear and to write what they see and hear. If the news ain't exciting like you want today that will be just too bad for you because Bentley and Lewis won't pep it up. They know their farmers—and plenty of city folks who like it the same as farmers."[30]

Behind this deliberate approach to newscasting was a quiet, tal-

[29] Agricultural Broadcasting Co., "FCC Clear Channel Hearings," Book IV, Section 5, p. 16.

[30] Clipping from the *Chicago Daily Times*, June 25, 1944.

ented young man named Julian Bentley, who headed the WLS news department. He came to WLS in 1933 from a dairy farm in northern Illinois via Knox College and the United Press. Bentley's main job at WLS was newscasting, except that between February, 1935, and June, 1938, he was responsible for editing an ill-fated WLS radio weekly magazine called *StandBy*. He chose, edited, wrote, and aired his own news material, as did his associate Ervin Lewis, who joined him in 1938. Their style was deliberate and straightforward, largely free from "flashes" and other techniques for suspense.

One of the station's most exciting newsbreaks bypassed Bentley and fell to two other staff members of WLS, Herbert Morrison and Charles Nehlsen, who were at Lakehurst, New Jersey, on May 6, 1937, to record the landing of the Hindenburg dirigible. What began as an unusual feature assignment ended as a report of one of the nation's shocking tragedies. Morrison's shout set off a compelling eye-witness account probably unparalleled in radio reporting to that date:

It's burst into flames! Get out of the way! Get out of the way! Get this, Charlie! Get this, Charlie! It's on fire! It's crashing! It's crashing terrible! Oh my! Get out of the way, please. And the folks—Oh! It's terrible! This is one of the worst catastrophes in the world! (*Explosion*) Oh—Oh—it's burning! The flames are going up four, five hundred feet into the sky. . . . It's a terrible crash, ladies and gentlemen! (*Sobs*) It's smoke and flames now, and the plane is crashing to the ground. Not quite to the mooring mast. Oh the humanity! Oh the passengers! All the people screaming around here. I can't even talk to the people. Those friends are out there. I can't talk, ladies and gentlemen.[31]

The blast of the main explosion disrupted Nehlsen's recording equipment, but he restored it while a shocked Morrison regained some composure. They then kept at a two-hour session of describing and interviewing amidst the bedlam to produce a 45-minute transcription. Listeners of WLS first heard the report the next morning, by which time the two staff members were surrounded by reporters and photographers. *Radio Guide* awarded them a special medal of merit as "radio's greatest heroes."[32] The national networks broke standing rules against airing recordings when they broadcast the transcription.[33] The National Archives later asked for and re-

[31] Robert St. John, *Encyclopedia of Radio and Television Broadcasting* (Milwaukee: Cathedral Square Publishing Co., 1967), p. 98.

[32] *Prairie Farmer*, 109 (May 22, 1937), 24.

[33] Agricultural Broadcasting Co., "FCC Clear Channel Hearings," Book IV, Section 6, p. 39.

ceived a complete sound recording of the Hindenburg disaster.

One of Julian Bentley's greatest strengths was in international affairs, and efforts by WLS in covering World War II reflected that interest. When the war broke out, WLS had access to three news services—Transradio Press, United Press, and Associated Press— plus coverage offered by the Blue Network. Eager for more coverage, Bentley worked closely with the British Broadcasting Corporation when he was in Great Britain in 1943 at the invitation of the British Minister of Information. When he returned home he checked with engineers of WLS about setting up a shortwave monitoring system which would allow WLS to hear broadcasts from the BBC and other foreign stations. The result was a new information source called the WLS Listening Post from which WLS could either broadcast foreign programs directly or record them for later use.

The station added to its war coverage in 1944 by sending Lewis to the western front, where he covered military action and the lives of residents in England, Wales, France, Belgium, Netherlands, Germany, and Luxembourg.

By 1946 WLS had four full-time newsmen (not counting a full-time weather specialist) and four teletypes which provided material for more than 14 hours of newscasts each week—a sharp contrast to the WLS of 1927 which used a local newspaper for the five minutes of news it broadcast each day.

Dr. John Holland, Staff Pastor

"I'm going to bring John Holland to WLS and he's going to be our station pastor," Butler announced to personnel of his station one summer day in 1933. In some ways the notice carried little impact because religious broadcasting was not new. As early as 1928 roughly one out of every 10 radio stations in the country was operated by a religious organization, wholly or in part. Half of all stations included some form of religious programming. Quin Ryan of WGN commented in 1928 that religion had "embraced the radio, and the sky pilots are cruising the skies." [34] He concluded, "After reverently weighing the listening public's reports on the matter, we may draw the compound conclusion that religious broadcasting is a great privilege and a great pest."

[34] Quin A. Ryan, "The New Sky Pilots," *Chicago Tribune Picture Book of Radio 1928* (Public Service Office, *Chicago Tribune*, 1928), p. 40.

Neither was religious programming new to WLS, which had begun a devotional program, the Angelus, in 1924. Chimes, violin, and cello music, a brief prayer, and an inspirational thought comprised this five-minute program of "rest and reflection" which Tony Wons (later Harlow Wilcox) conducted. By 1933 WLS was airing a regular program called Hymn Time, an early morning religious service from the Chicago Gospel Tabernacle, a weekly Little Brown Church of the Air, and a devotional segment on the Dinnerbell each day.

However, no commercial radio station had its own staff pastor. It is ironic that the idea came from a man so critical of organized religion, yet Butler knew the importance of religion to farm people and he had his own brand of faith. He explained in 1945: "Our ideas on the matter are very simple. We know that every time a seed sprouts, or a tree comes into blossom and fruitage, it is a manifestation of the power of God. This is so vital a part of everyday life that it does not seem strange to set aside space in the paper and time on the radio for a minister like Dr. John Holland to help us work in harmony with these great forces." [35]

The suggestion seemed even more natural to Butler because John Holland had been writing regularly in *Prairie Farmer* since February 18, 1922, and had first appeared on WLS May 26, 1924, only a few weeks after it began.[36]

In a manner typical of him, Butler approached the pastor with a promise of preaching to millions and an offer to "name your price." Holland, who was then serving at Court Street Methodist Church in Rockford, accepted the offer and stated a salary (which Butler asked Snyder to negotiate down to "a price we can handle"). On September 30, 1933, *Prairie Farmer* announced that Holland had joined the staff on a full-time basis. Dr. John—as staff members came to know him—was ideal for Butler's world-view because, although a Methodist, he was nondenominational. Fully one-third of his mail came from Catholics. A "practical application of the New Testament to our everyday lives" served as the entire basis of his preaching.

Holland also brought a farm orientation to his new job, for he had been born and raised on a livestock farm near Milton, Iowa; his brother and nephew both became Master Farmers. The urging

[35] *Prairie Farmer*, 117 (December 22, 1945), 1.
[36] *Prairie Farmer*, 96 (May 17, 1924), 6.

of an uncle caused him to begin studying law, but after a year he returned to his original plan of studying for the ministry and enrolled at Iowa Wesleyan College from which he graduated in 1902. Pastorates at New Lenox and Tinley Park, Illinois, followed his ordination from Garrett Biblical Institute. In 1908 he was appointed federal chaplain in Panama as the canal was being built, and when he returned, he served pastorates at Aurora, Illinois, Cedar Falls, Iowa, St. Paul, Minnesota, and Rockford, Illinois, before coming to *Prairie Farmer*–WLS.[37] Ten seasons on the Chautauqua circuit in addition to his 28 years of work in the pulpit provided him with an understanding of both rural and urban people.

Doctor John became one of the station's most popular personalities, especially through his part in Dinnerbell and the Little Brown Church of the Air, a nondenominational worship program on Sunday. It had begun on that Sunday evening in 1925 when Samuel Guard of the Sears-Roebuck Agricultural Foundation reported to listeners about devastation in southern Illinois. By 1928 it could claim attendance by persons of 21 nationalities and 17 religious creeds. Thousands of listeners held its membership card which promoted the nonsectarian motto: "I expect to pass through this world but once. Any good therefore that I can do, or any kindness that I can show to any fellow creature, let me show it now. Let me not defer or neglect it, for I shall not pass this way again."[38] Unlike many religious programs on radio, the Little Brown Church did not ask listeners for donations to support it.

Surveys in the late 1940's showed that more than 250,000 radios were tuned to it each Sunday morning. In 1938 when Holland spoke to an estimated 2,500,000 listeners during the dedication of a new transmitter for WLS near Tinley Park, he was within sight of the first little church at which he had preached to a congregation of 25 persons 30 years earlier. The station received an average of 400 requests a week for his sermons. These were in addition to several

[37] The following references include biographical information about John Holland: *Prairie Farmer*–*WLS Round-Up*, 5 (February, 1952), 1-2; Vernon L. Taylor, "Doctor John: Pastor to Millions," *Christian Advocate*, July 31, 1952, pp. 7ff.; Agricultural Broadcasting Co., "FCC Clear Channel Hearings," Book I, Section 2, p. 5; *Prairie Farmer*, 95 (November 10, 1923), 12; 105 (June 10, 1933), 6; 113 (June 14, 1941), 18; 119 (March 1, 1947), 40; *WLS Family Album*, 1941, p. 16; *WLS Family Album*, 1950, p. 3; *WLS Family Album*, 1955, p. 5.

[38] Grace Cassidy, "Way Back When," *Prairie Farmer*-WLS *Round-Up*, 2 (May, 1949), 2.

hundred thousand copies of *Prairie Farmer* containing his sermons twice a month plus the circulation of as many as 26 other farm papers which used his column for many years. Some small churches without regular pastors used his sermons during their worship hours, although the station stressed its desire not to compete with or replace regular worship in church.

Apart from an influence upon readers and listeners, the mere day-to-day presence of a staff pastor had an unmeasurable but marked effect upon staff members. His presence made religion and service a most natural part of the station's daily activities. When he closed the Dinnerbell program with a prayer, everyone in the studio prayed, just as everyone stood in respect during the national anthem which opened the program. WLS took on an atmosphere unusual among commercial radio stations of its day, an atmosphere which reinforced Butler's desire to operate a family station which stressed service. Some associates later maintained that Butler's decision to employ a staff pastor had the greatest effect for good of any action he instigated.

The relationship also may have had a strong effect upon Butler, who was a close associate of Holland for the 15 years that Butler lived after he hired his pastor. Holland filled a role that no other member of the staff could play toward the 65-year-old man for whom religion had been a source of turmoil and frustration since childhood.

Programming for Schools

WLS with its day-to-day contact was able to do more than *Prairie Farmer* in helping to serve the thousands of rural schools besieged with low budgets, poorly qualified teachers, aging facilities, and declining numbers of students. The Sears-Roebuck Agricultural Foundation soon recognized this problem and tried using WLS to help teachers of rural schools. In February, 1925, it started the Little Red Schoolhouse, a series of broadcasts conducted by "Uncle Ben" Darrow in cooperation with the Cook County Superintendent of Schools during school hours on Friday afternoons.[39] Each schoolhouse in Cook County had a radio and teachers were to use the programs as supplements to their teaching. The people at Sears

[39] *Prairie Farmer*, 97 (December 19, 1925), 16; Agricultural Broadcasting Co., "FCC Clear Channel Hearings," Book IV, Section 3, p. 1.

considered it the first program of its kind, but it lasted only one season because few schools outside of Cook County owned radios. Instead, the station turned to programs during nonschool hours: a program on Saturday noons called Junior Round-Up and weekly symphony concerts for children.

WLS tried schooltime programs again soon after *Prairie Farmer* bought the station. On December 21, 1929, *Prairie Farmer* announced that WLS would broadcast an opening exercise each weekday starting in January. The paper even agreed to share part of the cost in buying radios for schools that wanted them, but there is no further evidence of this program. Schedules of WLS for February, 1930, did not show it.

Seven years later, conditions were more suitable for helping rural schools through radio when WLS began a new program called School Time in February, 1937. This was a 15-minute series conducted at 9 A.M. each weekday by a staff member, John Baker, who had experience in educational radio. It featured current events with Julian Bentley on Monday, music appreciation on Tuesday, business and industry on Wednesday, practical geography on Thursday, and current topics on Friday. Many radio stations of the day granted time to school systems for broadcasting educational programs, but few attempted the entire job of planning, preparing, and presenting daily programs for the classroom in cooperation with state superintendents of public instruction. Pure Milk Association sponsored School Time for several years, although sponsorship only handled production costs; WLS paid administrative costs and donated the time.

Enrollment in School Time grew from 400 schools in 1937 to 6,000 schools in 1943-44 (see Table 11). It reached more than one million school children each day beginning in 1941, including those in one-fifth of all schools in Illinois and Wisconsin, one-fourth of those in Indiana, and one-third of those in Michigan. More than three-fourths of those schools were in rural areas: 64 per cent one-room rural schools and 14 per cent two-room village schools.[40]

WLS provided teachers with guides for each semester and a certificate of participation for schools which took part regularly. Baker continued as director for one and a half years, after which Harriet Hester—a former county superintendent of rural music—

[40] "17 Years of Farm Service," anonymous mimeographed report of activities by WLS between 1924 and 1941, p. 31.

TABLE 11. PARTICIPATION BY SCHOOLS IN WLS SCHOOL TIME PROGRAM, 1937–46

School Year	Number of Schools Enrolled	Estimated Number of Students
1936–37 (last half)	400	N/A
1937–38	1,200	N/A
1938–39	3,000	N/A
1939–40	4,220	650,000
1940–41	N/A	800,000
1941–42	5,834	1,500,000
1942–43	6,000	870,000
1943–44	6,000	N/A
1944–45	N/A	1,000,000
1945–46	3,000	N/A

SOURCES: *Prairie Farmer*, 109 (August 14, 1937), 20; 110 (February 12, 1938), 8; 111 (February 25, 1939), 6; 112 (May 18, 1940), 24; 113 (September 20, 1941), 24; 115 (September 18, 1943), 6; 116 (September 16, 1944), 1; 118 (September 28, 1946), 16; *WLS Family Album*, 1941, p. 35; *School Time Teacher's Program Guide*, first semester, 1943-44, p. 12.

took over for four years. E. Jerry Walker became director for two years, beginning in the fall of 1943. Arthur Page then became acting director until 1947 when Josephine Wetzler assumed the office which she held more than ten years.

Butler, keenly aware of the part which *Prairie Farmer* had played in forming the common school programs of Illinois a century earlier, took great pride in WLS School Time. In 1940 he wrote to Harold Safford, program director of WLS: "I am amazed to read that our School Time program is going to 6,000 schools and 30,000 classrooms. Isn't that wonderful? It gives me a thrill that I can't put on paper, but you would know I meant it if you could hear me dictating this note." [41]

Butler felt that he had upheld the traditions of *Prairie Farmer* in education. He explained in the program schedule of School Time for 1944, "The great work of our earlier leaders places upon us of this generation a responsibility we have been proud to accept, to keep in step with the on-coming generation." He did not live to see the program earn for WLS one of the outstanding awards in radio broadcasting, the 1948 DuPont Award for "outstanding and meritorious service in encouraging, fostering, promoting and developing American ideals of freedom, and for loyal and devoted service to the nation and to the community."

[41] Butler to Harold Safford, November 6, 1940.

The program later received the Freedoms Foundation Award for
"outstanding contribution to the American way of life," and Josephine Wetzler in 1956 was one of seven women broadcasters to
receive *McCall's* Gold Mike Award for her part in helping make
School Time a national example of in-classroom education by
radio.

Special Programming

An annual budget for programming of as much as $400,000 and
a staff of as many as 200 persons for a half-time station inevitably
resulted in special projects and experiments. These fall into three
categories: unique broadcasts, tradition-building programs, and
efforts to create goodwill between rural and urban segments of the
station's coverage area.

Like other early radio stations, WLS valued its "firsts," the more
unusual the better. One was a program presented 200 feet below
Lake Michigan in August, 1929, to cover the dedication of a water
tunnel which would supply Chicago with water from a new crib
two miles from shore. Staff members long remembered riding out
in a little tunnel car, sloshing around in boots and raincoats, and
being served an underground luncheon on a decorated table, "as
if we were in a private home." [42]

Another project in 1929 was a stunt broadcast from nine different
studios throughout Chicago. Highlighting the program was a double
quartet with each of the eight singers and the accompanist in a different studio. The following year, WLS recorded another first with
a three-way broadcast from plane-to-plane-to-ground during an
army show in Chicago.

In 1939 the station broadcast a series of programs from a one-
man submarine which crossed Lake Michigan from Michigan City,
Indiana, to Chicago. Listeners of WLS even heard the reaction of
a parachutist right after he made the world's record free-fall in
1941.

Among the programs by WLS designed to deepen the respect
which midwesterners felt for their heritage, "The Prairie President"
was first and perhaps most ambitious. It was the start of a two-part
dramatized biography of Abraham Lincoln and covered his youth
and career in Illinois through election to the presidency. A mid-

[42] *Prairie Farmer-WLS Round-Up*, 2 (May, 1949), 2.

western author and student of Lincoln named Raymond Warren wrote this series of half-hour dramas which began in November, 1929, and extended 31 weeks. He was assisted by P. C. Lund of the WLS staff. William Vickland, an actor and employee of WLS, portrayed Lincoln. Among the other participants was an actor named Butler Manville, who entered the studio one evening wearing a long black mantle with white-lined cape and carrying a cane so that he could do full justice to the part he was to play. An illustrated article about each radio drama appeared in *Prairie Farmer* during the period.

Sequel to "The Prairie President" was a 30-week series entitled "Now He Belongs to the Ages." It began in the fall of 1930 and covered the remainder of Lincoln's life.

A second major historical production arose from the centennial observance of *Prairie Farmer* in 1941. Called "Midwest in the Making," it consisted of 30 half-hour dramas about pioneer life in Illinois. Among other topics, this series covered the first run of the Galena and Chicago Union Railroad and the battle for an Illinois Central system, the first Illinois State Fair, the founding of public schools, the early grain reapers, and a craze in 1854 for exotic breeds of poultry. A continuation of the series, called "101 Years on the Prairie," began in October, 1941, and dealt with topics such as country doctors, lead mines of Galena, Jenny Lind, Chicago's fire of 1871, and meat packing in Chicago.

One project in 1935 to improve rural-urban understanding within Chicago was known as the *Prairie Farmer*–WLS Harvest Festival, a three-day exhibition at the International Amphitheater. Thousands of listeners from 30 states and Canada sent in 2,500 exhibits of fruit, vegetables, and grain for judging, and a schedule of varied activities attracted 25,000 guests, mostly from Chicago.

A series of goodwill programs just before World War II took WLS to various army camps for remote broadcasts, some as close as Chicago and some as distant as Camp Forrest, Tennessee. Beginning January 6, 1942, the station broadcast a weekly half-hour feature called Meet Your Navy from the Great Lakes Naval Training Center to help recruit servicemen, to sell war bonds, to entertain, and to inform listeners about life in the service. After the third week it became a regular program on the NBC Blue Network and continued for almost four years. A special Meet Your Navy night at the Chicago Stadium in 1944 raised more than $35,000 for the Chicago Servicemen's Center.

A Channel for Giving

Other radio stations in Chicago often looked upon the "crazy half-time station" with amusement because its methods sometimes were unpolished. For example, Butler—an enthusiast for building and remodeling—practically had carpenters hired by the year, and the sound of their pounding and sawing was common accompaniment for programs. The fact that listeners not only tolerated such distractions but even approved of them reflected in part the informal family spirit which soon dominated WLS, as it had *Prairie Farmer* after Butler bought the paper. Just as Butler considered WLS to be a neighbor of its listeners, the listeners responded in like terms. For example, a favorite folk singer of WLS, Bradley Kincaid, got a substitute singer one morning in 1930 because Kincaid's wife was in the hospital awaiting delivery. As the program proceeded, Kincaid called to report the birth of a girl whom they had named Barbara for the girl in his favorite song, Barbara Allen. When the substitute announced this on the air, telephones started ringing with messages of good wishes. Soon Kincaid called again, this time to report the birth of a twin daughter whose name would be Alene, also for the girl in the song. Listeners responded with a flood of mail and gifts which dramatized the personal interest which they took in the joys of this young man who visited their homes each day by radio.

Another pair at WLS, organist Ralph Waldo Emerson and his wife, did their pre-marriage wooing over WLS in a public courtship which listeners recalled for more than 25 years.

The public seemed to value a personal relationship as much as the staff members and responded with expressions which included poetry.

> The measure of *Prairie Farmer* and WLS
> Lies not in pomp and power—
> But the helpful, friendly humanness
> Through every day and hour.
> Could we measure the value of hopes renewed
> Or weigh the worth of a smile;
> In mansions, on farms or in cabins crude
> Your "bigness" we might hope to file.
> Like millions struggling toward a goal,
> Are hands that turn the dials
> To 870 kilocycles and hope the waves will roll
> WLS across the miles.

We find the tie that binds us in one great family,
That makes all creeds and colors one—
Your boundless Christian sympathy
When charity needs be done.
We hear you breathe, we feel the beating of your heart,
So near to us you are,
With story, song, report of mart—
Our bright and guiding Star.[43]

It was the same spirit as that of the crusades of *Prairie Farmer*,
enriched by the warmth of the human voice, and it created an unusually responsive audience. Table 12 summarizes the hundreds of
thousands of dollars which listeners of WLS donated through the
station for emergencies between 1925 and 1937, in addition to relief

TABLE 12. SUMMARY OF DISASTER RELIEF AND OTHER AID PROVIDED THROUGH
WLS (EXCLUDING CHRISTMAS NEIGHBORS CLUB AND WLS FOOD AND CLOTHING
STATION DONATIONS), 1925–37

Year	Project and Extent of Aid
1925	$216,905 for southern Illinois tornado relief
1926	$ 18,708 for Florida hurricane relief
1927	$ 86,760 for Mississippi flood relief
1928	$ 4,800 for Florida hurricane relief
1930	$ 18,300 and 32,000 baby chicks for Wabash Valley flood relief
1932	$ 652 for *Chicago Daily News* neediest family fund
1933	$ 800 for Moweaqua mine disaster relief
	$ 15,000 emergency crop seed grant from the Illinois Relief Commission to a tornado-stricken northern Illinois area arranged by *Prairie Farmer*-WLS, Pure Milk Association, and Illinois Agricultural Association
1934	21,435 children contributed one cent each for Warm Springs Foundation Fund.
	9,177 underprivileged children saw "A Century of Progress" as guests of WLS and its listeners.
1936	$ 22,083 for Eastern flood relief
1937	$ 94,382 for Ohio River flood relief

SOURCES: Agricultural Broadcasting Company, "Testimony and Exhibits of Agricultural
Broadcasting Company before the Federal Communications Commission Clear Channel
Hearings," Docket 6741, Book V, pp. 2-3; *Prairie Farmer*, 106 (April 14, 1934), 18;
"17 Years of Farm Service," WLS mimeographed report, undated; "WLS Flood and
Tornado Relief," typed summary, undated; George C. Biggar to author, February, 1967.

[43] Part of a poem entitled "An Appreciation" written by an unidentified
listener from Indiana and cited in *WLS Family Album*, 1931, p. 4.

following the tornado in southern Illinois. Several other expressions of generosity by listeners illustrate the confidence which they showed in the station.

One such project began in late 1930 when employees of *Prairie Farmer* and WLS became concerned about the 150,000 depression-ridden persons who were living on Madison Street, known as Skid Row, which ran parallel to and just one block south of Washington Boulevard. Many families in the area were destitute, so the company began a relief station in cooperation with the Volunteers of America, converted one large room into a receiving center for clothes and food, and called on listeners and readers for help. After only three days the WLS Community Kitchen, located a block south of the Prairie Farmer Building, had fed nearly 5,000 persons with food which listeners had provided. Hungry Chicagoans filed into the kitchen from 7 A.M. to 5 P.M. for meals of soup, sandwiches, tomatoes, bread and butter, cake, pie, and coffee.

Listeners offered refrigerators and the food to fill them, trucking firms offered free hauling, and local bakeries provided baked goods. One farmer drove 40 miles in a vegetable-laden Model T sedan that he had to "wish up every hill." When he got to the relief center and saw the line of hungry persons waiting in a large room warmed only by the heat of their own bodies, he delivered not only his vegetables but all the money he had with him. Farmers and businessmen of one community sent a truckload of 500 chickens for Christmas dinner.

Packages filled with clothing jammed the basement of the Prairie Farmer Building, allowing chilled men, women, and children to pick up more than 2,000 articles during the first three days. Staff members from Butler down took turns serving food and tending the clothing center.

By the end of February, 1931, donations from listeners in 45 states and seven provinces of Canada had provided the means for serving 144,607 meals and issuing 118,672 garments to 19,809 families.[44]

WLS undertook a second depression-centered project in 1934 when social agencies of Cook County announced that more than 10,000 underprivileged boys and girls in Chicago would not be

[44] Agricultural Broadcasting Co., "FCC Clear Channel Hearings," Book V, p. 5.

able to see the Century of Progress Exposition. The station turned to its listeners who responded with donations that allowed 9,177 children from 45 public welfare districts and settlement houses to attend the Exposition. Staff members of WLS arranged the daily excursions.

Christmas Giving Parties also started in 1934 as an effort by WLS to help needy children of Chicago during the holiday season. Stars of the WLS Barn Dance staged a special show which children could attend if each brought a toy or nonperishable food item for admission. These annual parties began in the Eighth Street Theater, but outgrew it by 1938 when 4,500 children attended the party in the ballroom of the Stevens Hotel and another 3,000 who wrote for tickets were refused because of limited space. By 1946 more than 40,000 had attended and contributed tons of toys and food items which the Salvation Army and Volunteers of America distributed.

Another project related to Christmas was the annual Christmas Neighbors Club, a project designed to help children in hospitals and other child-care institutions. The idea behind it began in 1925 when WLS stayed on the air all night accepting donations of dolls or money to buy Christmas dolls primarily for less privileged youngsters in the southern mountains. This program, called "Dolls and Dough," continued through 1929 and resulted in more than $15,000 worth of gifts. The Christmas Neighbors Club began in 1935 with a similar goal, except that donations helped buy equipment for hospitals rather than dolls. Proceeds averaged about $6,000 a year until 1943 when listeners doubled their donations. By the time Butler died in 1948, listeners of WLS were giving $46,000 a year for wheel chairs, inhalators, infant incubators, orthopedic walkers, fracture beds, radio-phonographs, and other needed items. Their total giving had exceeded $200,000 for this program alone since 1935 and thereby provided hundreds of child-care wards in the midwest with nearly 5,000 items.[45] The total was nearly one-third of a million dollars by 1952, after which records are not available.

[45] Agricultural Broadcasting Co., "FCC Clear Channel Hearings," Book V, pp. 9-10; *A Report on the Activities of Your Prairie Farmer–WLS Christmas Neighbors Club 1944* (Chicago: Prairie Farmer Publishing Company, 1945), pp. 26-27; "Dolls and Dough," typed WLS report, undated; *Prairie Farmer*, 119 (December 6, 1947), 5; 120 (December 18, 1948), 1.

Service at a Profit

WLS became one of the reasons that Butler and his business associates stood so firmly upon the stand that service has its rewards. The big staff and program budget indicate that the managers of WLS did not skimp on programming, even during the years of depression. Their decision proved to be justified by two developments: the emergence of advertising support to offset costs of programming and a growing audience for WLS.

Competing stations which scoffed at the methods of WLS found that they could not come close to matching its pull among listeners. Table 13 shows how mail from listeners rose to an average of more

TABLE 13. SUMMARY OF MAIL RECEIVED BY WLS, 1924–48

Year	Pieces of Mail[a]	Year	Pieces of Mail[a]
1924 (8 months)	54,416	1937	1,159,585
1925	123,217	1938	1,006,356
1926	189,316	1939	1,117,958
1927	205,625	1940	1,058,032
1928	256,820	1941	1,191,775
1929	415,072	1942	1,172,220
1930	619,980	1943	1,014,209
1931	734,523	1944	1,046,929
1932	1,021,208	1945	1,058,675
1933	939,796	1946	1,071,540
1934	1,051,041	1947	1,083,554
1935	1,300,312	1948	1,053,341
1936	1,515,901		

[a] Includes business correspondence, which averaged 17,000–22,000 between 1943 and 1946 but probably less before that.
SOURCES: "Presentation of WLS," scrapbook prepared by WLS, 1928, p. 5; Mildred Burton, "Report on Radio Mail Received for the Year of 1948," Ditto, p. 1, summarized for 1930-48. Mildred Burton was WLS mail department head.

than one million letters a year by 1932. It peaked in 1936 when WLS announced the largest mail count ever received by a single radio station—more than one million letters in the first six months.[46]

Thousands visited WLS each year to see the Dinnerbell program, Arthur Page, Dr. John Holland, and stars of the Barn Dance. One of the largest groups included 615 farm youths from Ohio who packed the cornstalk-insulated main studio one day in 1932, leaving room only for the announcer. Visitors from 34 states, Alaska, Can-

[46] *WLS Family Album*, 1937, p. 4.

ada, Mexico, Italy, Poland, Russia, England, and Syria signed the station's guest book that year. About 40,000 persons visited WLS during 1936.

Surveys attested to the popularity of *Prairie Farmer*'s radio station among farm people. When the U.S. Department of Agriculture surveyed farmers in Illinois, Indiana, Wisconsin, and Michigan during 1938 to learn which radio stations they used for getting market prices, WLS got 69 per cent of all mentions. The second-ranked station received 5 per cent. The Illinois Agricultural Association asked farmer-members about their radio listening habits and learned that WLS ranked first in every time period except the afternoon. (It was on the air only part of each afternoon.) An independent telephone survey of more than 3,600 rural homes in the four-state area around Chicago showed that WLS had 76 per cent of the total audience for radio between 5:30 and 6:30 A.M.

Among national advertisers, WLS became almost the automatic choice for coverage of the rich plains area within 100-150 miles of Chicago. They found that the station delivered a farm audience which few stations of its day could match for responsiveness.

Not only was WLS popular; it also was consistently profitable. Five months after Prairie Farmer Publishing Company bought a major interest in the station, Gregory could report to readers that WLS had broken even for the month. "To achieve that result in the fifth month that we have been operating the station is, we believe, a real accomplishment. We did not buy WLS with the idea that it would ever make us any money. We do not expect it to do so, and any increased income in the future will be used to improve programs and service to our listeners. We bought WLS because we believed that it should be maintained as a radio station dedicated to the service of agriculture."[47]

Future years—even years of depression—showed that WLS would do much more than break even. The managers of WLS were alert businessmen, accustomed to seeing enterprises produce profits. They were joined in 1928 by a young business manager named George Cook who had worked with *Prairie Farmer* as credit manager since September, 1927. Cook was from a farm in Missouri and got his first taste of publishing during high school when he worked on a local newspaper. An early interest in medicine faded after one

[47] *Prairie Farmer,* 101 (March 2, 1929), 10.

and a half years at St. Louis University, and in May, 1925, he came
to Chicago where he worked for Montgomery Ward and later
Transo Envelope Company before joining *Prairie Farmer*.[48] As a
part of the management group for WLS, Cook in turn became
assistant treasurer (1929), treasurer (1938), and a director of both
Agricultural Broadcasting Company and Prairie Farmer Publishing Company (1941).

Assets of WLS rose about $6,500 during 1929, the first full year
of management by *Prairie Farmer*. By 1932, total assets were
$331,132 compared with the original $250,000. Profits for that year
in the depths of depression were slightly more than $41,000, a
welcome offset for the losses of *Prairie Farmer*. Profits continued
to allow payments on the contract with Sears until it was fulfilled
ahead of schedule in October, 1935. *Prairie Farmer* then exercised
its option to buy all of the remaining shares, a $122,500 obligation
which it settled in another two years. By the time Butler died in
1948 the assets of his station had increased five-fold to more than
$1,200,000. The station's annual income tax alone was greater than
his original purchase contract of $125,000 with Sears.

[48] *Prairie Farmer*-WLS *Round-Up*, 3 (April, 1950), 4.

Good Times in Hard Times

CHAPTER 9

Dear editor:
I am a farmer and own a 300-acre farm with plenty of cattle, hogs, horses, and poultry. I would like to attend the Century of Progress Exposition in Chicago next summer, but in order to do so must arrange for a suit of clothes, pair of shoes and a hat. Here is what I want you to do—put me in touch with someone who will trade me a suit of clothes for a cow and calf; a pair of No. 10 shoes for a sow and pigs, and a hat for a fat goose. Besides this I would want to bring a couple of cases of eggs to exchange for a place to sleep while there. Will try to raise enough money for carfare and admission. I can make the trip in my "Flivver" providing the weather is fair, otherwise I would need a rain coat as the top is off it.[1]

It was like a step backward into the era of bartering, that age during which settlers dealt with native Indians using bright beads and calicos. Hardly anyone had money during the early 1930's, so farmers in the midwest traded wheat for haircuts, chickens for veterinary services, corn for dairy cows, and made other moneyless deals to get along. Scrip and wooden tokens practically replaced dollars and coins in many towns and trading areas. If it seemed

[1] *Prairie Farmer*, 105 (February 18, 1933), 6.

quaint in later years, it was anything but quaint at the time; it was a sign of a desperate attempt to meet the basic needs of life.

Farmers were especially tired of it because their depression had begun not with the crash of the stock market on October 24, 1929, but almost 10 years earlier. They had watched the value of their farm land drop more than 30 per cent between 1920 and 1924 alone. Prices for their products fell further and faster than those for industrial goods, then recovered more slowly.

The Illinois farmer of the 1930's was torn between ruinous prices and the horror with which a traditionally independent man of the soil viewed going "on relief"—between helpless frustration and the urge to react violently like his neighbors in Iowa through their Farmers Holiday. He pondered taking a job in town as some of his neighbors had done in the 1920's, but now they were coming back to the country, last hired and first fired under drastic cuts in industrial production.

A look at his urban neighbors heightened his frustration. Even in 1935-36, after the big depression had bottomed out, average annual income for each farm resident was little more than half that of nonfarm residents. He felt that something was wrong when 95 per cent of all urban homes had running water, compared with only 30 per cent of farm homes; 95 per cent of urban homes had electricity for lighting, compared with about 25 per cent of farm homes; and 85 per cent of all urban homes had indoor plumbing, compared with about 9 per cent of farm homes.[2]

If the problem was not unbelievably low prices that allowed burning corn for fuel cheaper than buying coal, it was a drouth in 1934 followed by millions of chinch bugs that streamed into his fields and even his home. His world seemed senseless and rickety to the point of numbness. The Lazy Farmer captured this feeling in a welcome to the new year:

> Hurrah for 1932
> There ain't no damage it can do
> To one and all that ain't been done
> To us in 1931.[3]

[2] N. H. Engle, *Housing Conditions in the United States* (Bureau of Foreign and Domestic Commerce, 1937), cited in U.S. Department of Agriculture, *Yearbook of Agriculture, 1940* (Washington: U.S. Government Printing Office, 1940), p. 389.

[3] *Prairie Farmer*, 104 (January 9, 1932), 4.

Corn Husking Contests

Gregory, sensing that farmers needed psychological relief if they could not have immediate economic relief, made human interest a distinct part of his editorial policy after 1920. He placed anti-stealing campaigns such as the chicken thief series in that category, "a desperate attempt to give the harassed farmer relief." [4]

Corn husking contests also became part of a program by *Prairie Farmer* to cheer its readers beginning in 1924. Harvesting corn by hand was one of the most detested, back-breaking jobs around the farm, demanding not only unending energy but also unending patience. Farmers knew that during the erratic corn husking season they were likely to be sweltering in heat one day, slogging through mud up to their ankles the next, facing frostbite from wintry winds of still another. Week after week the farmer worked alone, the quietness broken only by the rustling of dried-out corn leaves and husks as he worked each stalk, the creaking of his wagon, the sound of ears hitting a wooden bangboard, and his occasional call for the team to move ahead.

Some farmers tried to make a game of husking corn by keeping track of their daily take. Winter evenings often found farmers swapping stories around their stoves about corn picking exploits in the neighborhood. As early as 1916 *Prairie Farmer* had encouraged readers to send their results to the paper. However, Henry A. Wallace of *Wallaces' Farmer* deserves credit for starting the change of corn husking from a dreaded chore to a favorite sport. In 1922 Wallace conceived the idea of trying to put some substance into those tall tales by actually staging contests so a man could prove his championship by clear-cut action rather than by talk. Wallace printed an editorial in early October, inviting huskers to submit their records and take part in a contest. Only three men competed in the first contest on a cold December day in Polk County. Huskers earned points for volume, minus penalties for corn left in the field and husks left on ears.

Eleven huskers competed in the contest of 1923 on Wallace's farm, including one farmer from Illinois. In 1924 *Prairie Farmer* noted that "corn husking is the great fall sport on farms of the corn belt. The young man who can bring 200 bushels a day is the

[4] *Prairie Farmer*, 100 (July 14, 1928), 8.

hero of the community."[5] Meanwhile, both Illinois and Nebraska challenged Iowa's boast of having the best corn and corn huskers. *Prairie Farmer* sponsored the first state contest for Illinois in November with about 3,500 spectators on hand. Then state winners from Iowa, Nebraska, and Illinois competed in the first interstate contest which *Prairie Farmer* hosted in Sangamon County.

According to a later report in *Prairie Farmer*, Minnesota and Indiana took up the sport in 1925, South Dakota and Missouri in 1926, Kansas in 1927, Ohio in 1930, Wisconsin in 1937, and Pennsylvania in 1938. Sponsorship in the various states came from farm papers. For example, *Prairie Farmer* sponsored state contests in Illinois and Indiana, then took turns with other papers in hosting the national meet. Corn husking became recognized as a national sport in the *All-Sports Record Book* of 1935 which observed, "Corn husking is a sport for red blooded gentlemen with lightning fast and sinewy hands. If you are thinking of becoming a contestant for national honors the advice is offered that you first spend three years of wrestling grizzly bears as a period of training."[6] John Strohm, a staff member of *Prairie Farmer*, expressed the rigors and excitement of this new sport:

The corn field on Contest Day is a gridiron, a bull ring, a cinder track, basketball court, and boxing ring rolled into one. The husker must have the strength of a football player, the grace of a bull fighter, the speed of a sprinter, the accuracy of a basketballer, and the stamina of a boxer if he wants to go places in the corn husking contest field. There are no time-outs in corn husking. No rests between rounds. No trainers to work over aching muscles at the ends of the field. No coaches offering advice. The husker must go on his own for one hour and twenty minutes throwing corn every second. For eighty minutes huskers beat a steady tattoo on the bangboards, like a machine gun spitting bullets. Fast huskers can throw 50 to 60 ears a minute. Irv Bauman, national champ last year, threw an average of 50 ears a minute for the entire contest. That means that every six seconds he threw five ears. In the space of one second he spotted an ear, grabbed it, peeled it, broke it, threw it, and reached for the next ear while the other was on its way to the wagon.[7]

Butler had little to do with these contests and when he attended, the staff members felt he was more critical than complimentary. But Gregory liked them for several reasons. He felt they helped farm people forget their troubles, helped develop new and faster

[5] *Prairie Farmer*, 96 (August 30, 1924), 8.
[6] *Prairie Farmer*, 113 (October 18, 1941), 76.
[7] *Prairie Farmer*, 113 (October 18, 1941), 76.

husking methods, made a game of what formerly was plain hard work, and stirred teamwork within communities. For example, counties began to set up contests from which they sent winners to state meets. Often the county farm advisers, elevator operators, farm bureau groups, implement dealers, and other local businessmen took part, while groups of women set up food stands. The result was a cooperative effort which Gregory applauded.

Contests at the state level were far more complex; each required more than 1,000 volunteer workers. Sponsoring organizations such as *Prairie Farmer* invested staff time all summer to get ready.

Sizes of crowds varied with the unpredictable early winter weather, but Table 14 shows that state corn husking contests in Illinois were major crowd-drawers by 1930. Thirty thousand persons watched that contest on November 7 at the Funk farms in central Illinois—more than had attended even national meets of earlier years. Added thousands heard the account on radio because WLS broadcast the contest live as it had done since 1928. The National Broadcasting Company began on-the-spot coverage of national corn husking meets in 1929 with about 50 radio stations carrying the programs.[8]

TABLE 14. ATTENDANCE AT ILLINOIS STATE CORN HUSKING CONTESTS SPONSORED BY *Prairie Farmer*, 1924–41

Year	Number Attending	Year	Number Attending
1924	3,500	1933	35,000
1925	3,000	1934	25,000
1926	N/A	1935	N/A
1927	N/A	1936	45,000
1928	6,000	1937	70,000
1929	N/A	1938	85,000
1930	30,000	1939	95,000
1931	25,000	1940	50,000
1932	15,000	1941	7,000

SOURCE: Annual accounts in *Prairie Farmer*.

The system got more and more complex as crowds for the national contest grew to a peak of 125,000 in 1935 and 1936. Biggest crowd for a state contest in Illinois was 95,000 in 1939. Implement dealers became interested in these affairs and asked for a chance

[8] *Prairie Farmer*, 104 (October 29, 1932), 2.

to show their products. Farm papers began offering free space for exhibits to advertisers who carried a certain amount of advertising each year. Selection of sites became a major problem, for the contest required many acres for parking and exhibits, not counting space for plots of corn. Large crowds also made the championships highly competitive, so planners adopted detailed rules to cover every contingency. Between 20 and 40 volunteers followed the wagon of each contestant to see that the crowd did not interfere with his husking or give him help and to ensure that everything went according to the rules.

The crowds also attracted pickpockets who could—as Dave Thompson expressed it—lift a lot of leather. *Prairie Farmer* met this problem by stationing a livestock transport trailer on the grounds to serve as a jail manned by two guards. Officers from the pickpocket detail of the Chicago Police Department roamed the area to spot known pickpockets and herd them into the trailer. On one occasion Thompson (to the horror of salesmen for *Prairie Farmer* and WLS) even jailed a client's executive who broke a no-liquor rule.

An elaborate system allowed WLS to cover these "cornfield classics" live for listeners. During the national contest in 1941, for instance, Arthur Page was posted in a tower which rose high from the center of the contest field. A master chart of the field, past husking records, and various facts about each contestant gave Page information to undergird his own unfailing capacity for description. Page once confided that his most trying ordeal was during a state contest in which the starter's shotgun jammed after the warning shot and Page had to ad lib for 13 minutes until a state policeman ended the suspense by pulling out his revolver and starting the contest. From then on, *Prairie Farmer* used aerial bombs as starting signals.

Two field reporters supplemented Page's narrative by using portable shortwave sets to follow the huskers by wagon. Listeners thereby had access even to the sound of ears hitting the bangboards.

Excitement, color, and vigorous action made corn husking contests highly popular among farm people of the midwest through 1941, after which World War II and the mechanical cornpicker put hand husking on the shelf of farm memories. *Prairie Farmer* hosted the 18th and final contest before 100,000 spectators in

LaSalle County only a month before Pearl Harbor. Contests then were cancelled for the duration, never to revive. Mechanical pickers harvested roughly half of all corn in the major corn growing counties of Illinois by 1940. Within five years that share rose to more than three-fourths and spelled the end of hand husking and the knights of the husking peg.

Other types of sports appealed to Gregory who in April, 1926, joined with Edgar Bill of WLS (then owned by Sears) and Harry Butcher of the Illinois Agricultural Association to form a Middle West Farm Sports Committee. "It will take a long time to solve all our problems, but we can have a good time as we go along," Gregory insisted as he called for more contests: baseball, old fiddlers' and callers', horseshoe, hog calling, chicken calling, trap-shooting, milking, plowing, and horse pulling.[9] Some of them failed to materialize, but one which developed in 1936 was an Illinois Farm Sports Festival. *Prairie Farmer* supported this event with publicity, and stars of WLS performed before the 2,000 participants during two days of competition at Urbana. Gregory also introduced a regular sports page in May of that year.

Diversionary Dialogue Among Readers

Hard times occasionally stimulated some relaxing dialogue among readers of *Prairie Farmer* as they attempted to maintain a sense of humor. Gregory encouraged readers to write and sometimes a single letter triggered an entire chain of responses. One of these extended through the first half of 1928 and unearthed some rural folklore.

It began with comments by readers about natural curiosities such as doodlebugs, ground puppies, and hump-backed Joshuas. Other mysteries for debate were wart-witchery and the transforming of a horse hair into a living creature by immersing it in a running brook. Some readers swore by these stories; others scoffed. "I'd be sincerely grateful to anyone who would convince my children, the youngest of them now in his teens, that the wriggling threadlike creatures are native to shallow streams and that the belief that warts can be magically conjured away ought to be shelved. It's a never-ending source of mystery to me that among intelligent enlightened rural people, with their up-to-date homes

Prairie Farmer, 98 (April 3, 1926), 10.

and clubs and automobiles and children in high schools and colleges, so great a number should be found who cling to these age-old superstitions, and teach them to their children, and resent it if the modern disrespectful youngster laughs!" [10]

A string of letters contained testimonials about methods by which readers successfully called doodlebugs (to which Gregory responded by suggesting a doodlebug calling contest). About that time, someone wrote asking if other readers had ever seen joint snakes. One issue in April, 1928, contained two full pages of tales from readers about joint snakes—including one story which maintained that each section of such a snake has grease cups at the ends for lubrication. Gregory egged readers on by replying to each item with doubt but courtesy.

After the joint snake it was the hoop snake. "I wish to relate my experience with a hoop snake when I was a boy in Kentucky," wrote one reader from Champaign County. "As I was hoeing corn one day, I saw a large hoop snake come rolling toward me. I jumped to one side, but it hit the hoe handle with its horn, and in two hours the handle had swelled until it burst the eye of the hoe. What is your comment on that?" [11]

Gregory replied, "I am speechless," but his other readers were not. Another reader told about a hoop snake that swallowed more and more of its tail until, with one last gulp, the snake was gone. Gregory finally announced that he was closing discussion about snakes, explaining: "If we haven't settled the question by this time it can't be settled."

Other readers asked if cows sleep, why vines twine from right to left, and if foxes are friends or pests. This last question brought another two pages of response. The paper finally called for a straw vote on the question of foxes and even printed a ballot for readers to clip and return. Charmer black snakes, blacksmith bugs, and the genesis of weather were among other topics which readers wrote about. One reader argued that the reason for sunshine on Saturday was that Moses washed his shirt on that day, except now and then when he bought a new one. Water-witching was another bewhiskered favorite which always drew avid testimonials, both positive and negative.

[10] *Prairie Farmer*, 100 (January 7, 1928), 14.
[11] *Prairie Farmer*, 100 (April 7, 1928), 37.

Depression-sized Vacations

On February 15, 1930, *Prairie Farmer* announced that after threshing season it would sponsor a rail trip to "Adventureland"— the northwest and Canada—and invited readers to go along. More than 10,000 readers wrote for information but only 269 went, suggesting that many wanted a break but could not afford $300 for a 10-day to two-week trip. *Prairie Farmer* tried three more trips during 1931 before it gave up because of economic conditions. Instead, it shifted in 1932 to depression-sized outings—one-day trips by steamship across Lake Michigan for $1.25 a person. These were called *Prairie Farmer–WLS* Family Picnics, the first of which sailed to Michigan City, Indiana, on June 21. Musicians from WLS performed on the ship and at the destination.

People responded so warmly that the company scheduled a second trip for August 2 and a capacity group loaded the ship, as it did again on August 16 and August 30. *Prairie Farmer* and WLS closed the summer with a picnic by train to Lake Geneva, Wisconsin, and resumed the picnics with seven trips during 1933.

The major project of 1933, however, was a series of 51 conducted tours of the Century of Progress Exposition in Chicago. *Prairie Farmer* announced them to readers in March and tours ran at four-day intervals beginning in June. A person could spend three nights, two full days and two half-days in Chicago for $29. The paper arranged for rooms in a hotel near Lincoln Park and worked out a sightseeing program which members of the staff guided. Nearly 2,000 persons took the fair tour in 1933 in groups of between 30 and 96, and another 1,000 took part during 1934. Financially, a project designed merely to break even produced a profit of $15,000 to help recoup other losses which the paper was suffering. In turn, several thousand readers got low-cost "no-worry" vacations.

Prairie Farmer resumed its more distant tours in 1934 as farm prices began to inch their way upward. A six-day trip to the east coast in November introduced a series which still was active in 1968.

WLS Barn Dance—Call of the Country

Some people blamed radio for the depression of the 1930's. Notwithstanding that possibility, radio was perhaps the best salve with

which a society could treat the symptoms of its illness. It seems far
from coincidental that comedy and variety dominated radio programming in the United States when the depression was most
severe. On the networks, CBS was featuring Jack Benny, Fred Allen,
Burns and Allen, Howard and Shelton, and Stoopnagle and Budd.
The Red Network of NBC had Eddie Cantor, Ed Wynn, Rudy
Vallee, an Al Jolson series, Charles Winninger on Showboat, Jack
Pearl, and Ken Murray as the Royal Vagabond. The Blue Network
of NBC had the Marx brothers.[12]

Radio was experiencing what Erik Barnouw termed a "vaudeville
boom." [13] A song and a laugh helped Americans take their minds
off threats and problems, rather like whistling in the graveyard.
Networks and bigger stations (including WLS) were surprised to
find that hard times did not affect them as adversely as other segments of business. Somehow this new medium could offer the balm
that a hurting society needed and through huge audiences make a
place for itself on shrivelled advertising schedules.

WLS found its own type of vaudeville, tailormade for the millions of Americans who returned to the country in body and spirit
during the years of depression. It was the WLS National Barn
Dance, broadcast each Saturday night beginning in 1924 and already a national institution by 1928. Early radio programming in
the style of the potted palm made the Barn Dance stand out even
more starkly, for it was far from refined. In fact, its lack of elegance
nearly killed the program in infancy.

During the first month of operations, Edgar Bill called the staff
together and suggested that WLS try to assemble some fiddlers and
vocal talent to simulate an old-fashioned country barn dance.[14]
Farm people had enjoyed square dances and barnwarmings for
many years and Bill felt that a radio version might prove popular.
WLS over-rode a fear that farm families would be in town on
Saturday nights and scheduled its first Barn Dance for Saturday
evening, April 19.

The staff did not know where to find a square dance caller but
an announcement on the air produced a reply from Tom Owen,

[12] Erik Barnouw, *A Tower in Babel—A History of Broadcasting in the
United States* (New York: Oxford University Press, 1966), p. 273.
[13] Barnouw, p. 273.
[14] Based on an account from George Biggar, who was on the original staff.
Cited in "Forty Years in the Right Business," a speech by Biggar delivered at
the South Dakota Broadcasters Association Convention, Huron, South Dakota,
May 22, 1964.

who worked in a hospital in Chicago and who offered his services, saying that he had called dances in Missouri. A musician named Tommy Dandurand was in charge of the first little fiddling band. No one knew what to expect from a great silent audience gathered at earphones, accustomed to hearing light classical music which the managers of Sears felt befitted the company's image. One account states: "On the first Saturday night, a Sears vice-president had some guests in his home and with pardonable pride he tuned his crystal set to his spanking new radio station. He was known as a music lover. When his ears were assaulted by Turkey in the Straw rendered by a devil-may-care country fiddle, the National Barn Dance nearly died right then and there." [15]

George Biggar confirmed this reaction and added that Samuel Guard got called onto the carpet to explain why such disgraceful so-called music should be broadcast. His reply was that the Barn Dance was typical Americana. He also explained that hundreds of approving telegrams, letters, and cards showed that the common people who were mail order customers of Sears liked the program. Four hundred telephone calls had crowded into the studio that first night and caused the hotel manger to warn that if the phone kept ringing, WLS would have to put in its own lines.

When the fiddles, harmonicas, guitars, and accordions cut loose with "Arkansas Traveler" and other rollicking old-time tunes, it was as though the countryside had awakened.

"The Barn Dance brings happy memories of our youth."

"Mother and I pulled up the carpet and danced for the first time in years."

"Why, I'd never heard that song since I was a little girl." [16]

Executives of Sears grasped the appropriateness of this type of program for a radio station devoted to agricultural service, and the Barn Dance got its lease on life.

The Solemn Old Judge was the first announcer and pioneering stars included Ford and Glenn, Grace Wilson, Tommy Dandurand, Tom Owen, Chubby Parker, Walter Peterson, Ed Goodreau, Cecil and Esther Ward, Ralph Waldo Emerson, and Bob Hendry. Soon a new kind of musician began filing into Chicago seeking a spot on radio—folk artists and balladeers with their banjoes, cowboys

[15] Bernard L. Asbel, "The National Barn Dance," *Chicago*, 1 (October, 1954), 24.
[16] George C. Biggar, "Cowbells Ring Out on Saturday Night," in John Lair, ed., *100 Barn Dance Favorites* (Chicago: Cole, 1935).

with guitars and western songs. At first they performed without pay, but according to one of the tales at WLS, they started getting paid through some help from Al Capone. One of his girl friends reportedly sang in the College Inn of the Sherman Hotel and appeared one night on the Barn Dance at the request of the station. "Capone watched the performance with smiling approval which later turned to suggestive firmness when he asked the producer, 'Well, don't she get paid?' She was." [17]

Grace Wilson took this as a cue for demanding equal courtesy, whereupon WLS reportedly set up a full payroll for talent.

Early Stars on the Barn Dance

Records are somewhat sketchy about the progress and activities of the Barn Dance during the first six years, after which Prairie Farmer Publishing Company issued an annual *WLS Family Album* in response to the many requests for facts about performers. Barn Dances through 1930 took place in the Sherman studio with an adjoining auditorium from which up to 100 visitors could watch. The cast consisted of nearly 30 performers by 1928.

One of the early musicians who gained popularity largely through the Barn Dance (contrasted with Hay, Ford, and Glenn who had other programs) was a folk singer named Bradley Kincaid. Kincaid was a student in Chicago during 1926 when a classmate told WLS about this "hillbilly from Kentucky" who knew folk songs. At the urging of WLS, Kincaid borrowed a guitar, practiced a few ballads he had learned from his parents, and sang them on a 15-minute program. Response from listeners resulted in an invitation for Kincaid to be a regular on the Barn Dance. His tenor voice and "houn' dawg" guitar introduced many midwesterners to the wealth of southern folk ballads before he left WLS in January, 1931, to join WLW, Cincinnati. He felt that his popularity stemmed from the fact that he sang every word so that the listener could understand it.

Kincaid illustrates the surprise which most performers of the show felt when they first became aware of their popularity. Dave Thompson reported that Kincaid's first booking was at a theater in Peoria. When it was announced on the air, the young singer received a letter from a woman of that city who had been writing

[17] Asbel, p. 25.

him long, affectionate letters which he refused to read. Kincaid turned the letter over to Thompson who summarized its passionate essence as being ". . . now at last we can be together." That news nearly caused Kincaid to cancel the engagement, but instead he prevailed upon Thompson to go along and make sure he was not compromised in any manner.

The motion picture was still playing when the two men approached the theater in which Kincaid was to perform, but they saw a city policeman attending to a double line of people extending for more than a block. As Kincaid crossed the street he asked what the line was for and was slow to accept Thompson's suggestion that the people were there because they wanted to see him perform. Kincaid remained doubtful until he approached some of the standers and heard them explain that they were waiting to see and hear Bradley Kincaid, the mountain ballad singer from WLS. Thompson reported that an impressed singer performed well that night and even escaped his passionate admirer.

Thousands of aspiring guitar players began to dream about becoming good enough for a chance to play on the Barn Dance, so Kincaid met the demand for words and tunes to folk songs by publishing a songbook entitled "Bradley Kincaid's Mountain Ballads." By 1931 he had sold more than 100,000 copies at 50¢ each. He and his wife left WLS with twin daughters, a new Packard, more than $10,000 in the bank, and a decision to make a career in radio rather than the vocation in the Young Men's Christian Association for which he had studied.

Strange names became common in households of the midwest after 1924, names like Pie Plant Pete, Dynamite Jim, Arkie the Arkansas Woodchopper, and Walter Peterson, the Kentucky Wonder Bean. Harold Safford took the name Pie Plant Pete out of a Sears catalog and pinned it on a performer named Claud Moye from southern Illinois. Moye was one of a number of early stars on the Barn Dance whose equipment included a guitar plus a harmonica mounted on his chest. These were not merely guitars and harmonicas, however; Pete's combination was a "two-cylinder cob crusher." His favorite song was called, "It Can't Be Done."

> Now you might find a beggar who never does beg,
> You might raise a chicken without laying an egg,
> But you can't raise a cow from the calf of your leg,
> Don't try it, it can't be done.

You can't sail a ship without getting aboard.
Don't try it, it can't be done.
You can't take the rattle all out of a Ford,
Don't try it, it can't be done.
Now you might find a barber who could tell you just how
To get a good shave from the blade of a plow,
But you can't get milk from a prohibition cow,
Don't try it, it can't be done.[18]

Because speed and loudness were specialties of Pie Plant Pete, engineers needed a tighter grip on their control knobs when Pete approached the microphone. Listeners marveled at how he could play his guitar at lightning speed, sing a verse, switch to the harmonica, and never miss a beat.

Similarly, Dynamite Jim (a boy from Indiana named Harry Campbell) and the Kentucky Wonder Bean (Walter Peterson) stressed explosive country music. Instead of a "cob-crusher," Peterson used a "double-barreled shotgun" during his five years on the Barn Dance, and Campbell featured a "cap and fuse."

Other unlikely noises came from one of radio's early sound effects men, Tom Corwine. Corwine was reputed to have travelled Chautauqua with William J. Bryan, William H. Taft, and Theodore Roosevelt. His specialty was imitation and for 25 years he pleased audiences of the Barn Dance with sounds of almost every kind of animal. Corwine remained a WLS trouper until October, 1952, when he died at the age of 83.

Several comedy teams worked on the early Barn Dances, often combining music with comedy. One of these teams included Ralph Emerson, veteran organist with the station, and Hal O'Halloran, master of ceremonies. They had a comedy act which included a small, suitcase type of "haywire" organ that they could collapse at inopportune times during a routine. Emerson would start a tantrum, scolding and fussing, and O'Halloran would admonish him with advice that became a byword among listeners: "Don't lose your temper. Nobody else wants it." [19]

Hiram and Henry, another favorite team around 1930, specialized in a portrayal of Judge Hiram Higsby and Postmaster Henry Hornsbuckle, proprietors of a mythical Oatesville General Store (telephone: two longs and two shorts). At breakfast time each day they went through adventures scripted by Walter "Hank" Richards,

[18] Taken from verses published in the *WLS Family Album*, 1930, p. 46.
[19] Dave O. Thompson, unpublished memoirs, p. 132.

originator of Oatesville, who was a WLS writer-announcer. Merle
Housh was Henry and Trulan Wilder was Hiram in these frenzied
sketches into which they put great energy. When the Barn Dance
made its second major personal appearance before some 10,000
spectators at the International Amphitheater in November, 1930,
Hiram and Hank entered the arena riding mules. The plan called
for them to ride the mules around as a clown act. Hiram passed out
from exhaustion near the end of the program and had to be carried
from the ring, while the audience applauded it all as part of the
act.

Hiram and Henry also gained special note a few years later
when they were entertaining passengers on a trip across Lake
Michigan by steamship for one of the *Prairie Farmer*–WLS Family
Picnics. No one thought much about the rather high and rolling
waves until Hiram suddenly turned white and headed for the rail-
ing during one of their numbers. Henry finished as a solo artist.

One of Butler's favorite groups on the Barn Dance was a quar-
tette called the Maple City Four. The members had come to WLS
in about 1926 from LaPorte (The Maple City), Indiana. They
specialized in barbershop harmony, but clowned with novelty songs
and minstrel skits. One oddity was a homemade contraption something like a bagpipe which produced what became popular as the
"showerbath wheeze." They also had an act in which one member
lost his pants while their washboard orchestra was playing. Butler
allowed the act, but that was as far as he would go in permitting
any blue notes on the Barn Dance, and he insisted that the quar-
tette sing "The Old Rugged Cross" as a sort of atonement for their
riotous act.

Hymns became a traditional part of the Barn Dance early in the
series. One night Ford and Glenn decided to slip a couple of hymns
into the middle of the program, despite a fear of Edgar Bill that
they might slow up the pace. Response from listeners showed that
hymn time was one of the highlights of each program.

Two other comedy teams were among many which whisked
briefly before the microphones of WLS. One was a harmony team
on WLS every Friday night for a while in the late 1920's, "singing
and doing some puny patter." [20] Its members were Charles J.
Correll and Freeman F. Gosden. Glenn Rowell explained: "When
Ford and I came back from vacation, they were doing a strip show

[20] Glenn Rowell, "Glenn Rowell Recalls Early Days," undated manuscript.

on WGN calling themselves 'Sam and Henry.' Then later when
WGN objected to them plugging some personal appearances . . .
they left WGN and started the following week as 'Amos 'n Andy'
doing the same characters. The rest is history." [21]

A second team was known as the Smith Family on WLS in 1927
and featured Marian and Jim Jordan, known nationwide later as
Fibber McGee and Molly.[22] They later attracted from WLS a staff
member named Harlow Wilcox who became their announcer.

Men made up most of the cast of early Barn Dances. A photograph of the cast in 1928 showed only four women in the group
of 28, but one of them outlasted all of the men. She was Grace
Wilson, the former vaudeville trouper whose song, "Bringing Home
the Bacon," had greeted listeners on the station's first test program.
Announcers of the Barn Dance always introduced her as "the girl
with a million friends," but neither they nor the series of *WLS
Family Albums* which featured her between 1930 and 1957 ever
explained her background. Her specialties were blues and sentimental tunes.

Another pioneer on the Barn Dance was a Missourian named
Luther Ossenbrink who called himself Arkie the Arkansas Woodchopper when he arrived at WLS in mid-1929, after getting a start
on Sears programs at KMBC, Kansas City. Good nature and a
wide range of musical skills were his chief assets, for his voice was
somewhat raspy. Friendly hecklers accused him of having never
sung on key, but he could call square dances and play the guitar,
fiddle, or banjo. Probably best of all, he could laugh. Fellow performers found they could break him up while he was singing, and
listeners became accustomed to hearing him burst out laughing in
the middle of a song. The Maple City Four might be down on
hands and knees like a drove of pigs with Ralph Emerson waving
his arms and chasing them in front of Arkie. Some of the girls might
be removing his boots and tickling his feet or wrapping his head
with gauze while he tried to sing. "Let's fix Arkie" became a favorite
slogan of the Barn Dance gang as it stretched its imagination for
new ways to heckle him while he sang his favorite song, "A Dollar
Down and a Dollar a Week." His laugh had an infectious quality

[21] Rowell.
[22] George C. Biggar, "Now WLS Is Grown Up—We're 25 Years Old,"
Prairie Farmer, 121 (May 7, 1949), 40; Jack Holden, "Many WLS Artists
Have Made Movies in Hollywood," *Prairie Farmer*, 116 (May 13, 1944), 22.

that inspired loyalty—even fan clubs—during a tenure on the Barn Dance that is approaching 40 years.

Except for the hymns, every part of the Barn Dance was devoted to fun, taking people's minds off their worries for several hours every Saturday evening. Soon it became a regular part of the weekly routine for farm families and others.

On Saturdays, when supper's through, and all the chores are done,
Dad says, "Turn on the radio, Mom, it sure is fun
To listen to that Hayloft Gang, as they go on the air."
And to our faithful radio set, he drags his rockin' chair;
I sit and knit, or hold the youngest baby to my breast,
The other young'uns long ago have settled down to rest.
Dad lights his pipe and turns the knobs and gets her set just so,
And then leans back, contented like, there in the lamplight's glow.
You-all can have your orchestras, 'n jazz in minor key,
But Brad Kincaid's Houn'-Dawg Guitar's Grand Opera for me.
And me, although I like the fun, and think the singing's fine,
I get a lump here in my throat, turning back ten years of time.
When Dad would crank the flivver, and through a foot of snow,
Down to the old red schoolhouse, we'd jolt six miles or so;
Where Saturdays at eight P.M., from all the country round
From babies to granddaddies, all the ranch folk could be found.
And after Literary, I remember yet, the thrill
When Dad asked "for the pleasure" of the first quadrille.
The music of the fiddles, the banjos ringing sweet,
As he swung me on the corners, and most nigh off my feet.
And how he drove the flivver home, one-handed through the snow,
For his other arm was round my waist—yes Dad was my first beau.[23]

In the days of radio receivers with headsets, more than one farm family spent Saturday evenings lying on the floor of the living room around a set of headphones which rested in a dishpan so that all could hear the Barn Dance. The growing popularity of country music led John Turnipseed to observe in *Prairie Farmer*: "Speeches are out of date. . . . In these days folks that want to appear before the public and git away with it has got to learn to sing or play a steel guitar."[24]

25-year Run at the Eighth Street Theater

When *Prairie Farmer* took ownership of WLS, it found that re-

[23] Evelyn Calhoon, "Turning Back the Years of Time," *WLS Family Album*, 1931, p. 4.
[24] *Prairie Farmer*, 101 (April 27, 1929), 6.

quests for tickets to the Barn Dance were being filled seven months in advance and performers had many more requests for appearances than they could meet. Another sign of popularity appeared on October 25, 1930, when nearly 20,000 fans from Chicago and a dozen states came to see a broadcast of the Barn Dance from the International Amphitheater; 10,000 others who came were turned away for lack of space. Officials of the Union Stock Yards termed it the biggest crowd which had ever assembled at the stockyards for any event.[25]

Crowds followed the program from the Sherman Hotel with its small 100-seat theater to the new studios in the Prairie Farmer Building, which still could not handle them. In 1931 Glenn Snyder and Earl Kurtze of WLS Artists, Inc., met to discuss ways by which the National Barn Dance might become a stage show with paid admission. Their search for a theater which would accept the show at a price they could afford ended at one of the city's "jinx houses." It was the Eighth Street Theater, located on the south edge of Chicago's Loop at Eighth Street and Wabash Avenue. The theater first opened in 1908 as the Garden Theater and later became the American Music Hall. Snyder contracted to put the Barn Dance into the Eighth Street Theater for two weeks during which the owners would get 60 per cent of the proceeds, WLS 40 per cent.[26]

Snyder and some of the talent went to the theater early on the afternoon of March 19, 1932, the date of the first performance there. Already, several persons from downstate Illinois were waiting to get in and by the time the theater opened Wabash Avenue was clogged with people. The theater seated 1,200 persons who filled it twice, first for a performance from 7 to 9:30 and then for the final performance from 9:45 to midnight. Adults paid 50 cents and children 25 cents during the first few months, after which the cost of tickets rose to 75 cents and 35 cents.

What the managers of WLS thought might be a fast-fading curiosity actually grew steadily through the years. Table 15 shows cumulative attendance through August 31, 1957, when high costs for talent forced the Barn Dance to close the doors of what was by then its own Eighth Street Theater. During more than 25 years, few seats were empty at either performance. Crowds even filled the orchestra pit, and tickets were sold out five to eight weeks in

[25] *Prairie Farmer,* 102 (November 8, 1930), 18.
[26] Glenn Snyder, personal interview, June 15, 1967.

TABLE 15. CUMULATIVE ATTENDANCE AT EIGHTH STREET THEATER PER-
FORMANCES OF THE WLS NATIONAL BARN DANCE, MARCH 19, 1932, THROUGH
AUGUST 31, 1957

Date	Cumulative Attendance Record
January, 1933	100,000 paid admission since March 19, 1932
December, 1934	304,000 paid admission to date
Early 1937	600,000th paid visitor honored
1939	800,000th paid visitor honored
October, 1940	900,000th paid visitor honored
November, 1941	1,000,000th paid visitor honored
December, 1942	1,107,000 paid admission
July, 1946	1,500,000th paid visitor honored
1950	2,000,000th paid visitor honored
September, 1955	2,500,000th paid visitor honored
August, 1957	2,617,000 paid admission through August 31, final performance in the Eighth Street Theater

SOURCES: Harry Steele, "Swing Your Partners," *The Chicago Visitor*, 5 (January, 1933),
34; *WLS Family Albums* for 1935, 1937, 1938, 1940, 1941, 1942, 1943, 1951, 1956;
Prairie Farmer-WLS Round-Up, 10 (August, 1957), 9; *Prairie Farmer*, 118 (August 3,
1946), 28.

advance. The only Saturday nights that the theater was dark were
those during which the Barn Dance entertained at special events
such as state fairs in Illinois, Wisconsin, and Indiana. However,
the Chicago Civic Theater housed the Barn Dance from September,
1942, to September, 1943, when the U.S. Army took over the Eighth
Street Theater.

Its popularity became a puzzle to show business, which watched
a run in live theater that seemed to have no end. Every Saturday
evening Wabash Avenue had a half-block line of patrons carefully
guarding their places. Bernard Asbel commented in 1954:

After 26 years, the theater management still can't convince the customers they can go somewhere and relax, that every ticket represents
a reserved seat. . . . Often at 5 or 6 in the afternoon a carload of people
will show up for admittance and present tickets for the 10 o'clock show.
When "Tim" Timpone, the theater manager, informs them that they
can't get in until after 9:30, the head of the family exclaims, "Nine-
thirty! But we just drove up from below Springfield. What'll we do?"
Obviously, they came with no other plans. Tim, in the neighborly
fashion he's acquired for Saturday nights, suggests, "There's some nice
soft seats down in the lobby of the Conrad Hilton Hotel. Why don't you

sit and visit a while?" It's a solution that's usually quite satisfactory to the customer, if not to the Hilton management.[27]

Who were these 2,617,000 people who paid to see the WLS National Barn Dance in its hayloft on Eighth Street? Snyder termed them "common people of all kinds—city people, country people, all kinds of people who work for a living." [28] Between 50 and 60 per cent were from outside of Chicago. One survey in the early 1950's showed 122 occupations represented by patrons.

Development of National Stars

From the beginning of radio, stations had been intent upon attracting big-name stars to the microphones. However, the idea of putting radio personalities upon the public stage was a new twist, the effect of which was to make WLS a spawning ground for many performers who gained national recognition. This was especially true after NBC began broadcasting part of the National Barn Dance. As early as May, 1932, NBC was picking up the last half-hour of the program at the Eighth Street Theater.[29] A year later one of the sponsors of the Barn Dance, Dr. Miles Laboratories, used WLS with such success that it decided to use the Barn Dance as a vehicle for national advertising of its product, Alka-Seltzer. On September 30, 1933, 18 stations of NBC Blue aired the first Miles-sponsored broadcast on a late evening pickup which was not truly national because the stations were all from Omaha eastward. A year later, 30 stations from coast to coast were carrying the show, and at an earlier time—8:30 in the midwest. Sponsorship by Miles continued 13 years, until 1946. ABC-TV televised the Barn Dance for 39 weeks beginning in February, 1949.

Between 70 and 100 performers appeared in each program after 1933 and the names of many became common in homes across the country. Two performers who came to the Barn Dance in the early 1930's were Gene Autry and Smiley Burnette. Autry appeared on WLS starting in 1930 as the Oklahoma Yodeling Cowboy, although he was employed by Sears and the American Record Corporation rather than the station.[30] His favorite song, "Silver Haired Daddy of Mine," soon was a favorite among listeners, and the *WLS Fam-*

[27] Asbel, pp. 20-21.
[28] Asbel, p. 21.
[29] *Prairie Farmer*, 104 (May 14, 1932), 18.
[30] Anna Rothe, ed., *Current Biography* (New York: H. W. Wilson Co., 1948), p. 24.

ily Album of 1933 observed that "no program with Gene Autry is quite complete until he sings it."[31] In those days WLS could hire the smooth-singing cowboy for $35 a week. Not many years later, as the nation's number one cowboy, he could not afford to make an appearance with the Barn Dance at a state fair for $1,500 plus traveling expenses. However, he made other guest appearances in the hayloft which he had frequented for between three and four years. Burnette, known for many years as "Frog" in western movies and unique for his turned-up western hat, made his first appearance on WLS with Autry.

Another regular in 1933 was a youngster of about 13 who appeared on the Barn Dance as the Little Cowboy. His name was George Goebel and his mother brought him to the theater for his performance which earned him about $5. He had a clear soprano voice, and WLS proudly adopted him because he enjoyed singing cowboy ballads while wearing a five-gallon hat and strumming a ukelele that almost dwarfed him. His early appearances were made possible by the fact that the ukelele was not a union instrument, so he did not have to pay union dues or work for scale. A change of voice in 1935 made staff members uneasy about calling him Georgie any more and killed his role as a soprano. By 1940 Goebel had his own touring group called Georgie Goebel's Barn Dance Band and when World War II came, listeners heard him sworn into the Army Air Corps during one of the programs in the hayloft which had given him his first years of experience in show business. The WLS "family" always felt it had helped raise him.

Red Foley made his first appearance on the Barn Dance in March, 1931. The young, curly-haired Kentuckian played with the Cumberland Ridge Runners and performed as Burrhead, the beau of a bashful, giggling, bedimpled new starlet named Lulu Belle. He continued at WLS for several years, then went on his own to Cincinnati, starring on NBC Avalon Time and the Plantation Party on Mutual. In March, 1940, he returned to WLS where he performed during the war years.

Meanwhile, Lulu Belle (whom spectators found much prettier than her name implied) began to bounce her way to nationwide popularity as a gum-chewing, little-girl upstart who wore an old-fashioned frock, high-top shoes, and a big bow in her hair. Boy friends always fit into her routine—first Red Foley, then a tall,

[31] *WLS Family Album*, 1933, p. 33.

lean, and shy banjo picker named Skyland Scotty Wiseman who
joined the Barn Dance in 1933. "Madam, I've Come to Marry You"
was the first song which Lulu Belle and Scotty sang together; in
December, 1934, he did marry her. They feared that marriage would
end their sweetheart routine on the Barn Dance, but listeners
seemed to like the team even more. Thousands of gifts arrived after
they informed audiences by song that "Somebody's Coming To
Our House." Lulu Belle and Scotty were regulars on the Barn
Dance for a quarter-century and in 1936 she was voted National
Radio Queen. He wrote a number of songs, the most popular of
which was "Have I Told You Lately That I Love You?"

Pat Buttram came to WLS in 1934 full of tall tales about his
kinfolk in Alabama. Another of his early specialties on WLS was
a Buttram Radio School for New Beginners Just Starting. Barn
Dance audiences welcomed his dry humor and on-stage chicanery.
One of his self-appointed duties was to step to the front of the
stage, snap his suspenders, and assure audiences, "You can dance
in the aisles or tear up the place if you want to. It don't belong to
us." *WLS Family Albums* showed him as a regular on WLS between
1934 and 1942.

A complete review of stars on the National Barn Dance is necessarily beyond the scope of this effort. However, millions of radio
listeners enjoyed other stars of the Barn Dance such as:

Uncle Ezra, the Old Jumpin' Jenny Wren who owned Station
E-Z-R-A, "a powerful little five-watter down in Rosedale," and who
invariably rushed in late asking, "Hain't missed nothin' have I?"

Patsy Montana and the Prairie Ramblers, chosen as one of the
three most popular acts on WLS in the mid-1930's.

Hoosier Hot Shots, whose tooting, scraping, and pounding on a
weird menagerie of instruments created a unique and popular
musical sound. Their specialty was what they called the "Zither,"
a glorified washboard adorned with bells, horns, and other gadgets.
Paul Trietsch (of "Are you ready, Hezzie?" fame) played it with
thimbles on his fingers.

Rex Allen, a regular on WLS for several years after 1945. Soon he
began to make movies and gained billing as "King of the Cowboys."

Homer and Jethro, musical satirists who gave a backwoods twist
to popular tunes (for example, "How Much Is That Houn' Dawg
in the Winder?"). Audiences of the Barn Dance watched this pair
from Hoot 'n Holler, Tennessee, starting in about 1951.

The Cumberland Ridge Runners, first authentic southern playing-singing act on WLS. They appeared during the 1930's.

Henry Burr, an early recording star known as the dean of the ballad singers. He made his comeback on WLS in 1934 and remained until 1941.

Hoosier Sod Busters, considered the outstanding harmonica act in the history of the Barn Dance.

Louise Massey and the Westerners, a family group from New Mexico which got its start in Chautauqua and lyceum appearances. The group appeared regularly on WLS in the mid-1930's and again in the early 1940's.

Max Terhune, known to fans as the Hoosier Mimic. During his stay between 1931 and 1935, he supplied audiences with any sound, from that of a cat and dog fight to a street car on an icy track. He later appeared in several movies and created voices for Walt Disney's cartoons.

Donald "Red" Blanchard, who appeared on Barn Dances of the early 1930's as one of Rube Tronson's Texas Cowboys, but who came into his own after World War II as a quick-witted spinner of yarns and a congenial master of ceremonies.

Dolph Hewitt, a yodeller and singer whose robust strains made believable the claims by press releases that he learned to sing while clearing timber. He first joined the Barn Dance after his release from wartime duty in the Marines and helped lead it to WGN after the new owners of WLS changed to a music-news format in 1960.

Ted Morse, talented 250- to 300-pound trumpet player who pleased audiences by donning a ruffled, silken baby dress and bonnet to portray Little Genevieve, the Barn Dance's cute, teddybear-toting crybaby of the 1940's.

Holly Swanson, a 5-foot 22-inch stringbean whose wide-eyed role as Cousin Tilford made him a striking partner for the roly-poly Morse. They teamed up with another musician named Jimmie James for a comedy instrumental group known as the Virginia Hams.

Bob Atcher, another star of the 1950's, who came to WLS with more than 300 recordings to his credit. The handsome singer was known for his pleasing voice and resplendent wardrobe which reportedly included about 100 ornate shirts costing some $250 each. A $25,000 palomino and handmade silvermounted saddle completed his ensemble.

Captain Stubby and the Buccaneers, a versatile group of five, who performed on WLS during the 1950's and then moved with the Barn Dance to WGN.

Listeners extended to the performers of WLS a loyalty which bordered on fanaticism. One listener in Iowa kept track of every song she ever heard Louise Massey and the Westerners sing: 3,292 songs in person and 501 recordings. Another listener in Kentucky tallied the 2,664 songs that she had heard Mac and Bob sing.

By one count in 1944, nearly 30 performers from the WLS National Barn Dance had been to Hollywood to take part in movies, a trend which Burridge Butler watched with increasing concern.

Butler and the Barn Dance

In evaluating the ways in which Butler influenced the Barn Dance, one needs to keep several points in mind: (1) the program was well established when he bought WLS, (2) he was more than 65 years old when the Barn Dance went into its period of greatest growth, (3) he and Mrs. Butler were spending half of each year away from Chicago by that time, and (4) he had—in turn—two station managers who ran their operations largely autonomously. Edgar Bill and Glenn Snyder exercised more freedom on WLS than staff members on *Prairie Farmer,* probably for two reasons. First, Butler likely understood his limited prowess in this new medium, especially the entertainment part which made up half of the total programming time of WLS. Publishing was his first love and radio had less call for his 40 years of experience with printer's ink. As long as WLS kept showing notable profits, Butler was not inclined to interfere in the management of it.

Second, Bill and Snyder were naturally independent and they rejected the type of paternalism that many other employees accepted. Butler once tried to steer Bill into a clothing store to buy the young station manager a new suit, but earned only a rebuke. "Mr. Butler, I do not want you to buy my clothes. I want you to pay me enough money so that I can buy the kind of clothes that the job I am doing for you demands that I wear." [32] Snyder, just as short as Bill, also was as independent, and differences often arose between a fiery Snyder and a Butler who hated for anyone to argue with him. The two men molded a mutual understanding that

[32] Thompson, p. 75.

was sometimes strange to observe. One of the favorite stories among executives at WLS was about an especially turbulent session between Butler and his station manager. As the story goes, their heated exchanges reached a fever pitch, for neither man would give in. Finally, Snyder announced that he was quitting WLS. Butler sealed the pronouncement by firing Snyder, who returned to his office on the third floor. Shortly thereafter, George Cook called Snyder and asked, "What happened between you and Mr. Butler? He just came here and said, 'Snyder is sure cranky today'."

The result of these forces was that staff members on WLS knew Butler as a myth as much as a man. During visits to the third floor he sometimes stepped up to an employee and asked, "What do *you* do here?" More often than not, after Butler left, the surprised worker had to ask others who he was.

This is not to suggest that Butler lacked influence either on the Barn Dance or around WLS. He felt strongly about the Barn Dance, and his influence on it—often indirect—is clearly discernible. Butler conceived of the National Barn Dance as a big, wholesome country party. His own regular visits to the Eighth Street Theater pleased him; he liked to laugh during the program and go backstage to greet his "boys and girls." It was the kind of honest, down-to-earth fun that fit Butler's view of life in the country, a view which most owners of stations rejected as out of date.

One outgrowth of Butler's view was that artists of WLS learned that they should act naturally and "ring true." WLS studiously avoided becoming what Snyder termed "hungry hillbilly," because neither Butler nor his associates wanted the toothy, slicked-up aura which characterized many hillbilly bands of the tavern trade. They wanted a re-enactment of something natural to the midwest. Whenever Butler saw one of his performers stride on stage in an expensive cowboy outfit, he quickly ordered the star to get rid of the "fancy get-up" and wear overalls and the calico shirt which Butler considered more in keeping with a barn dance.[33]

If Butler noticed a female performer doing little dances with a fringed cowgirl skirt two or three inches above the knee, he would protest: "That isn't us. That's Hollywood. People didn't drive hundreds of miles to see a girlie show. They came to see their friends on WLS, friends they have faith in and think are nice people."[34]

[33] Unpublished manuscript by George Biggar, February, 1967.
[34] Bill Lester, personal interview, December 28, 1966.

"Hollywood," "show business," and "show people" were swear terms
in Butler's vocabulary, epithets which he reserved for moments of
coldest contempt.

Along with simple garb, Butler also favored simple music on
WLS and the Barn Dance. His stated policy was that "we want
music that our listeners would like to play or sing for themselves." [35]
Kate Smith was one of his favorites. In fact, when he first heard
her—without knowing who she was—he got in touch with Snyder
and said she should be on the staff of WLS. His highest compliment
for a vocalist was, "She (or He) sure gets the moon over the mountain."

Disapproval of musical style sometimes brought even more ex-
pressive reactions. One afternoon at the Prairie Farmer Building he
paused attentively to hear a girls' trio. The girls were singing a
modern, unfamiliar tune with little melody, and Butler startled
them by bursting into the studio, stepping to the microphone, and
instructing them to replace such songs with something like "My
Old Kentucky Home" that everyone could enjoy.

Butler also wanted the Barn Dance to be lively and emphasized
the point one evening by grabbing a chair and throwing it across
the stage to demonstrate that things were too quiet.

As artists on WLS became national stars, Butler grew more and
more fearful that the Barn Dance was losing the friendliness, sincerity, and simplicity of a midwestern rural barn dance or barn-
warming. He confided in 1943, "The Barn Dance is my adopted
baby and I love it, but it is being buffeted around by 'show people'
. . . and . . . is dominated too much by the vaudeville and the commercial spirit." [36]

The strength of his philosophy perhaps contributed to a stability
in staff and a sense of camaraderie which was noticeable. For
some performers the Barn Dance was only a part-time job, yet the
family spirit that characterized every latter-day enterprise under
Butler grew among them. They considered themselves "a happy
crew," partly because some members were as entertaining off stage
as on, and sometimes because tight schedules created intense re-
lationships. A performer might be at WLS for the first three days
of the week, taking part in programs throughout the day. Then he
or she might join a group of perhaps 20 others for local appear-

[35] *WLS Family Album,* 1935, p. 10.
[36] Butler to George Biggar, March 1, 1943.

Good Times in Hard Times   231

ances booked by WLS Artists, Inc., which Butler had established
to help supplement their incomes. On Saturday they would return
to Chicago for the Barn Dance and the start of another busy week.

Experiences crowded in, large and small, and left lasting impres-
sions with those who took part. Like having someone stay alert to
keep George Goebel awake at the wheel during long drives at
night. Like the time that one theater in southern Michigan scheduled all the cast to dress in a single coal bin. Like many other times
under poor dressing conditions when Arkie would assign girls to
one side, boys to another, then stand in the middle with a stern
warning and a watchful eye toward the males.

Like one night at the Illinois State Fair of 1936 when a 50-mile-
an-hour gale and rainstorm struck while the Barn Dance was on
the air, coast to coast. They piled bales of straw around the small
makeshift control booth to keep it from blowing away, and one staff
member—Al Boyd—ran into an elephant as he dashed through rain
and darkness.

Like during the performance a year earlier at the Illinois State
Fair when Lulu Belle almost wrecked the show by rushing up and
kissing Governor Henry Horner at the close of his brief speech.

Like the five special wartime Barn Dances at Normal, Danville,
Decatur, Mt. Morris, and Ottawa for which people "paid" 3,500,000
pounds of scrap metal and rubber as admission.

Like looking out upon 110,000 faces at the 1935 National Corn
Husking Contest in Indiana.

Most of these experiences were heady, for applause showered
upon the Barn Dance from a public which welcomed a chance to
laugh. The Barn Dance was ideal for its times, not only because
it brought a song and joke but also because its genuine rural flavor
was in lock-step with a fast-urbanizing America's longing glance
backward at an agrarian heritage. A lack of polish and refinement
probably was its greatest strength, not for the sake of those traits
but for the genuineness which they signalled. An obituary in the
Peoria Star caught this idea: "Burridge Butler created at WLS a
unique style of broadcasting which, if not great art, is at least
authentic art."[37] In truth, Butler did not create the style, but he
helped shape it and fought zealously to keep it authentic.

[37] *Peoria Star*, April 5, 1948.

A Third Career

CHAPTER 10

It was as regular and unfailing as the crowds in the Eighth Street Theater on Saturday night. It was something like spring fever, except that it came in the fall, in September and October when chilly, moist winds began to whip through the Loop from Lake Michigan. Employees of *Prairie Farmer* and WLS would become aware of it through rumblings from the southeastern corner of the second floor. Word would spread that the Chief was unhappy, and staff members would be called into Butler's office to explain why this project and that seemed to be faltering. Others would look up from their desks with surprise as Butler approached with instructions to discard those big stacks of papers, put their feet up on their desks, and think. His favorite plea was, "Let's start something!"

It was stir-up time, for Butler was about to leave his Chicago family for a winter in Arizona, and he always felt more comfortable if he thought he was leaving his staff on its toes. Moreover, his autocratic pride probably dictated that he emphasize his power to staff members who would be out of his direct control for six or seven months.

232

This routine—which inevitably repeated when he returned—extended for 20 years, between about 1928 and his death. At least some associates knew what Butler was doing, but the effect was always the same. Butler was so perpetually restless that even a 90-year-old farm paper had little chance to grow stale.

To Camelback

Arizona represented Butler's second retirement, this one dictated by poor health rather than by a tradition of E. W. Scripps or an internal power play. A form of arthritis had begun to bother Butler and, according to one report, his doctor told him in the late 1920's that if he moved to Arizona he might prolong his life a few months.[1] Another version was that doctors sent Butler to Arizona to die, expecting him to live only a year or two.[2] No evidence outlines the degree or nature of such a crisis, however, and he seemingly was not bedridden because in a letter of late 1942 Butler wrote that his confinement to bed was the first in 40 years.

Mrs. Butler also had a respiratory ailment which the climate of Arizona helped relieve.

They settled in Phoenix where Butler might—like the immortal bird—rise in youthful vigor from his own ashes. An estate of about one and a half acres some 10 miles northeast of downtown Phoenix gave them a view from the southern foot of Camelback Mountain in one of the city's finer residential areas. After tearing down the existing home, Butler placed himself typically in the center of a home-building project. It was an adobe-type structure of southwestern colonial style with tile floors and beam rafters. A massive iron gate from a railroad company greeted visitors at the entrance.

Casa Davenal was clearly a man's piece of work, even to the furnishings. The downstairs portion was filled with furniture that Butler had brought from Mexico—massive, crudely ornate pieces, chairs with rawhide or leather seats and buckskin binding, bright Indian rugs, blankets, pots, and baskets. A hired gardener maintained the grounds which included about a half acre of grapefruit trees. Cacti of all types surrounded the home and Butler became a devoted collector of them, gaining some respect in the southwest

---

[1] *Arizona Farmer*, 27 (April 17, 1948), 2.
[2] *Tucson Daily Citizen*, clipping from March 30, 1948.

by assembling 180 varieties before he died. One spring he reportedly returned to Chicago and announced proudly that he had found and identified a previously unrecorded variety of cactus. It had been named *Cacti Butlerii,* he explained, adding, "And it is to be spelled in italics."[3]

Phoenicians looked upon Butler as an "almost legendary Horatio Alger success myth of the middle west."[4] At noontime gatherings around the big table in the Arizona Club, local businessmen found Butler a jovial, affable cohort. They knew him as a capitalist and during the ensuing 20 years came to respect him as a shrewd businessman and humanitarian. They never considered him a leader in business or agriculture, but many knew him or knew about him.[5]

Butler and KOY, Phoenix

Gardening and home-building, mixed with periodic camping and sightseeing tours, could contain Butler for a while, but soon he began to see opportunities for profit and diversion. By the early 1930's Butler was preaching to his associates in Chicago that Arizona held the promises of an expanding frontier. One Saturday morning in the summer of 1936 he insisted to Glenn Snyder and George Cook that they should own something themselves, then told them about a station in Phoenix that might be for sale. One of two stations in the city, KOY had gone broke twice and was floundering. Only weeks earlier its antenna had even blown down.

With encouragement from Butler, the two executives drove to Phoenix and began bargaining with the owner who suffered from migraine headaches and could talk only briefly at each session. Presiding over their negotiations was the fallen antenna which still stretched over Central Avenue and rested on the top of the hotel in which they were staying. The frustrations of bargaining and temperatures of 112 degrees left them wondering if their impulse had been poorly conceived.

Butler had instructed Snyder and Cook to pay no more than $50,000 for KOY, but a deadlock led them to compromise on an option of $55,000. Butler never let his younger associates forget

[3] Dave O. Thompson, unpublished memoirs, p. 67.

[4] Emmett McLoughlin, *People's Padre* (Boston: Beacon Press, 1954), p. 112.

[5] Walter Bimson, personal interview, December 28, 1966.

that "weakness," even though he lived to see its value climb to an estimated $300,000.[6] They and other stockholders sold KOY in 1967 for more than $2 million.

Butler had talked with them about a station of their own, but he paid for it and held most of the stock as long as he lived. Furthermore, KOY became his main wintertime project, a re-creation of WLS—this time on his own and with no one making decisions without his knowledge. As he once exulted to Snyder in Chicago: "You fixed this up so I can't move anything, but out in Phoenix I can pick up a piece of board and nail it on the wall. That's mine out there. You can't interfere with it."[7]

His employees in Phoenix understood this possessive passion and realized that they were part of Butler's toy collection. KOY let him thumb his nose at the tight unions in Chicago that he felt were squeezing him. In Phoenix he did not need a dozen experts and a costly blueprint to lay out a transmitter building. He simply walked out into the 20-acre plot that he had bought on Camelback Road, traced marks here and there with his size 12 shoe, voiced orders about what should go where, and awaited the action. He could give on-air rules at KOY and expect them to be observed, rules he probably could never have enforced in Chicago.

In a sense, Phoenix saw the latter-day Butler unleashed. It saw him at some of his best and at some of his worst, because the lack of fetters and perhaps his age let him range further toward both extremes. Staff members of KOY, especially, saw the eccentric side. Butler promised to keep all employees after he bought KOY, but gradually most of them drifted away because they could not take the new and rather sharply defined rules that he enforced.

For example, Butler insisted that all announcers stand while they were on the air. If he saw a seated announcer, he would walk into the studio and jerk the chair out from under the man. So strong was his effect upon associates that if the program director was home listening at 10 P.M. and suspected that an announcer was sitting down, he drove to the station and checked.

Announcers at KOY also were not allowed to use the expression, "ladies and gentlemen." You would not walk into a friend's home and say that, Butler argued, but rather you would say "good evening," as to a friend. Rejecting a formal style which was popular

[6] *Phoenix Gazette,* clipping from April 7, 1948.
[7] Glenn Snyder, personal interview, June 15, 1967.

on the networks, Butler wanted his announcers to say, "This is the friendly station, KOY, Phoenix." Talk to *people*, he urged again and again.

One night Bill Lester, who was announcing, answered the phone and heard a voice growl, "Did you look at the moon?" Thinking it was a prank, the busy announcer answered impatiently, "No, I didn't look at the moon. Why should I look at the moon?" He learned only then that Butler was on the other end of the line, trying—in his gruff way—to suggest that the evening's beautiful blood-red moon might be of interest to listeners.[8] Butler wanted a warmth in his station that he often could not convey himself.

Even the pronunciation of the call letters and the rate of speech came under close scrutiny. He had tried without success to get announcers at WLS to pronounce "Chicago" in a certain way. He was more successful in his demand that announcers at KOY pronounce each call letter distinctly, K-O-Y. They still were doing so almost 20 years after he died. And as his hearing became poorer he became sensitive to the rate of speaking. A 19-year-old fledgling announcer once looked up from the microphone and saw Butler staring at him from the adjoining studio. The boy got more nervous and automatically talked faster, which was what bothered Butler in the first place. Butler raised his arms like a gorilla and began shouting, "Too damn fast." The frightened announcer was about to break down on the air when a bystander assured the waving owner that his message would get to the announcer.[9]

Butler was prone to enter the station at strange hours and berate associates if he found anything wrong. One night he came in and could not find the key to enter his office, a matter about which he addressed his program director, Jack Williams (later governor of Arizona), the next morning. When the station manager, William Baldwin, suggested that the office manager or custodian should deal with office keys—not the program director—Butler replied coldly that even rats in the attic were the responsibility of the program director.[10]

One Saturday evening while attending a football game Butler got chilly, called the station, and asked his program director to deliver a coat. The request meant driving from KOY to Butler's

[8] Bill Lester, personal interview, December 28, 1966.
[9] Bill Lester, personal interview, December 28, 1966.
[10] Jack Williams, personal interview, December 26, 1966.

home 10 miles away, then to the stadium, then finding Butler in
the crowd of 10,000 to 15,000 people. Williams gave up his plans
for the evening to fulfill Butler's request. The next morning Butler
called Williams to his office and offered to buy the young man a
tuxedo in return for the favor. An associate from Chicago later
suggested that Williams erred in accepting the offer, for he never
would get a raise (which was true for some time).[11]

Executives at KOY were under no set rules for office hours, but
Butler believed they should be on the job before 9 A.M. One morning—with mischief most likely on his mind—he managed to rouse
himself, eat breakfast, and have his chauffeur drive him to KOY
by 8 A.M. Employees later felt sure that he expected to find the
offices dark, then criticize others as they came in. Unfortunately for
his plan, all of the top executives were busy at their desks when
Butler climbed the stairs. Visibly disappointed, he sat in his office
a while, then left the building, never to arrive that early again.

Such incidents made staff members at KOY stand in fear of this
ogre, this immense man of unlimited power. He reacted so violently
to small matters that they shuddered to think what would happen
if they really blundered. Butler's range of emotions startled them.
He could be the jovial companion, taking a roll, buttering it carefully, but then throwing it across the dining room. He could be
the bully, intentionally jostling men on elevators and then asking:
"Aren't you going to hit me?" His explanation: "I just wanted to
see what kind of man you are." [12]

He could be the childish Butler who spit his tobacco in a corner
of the stairs, then watched for a chance to berate the custodian for
failing to remove his mess quickly. He could be the irate old man
who raised his cane as if to strike an engineer at KOY who talked
back to him.

He could be the fussy Butler who ordered a new car of a certain
color, then refused delivery because it was not the color he wanted.
He could be the agile 75-year-old who each day happily climbed a
step ladder and crawled through a second-story window to reach
his office during one of his remodeling sprees. Tobacco juice on
the stairs angered him, but he was happy when the whole studio
was in shambles with dust floating and carpenters banging.

His employees earned frugal salaries, but for years KOY had

[11] Jack Williams, personal interview, December 26, 1966.
[12] Bill Lester, personal interview, December 28, 1966.

on its payroll a man too crippled to work. Butler had brought to
Phoenix an announcer from WLS who was suffering from arthritis
and whose recovery Butler financed.

And about the time staff members concluded that the Old Man
was impatient, he would surprise them with a display of calmness.
In one instance, Butler remained unbothered when employees
from KOY smashed the fender of his car twice while returning it
from Chicago.

A legend about Butler began to form in Phoenix as it had in
Chicago, at first a legend growing out of his unusual actions.
Gradually, however, his associates at KOY began to see that the
actions themselves were not the guidelines to use in measuring
this man; rather, they needed to look at the effects of those actions.
A radio station in serious condition returned to health soon after
Butler bought it—financially and as a force in the community. Part
of the change came from Butler's efforts (through Glenn Snyder)
to get KOY on a more desirable frequency. Those efforts resulted
in a change from 1390 kilocycles to 550, which gave KOY bigger
audiences and more leverage in competing for national advertising.

Another source of success was Butler's willingness to spend
money on programming. Employees maintained that although his
salaries were minimal, he spared little money in trying to build
KOY. Butler's only requirement was that the station stay in the
black.

A renewed sense of community involvement also helped account
for the vigor of KOY after Butler bought it. He challenged his
employees at KOY to hold a mirror in front of the community and
reflect back what was happening. They should probe into the
community to determine what it needed and invest not only the
resources of KOY but also their own abilities by working personally
in local affairs. The station devoted hundreds of hours to producing
shows for wartime bond drives and sponsored a Fourth of July
celebration with admission by war bonds only. Like WLS, KOY
formed a Christmas Neighbors Club to provide wheel chairs and
other items for children in hospitals. If a family got burned out,
KOY conducted a fund-raising drive, and it once raised money to
provide a funeral for an itinerant preacher.

Other similarities between WLS and KOY included the "invited
guest" gospel which Butler preached with all the vigor he could,
even if it meant pulling chairs out from under announcers and

outlawing references to "ladies and gentlemen." KOY had a Dinnerbell program, a staff organist, and musical groups with a country
flavor similar to that of WLS. Butler printed a *KOY Family Album*
for several years and tried to build the family spirit by staging an
annual Christmas party for staff members and families.

Mrs. Butler attended the Christmas party each year, but in
Phoenix as in Chicago no one got close enough to know her as any
more than a beautiful and gracious woman. Descriptions could go
no deeper. Butler had called her his rose, which probably meant
that she was the boutonniere which he wore when he dressed up
to go out. She helped legitimize him by unspoken assurance to
doubters that a man with a wife as kind and refined as she could
not be as rough-shod as he often appeared. Poised, gracious, and
beautifully white-haired, she was the kind of woman (as one man
put it) whose picture one would put on a Mother's Day card.

"Burridge is my boy," Ina Butler would say with a laugh. Evidence suggests that her boy dominated in all outward matters.
They apparently were devoted to one another in their mutual
understanding, however, and she probably helped steady him. Her
full effect cannot be measured because his own tidal wave kept
her nearly submerged.

Covering Arizona

Butler had not owned KOY long before he also bought radio
station KTUC in Tucson. He left no statements about his reasons
for this move, but the general feeling of associates was that he
wanted to be a major force within Arizona and could not be so
with a small station located at a modest 1390 on the dial. In those
days, the areas around Phoenix and Tucson accounted for most
of the population of Arizona, so Tucson was a logical market for
Butler's second buy. He bought KTUC from the same man who
had owned KOY and—as in Phoenix—sold some of the shares to
Glenn Snyder and George Cook. Housed in a garage next to the
fire department, KTUC was even less pretentious than KOY.

Staff members of KTUC hardly knew Butler, for he came to
the station only once or twice a year. One of his managers at the
station, Lee Little, made occasional trips to Phoenix for confer-
ences, but the station manager largely arranged his own programming. Little reported being aware of only two definite interests

which Butler expressed for the station in Tucson: (1) doing things for local people and (2) promoting the state.[13] Cook and Snyder were more involved in operations of KTUC than Butler.

A direct line between Phoenix and Tucson allowed KOY and KTUC to share some programs. Another station, KSUN in Bisbee-Lowell, became part of this hook-up (although Butler held no financial interest in KSUN), and together they formed what was known as the Arizona Network. The daily Dinnerbell was among those programs which all three stations carried. At one time in the early 1940's Butler conceived of using this network to provide programs for schools in rural areas, similar to WLS School Time. He arranged air time on the stations, but teachers at the University of Arizona who were to produce the programs found that demands on their time were too great and the idea never worked out as intended.[14]

Arizona Farmer

By 1940 Butler owned not only two radio stations in Arizona but also the *Arizona Farmer,* a state farm paper similar to *Prairie Farmer.* It rounded out a combination very much like that in Illinois—on a smaller scale—except that he had worked the formula backwards, starting with a radio station rather than a farm paper.

The *Arizona Farmer* was in financial trouble and not for the first time in its turbulent 18-year life. Arizona Pima Cotton Growers in 1922 had paid original expenses of what was known as the *Associated Arizona Producer.*[15] Bankruptcy of the cooperative shifted the paper to the Salt River Valley Water Users' Association, which had sent it free to all shareholders and all members of the state Farm Bureau. Just as the publication was getting started again, the depression hit and the Association dropped its support, leaving the stranded paper in the hands of its editor, Ernie Douglas, and an advertising director named Ward Powers. Despite the depression, they managed to switch what was by then named *Arizona Farmer-Ranchman* to paid circulation, but in the late 1930's Powers sold out to an insurance man named Joseph Haldiman.

[13] Lee Little, personal interview, December 29, 1966.
[14] Jack Williams to author, March 6, 1967.
[15] Ernie Douglas, "A Brief History of *Arizona Farmer-Rancher,*" special edition of *Arizona Farmer-Ranchman,* 45 (September 3, 1966), 1.

Douglas had decided to abandon what Haldiman renamed the *Arizona Farmer* when Butler became interested in it. A weekly 15-minute farm program by Douglas over KOY gave Butler the idea of using the same approach in Arizona as in Illinois, so he initiated contact with Haldiman and bought the paper. The first issue under his ownership appeared on February 17, 1940, and Douglas returned as editor.

A lean, long-strided native of Arizona, Douglas had a writing style which ranged from withering contempt to hilarious wit, something like Clifford Gregory in his prime. Whereas Gregory had the Lazy Farmer and John Turnipseed, Douglas had Foxtail Johnson and a mythical homestead called Squawberry Flat. Like Gregory, he had a passion for bright writing. "We are easily excited by any development bearing on farming or stock-raising in the irrigated Southwest, and we try to let that excitment show through in every story," Douglas explained.[16]

A regular column, Foxtail Johnson Objects, added to the vivid personal imprint which Douglas stamped on every issue. Each column consisted of 15 or more brief homespun maxims in what Douglas called his "ditchbank English":

Skink Fluper has decided to sell his cotton farm, buy stock in a rayon mill and take it easy the rest of his life.

After a Phoenix test, Clab Huckey reports that two bandannas tight over the nose'll strain out 3% of the smog and 98% of the air.

Our state university is makin' a plumb useless study of how much water costs. Shucks! Everybody knows it costs too much to irrigate with, but for use around a moonshine still it's dirt cheap.

Bart Whepley got his name into a county seat paper last week and it was spelt right, bein' coppied off a police blotter.[17]

The *Arizona Farmer* was not making money when Butler bought it, and it had a circulation of about 12,000, mostly to members of the state Farm Bureau. A staff of five consisted of Douglas as editor and publisher, C. H. Powell as business and advertising manager, a circulation manager, an office manager, and a secretary-treasurer from Chicago.

Butler's stated intent was to buy the paper and turn it over to capable people. "Now you're on your own," he told staff members at the start, but evidence suggests that 55 years of experience in

[16] *Arizona Farmer-Ranchman,* 45 (September 3, 1966), 12.
[17] *Arizona Farmer-Ranchman,* 45 (September 3, 1966), 2-3.

publishing did not allow him to remain aloof.[18] Members of the
staff hand-delivered complimentary copies and sold subscriptions
throughout the nearby area after Butler's first edition appeared.
Paid circulation had to grow, he felt, because he wanted the paper
to move toward audited circulation. Table 16 shows that the circulation declined between 1942 (when *Arizona Farmer* first joined
the Audit Bureau of Circulations) and 1946 as the paper cleaned
up its lists, then rose to a peak of nearly 14,000 in 1949.

TABLE 16. TOTAL NET PAID CIRCULATION OF *Arizona Farmer* FOR THE FINAL
SIX MONTHS OF EACH YEAR, 1942 THROUGH 1950

Year	Total Net Circulation for Six Months Ending December 31
1942	11,472
1943	11,049
1944	9,385
1945	9,373
1946	12,455
1947	12,686
1948	13,003
1949	13,963
1950	13,684

SOURCE: *Audit Bureau of Circulations Blue Book*, publisher's statements for the years
cited.

Butler used KOY to help boost the paid circulation of *Arizona
Farmer* through promotional announcements on Dinnerbell. Conversely, a half-page advertisement promoting KOY in every issue
helped increase listenership among readers.[19] In July, 1946, the
Arizona Farmer even moved to the KOY Building from its former
offices with the Salt River Valley Water Users' Association. However keenly Douglas and Powell wanted to transform their paper
into something as ambitious as *Prairie Farmer,* their market imposed severe limits because Arizona had only a fraction of the
213,000 farmers in Illinois. Also, wartime shortages took some of
their advertisers out of the paper. After deficits in 1940, 1941, and
early 1942, the *Arizona Farmer* earned its first profit under Butler's
ownership in September, 1942.

He was pleased with progress that year, not only in finances

[18] *Arizona Farmer,* 18 (February 17, 1940), 1.
[19] Al B. Pote, personal interview, December 27, 1966.

but also in editorial work. *"Arizona Farmer* in the past year has grown in stature faster than any publication I ever knew," he observed in early 1943. "It has been raising hell in true Western style about a lot of things that ought to be corrected. . . ."[20]

His ditchbank editor probably never was aware of this confidence and pride because—like other employees—Douglas got more criticisms than compliments from Butler. "Now that's the way to write a lead," Butler would say to Douglas as he pointed at an article in *Prairie Farmer* (whose editor was getting the same treatment in reverse).[21] Such remarks offended Douglas, who took pride in his writing and had seen no signs that Butler was in any position to teach skills in it. Often the editorial suggestions which Butler offered during regular but brief visits to the paper fell on forgetful ears.

Fascination with the Past

A letter in late July, 1937, opened another facet of Butler's fast-spreading interests in Arizona. It was from Emil W. Haury, head of the anthropology department at the University of Arizona, who described to Butler a 350-piece collection of Maricopa pottery in Phoenix and asked if Butler would be willing to pay $750 to buy it for the Arizona State Museum. Butler got many requests from philanthropies in his latter years and did not reply immediately, but within a few months the two men chanced to meet and Haury restated the need. After another meeting, this time in Phoenix, Butler donated funds to buy the collection. Half of the pieces went to the Arizona State Museum and the other half to the Arizona Anthropological Association at Pueblo Grande.

This was the beginning of a 10-year personal friendship during which Butler became interested in those who had peopled the southwest in earlier centuries. What kindled his interest was the fact that pre-Columbian civilizations of the southwest were agricultural, that they irrigated and grew corn, beans, and squash. He could sense that their tilling of the soil gave them a stability not seen among nonagricultural groups, for they could store food for winter rather than roam with the seasons. As Professor Haury later observed, this was "in harmony with his deep interest in the wel-

---

[20] Memorandum from Butler to Ralph Ammon, January 25, 1943.
[21] Ernie Douglas, personal interview, December 27, 1966.

fare of the farmer today and the effects of an agricultural economy on American culture." [22]

Butler first visited a site of diggings by the University in the summer of 1938. He loved to explore ruins of the ancient Indians and was struck by the thought that man was in southern Arizona 10,000 or 15,000 years ago. "It's a lot of fun isn't it, checking up on him?" Butler once asked Haury by letter.[23] He also marvelled at the sight of a skeleton with the mark of arthritis on its spine, for here was a person from centuries past who had suffered the same miseries as he. Butler never developed any detailed understanding of what Haury and his associates were doing, but they found that he was boyishly happy in the field examining and talking about new discoveries. One of his main effects upon the researchers was to stimulate and encourage them. His face would get flushed and tears might come to his eyes during the excitement of a finding. "We needed that, too," Haury recalled. "We needed to have somebody on the outside that was interested, not just in a monetary sense but in other ways." [24]

The professor sometimes accompanied Butler's party on camping trips, and during several days at Lake Mead he and Butler had a chance to talk about the University's program for giving field training to archaeology students. Students had been getting field experience since 1915 on a mobile basis, but Haury felt the need for a permanent camp. The value of this training appealed to Butler, and he suggested on the trip back from Lake Mead that Haury draft a prospectus for such a camp. Haury did so, but World War II intervened and it was late 1944 before the matter got revived. A survey by Haury and an assistant revealed an area on the San Carlos Indian Reservation which showed promise for a long-range historical study of ruins dating perhaps before 1400.

In early 1945 Butler accompanied Haury to the site and consented to help finance what became the Point of Pines Archaeological Field School located at about 6,000 feet on the edge of a large grassland area with a forest of ponderosa pines behind it. He gave $5,000 in November, 1945, to start building. Digging began in 1946, and Butler—by then 78 years old—came up several times before

[22] John W. Holland, "Let's Start Something," unpublished eulogy of Butler, p. 63.
[23] Butler to Emil Haury, December 20, 1938.
[24] Emil Haury, personal interview, December 29, 1966.

he died, although his failing health did not allow full pleasure from his part in the project. He donated another $1,000 in 1947, and after he died Mrs Butler gave $1,500 to fulfill a verbal commitment which he had made before his death.[25]

Point of Pines Camp continued for 15 years, during which time it housed more than 300 students from 45 colleges and universities of the United States and more than a dozen other nations.[26]

Roaming the Country

Camping became one of Butler's main pleasures during the latter part of his life. As early as 1921 he and a few employees of *Prairie Farmer* would leave the office during slack summer months and travel westward. For some, such as Gregory, these trips were no vacation. He noted wryly in a diary account from the mountains of Wyoming, "We have been getting ready for a week and are about all set to start our vacation."[27] By that time they had slept among the sage brush on bumpy ground and twisted a rear axle of one car. "They say the scenery is great out here, but about all the scenery we have seen so far is the inside of a Dodge car," Gregory disclosed.

James Edwards was another apparent sufferer on that trip, for he reportedly concluded that a vacation is only another way of getting tired. Through it all, Butler assured his companions that they would adjust to the routine and served as an example by maintaining his composure through trials which included one dunking in a river and an overturned car.

Gregory and Edwards accompanied Butler on a number of such trips into the Rocky Mountains, although they did not become avid campers. C. P. Dickson refused to camp with Butler, as did Gus Holt who "did not think he would have any fun from flunkying for Mr. Butler out in the mountains and woods for . . . three weeks."[28] Butler's most regular companions were Fred Orlemann and Roy Lynnes, both of whom enjoyed the trips and accompanied Butler as long as he lived. Lynnes, a favorite who seemed to arouse Butler's fatherly concern, came to *Prairie Farmer* as an office boy

[25] "Burridge D. Butler Contributions to the University of Arizona," summary compiled by Dr. Emil Haury, December, 1966.

[26] Emil Haury, personal interview, December 29, 1966.

[27] *Prairie Farmer*, 93 (August 6, 1921), 4.

[28] Thompson, p. 66.

around 1920 and became editor of the *Poultry Supply Dealer,* a small hatchery periodical which Butler published.

During the early days of camping, their touring car was a big Buick with a fabric top and side curtains. Butler was the chief packer and they loaded it with canned goods, food, blankets, and a tent. One of the tales which returned with them concerned a sudden cloudburst which soaked everything, including labels on the cans. For the rest of the trip Butler and his partners never knew whether they would have beans or peaches until they opened the can.

His roaming grounds shifted to the southwest after the Butlers began living in Arizona. Fred Orlemann and Roy Lynnes remained his most frequent traveling companions from Chicago—supplemented by George Cook and Glenn Snyder—and he added staff members from KOY and the *Arizona Farmer* on occasion. A. A. Nichol, a faculty member of the University of Arizona, sometimes accompanied the group, and the handyman on most trips was Padraic McArdle. A used truck and the old Buick marked their regular processions into the mountains.

Native Arizonians who heard about the millionaire camper from Chicago conjured visions of Butler with expensive equipment, but they were due for bafflement because he resisted camping that way. He had what one veteran termed "the rattiest mess of equipment that I ever saw." Apparently, camping was not camping to Butler unless he could rough it. In fact, when he went to the new Point of Pines Camp in 1947 as an ailing man more than 79 years old, he rejected the use of a dormitory and running water. Instead, he insisted upon driving a half-mile away and pitching a dry camp. The old familiar double-sized folding cot supported a back which ached so badly that when mornings came one of his men had to set him up, turn him around, and help him dress.

It was the same Butler who, whenever he came upon what looked like an impassable trail, insisted on taking it. He never drove, for even in younger days he was a notoriously dangerous driver. As one staff member at WLS explained, Butler did not drive a car— he only aimed it. His driving was highly erratic and he frightened passengers by a refusal to keep his mind on the road. He would roar down the road wide open in low gear reading a newspaper which he spread out on the steering wheel. Accidents were common whenever he drove (which may explain why he was tolerant of others who banged the fenders of his car), but he never wanted Mrs. Butler to know what he had done. He would position the car so that she could not see the damage, then call someone from KOY, have him come out to Casa Davenal, pick it up, have it fixed, and return it so Mrs. Butler would not know. Men at the garage reportedly got to the point of insisting they had rolled out the fenders so many times that there was nothing left to roll out.

If Butler did not drive in any physical sense, he drove by suggestion. On camping tours he had the habit of heckling drivers. Once, as the open Buick started across a desert from Boulder Dam toward Phoenix, Butler pointed to a trail and suggested seeing where it went. The driver, Glenn Snyder, usually ignored such advice but in this case decided to follow Butler's pointing arm. The trail wound along a dry wash and started up a steep mountainside, and Butler, sitting on the outside, could look almost straight down the sheer slope. At the top he sighed in relief and promised never to request another such detour—a promise soon forgotten.[29]

Nothing looked impossible to Butler on camping trips and usually he emerged unscathed, but the exceptions were notable. For years, acquaintances in Arizona continued to tell about his return from one camping trip during the 1940's. Butler and his party were riding in his Chrysler convertible when they approached a flowing creek. Heavy rain had fallen and those in the car decided that this was the start of a flash flood. Butler settled the debate by ordering the driver, Clarence Powell, to cross, despite the concern of others. Soon they were stranded in a rising stream because the far bank had been undercut by running water and the wheels hit a solid wall. The riders got Butler out of the car and staggered to shore, losing his briefcase, while the flood crested and took his Chrysler downstream end over end.[30]

Some of his actions on camping trips showed no rationale except for the storytelling pleasure they would offer in later years. On one trip, Butler felt an urge to stop, build a fire, and boil water for tea. It was high noon under a scorching August sun, and his companions did not relish the thought of boiling water on a dusty roadside—especially with a lunchroom a half mile ahead—but they stopped and had hot tea.

[29] Glenn Snyder, personal interview, June 15, 1967.
[30] Jack Williams, personal interview, December 26, 1966; Al B. Pote, personal interview, December 27, 1966.

He liked to give instructions about how to cook, especially in the mornings. He would poke the fire with his cane, then jiggle the coffee pot as he sat with his breath steaming in the cold mountain air. One morning he was enjoying the chance to pester his companions in their efforts to fix breakfast. They were doing everything wrong. The whole camp was dirty, the coffee pot was too black, the coffee was not boiling right—it needed more egg shells in it— and so on. Butler began to ladle out the mush, but they could not find the grimy but useful rag for holding the hot handle. They ate until they got to the bottom of the mush pan, where they found their lost rag. One companion observed that Butler was quiet for a while.

Fellow campers joked about the rough-out living, but mostly in good humor, for they enjoyed it. Butler often was willing to slow the pace during tours, for he criticized those who "travel like the Irishman's flea." They would spend evenings talking around the campfire, sometimes discussing news from a newspaper which someone had obtained, playing hearts, listening to the WLS Barn Dance, or talking business. Butler was known to call Chicago from a hundred miles in the desert and ask executives to come down and join him for a discussion. They devoted part of their days to scanning the countryside for certain kinds of cactus, enjoying the sights, or taking what Butler called a "big sleep." That meant resting, hiking, shooting at targets, and generally relaxing for several days. Hunting and fishing were not major features of outings with Butler.

"I have been roaming around the country all my life," he once remarked. "I enjoy this life, and that's the reason I like to do it."[31] It made him the pioneer who took trails no one else took, camped without the fineries, and in general tried to set himself apart.

[31] F. W. Orlemann, personal interview, June 20, 1967.

Butler's Heirs

CHAPTER 11

"How I envy you with that boy." It was more than a casually courteous remark from the 50-year-old Butler to the wife of a staff member. Instead, the comment came from a man who had an immense capacity to love but no children upon which to lavish it, a man proud of the Butler name in publishing and crushed at the thought of having it vanish. Butler might have been a different person if he had had children, for perhaps they would have rechanneled his drives, calmed him or, conversely, even heightened his frustration because he was so demanding and domineering. In any case, the fathering instinct was one of the most persistent forces within him, a force which seemed to help account for much of what *Prairie Farmer*, WLS, and other enterprises did under his ownership.

Close associates confirmed that a lack of children hurt Butler deeply. One son by his second wife died at birth. Later he wanted to adopt a son, but Mrs. Butler—who could see ramifications which bothered her—would not consent.[1] Butler reportedly then visited the sister of his first wife and cried in disappointment.

[1] Davenal Hardy, personal interview, April 28, 1967.

His frustration, which probably began by 1890, made him highly emotional about the role of families. "The family is the first and greatest institution in America," Butler often said. "There is no greater calling than that of father and mother, who are bringing up fine boys and girls to be honest citizens." [2] Especially on camping trips he pondered the pleasure of having a son to replace him, apparently unmindful of the inconsistency of his views as they applied to others. Late in 1935 Butler expressed concern when Gregory indicated an interest in hiring his son, Merrill—a recent journalism school graduate, then working on a small publication in Springfield—for an editorial position on *Prairie Farmer*. "When I told you that I did not favor having Merrill come on *Prairie Farmer* I had two points in mind on which I based my objection. The first point, of course, was that I don't think that any organization should be the lodging place for young relations because nepotism is a dangerous thing in business. . . . My second point was that it would be unfair to Merrill to break into the game 'working for dad'. . . . Unless Merrill is a very exceptional boy he will develop less personally under your hand than if he was fighting his battle among strangers." [3]

Butler's fears leave open the question of how he would have handled a similar case with his own son.

Adopted Family

His response, conscious or unconscious, was to "adopt" a much larger family—all those he served and who served him. *Prairie Farmer* and WLS were part of that family. "As I look upon this work of *Prairie Farmer*, I regard it as my child," he explained to readers in 1919. "A father or mother will understand this feeling as being above all other considerations." [4] Some employees were cool to his paternalism, but in general the staff accepted the role he suggested. A birthday note to Butler from 29 office girls in 1921 illustrates that acceptance: "Your expression that we of *Prairie Farmer* are all like one big family really makes each one of us feel that she is a part of this big family, a sort of daughter as one of us

[2] John W. Holland, "Let's Start Something," unpublished eulogy of Butler, p. 48.
[3] Butler to Clifford Gregory, December 19, 1935.
[4] *Prairie Farmer*, 91 (January 11, 1919), 5.

put it. You, as head of our family, Mr. Butler, have the esteem of each one of your business daughters. . . ."[5]

The introduction to one *WLS Family Album* (a title which also testifies to the point) explained, "We often refer to our listeners and ourselves as the *Prairie Farmer*–WLS family circle." It introduced Butler as he "who sits at the head of the table."[6]

Even when Butler neared the end of his life and spent most of each year away from Chicago, the family spirit seemed to persist. He hired a new assistant publisher in late 1942 and within four months the executive was referring to the *"Prairie Farmer*–WLS family." Less than six months before Butler died the paper announced a new editor with the headline, "Paul Johnson joins *Prairie Farmer* Family."[7]

Butler explained the spirit in terms of "practical altruism which dominates every activity of *Prairie Farmer*. This has made one family of our entire organization."[8] Undoubtedly, a goal of serving readers provided part of the spirit because it enmeshed even those staff members who spurned Butler's paternal claim, but probably an even more important source was his personal need for a family relationship.

Editorial crusades under Butler suggest that in adopting *Prairie Farmer* and WLS as part of his family, he also embraced all readers and listeners. "We're one of the family in Midwest America," a booklet about WLS School Time assured in 1943. Butler probably never had quite the same personal feeling about rural people in Arizona as those in the midwest because he did not get really close to southwestern agriculture. No evidence indicates that he tried to possess Arizona or its farm people in the same sense that he championed those midwesterners who lived on 80 acres at the end of the road. Butler's closest concern in Arizona was with the staff members of KOY and the *Arizona Farmer*, some of whom he regarded with active fatherly concern.

Looking for Another Lincoln

A strong interest in young people stands as another signal of the strength of Butler's paternal drive. In fact, children may have

[5] *Prairie Farmer*, 93 (February 12, 1921), 18.
[6] *WLS Family Album*, 1933, p. 3.
[7] *Prairie Farmer*, 119 (October 11, 1947), 5.
[8] *Prairie Farmer*, 91 (January 11, 1919), p. 5.

been closer to his heart than co-workers, readers, or listeners.

"If you help a grown man you are helping one individual who is set in habits and hard to break," Butler believed. "But if you help to inspire a boy to make the most of his abilities, you may be helping thousands of people through the life of that one boy."[9] Children found him humble, kind, and generous. Among younger relatives he gained the reputation for always bringing surprises and gifts when he visited. However, Butler's main contributions to youth remained outside of the few relatives he had, and they deserve attention.

Winnie, his first wife, perhaps got him started helping children. Back in Grand Rapids she had begun a hobby of dropping every dime she got into a small barrel with the thought that the money might help some child. Butler always expected her to go through his pockets and remove the dimes; her habit became a game between them. When she died in 1904 the barrel held $500 worth of dimes, so Butler asked a friend in Grand Rapids for ideas about using it. The friend told of his own son who had died the same year and in whose memory the father had presented a box of books to the Grand Rapids Library as a portable library which sick and crippled children could use in their homes. Nothing had pleased the man's son more than illustrated picture books in color, so Butler's friend suggested using the money to buy picture books in colors for boys and girls of Grand Rapids.

That was the beginning of a Winnie Whitfield Butler Collection of Picture Books in Colors, housed in the Grand Rapids Public Library. When the $500 was gone, Butler instructed the librarian to continue buying books and send him the bill. His total donations between 1905 and 1948 are unknown, but were averaging $300 to $500 a year by 1940.[10] Three other donations resulted in a permanent fund still active in 1968.

One was a bequest of $400 from Winnie's sister, Mrs. George E. Hardy, in 1922. Butler and Hardy, having married sisters on the same day, celebrated their 10th anniversary by presenting their wives with one share each of stock in the Tin Plate Company. Mrs. Hardy's $25 share had grown to a value of $400 by 1922 when she donated it as a memorial to her sister.

[9] Holland, p. 27.
[10] Minutes of the Grand Rapids Board of Library Commissioners, November 28, 1941, p. 289.

Two other donations—$2,000 and $5,710—came in 1941 and 1943, respectively, when Butler settled the estate of his sister, Fannie, in Grand Rapids.[11] He asked that these funds become a Winnie Whitfield Butler Trust, the interest from which would provide funds for new books each year. The fund has remained intact and provides about $500 each year, mostly for Caldecott Medal picture books, each of which carries a bookplate identifying it as part of the collection.[12]

By August 1, 1943, Butler had bought 10,199 books directly and through the Trust. Total circulation of books from the collection at the main (Ryerson) library and branches amounted to 265,000, which did not include use within the libraries.[13] Figures are not available for later years. Librarian Samuel H. Ranck sometimes sent Butler copies of worn-out books from the collection to show how much the children used them. Ranck once remarked, "For many years I have always been saying in referring to this collection that I believe there is no similar amount of money expended in Grand Rapids that has given and continues to give so much joy and pleasure to so many children, a joy and pleasure of the highest character, as has developed from this collection of picture books." [14]

This was one case in which Butler specifically asked for no personal publicity.

U.S. Boys' Working Reserve

Butler's first large self-chosen youth project was during World War I when a shortage of food coupled with a shortage of labor presented farmers with a need for help. "Food will win the war!" was the battle cry from Washington, but farmers were asking how they would be able to produce that food without manpower. Early in 1917 President Woodrow Wilson issued a call for volunteer workers to go to the farms and help produce needed food for the world. Recruiting stations for farm labor appeared in towns and cities while appeals went out to men who were unfit for military duty and to boys over 14.

[11] Minutes of the Grand Rapids Board of Library Commissioners, November 28, 1941, p. 289; September 24, 1943, p. 95.
[12] Eleanor Burgess, personal interview, May 13, 1967. The fund amounted to $8,110 as of May, 1967.
[13] Minutes of the Grand Rapids Board of Library Commissioners, July 30, 1943, p. 84.
[14] Samuel H. Ranck to Butler, July 21, 1941.

The United States Boys' Working Reserve was one of the organized projects arising out of this need, a project aimed at enlisting the help of America's five million boys who were over 16 and under military age. At a national conference in early June, 1917, leaders laid out a plan for organizing by states, each state headed by a federal state director.

Butler became director for Illinois, a full-time volunteer position which he assumed on July 1 in headquarters provided by the Illinois State Council of Defense at 120 W. Adams Street. This meant an absence of more than a year from *Prairie Farmer*. During some especially busy periods of 1918 he did not appear at the office more than once every two weeks.

Butler and the other volunteer businessmen who worked with him tailored their program after a pilot study in Chicago. That project, conducted among high school boys of the city in 1917, offered credit for farm work and resulted in placing 700 boys in 29 states and three provinces of Canada.[15]

A five-point program by the Reserve consisted of enrollment, education, placement, welfare, and credits. Eighty-two of the 102 counties in Illinois set up local operating units which worked with schools, YMCA's, and other agencies. A curriculum committee prepared 22 lessons in farm crafts such as harnessing and driving horses, cultivating corn, shocking wheat, and feeding livestock. About 20,000 youths in the state studied the series of one- to six-hour lessons in place of other classwork before the work season of 1918.

Butler's big problem was getting farmers to employ boys who had volunteered and been trained, a problem which suggests that farmers were not convinced that inexperienced boys would be able to help much. He used *Prairie Farmer* to assure readers that boys from the Reserve were capable.

His final report for 1918 showed that the project had placed 21,000 boys on farms in Illinois (compared with 45,000 who volunteered and 105,000 who had been eligible to volunteer). The boys had helped produce crops worth $23,000,000 while earning $1,200,000 for themselves in wages.[16] Butler closed out his assign-

[15] Dudley Grant Hays, *To the Farms for Victory: The Campaign of the Chicago High School Boys in Food Production—1917* (Chicago: Board of Education, September, 1917), p. 55.

[16] Illinois Council of Defense, *Final Report of the State Council of Defense of Illinois, 1917-1919* (Springfield, no date), p. 211; Edward F. Dunne,

ment on July 1, 1919, with the conclusion that the boys who had taken part left a record of which they could be proud.

Butler and Blackburn College

A tall, wiry man entered Butler's office one day during 1914 and—in a clipped, quick-spoken manner—introduced himself as William Hudson, president of Blackburn College at Carlinville, Illinois. After a few minutes of cordial exchange, Butler startled the visitor by asking bluntly, "And what do you expect of me?" [17] Hudson, it turned out, had a thousand ideas, and that date marked the start of Butler's 34-year involvement with Blackburn College.

A unique self-help plan was one of two major appeals which Blackburn held for Butler. Hudson had arrived at Carlinville in 1912 with an idea that students could work their way through Blackburn by maintaining its physical plant and the daily needs of its own community. Students each worked 15 hours a week at firing furnaces, cooking and serving meals, laundering, choring on a farm which the college owned, erecting buildings, and even serving as secretaries for faculty members. Assignments came from a work committee of students. Hudson's philosophy was that self-help was more than a means by which a student could pay his way through school. He believed it was a good thing for students to work out with their hands the theories they learned in the classroom.[18]

Butler, a staunch self-helper, commended the program to readers of *Prairie Farmer* in 1919: "I have said before that if Abraham Lincoln were a poor boy in Illinois today he would find his way to Blackburn, and of that I am sure. . . . It demonstrates in its humble way what is but the beginning of the secret of character building. It teaches the purifying process of the sweat of intelligent labor and that self-help and self-reliance are the cornerstones of manhood and womanhood. And that service is the capstone of high character and the greatest thing to which we can be called." [19]

Illinois—The Heart of the Nation, II (Chicago: Lewis Publishing Co., 1933), p. 393; Ernest L. Bogart and John M. Mathews, *The Modern Commonwealth, 1893-1918,* vol. V of *The Centennial History of Illinois* (Springfield: Illinois Centennial Commission, 1920), p. 466.

[17] William H. Hudson, "The World Needs Such Men," *Prairie Farmer,* 90 (February 9, 1918), 6.

[18] Harriet Stoddard, personal interview, April 14, 1967.

[19] *Prairie Farmer,* 91 (February 8, 1919), 33.

He loved to see the students working and once advised alumni of the college, "If you want a real kick go down there and see those young men and women at work." [20] When the depression was at its worst, he commented that "it is always hard times at Blackburn, or it is never hard times—whichever way you look at it." [21]

The president of Blackburn was its second main attraction for Butler, who always respected a good salesman. Hudson was precisely that, a man who had raised the assets of Blackburn from about $100,000 in 1912 to nearly $2 million when he retired in 1945.[22] He shared with Butler a nervous energy, touchy emotions, and a bent for intuitive decisions. Butler admired what Hudson was doing, ". . . pulling his farm and his college out of the Carlinville mud with the lever of true service to God and country." [23] The admiration was mutual, for Hudson had what one member of his faculty described as a halo around money and respected those who possessed it. His contact with Butler not only served that need but also fed his flair for publicity through *Prairie Farmer* and WLS. The two outlets produced thousands of inquiries for Blackburn College starting in early 1915.[24]

In mid-1916 the college recommended to the Presbyterian Synod that Butler become a member of the board of trustees, an action which led to his joining the board on June 5, 1917.[25] He remained on the board until his death, although in late years he was not active.

Butler's strongest support for Blackburn came during the late 1920's. First, he announced on July 2, 1927, that he was offering 10 scholarships at the college. "If I can help the young men and women of the farm to grow up and become better farmers or wives —better neighbors—better morally and physically—then I have achieved something worth while," he explained.[26] Strictly speaking, these were not scholarships at first because Butler gave the money to Blackburn, which in turn loaned it to incoming students. Arthur

[20] *Blackburn College Alumni Bulletin*, 21 (November, 1927), 3.

[21] *Blackburn College Alumni Bulletin*, 25 (September, 1931), 1.

[22] *Catalogue of Blackburn College, 1967-68*, 61 (March, 1967), 13.

[23] *Prairie Farmer*, 91 (February 8, 1919), 33.

[24] See, for example, *The Blackburnian*, 63 (March 26, 1936), 1; 70 (January 17, 1948), 1; *Blackburn College Alumni Bulletin*, 23 (May, 1929), 2; 23 (September, 1929), 4; 25 (February, 1931), 2; 25 (December, 1931), 4.

[25] Minutes of the Board of Trustees, Blackburn College, for meetings of May 30, 1916, and June 5, 1917.

[26] *Prairie Farmer*, 99 (July 2, 1927), 5.

Page traveled 2,000 miles during mid-1927 interviewing 27 finalists among the 300 who applied. Each agreed to repay the $200 to Blackburn College within 10 years after graduation, with no charge for interest. Hudson and Butler apparently thought they could thereby build a permanent rotating fund, but the plan did not work out because many loans never got repaid; students were not of age when they signed. In 1967 the Burridge D. Butler Scholarship Fund contained $17,157, interest from which continued to provide scholarships each year.

After the first year, Blackburn College took over the job of choosing what it called its Butler Scholars. By 1941, the last date for which a count existed, Butler had provided loans for 78 students whose records he kept in a loose-leaf notebook which he often scanned with pleasure. "I'm not interested in big granite tombstones for they are often but the expression of post-mortem vanity and a waste of money. . . . I am building my monument in the lives of young men and women who might be denied a chance for an education, except for the little help I am able to give them." [27]

Even so, Butler's most visible contribution to Blackburn proved to be a monument of brick and stone. It began after fire destroyed "Old Main" at the college just before classes began in the fall of 1927. Trustees arranged temporary space (four Pullman railroad cars and two portable buildings) while President Hudson started a drive for $200,000 to replace the burned building and provide a new dormitory for men. *Prairie Farmer* helped promote the campaign, but of greater impact was an offer from Butler to contribute $50,000 after it reached the half-way mark. The result was a new Burridge D. Butler Hall, housing 110 men, which the college dedicated October 6, 1928. Built of red brick and trimmed with Indiana limestone, it cost $73,000 "through student work and generous prices." [28] The building contained 55 rooms, a large living room with fireplace, and classrooms for the department of agriculture. Mrs. Butler used a flaming torch that evening to light a fire on the hearth, dedicating the living room to friendship. A plaque inside the main entrance honored Butler's mother and grandmother with the statement, "May those who enter here know of two noble women who exemplified the virtues of truth, courage and sympathy."

[27] Holland, p. 36.
[28] *Blackburn College Alumni Bulletin*, 22 (November, 1928), 1.

Students dedicated their yearbook, *Blackburnia,* to Butler in 1930 and featured him in their campus newspaper, *Blackburnian.* Two years later—on June 8, 1932—the college conferred upon him the honorary degree of Doctor of Law. His reported restiveness before and during the ceremony may have arisen partly from a recollection of his father's ringing denouncement of honorary titles: "Really great men do not need them and will not have them and where otherwise able men have been constrained to accept them they have thereby manifested a weakness in that direction." [29]

Observers offered several explanations for a parting between Hudson and Butler in later years. His associates in Chicago suspected that Butler tried to dictate policy at Blackburn. Faculty members felt that use of Butler Hall as a dormitory for girls during the war may have disturbed him and that he disagreed when the college shifted from a two-year to a four-year program.

Personal differences also may have cooled the relationship, for both men were strong-minded. Hudson probably was upset in 1946 when Butler began offering four $500 Ina H. Butler Citizenship Awards each year to rural girls for use in colleges of their choice. Hudson clearly was disturbed by a feeling that Butler had not lived up to his promises about the $50,000 for a new building. Butler had sold a stamp collection to provide part of the money, then added to the total from other sources, according to Mrs. Butler.[30] However, during a series of exchanges with Mrs. Butler after the death of her husband, Hudson insisted that an unpaid balance of $31,000 remained.[31] In turn, she was certain that Butler had paid in full. Apparently neither could produce evidence to settle the matter, and both parties ended the relationship disgruntled, leaving some tarnish on Butler's part in promoting a self-help concept which commanded his enduring respect.

Butler's Boys in Chicago

Butler had one major lament when he completed work with the U.S. Boys' Working Reserve in 1919: the Reserve "could not help the boys who most needed help because it dared not send such

[29] T. D. Butler, "What Are Titles Worth?" *Christian Evangelist,* July 23, 1891, p. 468.
[30] Ina Butler to Robert P. Ludlum, July 6, 1953.
[31] William Hudson to Ina Butler, April 12, 1955.

boys into farm homes."[32] At that time Chicago had about 180,000 underprivileged boys. In an effort to do something for them he and three friends arranged a dinner meeting at the Blackstone Hotel on June 12, 1919, and invited 25 leading businessmen in Chicago to attend.[33] The hosts also invited two men from New York— William E. Hall and C. J. Atkinson, president and executive secretary of the Boys' Club Federation (International)—plus John H. Witter, general superintendent of the Chicago Boys' Club.

Butler had become acquainted with Hall during the two prior years, for Hall had conceived the idea of the U.S. Boys' Working Reserve. Hall and other speakers during the dinner urged businessmen to help the 66 per cent of all boys in Chicago who were "without the proper advantages which should be theirs by right of national heritage."[34] Speakers explained that such boys rarely went beyond the fourth or fifth grade and sooner or later started a record of crime.

The meeting stimulated another, this time before the public affairs committee of the Union League Club. Butler helped plan that meeting too, and he used a businessman's approach by inviting not only Hall and Atkinson but also Judge Victor P. Arnold of the Juvenile Court and Judge Daniel H. Trude of the Municipal Court.[35] They reported that 16,000 boys had appeared in their two courts during the past year and maintained that preventing crime through boys' clubs would cost far less than the courts, jails, and police forces required to correct crimes already committed.

By December, 1919, the Union League Club had formed its own boys' club in Chicago under a corporation known as the Union League Foundation for Boys' Clubs. Forty-two charter members, including Butler, paid $1,000 each to start the project. Butler also became one of ten trustees for the new Foundation.[36]

A three-story brick building known as the "Bucket of Blood" at

[32] Illinois Council of Defense, *Final Report*, p. 214.
[33] Bruce Grant, *Fight for a City* (Chicago: Rand, McNally and Co., 1955), pp. 214-215. Also, see William E. Hall, *100 Years and Millions of Boys: The Dynamic Story of the Boys' Clubs of America* (New York: Farrar, Straus & Cudahy, 1961), pp. 38-39.
[34] Grant, p. 215.
[35] Grant, p. 215.
[36] "A 35-Year Summary of the Union League Foundation for Boys' Clubs," mimeographed report, 1955, pp. 14-15.

19th and Leavitt Streets in Chicago's eleventh ward housed the first boys' club. Earlier occupants had included a saloon, a dance hall, and "other institutions of a character that contributed nothing to the making of good character." [37] Eighty thousand persons representing 22 nationalities lived within a square mile and made it one of the most congested areas of the nation.[38]

One thousand boys had joined the new club within a few weeks after it was dedicated on May 29, 1920, and the number soon doubled to more than 2,000. Two-thirds of them had never seen a circus, half had never ridden an elevated train, and many did not speak English.

Butler was extremely pleased with the club's dramatic effect upon crime in the eleventh ward. In 1919 the ward had more juvenile delinquency than any other within Chicago, totaling 1,344 arrests.[39] The number of arrests fell to 802 in 1920, 592 in 1921, then only 276 in 1928. Butler balanced this reduction against $17 that the club invested in each boy during a year, then added: "A normal boy is never a bad boy. He is only a good boy doing the wrong thing. Give him a simple club for the activities of his leisure time—between school time and bed time—and he is taken off the streets. . . . Through supervised games he learns to play fair; and the boy who learns to play fair develops an alertness, honesty, and truthfulness that makes a man of him. That is the net of it." [40]

His interest in the Union League Foundation continued through the 1920's as it expanded programs. In May, 1924, the Foundation bought an 80-acre campsite near Salem, Wisconsin, and in April, 1927, it opened a second club at 524 N. Wolcott Avenue. Butler served as president of the Foundation for two years, 1929 and 1930, just before his interests began to shift toward Arizona.

In the meantime, he had been elected a member of the national board of Boys' Clubs of America in 1920 for a term which extended until he died.

[37] Grant, p. 216.
[38] "Union League Club Creates Foundation for Boys," *Fort Dearborn Magazine*, 2 (September, 1920), 7.
[39] Burridge D. Butler, "Boys' Clubs and Crime," *The Review of Reviews*, 79 (April, 1929), 74; John C. Shaffer, "Service for City, State and Nation," *The Spirit of the Union League Club, 1879-1926* (Chicago, 1926), p. 89; Grant, p. 221.
[40] B. D. Butler, "Boys' Clubs and Crime," p. 74.

Butler took less part in the Boys' Clubs of Chicago after 1930 but lived to see the time when they had an alumni roster of nearly 50,000 boys.

Boys' Clubs of Phoenix

Even 20 years after Butler died, he was in the minds of youths and others connected with the Boys' Clubs of Phoenix. Boldly lettered words, "Burridge D. Butler Boys' Club," on the building at 1652 E. Moreland Street offered daily testimony to his support.

Phoenix had no boys' club program when Butler came to Arizona. In 1943 he explained to Alfred Knight, president of the local Optimist Club, how successful such clubs had been in aiding underprivileged boys. The result was a meeting in Butler's office at which members of the Optimist Club began plans for such a program in Phoenix. Butler became a member of the original 11-man board, as did his program director, Jack Williams.[41]

Progress was slow until 1946 when a gift of $10,000 from Butler renewed interest and stimulated other donations. The board leased a nursery school at 926 E. Van Buren Street and a playground with buildings at 815 S. Seventh Avenue. These sites became the Eastside and Westside clubs, both of which were dedicated on December 7, 1946. Butler, by then 78 years old, attended the ceremonies and KOY broadcast them.

Within a year the juvenile department reported a 50 per cent decline in delinquency in areas around Eastside and Westside clubs. After three years juvenile courts were handling only 25 per cent as many cases from those two districts as before the clubs began.

A settlement of Butler's estate provided another donation to the Boys' Clubs of Phoenix in 1950. The $30,000 became the nucleus for a new club on Moreland Street in one of the major delinquency areas of the city. Officials named the new $150,000 club in Butler's memory and dedicated it November 30, 1952, at a ceremony in which Governor Howard Pyle delivered the main address. Burridge D. Butler Boys' Club was designed to handle 2,000 boys with its gymnasium, game and reading rooms, kitchen, and office. A later addition gave it the state's largest indoor swimming pool. By 1967

[41] George F. Miller, "Boys' Clubs of Phoenix, Inc.," manuscript dated September 19, 1966.

its annual operating budget was $30,000 and it was one of four Phoenix Boys' Clubs serving more than 4,000 boys.

Involvement with Boy Scouts

Butler's interest in boys extended into the Boy Scout movement, although his personal part in it is not well documented. He was a member of the national council of Boy Scouts of America from 1925 to 1930 and a member of the original Rural Scouting Committee from 1927 until 1946.[42]

One of his efforts took the shape of a Lone Scout Department which appeared in *Prairie Farmer* beginning January 31, 1925. Lone Scouting was for boys from farms and small towns where troop scouting was not possible. Butler wrote for the department as "Chief Medicine Man" of the *Prairie Farmer* Lone Scout Wigwam, an organizational cluster which paralleled those which several other state farm papers were sponsoring. Membership in the Wigwam reached 1,388 by April 10 when interest appeared to level off, causing the Lone Scout Department to vanish in less than a year.

In general, Butler felt that Scouting was a program designed more for affluent boys—those who could afford to buy uniforms and pay their way on camping trips—than for boys in slum areas. The idea that any youngster could use a boys' club daily for only 50¢ to $1.50 a year appealed more to Butler and captured his deeper involvement.

Helping the People's Padre

Butler's respect for crusaders probably explains his interest in the work of a Franciscan priest, Father Emmett McLoughlin, whose parish was the southside poverty area of Phoenix. The young priest had arrived in Phoenix during 1934 to find a shocking pocket of poverty "south of the tracks," between the warehouse district and the city dump. Thousands of Negroes, Mexicans, and "white trash" lived in shacks, "many without electricity, most without plumbing and heat. They were built of tin cans, cardboard boxes, and wooden crates picked up by the railroad tracks."[43] Outlaws,

[42] Howard R. Patton to author, April 14, 1967; minutes of the first meeting, National Committee on Rural Scouting, May 10, 1927.

[43] Emmett McLoughlin, *People's Padre* (Boston: Beacon Press, 1954), p. 41.

prostitutes, and "glassy-eyed victims of denatured alcohol" lived in a "cesspool of poverty and disease." [44] McLoughlin approached the problem by raising funds to buy an abandoned grocery store in the heart of the neighborhood and remodel it as a church and social hall. Its formal name was St. Monica's Community Center, but people more commonly called it Father Emmett's Mission. It became the start of a program which expanded in 20 years into social work, medical clinics, three housing projects, and one of the largest hospitals in Arizona.

Butler got involved when the priest approached him (on a dare) about providing floodlights for a playground. Friends had told McLoughlin that when Butler saw his Roman collar he would curse vigorously and throw the priest out. "He did curse," McLoughlin later reported, "but when I responded in kind he bought the floodlights." [45] Butler also helped get poles, fixtures, wiring, and other scarce items.

This experience led McLoughlin to turn to Butler in 1943 when he had approval by the War Production Board to build a hospital but not a nurses' home or nursing school. Materials were too scarce for the Board to give needed approval, but it agreed to approve the projects if McLoughlin could get the most critical materials through second-hand channels.

McLoughlin feared that was impossible, but on the way home from Washington he stopped in Chicago to visit Butler, "one man who had never heard of the word 'impossible'." [46] Butler listened, swore, picked up the phone, and called a friend who was president of a power company. He asked his friend to gather some engineers, meet McLoughlin the next day, find out what items the building would require, and try to get them. [47]

The meeting took place and about the time McLoughlin got back to Phoenix, trucks from Chicago started rolling into the Mission loaded with wire of various sizes. McLoughlin rounded up pipe, fixtures, and other materials which led to the approval which he had sought.

Butler soon became a member of the board of directors of the new St. Monica's Hospital and served until he died. Failing health did not allow an active part, but he helped with donations of various kinds.

[44] McLoughlin, pp. 41-42.   [45] McLoughlin, p. 112.   [46] McLoughlin, p. 112.
[47] Emmett McLoughlin, personal interview, December 30, 1966.

The drive and vigor of McLoughlin impressed Butler, who often lectured the young priest against all religion. At a party celebrating his eightieth birthday Butler urged McLoughlin to quit the church and get married. Accustomed to Butler's brashness, McLoughlin asked what he would do for a living and Butler countered with an offer to give him KOY. As far as getting married was concerned, Butler proposed: "I'll start advertising it on the air this afternoon and I'll have a hundred of them there in the morning and you can take your pick."[48]

His suggestion would have been outrageous except that by 1948 McLoughlin was having doctrinal and moral doubts which led to his resignation from the Franciscan Order and from active ministry eight months after Butler died. He refused to abide by an order of the Provincial Council that he leave his duties as superintendent of St. Monica's Hospital.

Parade of Crown Princes

Butler's offer to give KOY to Emmett McLoughlin illustrates another sequence in the drive by Butler to perpetuate his family. Years of searching for a successor in his business left a weaving trail which ended in frustration, not only for Butler but also for more than a half-dozen candidates who paraded before him at *Prairie Farmer*–WLS over a period of 28 years. He always kept looking for another B. D. Butler, yet probably could not have tolerated the man if he had appeared. James Edwards often told Butler that the pattern had been broken when Butler was born.

This did not deter the strong-minded publisher who prided himself in being an effective salesman. His most common (and frustrating) device for attracting likely crown princes was what employees came to describe as mountain-top promises. Whenever Butler found a man he liked, he took the prospect up on the mountain to survey the wonders of a future with him. Offers of power, ownership, and wages usually much above those of other employees proved difficult to refuse.

Some persons regarded this tactic as outright fraud and pointed toward a string of broken promises. Others believed that Butler honestly meant what he promised, but never found the man who really earned it.

[48] Emmett McLoughlin, personal interview, December 30, 1966.

No one knows for sure when the parade of crown princes really began. His first editor, C. P. Reynolds, may have been the first candidate, because after Reynolds died, his wife reportedly felt that Butler had not abided by all of the promises he allegedly had made to her husband. Stock ownership was clearly an incentive which Butler used to attract C. V. Gregory as editor in 1911. Butler apparently withheld stock for more than a year, then offered Gregory a share in the ownership when convinced that the new editor was sound.

Herman Steen, who had left *Prairie Farmer* in 1923, was another mountain-top candidate. For 20 years afterward Butler urged Steen to come back to the organization. Several others came to *Prairie Farmer* as prospects during the 1920's, including Arthur Page (who proved himself more philosopher than businessman) and a man named Pete Fleming from the state Council of Defense. Butler reportedly promised Fleming that the two of them would "run this place," but the new man left shortly when he felt that he was being used to stir up trouble around the office. On the radio side, Butler often brought in men who soon found they had nothing to do. It seemed as if he hired them to show off, to prove that he could hire a man whenever he pleased. Some stayed, but many moved on when they saw that WLS had no place for them.

The parade increased in tempo during 1935, headed by Conklin Mann, who got involved in the conflict between Butler and Gregory. His role was even more complicated by Butler's lengthy absences from the office, which meant that the new general manager had to establish himself among associates who saw him as a highly paid outsider who had entered over their heads. Mann left in March, 1938, after what employees described as a "running battle" with Butler. He later said that Butler was pleased with the improvements he had made in *Prairie Farmer*, "but the other publishers of the Midwest Unit began to tell Mr. B. that I would wreck them with extravagance. . . ."[49] By 1938 Mann agreed with Floyd Keepers, one of Butler's perceptive critics, who years earlier had given Mann a personal view of what ailed *Prairie Farmer*: "There isn't a thing around here that wouldn't be cured in 10 minutes if Mr. Butler would just move out to Arizona and stay."[50]

Soon after Mann left, Butler felt that he needed someone else to

[49] Conklin Mann, cited in Dave O. Thompson, unpublished memoirs, p. 208.
[50] Floyd Keepers, personal interview, January 24, 1967.

dress up the paper. This time he wanted someone who was an expert at handling news, so in February, 1939, he hired as managing editor a mild-mannered and congenial former city editor named Rowland Wood. Butler made it clear that Wood's job was to produce an attractive paper; apparently the agreement carried few mountain-top promises. Wood was what Dave Thompson described as a good managing editor, but "like a fish out of water at *Prairie Farmer*. He did not know anything about agriculture. . . . He also knew none of the people in agriculture. Therefore, he had a hard task." [51]

Wood stayed until November, 1941, which helped the editorial staff surmount a record centennial issue of 196 pages on January 11, 1941. By that time Butler had decided Wood would not fit into a position of management and informed Thompson "that it would be desirable if Mr. Wood were no longer there" when Butler returned from Arizona the following spring.[52] Wood resigned and returned to newspapering in Chicago.

Butler's next prospect had not only experience in newspapering but also a long record of leadership in midwestern agriculture. Ralph Ammon had studied journalism at the University of Wisconsin before becoming farm editor of the *State Journal* in Madison. He proved to be an avid promoter whose campaigns included drives to hire a county agent in Dane County and improve the county fair. He soon became secretary of the Dane County Fair, and his success led to appointment in 1930 as manager of the Wisconsin State Fair. Ammon cleaned up what the governor described as a "political football" and held that position for more than 12 years, the last five of which he also served as director of agriculture for Wisconsin.

The combination appealed to Butler—farm background, newspapering experience, business skill, a crusading spirit, and a respected name in agriculture—so he invited Ammon to his home in Hinsdale where he took his guest to the very peak of Butler mountain. All of this will be yours, Butler reportedly assured Ammon, pointing to the opportunity to become a great publisher and radio station manager. Ammon joined *Prairie Farmer* in a loosely defined position as assistant to the publisher in November, 1942, with an understanding that when Butler returned from Ari-

[51] Thompson, p. 284.
[52] Thompson, p. 284.

zona in early January, they would arrive at terms on salary and ownership of stock. Other officers of the company knew about the agreement but had not taken part in reaching it. Butler's charge to Ammon was: "Analyze the whole setup from the Publisher's standpoint. You have two months to go into the whole situation, and when I return, you will have an opportunity to talk with me."[53]

Within a month Butler was showing some impatience with Ammon's editorial direction. "You are a man who looks before he leaps but that doesn't mean that we should try to travel right down the middle of the road," he chided in December.[54] He also was editing the editorials which Ammon wrote. Butler's back began bothering him around Christmastime, delaying his visit to Chicago and allowing time for other problems to appear.

In late January Ammon submitted his plan for reorganizing *Prairie Farmer* and WLS. Under the plan, Ammon would supervise *Prairie Farmer*, Glenn Snyder would remain manager of WLS, and both groups would share a proposed new promotion department. Editorially, John Strohm, formerly assistant editor, would shift to the managing editorship over Thompson and Page, who would remain associate editors. This plan went into effect on February 20, but relations between Butler and Ammon kept cooling. Butler felt that business news should be secondary; Ammon argued that "in the past twenty years farming has moved very much into a business."[55] Ammon started a "Food for Humanity" program; Butler was not sure what it was and feared that *Prairie Farmer*–WLS would gain little from it. Ammon made a sales trip to the east coast and failed to see most of the advertising executives whom Butler had suggested visiting.

Furthermore, when Butler finally returned to Chicago in May, he changed the organization which Ammon had set up, undercutting Ammon's central role and allowing department heads to work autonomously. Pressure for this change probably came from the department heads, all of whom had worked at the paper more than 20 years and had become irritated by actions of the new man. They charged that he used their ideas to improve his own standing with Butler.

[53] Memorandum from Butler to Ralph Ammon, November 16, 1942.
[54] Memorandum from Butler to Ralph Ammon, December 10, 1942.
[55] Memorandum from Ralph Ammon to Butler, March 15, 1943.

For his part, Ammon was clearly disgruntled by June, for the board of directors had not elected him a member or offered him stock. He also was tired of having no office and only limited authority.

Butler asked Thompson to ease Ammon out of the organization, a chore to which Thompson agreed after delivering his own ultimatum: the day Butler's next expert walked into *Prairie Farmer,* Thompson would walk out. Butler felt that he had a competent workman in Thompson, but not a first-rate editor, so Thompson never got the editorial title even though he filled the position steadily between 1937 and 1945. He, Page, and Strohm continued in the major editorial positions after Ammon left in 1943.

Nearly two years passed before the next crown prince emerged from a respected daily newspaper in central Illinois, the *Bloomington Pantagraph.* Arthur Moore, its editor, had written a book, *Farmers and the Rest of Us,* which *Prairie Farmer* reviewed favorably in April, 1945. Thompson maintained that the part which struck Butler's fancy was a reference to Earl Smith of the IAA as having spaniel-brown eyes. Butler was highly critical of Smith at the time.

He invited Moore to Arizona where they agreed on a clear-cut title, an arrangement for buying stock in the company, and a salary higher than any other employee was getting. Moore became editor and a member of the board of directors on May 10, 1945. In turn, Dave Thompson fulfilled his own promise by resigning the same day.

Where Ralph Ammon had been most interested in promotion and advertising, Arthur Moore was an editor. He suffered somewhat from a lack of farm background but soon pumped into *Prairie Farmer* some of its long-missing dialogue with readers. Not since Gregory left had the paper contained so much content from readers as in 1946. Moore, like Gregory, thought of *Prairie Farmer* as "the greatest farm forum in the world." [56] He contended that the paper was printing more letters from farmers about issues of the day than any publication he knew: 344 letters over an eight-month period. His hobby, Moore confessed to readers, was getting and printing letters from readers. They wrote 24,106 letters to *Prairie Farmer* during March, 1946.

Moore did not mix with farmers as much as Gregory, but his

[56] *Prairie Farmer,* 118 (May 11, 1946), 12.

issues showed an editorial vigor. They also contained more news about farm legislation than *Prairie Farmer* had used for a decade, and less about fairs, sports festivals, and other specialties of previous editorial staff members.

On January 3, 1947, Moore resigned to join McGraw-Hill in a move which onlookers interpreted as a sign that he was "bound for bigger things." His was not a case of quitting in disgust or under pressure; rather, members of the staff felt that *Prairie Farmer* simply was not able to hold him. Moore's resignation left Butler with no editor or managing editor, for John Strohm had resigned in early 1946. Strohm was among those who had taken trips up the mountain to look at the wonders of Butlerland, but the view became less appealing after Butler bypassed him to hire Moore.[57]

Arthur Page, by then a perennial standby, supervised editorial work as associate editor while the editor's chair went vacant again.

Conditions nearly forced Butler to turn the search for a replacement over to his associates this time, for his health was failing fast and he was in the Chicago area only a few months each year. By now Butler had a reputation in farm publishing as a man with whom no editor could get along. The parade of editors at *Prairie Farmer* since 1937 had convinced others that he was a man to avoid.

One evidence of this strength of feeling about Butler was a spontaneous informal group which called itself the Prairie Farmer Alumni Association. Members were those who either had quit *Prairie Farmer*–WLS or been fired by Butler, and its mere existence is a meaningful testimony to his personal impact. The association formed in 1938 when a group of Butler's former employees met for dinner in Chicago during the International Livestock Exposition. Inevitably, discussion centered around Butler, and the session was so much fun that the men decided to meet again the following year. *Prairie Farmer* and WLS had more than 30 "alumni" of Butler's era by then, so the dinners were well attended. Each program consisted of having members relate stories they had heard about Butler during the past year. As one member recalled, it was always "a hullabaloo telling each other what a louse Mr. Butler was." Members kept alert year-around to find tales which they could share at this annual event.

Whether Butler knew about the group or not, he never failed

[57] John Strohm, personal interview, February 25, 1967.

to furnish plenty of stories for an evening of fun. The result was
that his more bizarre actions got broadcast far and wide by this
informal publicity agency. (Significantly, the group dissolved when
he died.)

Therefore, as James Edwards and Fred Orlemann searched for
a new editor, they were trying to sell what those in farm publishing
considered to be a hot-seat. Their search took them to an extension editor named Paul C. Johnson at the University of Minnesota.
Johnson had grown up on a farm in Minnesota, graduated from
St. Olaf College, edited four community newspapers (one of which
he also published), and then joined the staff of the university. He
was well settled there, but the prospects of talking to 350,000
readers of *Prairie Farmer* quickened his newspaperman's instincts.
Warnings descended upon him from all directions when friends
learned that he was thinking about the job in Chicago. Stay away
from there, they insisted. The old man has fired three editors already, WLS has had a big blow-up, and the whole place is going
to the dogs. Before he dies, Butler may kill this thing that he built.[58]

Despite such warnings, Johnson went to Chicago in August, 1947,
for an interview with Butler. Probably very wisely, Johnson refused
to become a candidate as crown prince. He told Butler and the
other directors that he did not want to own and manage the business; he wanted to edit the paper and work closely with heads
of other departments. This is exactly what Edwards, Orlemann,
and Holt wanted to hear, for they were tired of having outsiders
come in over them. *Prairie Farmer* offered Johnson the job, which
he refused at first because he felt that Butler was only lukewarm
to him. After Butler and other directors assured him of their interest, he assumed the editor's chair on October 25, 1947, to end
the parade of crown princes and begin a new editorial era.

End of the Butler Years

Clearly, Butler was lonely late in his life. Employees—even his
directors—looked upon him with mixed awe and fright, so no one
at the paper really was close to him. During and after the depression he isolated himself from more conservative members of the
Union League Club. He also was not content to stay home, even
on weekends. When he began taking naps each afternoon on a big

[58] Paul C. Johnson, personal interview, January 13, 1967.

couch in his office, employees suspected that he did not want his wife to see that he was having to slacken his pace, for she was still quite spry. Activities which he had loved in former years had lost their appeal. He told John Holland when he was 78: "Have you sensed a little feeling of rest as one by one nature cuts the cords that tie you to this earth? I always rode horses and did whatever I wanted to do. For sixty-five years I have never really known what it was to be tired out. It is getting different with me now. I used to look forward to climbing these Arizona mountains and of poking around in the deserted houses of the cliff dwellers to find out how they lived, and how they did their farming. Golf was my finest relaxation. Now it is a pain in the neck. I once loved to go to banquets but now I'd rather sit in a corner with a good bowl of bread and milk." [59]

His big frame was growing more and more unsteady. The back caused constant pain, and he was so miserable during the entire winter of 1947-48 that he wished not to live if he could not get better. His mind turned more and more to Grand Rapids and associations at the beginning of his career.

He was discouraged because *Prairie Farmer* and WLS were growing further apart, despite his constant appeals, and because too many staff members had what he termed "radioitis." By then the future of radio looked uncertain to him as television approached. Under Butler WLS did not get involved in television because he and his manager believed that television—with its confined line-of-sight signal and heavy reliance on cigarette and other consumer-oriented advertising—simply did not fit their concept of serving farm people. They feared that there would be open criticism even if they started or bought a television station and ran it as a separate, nonagricultural unit.

On the publishing side, Butler knew that he had failed to find a successor. Members of his old guard had tried for years to convince him that they could run the business as a group, that they had been with him long enough to know how he would act at given times. Their reasoning was that together they—better than outsiders—could keep *Prairie Farmer* moving in the direction he wanted. Butler agreed that they knew him from long experience but feared that without him they might not have enough fresh

[59] Holland, pp. 40-41.

ideas of their own. Somehow he sensed that his dominance might have taken a toll in the creativity of those who had stayed with him.

General business conditions also confused Butler after 1946. Partly influenced by Eugene Davenport, Butler had been convinced that the country would enter a severe depression after World War II. His response had been to shore up the cash position of *Prairie Farmer* and WLS pending the expected letdown. By 1947, WLS alone had more than $1 million in cash and government bonds to meet a depression which did not come.

Prospective buyers were offering Butler what seemed like astounding prices for his properties, which heightened both his pleasure and frustration. Rumors in the trade reported that ABC, Marshall Field, and other interested parties had offered about $4 million for *Prairie Farmer* and WLS.[60] Butler's uncertainty about whether or not to sell before the break which he expected created uncertainty among members of his staff.

On March 23, 1948—less than seven weeks after his eightieth birthday—Butler fell backwards from a knoll while walking in his citrus grove at Casa Davenal. The fall either knocked him unconscious or left him thrashing helplessly because he was there more than an hour before his cries brought help. He entered St. Monica's Hospital too ill for questioning. The admitting diagnosis was cardiac and back injury, although the final diagnosis was uremic poisoning (kidney failure). For seven days he was partially conscious in the hospital he had helped build, under oxygen for two of them. He died during the morning of Tuesday, March 30.

Dr. John Holland officiated at a memorial service on April 2 in Phoenix and at an interment of ashes on May 27 at the North Shore Garden of Memories, Chicago. Brevity characterized both services, for Butler had instructed Holland beforehand: "Say a few words, and I do mean a few. I do not want to suggest what you say, when and if the time comes. But for heaven's sake, don't turn on the oratory and praise me to the skies. And certainly, I do not want you to tell all the mean things you know about me. Better just read a few verses from the Sermon on the Mount, have my friends repeat the Lord's Prayer, and make it all short." [61]

[60] *Broadcasting Magazine*, April 12, 1948, 30; Addison Warner to author, July 6, 1967.
[61] Holland, p. 42.

Legacy

Many people wondered what the childless millionaire with no close living relatives would do with his fortune. Butler had once introduced himself to a visitor by putting his arm around the man and saying, "I have a million dollars. What should I do with it?" Butler's unabashed guest had replied just as quickly, "Spend it." However, Butler had acquired his wealth by careful attention, and his 13-page will revealed that he wished to handle it with the same care. He had long maintained that it is a good idea to "make up your mind about what you want to have done with your property after you are gone and settle the matter yourself while you are living, rather than to leave your estate to be juggled around through the courts." [62]

Disadvantaged children of Illinois proved to be major heirs under Butler's will. Much of his estate went into the Burridge D. Butler Memorial Trust of Chicago. Holt, Orlemann, Edwards, Cook, Page, and Murphy became trustees, charged to hold all net income for uses named by the Chicago Community Trust. The Chicago Community Trust, in turn, was directed to use all funds for charitable purposes. Butler specifically asked that 20 per cent go to the Illinois Children's Home and Aid Society, especially for that part of its program to help children in rural districts of Illinois.

This meant many thousands of dollars for charitable and educational uses each year—in perpetuity. For example, the principal of the Butler Trust on October 31, 1965, was $4,288,474. A second trust called the Burridge D. Butler and Ina H. Butler Fund, which Mrs. Butler established later, comprised another $526,451.

As of December, 1966, the Butler Trust alone had provided $1,546,260 for 89 recipient organizations since it became operative in June, 1951. The Illinois Children's Home and Aid Society, as main beneficiary, had received more than $300,000 of that total.

Butler's interest in the Society dated back to at least 1919, by which time *Prairie Farmer* was helping it place children in the homes of readers.[63] Since it was founded in 1883, the privately supported agency had served thousands of dependent and neglected children—about 1,700 children and families each year. The Illinois Children's Home and Aid Society was well suited to Butler's in-

[62] *Prairie Farmer*, 91 (March 8, 1919), 13.
[63] *Prairie Farmer*, 91 (August 23, 1919), 11; 96 (December 13, 1924), 8; 107 (April 27, 1935) 6.

terests in several ways. First, it offered an unusually wide range
of services: foster family, adoption, residential treatment for serious
emotional problems, therapeutic group home living for adolescents,
and counseling help for children and parents. Second, it served
children in both rural and urban parts of Illinois (Butler's funds
have always been earmarked for downstate programs). Third, it
was nonsectarian and had a long record of service.

Youth-centered charities in Arizona also gained from Butler's will,
for his share of stock in the Salt River Broadcasting Company
(parent firm for KOY) provided $94,890 to eight welfare groups
for youths in Arizona. Table 17 shows that the Boys' Clubs of
Phoenix got the largest share, which helped build the Burridge
D. Butler Unit.

TABLE 17. RECIPIENTS OF FUNDS FROM THE BURRIDGE D. BUTLER TRUST
OF PHOENIX, ARIZONA, JUNE, 1950

Recipient	Amount
Boys' Clubs of Phoenix	$30,000
Arizona Boys Ranch	22,390
Boy Scouts of America (Roosevelt Council, Phoenix)	10,000
Girl Scout Council	7,500
Jane Wayland Home	7,500
Maricopa Council, Inc., Camp Fire Girls	7,500
Boy Scouts of America (Catalina Council, Tucson)	6,000
Arizona Children's Home Association	4,000
Total	$94,890

SOURCE: First and final account and report of trustee and petition for discharge in the
Superior Court of the State of Arizona, October 23, 1950.

Arizona Boys Ranch used its $22,390 to construct its first build-
ing, a 10-boy cottage built in 1951. According to the superintendent,
this gift was the pioneer effort in building a ranch which in 1966
included 25 buildings and provided homelife experience for 80
boys.[64]

Boy Scouts of Phoenix applied funds from the will to a new
Scouting center dedicated October 21, 1950.[65]

[64] Wendell R. Newell to author, January 16, 1967; *Brand of Excellence—
Arizona Boys Ranch and Arizona Boys Ranch Foundation,* brochure, 15 pp.,
no date.
[65] George Miller, personal interview, December 30, 1966.

Other portions of the will gave all stock for the *Arizona Farmer* to Clarence Powell (60 per cent) and Ernie Douglas (40 per cent). Butler also gave Roy Lynnes all stock in the baby chick company which included the *Poultry Supply Dealer* that Lynnes edited.

Mrs. Butler received an annual salary under the will, a provision which she protested. On June 1, 1948, she filed a renunciation of the will and petitioned the court for the widow's half.[66] The court supported her petition, which opened a three-year chain of legal maneuvering. In the end she got half of the shares in her husband's firms, but was legally forced to sell them and thereby prevented from exercising control over their management. Some of Butler's former staff members nodded knowingly when they heard about his provision for Ina Butler; they figured that it proved Butler wanted to keep his dead hand on his widow. Others said that she had agreed earlier with her husband's will but that outsiders encouraged her to renounce it after he died. Clearly, Butler did not intend for his wife to become involved in the management of any properties, a view which mirrored his general opinion about women in business.

Facts also suggest that her action in rejecting the will held no deep personal resentment, because when she died she willed the money to a nearly identical trust which the Chicago Community Trust administers along with that of her husband.

In addition to the money which he left, Burridge Butler left some enduring imprints upon the organizations which he had owned. Employees and outsiders alike agree that the spirit of Butler still pervaded the Prairie Farmer Building 20 years after he died. His large portrait beside that of John S. Wright in the second-floor lobby was a silent witness to that spirit. Furthermore, no one ever moved into his corner office. It became a conference room, fitting symbol of the managerial approach which guided Prairie Farmer Publishing Company after he died.

One of two philosophies which endured with greatest strength was that in order to profit, an institution must serve. Onlookers never could agree about which motive really drove Butler—profit or service. Evidence suggests that the motives were so intertwined in his personality that they defy separation. It appears that he often considered service as a device for personal gain. Perhaps the most

[66] Renunciation and petition from Ina Butler to the Probate Court, DuPage County, Illinois, June 1, 1948.

graphic expression of this philosophy was his remark, "I believe if you meet a man who has no coat, and you give him yours, in the true spirit of Christ, that more coats will be put on your own shoulders as fast as you can give them away." [67] It is possible that his motives shifted as he grew older. Perhaps the Butler who found a formula of using service to make money early in his manhood lived with the service portion long enough that the money became less important. Some evidence points toward this possibility. One example comes from a letter in 1943 to a former associate. "I always have in mind directness and simplicity, and real sincere honest to God friendship between the station and the people who are listening. Perhaps I over-estimate this attachment because I am 75 years old and sentimental. But I feel at times the station is too commercial, making too much money, and that our friendship is alloyed with too much materialism and selfishness."

Whatever Butler's motives, his philosophy remained strong in the minds of executives who followed him.

A second principle still much alive at *Prairie Farmer* 20 years after he died was that the editor should have a strong franchise. Members of the editorial staff credit Butler with creating an environment in which editors are consulted and their opinions respected in all phases of operations. They feel his influence has given them unusual freedom from advertisers and others because management absorbed this Scrippsian belief.

And what of the impact of *Prairie Farmer* and WLS out on the prairies of the midwest during these years? No one can measure the effect upon schools, crops, farm groups, community life, roads, and a hundred other interests to which *Prairie Farmer* and WLS directed attention during their crusading years. However, in 1968 Butler's family spirit still lived in the eyes of midwestern farm people, many of whom seemed to brighten at the mention of WLS Dinnerbell or the chicken thief campaign.

"Sure, Art Page and his newlyweds. That's right—and the national anthem. I'd almost forgotten. We listened every day. And Dr. John Holland with his Little Brown Church of the Air. Who was it? Oh—Jim Poole. When he came on with the markets, my dad would crown anybody that made a noise.

[67] Holland, p. 48.

"And the chicken thieves. Why, that was a big thing—exciting—we kids saw thieves behind every bush. I think we were really disappointed when they didn't come to our place.

"I liked the Lazy Farmer. Yes, and the Protective Union. We still have a sign out front.

"Oh, yes, and the National Barn Dance every Saturday night. Do you remember Lulu Belle and Scotty? Gene Autry. Didn't he start on the Barn Dance? And who was that big fat man who always dressed up like a baby? Sure, and I remember when our family used to go to the state fair and leave our lunch basket at the *Prairie Farmer* tent. All of us would meet there at noon for picnic dinner. I don't know, they just seemed like our type of people. Kind of like a part of our family.

"Burridge Butler? No, I don't believe I remember him."

BIBLIOGRAPHY

A. Collections

Biggar, George C., Laguna Hills, California. Personal papers include Biggar-Butler correspondence from December, 1933, through September, 1947; unpublished manuscripts and facts about WLS programming. Other items in this collection are cited individually.

Blackburn College, Carlinville, Illinois. Files include correspondence among President Robert P. Ludlum, President-Emeritus William Hudson, and Mrs. Ina H. Butler, June 10, 1953, through November 29, 1956; minutes, Blackburn College Board of Trustees.

Cassidy, Grace E., Crystal Lake, Illinois. Personal papers include facts about WLS, Chicago, from 1924 through 1959: listener mail, dates, special events, court briefs involving WLS cases, reports of fundraising efforts, reminiscences by early WLS staff members Glenn Rowell and Bradley Kincaid, an account of the March, 1925, tornado relief effort in southern Illinois, and other items.

Grand Rapids Public Library, Grand Rapids, Michigan. Records pertaining to B. D. Butler include minutes and annual reports of the Board of Library Commissioners, April, 1921, through September, 1943; financial statements for the Winnie Whitfield Butler Trust Fund; correspondence involving library staff members, Butler, Thomas Murphy, and the president of the Board of Library Commissioners.

Gregory, C. V. Personal papers held by his wife, Des Moines, Iowa, include correspondence with Butler, *Prairie Farmer*-WLS staff members, agricultural leaders, and others, December, 1910, through October, 1936.

Haury, Dr. Emil. Papers in the Department of Anthropology, University of Arizona, include correspondence with Butler from July 28, 1938, through September 23, 1947; with Mrs. Butler, June 3, 1948; undated manuscript entitled, "To the late Burridge D. Butler," summarizing the Point of Pines field school; summary of Butler donations to the University of Arizona, 1938 through 1951.

Horner, Henry. Papers at the Illinois Historical Library, Springfield, include correspondence between the Illinois governor and C. V. Gregory between August, 1933, and August, 1937.

Illinois Children's Home and Aid Society, Chicago. Files include correspondence of the Society, Burridge D. Butler Memorial Trust of Chicago trustees, and the Chicago Community Trust, 1948 through 1967.

Johnson, Paul, Prospect Heights, Illinois. Personal papers include correspondence with *Prairie Farmer* executives during negotiations for employment, July-September, 1947.

Kellogg, F. W. Personal papers held by his son, William Scripps Kellogg, LaJolla, California, include some biographical information about F. W. Kellogg, but mostly material (promotion brochures, clippings, and trade paper articles) about the Clover Leaf Newspapers between 1902 and 1910.

Lee Brothers Historical Collection of Portraits of Prominent Citizens of Minnesota of the Twentieth Century, in the Galleries of the Minnesota Historical Society, St. Paul. Contains a brief biography of John Burgess, dated November 22, 1917.

Lowden, Frank O. Papers at the University of Chicago Library include personal correspondence with Butler between October, 1931, and April, 1942; with Gregory between December, 1925, and July, 1936; with Herman Steen between December, 1928, and August, 1937; with Henry A. Wallace during September, 1931; with E. O. Sykes of the Federal Radio Commission in November, 1928, concerning WLS; and others.

Orlemann, Fred W., Delray Beach, Florida. Personal papers include correspondence with Butler and *Prairie Farmer*-WLS staff members between May, 1922, and June, 1943; a financial analysis of Prairie Farmer Publishing Company operations 1928-33 by the First National Bank of Chicago, dated July 12, 1934.

Prairie Farmer Publishing Company, 1230 Washington Boulevard, Chicago. Files include minutes of Prairie Farmer Publishing Company from January 19, 1882, through August 13, 1946; minutes of Agricultural Broadcasting Company from October 23, 1928, through dissolution on December 12, 1957; some business statements of the

1909-48 period; assorted office memoranda and correspondence; contracts involving *Illinois Farmer* purchase; minutes of the Farmers Publishing Company (*Farmers Voice*), May 9, 1911, through May 12, 1913; records of payments by B. D. Butler trustees to Chicago Community Trust from June, 1951, through December, 1966.

B. Correspondence

Babcock, James M., associated with Burton Historical Collection, Detroit Public Library, to author, June 2, 1967.

Bakken, Douglas A., of the Nebraska State Historical Society, to author, March 16, 1967.

Bennett, C. O., of the Audit Bureau of Circulations, to author, July 28, 1967.

Benson, Thomas, of Webb Publishing Company, St. Paul, to author, August 29, 1967.

Biddy, Ben R., of the Disciples of Christ Historical Society, to author, March 17, 1967; April 7, 1967; May 2, 1967.

Biggar, George C., of Laguna Hills, California, to author, November 24 and December 8, 1966; February 18, March 4, March 6, March 10, March 17, May 8, and June 3, 1967.

Biggar, George C., of Laguna Hills, California, to Paul Johnson, January 10, 1967.

Buck, Glenn, of Nebraska Farmer Company, to author, March 20, 1967.

Cartwright, Lin D., of St. Louis, Missouri, to author, May 19, 1967.

Cassidy, Grace E., of Crystal Lake, Illinois, to author, January 26, March 9, and March 21, 1967.

Cosgrove, Nancy, of the Grand Rapids Public Library, to author, July 11, 1967.

Cottier, Hamilton, of Princeton, New Jersey, to author, May 29, 1967.

Duncan, Mrs. Edgar H., of Belmont College, Nashville, Tennessee, to author, April 29, 1967.

Estill, Allen S., of the Tennessee Association of Christian Churches, to author, April 13, 1967.

Germain, Mrs. Marvin L., of East Grand Rapids, Michigan, to author, June 9, 1967.

Gleason, John M., of Boys' Clubs of America, New York City, to author, April 4, 1967.

Green, Dr. J. Frank, of Cascade Christian Church, Grand Rapids, Michigan, to author, April 12, 1967.

Hardy, Davenal W., of Cos Cob, Connecticut, to author, April 16, 1967.

Hay, Taylor, of the Union League Club of Chicago, to author, May 16, 1967.

Hinshaw, William W., Jr., of Highland Park, Illinois, to George Cook, January 16, 1967.

Hopkins, Cyril, of the University of Illinois, to B. D. Butler, no date.

Howard, Mrs. M. C., of Benton Harbor, Michigan, to author, April 2, July 24, August 11, August 13, 1967.

Hughes, Charles E., of Armour and Company, to author, April 7, 1967.

Johnson, Eloyse A., of the Ellen Browning Scripps Foundation, San Diego, California, to author, April 12, 1967.

Judah, Stillson, of the Pacific School of Religion, to author, April 19, 1967.

Kellogg, William S., of LaJolla, California, to author, April 28 and October 18, 1967.

Knight, Oliver, of the University of Wisconsin, to author, April 1, 1967.

Lagessie, Lee, of the Chicago Area Council, Boy Scouts of America, to author, April 6, 1967.

Lemmon, Paul, of Boys' Clubs of America, Chicago, to author, March 21, 1967.

Maines, Lawrence, of the Michigan Association of Christian Churches, to author, April 7, 1967.

Martin, Dr. E. M., of the Union League Club of Chicago, to Taylor Hay, March 22, 1967.

Mason, Norman, of Mecosta County, Michigan, Clerk's Office, to author, June 2, 1967.

McCully, O. W., of the Pennsylvania Association of Christian Churches, to author, April 25, 1967.

McKeene, H. A., of the Illinois State Farmers' Institute, to B. D. Butler, no date.

McMillen, Wheeler, of Moorestown, New Jersey, to author, August 26, 1967.

Million, Lucille, of the *Kentucky Christian,* to author, April 20, May 11, 1967.

Muller, C., of the Central Christian Church, Grand Rapids, Michigan, to author, April 12, 1967.

Newell, Wendell R., of Arizona Boys Ranch, to author, January 16, 1967.

Patton, Howard R., of the National Council, Boy Scouts of America, to author, March 17, March 21, and April 14, 1967.

Porter, W. M., of Scripps-Howard Newspapers, to author, July 16, 1967.

Portschy, Dale, of the Omaha Public Library, to author, July 17, 1967.

Pullin, Morris H., of the Illinois Disciples of Christ, to author, April 3, 1967.

Rader, Mrs. Wm. E., of the First Christian Church, Modesto, California, to author, April 20, 1967.

Rumble, Cleve, of the *Louisville Courier-Journal* and *Times*, to author, June 1, 1967.

Sachs, Lois, of the Union League Club of Chicago, to Taylor Hay, March 31, 1967.

Shugard, Harold, of Hastings, Minnesota, to author, July 12, 1967.

Steen, Herman, of Wheaton, Illinois, to author, January 30, February 14, February 26, 1967.

Warner, Addison W., of Ft. Worth, Texas, to author, July 6, 1967.

Williams, Jack, of KOY, Phoenix, to author, March 6, 1967.

C. Books and Pamphlets

Arizona Boys Ranch and Arizona Boys Ranch Foundation. *Brand of Excellence*. Brochure, no date, 16 pp.

Baker, Rob H., ed. *The City of Grand Rapids*. Grand Rapids: B. F. Conrad and Co., 1889.

Bardolph, Richard. *Agricultural Literature and the Early Illinois Farmer*. Urbana: University of Illinois Press, 1948.

Barnouw, Erik. *A Tower in Babel—A History of Broadcasting in the United States*. Vol. I. New York: Oxford University Press, 1966.

Baxter, Albert. *History of the City of Grand Rapids, Michigan*. New York: Munsell and Co., 1891.

Bell, John T. *Omaha and Omaha Men*. Omaha, Nebraska, n.p., 1917.

Bennett, Charles O. *Facts Without Opinion*. Chicago: Audit Bureau of Circulations, 1965.

Block, William J. *The Separation of the Farm Bureau and the Extension Service*. Urbana: University of Illinois Press, 1960.

Bogart, Ernest L., and John H. Mathews. *The Modern Commonwealth, 1893-1918*. Vol. V of *The Centennial History of Illinois*. Springfield: Illinois Centennial Commission, 1920.

Bogue, Allan G. *From Prairie to Corn Belt—Farming on the Illinois and Iowa Prairies in the Nineteenth Century*. Chicago: University of Chicago Press, 1963.

Brink, Carol. *The Twin Cities*. New York: Macmillan Co., 1961.

Britt, Albert. *An America That Was—What Life Was Like on an Illinois Farm Seventy Years Ago*. Barre, Mass.: Barre Publishers, 1964.

Brown, John T. *Churches of Christ*. Louisville: John P. Morton and Co., 1904.

Bryan, William Jennings. *The First Battle: A Story of the Campaign of 1896*. Chicago: W. B. Conkey Co., 1896.

Buck, Solon J. *The Granger Movement*. Lincoln: University of Nebraska Press, 1913.

Butchart, Reuben. *The Disciples of Christ in Canada since 1830*. Toronto: Canadian Headquarters Publications, 1949.

Butler, Thomas D., ed. *Poetry and Prose of Marie Radcliffe Butler*. Cincinnati: Standard Publishing Co., 1884.

Butterworth, Julian E., and Howard A. Dawson. *The Modern Rural School*. New York: McGraw-Hill Book Co., 1952.

Campbell, Christiana McFayden. *The Farm Bureau and the New Deal*. Urbana: University of Illinois Press, 1962.

Capper, Arthur. *The Agricultural Bloc*. New York: Harcourt, Brace and Co., 1922.

Carney, Mabel. *Country Life and the Country School*. Chicago: Row, Peterson and Co., 1912.

Carruth, Gorton, and associates, eds. *The Encyclopedia of American Facts and Dates*. 3rd ed. New York: Thomas Y. Crowell Co., 1962.

Castle, Henry A. *History of St. Paul and Vicinity*. Chicago: Lewis Publishing Co., 1912.

Chicago Tribune. *Chicago Tribune Picture Book of Radio 1928*. Public Service Office, Chicago, 1928.

Christianson, Theodore. *Minnesota—The Land of Sky-Tinted Waters*. Vol. 3. Chicago: American Historical Society, 1935.

Church of the Transfiguration. *Illustrated Guide Book of the Church of the Transfiguration, New York City*. Booklet, 1963, 32 pp.

Cole, Cyrenus. *I Remember, I Remember*. Iowa City: State Historical Society of Iowa, 1936.

Demaree, Albert L. *The American Agricultural Press, 1819-1860*. New York: Columbia University Press, 1941.

Dunne, Edward F. *Illinois—The Heart of the Nation*. Vols. II, III. Chicago: Lewis Publishing Co., 1933.

Farlow, Lawrence. *The Farmers Elevator Movement in Illinois*. Farmers Grain Dealers Association of Illinois, 1928.

Faulkner, Harold U. *American Economic History*. 6th ed. New York: Harper and Brothers Publishers, 1949.

Federal Writers' Project. *Nebraska—A Guide to the Cornhusker State*. New York: Viking Press, 1939.

Gernon, Blaine B. *The Lincolns in Chicago*. Chicago: Ancarthe Publishers, 1934.

Girls' High School, Louisville. *Girls' High School 50th Anniversary*. Louisville: C. T. Dearing Printing Co., 1958.

Grant, Bruce. *Fight for a City*. Chicago: Rand, McNally and Co., 1955.

Hall, William E. *100 Years and Millions of Boys—The Dynamic Story of the Boys' Clubs of America*. New York: Farrar, Straus and Cudahy, 1961.

Haynes, Nathaniel S. *History of the Disciples of Christ in Illinois, 1819-1914*. Cincinnati: Standard Publishing Co., 1915.

Hays, Dudley Grant. *To the Farms for Victory: The Campaign of the*

284

Prairie Farmer and WLS

Chicago High School Boys in Food Production—1917. Chicago: Board of Education, September, 1917.

Hennessy, W. B. *Past and Present of St. Paul, Minnesota.* Chicago: S. J. Clarke Publishing Co., 1906.

Hewitt, Richard. *A History of Omaha 1854-1954.* Omaha: P. C. Doss and Co., 1954.

Hoffer, Charles R. *Introduction to Rural Sociology.* New York: Farrar & Rinehart, 1934.

Hudson, Horace B. *A Half Century of Minneapolis.* Minneapolis: Hudson Publishing Co., 1908.

———. *Hudson's Dictionary of Minneapolis and Vicinity.* Vols. 8, 10. Minneapolis: Hudson Publishing Co., 1904, 1906.

Hutchinson, William T. *Lowden of Illinois.* Vols. I, II. Chicago: University of Chicago Press, 1957.

Illinois Agricultural Association. *Report of the Illinois Agricultural Association School Committee,* November, 1944.

Illinois Children's Home and Aid Society. *A Share in the Life of a Child.* Brochure, Chicago, no date, 16 pp.

———. *Teacher-Mechanic-Bookkeeper-Marine-College Student-Homemaker.* Brochure, Chicago, 1967, 12 pp.

Johnston, J. Stoddard. *Memorial History of Louisville from Its First Settlement to the Year 1896.* Vol. II. Chicago: American Biographical Publishing Co., 1896.

Keller, Helen R. *The Dictionary of Dates.* Vol. II. New York: Macmillan Co., 1934.

Kile, Orville M. *The Farm Bureau Movement.* New York: Macmillan Co., 1921.

———. *The Farm Bureau Through Three Decades.* Baltimore: Waverly Press, 1948.

Knight, Oliver, ed. *I Protest: Selected Disquisitions of E. W. Scripps.* Madison: University of Wisconsin Press, 1966.

Kolb, John H., and Edmund deS. Brunner. *A Study of Rural Society.* 4th ed. Boston: Houghton Mifflin Co., 1952.

Lacey, John J. *Farm Bureau in Illinois.* Bloomington: Illinois Agricultural Association, 1965.

Lewis, Lloyd. *John S. Wright—Prophet of the Prairies.* Chicago: Prairie Farmer Publishing Co., 1941.

Louisville Courier-Journal. The Story of Your Newspaper. Undated booklet, 33 pp.

Lydens, Z. Z., ed. *The Story of Grand Rapids.* Grand Rapids: Kregel Publications, 1966.

Marquis, Albert N., ed. *The Book of Minnesotans.* Chicago: A. N. Marquis and Co., 1907.

McLoughlin, Emmett. *People's Padre*. Boston: Beacon Press, 1954.

Minneapolis Journal. Fiftieth Birthday, 1878-1928. Minneapolis, 1928.

Morison, Bradley L. *Sunlight on Your Doorstep, The Minneapolis Tribune's First Hundred Years, 1867-1967*. Minneapolis: Ross & Haines, 1966.

Nicoll, Bruce H., and Ken R. Keller. *Sam McKelvie—Son of the Soil*. Lincoln: Johnsen Publishing Co., 1954.

Ogilvie, William E. *Pioneer Agricultural Journalists*. Chicago: Arthur G. Leonard, 1927.

Parsons, E. Dudley. *The Story of Minneapolis*. Minneapolis, 1913.

Peterson, Theodore. *Magazines in the Twentieth Century*. Urbana: University of Illinois Press, 1964.

Peterson, William J. *The Pageant of the Press*. Iowa City: State Historical Society of Iowa, 1962.

Prairie Farmer Publishing Company. *A Report on the Activities of Your Prairie Farmer-WLS Christmas Neighbors Club, 1944*. Booklet, Chicago, 1945, 48 pp.

————. *Buckarooing in the West*. Chicago: Prairie Press, 1937.

————. *Mr. and Mrs. Butler's Second Annual Prairie Farmer-WLS Children's Party*. Program of events, Chicago, 1937, 4 pp.

Proceedings of the Governor's Conference on Rural Education. Springfield, Illinois, January 18-19, 1946.

Regan, James L. *The Story of Chicago in Connection with the Printing Business*. Chicago: Regan Printing House, 1912.

Russell, A. J. *Goodbye Newspaper Row*. Excelsior, Minn.: Minnetonka Record Press, 1943.

St. John, Robert. *Encyclopedia of Radio and Television Broadcasting*. Milwaukee: Cathedral Square Publishing Co., 1967.

Saloutos, Theodore, and John D. Hicks. *Agricultural Discontent in the Middle West, 1900-1939*. Madison: University of Wisconsin Press, 1951.

Scott, Roy V. *The Agrarian Movement in Illinois, 1880-1896*. Urbana: University of Illinois Press, 1962.

Shaw, L. Lloyd, ed. *The Industries of Grand Rapids*. Grand Rapids: J. M. Elstner and Co., 1887.

Shideler, James H. *Farm Crisis, 1919-1923*. Berkeley: University of California Press, 1957.

Shutter, Marion D., ed. *History of Minneapolis*. Vol. I. Chicago-Minneapolis: S. J. Clarke Publishing Co., 1923.

Smith, Clarence B., and Meredith C. Wilson. *The Agricultural Extension System of the United States*. New York: John Wiley and Sons, 1930.

Sorenson, Alfred. *The Story of Omaha*. Omaha: National Printing Co., 1923.

Swanberg, W. A. *Citizen Hearst.* New York: Charles Scribner's Sons, 1961.

Teal, Marion Pedersen. *The Earth Is Ours.* New York: Thomas Y. Crowell Co., 1948.

Tebbel, John. *The Life and Good Times of William Randolph Hearst.* New York: E. P. Dutton and Co., 1952.

Union League Club of Chicago. *Union League Foundation for Boys' Clubs, Inc.* Brochure, Chicago, 1955, 16 pp.

U.S. Country Life Commission. *Report.* New York: Sturgis & Walton Co., 1911.

Wakeley, Arthur C., ed. *Omaha: The Gate City and Douglas County, Nebraska.* Chicago: S. J. Clarke Publishing Co., 1917.

Wallace, Henry A. *New Frontiers.* New York: Reynal & Hitchcock, 1934.

Ware, E. B. *History of the Disciples of Christ in California.* Healdsburg, Calif.: F. W. Cooke, Publisher, 1916.

White, Arthur Scott, ed. *Incidents in the Lives of Editors.* Grand Rapids: White Printing Co., 1920.

Whitney, Carrie W. *Kansas City, Missouri—Its History and Its People, 1808-1908.* Vol. I. Chicago: S. J. Clarke Publishing Co., 1908.

Who's Who in Radio. Chicago: Charles P. Hughes Publishing Co., 1925.

D. Public Documents

Cook County, Illinois. *Tract Book,* Vols. 231, 340, 451c.

Douglas County, Nebraska. *Corporation Record,* Book K, pp. 55-60; Book R, pp. 352-354; Book 3, pp. 424-425; Book 5, pp. 518-519.

DuPage County, Illinois. Last will and testament for Burridge D. Butler, and Probate Court records concerning the estate, April 8, 1948, through December 3, 1951.

Federal Reporter. 2nd series. Vols. 37 (March-April, 1930), 70 (May-July, 1934), 82 (April-June, 1936), 88 (April-May, 1937). Washington: U.S. Government Printing Office.

Gaumnitz, W. H. "Salaries and Salary Trends of Teachers in Rural Schools." Bureau of Education, Bulletin 6. Washington, 1929.

Gregory, C. V. "Pure Seed Investigations." Iowa Agricultural Experiment Station, Bulletin 99 (popular edition), Ames, Iowa, 1908, 14 pp.

Hennepin County, Minnesota. *Miscellaneous Record,* 95, pp. 133-135; 136, 270-271; 189, 7-8; 259, 624-625.

Illinois Department of Public Instruction. "The One-Room Country Schools in Illinois," Circular 51. Springfield: Illinois State Journal Co., 1910.

————. "The One-Room Country Schools and Village Schools," Circular 65. Springfield: Illinois State Journal Co., 1912.

Illinois Highway Commission. *Fourth Report of the Illinois Highway*

Commission—1910, 1911, 1912. Springfield: Illinois State Journal Co., 1913.

———. *Fifth Report of the Illinois Highway Commission, 1913-1916.* Springfield: Illinois State Journal Co., 1917.

Illinois Department of Public Works and Buildings. *Fifth Annual Report of the Department of Public Works and Buildings—Division of Highways—January 1, 1921–December 31, 1922.* Springfield, Illinois: Illinois State Journal Co., 1923.

Illinois Council of Defense. *Final Report of the State Council of Defense of Illinois, 1917-1919.* Published by authority of the State of Illinois, Springfield, no date.

Jefferson County, Kentucky. *Marriage Register,* 1 (February 16, 1784, through May 10, 1842) and 8 (July 11, 1860, through May 29, 1864).

Kent County, Michigan. *Death Record,* Book 6, p. 159.

Kent County, Michigan. *Marriage Record,* Book 10, p. 244.

Office of Vital Statistics, Bureau of Records and Statistics, Kentucky State Department of Health. *Death Register,* Book 6, p. 275.

Oldham County, Kentucky. *Marriage Register,* Book 1857, p. 166.

Ramsey County, Minnesota. *Book of Incorporations,* Book I, pp. 124-126.

Stuntz, Stephen C. "List of the Agricultural Periodicals of the United States and Canada Published During the Century July 1810 to July 1910." U.S. Department of Agriculture, Miscellaneous Publication No. 398. Washington: U.S. Government Printing Office, 1941.

True, Alfred C. "A History of Agricultural Education in the United States, 1785-1925." U.S. Department of Agriculture, Miscellaneous Publication No. 36. Washington: U.S. Government Printing Office, 1929.

———. "A History of Agricultural Extension Work in the United States, 1785-1923." U.S. Department of Agriculture, Miscellaneous Publication No. 15. Washington: U.S. Government Printing Office, 1928.

U.S. Department of Agriculture. *Agriculture Yearbook,* 1923. Washington: U.S. Government Printing Office, 1923.

———. *Yearbook of Agriculture,* 1940. Washington: U.S. Government Printing Office, 1940.

———. *Yearbook of Agriculture,* 1956. Washington: U.S. Government Printing Office, 1956.

———. *Yearbook of Agriculture,* 1962. Washington: U.S. Government Printing Office, 1962.

———. "Soybeans, Cowpeas, and Velvetbeans, By States, 1924-1953," Statistical Bulletin 211. Washington, June, 1957.

U.S. Department of Commerce. *Census of Agriculture.* 1925, Part 1 (Northern States); 1945, Vol. 1, Part 5 (Illinois); 1950, Vol. 1, Part 5 (Illinois). Washington: U.S. Government Printing Office.

quality

————. "Characteristics of the Population," in *Sixteenth Census of the United States*, Vol. II. Washington: U.S. Government Printing Office, 1940.

————. "Population Characteristics," in *Current Population Reports, Series P-20*, No. 19. Washington: U.S. Government Printing Office, 1948.

U.S. Reports. Vols. 281 (October term, 1929), 293 (October term, 1934), 299 (October term, 1936), 301 (October term, 1936), 302 (October term, 1937). Washington: U.S. Government Printing Office.

University of Illinois. "College of Veterinary Medicine," in *University of Illinois Bulletin*, 58 (June, 1961).

E. Newspapers

Arizona Farmer-Ranchman, February 17, 1940; April 17, 1948; special edition of September, 1966.

Arizona Times, February 5 and April 8, 1948.

Blackburnian, student semi-monthly newspaper of Blackburn College, Carlinville, Illinois; selected issues from January 27, 1928, through April 9, 1949.

Chicago Daily News, March 30 and March 31, 1948.

Chicago Daily Times, June 25, 1944.

Chicago Tribune, May 30, 1906; March 31 and April 8, 1948; July 14, 1956; November 18 and 19, 1959.

Christian Evangelist, November 18, 1920; January 20, 1921.

Christian Standard, May 5, 1866, through June 25, 1887; May 7, 1921. Contained 103 articles by Thomas D. Butler.

Daily Illini, November 3, 1956.

The Farmer's Review, October 24, 1908; May 15, 1918.

The Farmers Voice, May 15, 1913.

The Farmers Voice and Rural Outlook, June, 1905.

Grand Rapids Daily Democrat, selected issues from January 6, 1886, through June, 1894.

Grand Rapids Press, July 29, 1904; May 7, 1932; December 10, 1934; January 24, 1941; June 3, 1948.

Hinsdale Doings, April 8, 1948.

Hoard's Dairyman, March 3, 1916.

Illinois Farmer and Farmer's Call, January, 1856; July 1, 1916; April, 1924.

Illinois Farmers Guide, January through August, 1939.

Louisville Evening Times, January 22, 1885.

Minneapolis Journal, August 5, 1903; March 8, 1923; December 26, 1933.

Minneapolis Tribune, August 1, 1903; August 5, 1903.

New York Times, March 31, 1948.

Omaha Daily Bee, selected issues from October 9, 1899, through October 9, 1903.

Omaha Daily News, selected issues in all volumes from October 9, 1899, through October 9, 1909; selected volumes through February 13, 1927.

Omaha Examiner, September 8 and September 15, 1900.

Omaha Morning World-Herald, selected issues from September 12, 1899, through May 1, 1900; May 21, 1932.

Orange Judd Farmer, selected issues from May 5, 1900, through July 1, 1930.

Peoria Star, April 5, 1948.

Phoenix Gazette, selected issues from March 31, 1948, through December 12, 1966.

Phoenix Republic, selected issues from December 8, 1946, through December 1, 1965.

Prairie Farmer, selected volumes from 1841-51; selected issues of all volumes, 1852-1908; all issues of all volumes, 1909-48.

St. Paul Daily News, selected issues, March 1, 1900, through March 1, 1908.

St. Paul Daily Pioneer Press, March 1, 1900.

St. Paul Dispatch, March 1, 1900; March 8, 1923; December 26, 1933.

St. Paul Globe, March 1, 1900.

St. Paul Rural Weekly, December 28, 1904; February 8, 1905.

Tucson Daily Citizen, March 30 and April 7, 1948.

Wallaces' Farmer and Iowa Homestead, October 26, 1929; July 17, 1937; November 29, 1941.

Wisconsin Agriculturist and Farmer, June 1, 1929.

F. Periodicals

Agricultural Advertising, selected issues from May, 1908, through April, 1910.

American Highway Association. *Good Roads Yearbook,* 1912-17. Washington, D.C.

American Newspaper Directory, 1879-80, 1893. New York: George P. Rowell and Co.

Audit Bureau of Circulations Blue Book. Periodical publishers' statements, 1914 through 1948, for 20 farm publications with Illinois circulation. These reports were identified as *A.B.C. Auditor's Reports* before December, 1924.

N. W. Ayer and Son's American Newspaper Annual, selected volumes, 1890 through 1925. Philadelphia: N. W. Ayer and Son.

Blackburn College Alumni Bulletin. September, 1927, through May, 1948.

Blackburn College Catalogue, March, 1967. Carlinville, Ill.: Blackburn College.

The Blackburnia, 1930. Yearbook of Blackburn College, Carlinville, Illinois.

Boys' Clubs of Phoenix 1966 Annual Report. Published by Community Relations Department, 1967, 9 pp.

Country Gentleman. February, 1927.

Des Moines Directory, 1898 through 1903. Des Moines: R. L. Polk and Co.

Grand Rapids City Directory, 1877-81 and 1886-1900. Grand Rapids, Mich.: R. L. Polk and Co.

Homelife for Children, Spring, 1967. Periodical of the Illinois Children's Home and Aid Society.

Illinois Children's Home and Aid Society 1965 Annual Report. Mount Morris: Illinois Children's Home and Aid Society, 1966.

Lakeside Directory of Chicago, selected volumes, 1852 through 1910. Chicago: Lakeside Press.

Louisville City Directory, 1836-89. Louisville: C. K. Caron and other publishers at various times.

Men of Minnesota, 1915. St. Paul: R. L. Polk and Co.

Minneapolis City Directory, selected volumes, 1898 through 1911. Minneapolis: Minneapolis Directory Co.

Nebraska Blue Book, 1899-1900, 1901-2, 1920. Lincoln: State Journal Co.

Omaha City Directory, 1899 through 1909. Omaha: McAvoy Directory Co. and Omaha Directory Co.

Prairie Farmer's Half Acre, December 27, 1930; March 7, 1931; March 12, 1932. Prairie Farmer Publishing Company house organ.

Prairie Farmer–WLS Round-Up, selected issues, August, 1948, through August, 1957. Prairie Farmer Publishing Company house organ.

Printer's Ink, January 24, 1924.

Current Biography. New York: H. W. Wilson Co., 1948.

'Round the Clock with Prairie Farmer–WLS, March, 1944. Prairie Farmer Publishing Company house organ.

St. Paul City Directory, 1898-1910. St. Paul: R. L. Polk and Co.

StandBy, April 12, 1949. Radio weekly. Chicago: Prairie Farmer Publishing Co.

Union League Men and Events, July, 1948. Chicago: Union League Club of Chicago.

Union League Club of Chicago Yearbook, 1910. Chicago: Union League Club of Chicago.

Webster's Biographical Dictionary. Springfield, Mass.: G. and C. Merriam Co., 1958.

Who's Who in America, 1948-1949. Chicago: A. N. Marquis Co., 1948.

Wilson's Directory of the Extension Service in the United States, 1924-1925. Cambridge, Mass.: Wm. G. Wilson, Publisher, 1925.

WLS Family Album. Annual volume, 1930 through 1957. Chicago: Prairie Farmer Publishing Co.

Yearbook of the Churches of Christ, 1892, 1897, 1900-1903, 1909, 1913. Cincinnati: American Christian Missionary Society.

G. Periodical Articles

Anonymous. "The Cities of the South—Louisville," *Southern Quarterly Review,* 1 (April, 1868), 33ff.

———. "Burridge D. Butler," *Little Sketches of Big Folks—Minnesota 1907,* p. 64.

———. "Union League Club Creates Foundation for Boys," *Fort Dearborn Magazine,* 2 (September, 1920), 6ff.

———. "Radio and Farm Life," *Literary Digest,* 74 (September 23, 1922), 28.

———. "Price Reporting to Farmers by Radio," *Literary Digest,* 77 (June 30, 1923), 25.

———. "Lawrence V. Ashbaugh," in *Proceedings of the Fifty-Eighth Annual Convention of the Minnesota Editorial Association,* Minneapolis, February 15-16, 1924, p. 57.

———. "Broadcasting Station Directory," *Wireless Age,* 12 (April, 1925), 79-80.

———. "Frederick William Kellogg," in Winfield S. Downs, ed., *Encyclopedia of American Biography.* New York: American Historical Co., 1941, pp. 453-455.

———. "Passing of Burridge Butler," *Variety,* March 31, 1948.

———. "Burridge Butler, Veteran Publisher-Broadcaster Passes," *The Advertiser,* April, 1948, p. 29.

———. "Burridge Davenal Butler," *Broadcasting,* April 5, 1948, p. 56.

———. "Butler's Will," *Broadcasting,* April 12, 1948, p. 30.

Asbel, Bernard L. "The National Barn Dance," *Chicago,* 1 (October, 1954), 20-25.

Biggar, George C. "Cowbells Ring Out on Saturday Night," in John Lair, ed., *100 Barn Dance Favorites.* Chicago: Cole, 1935.

Blythe, Stuart O. "Farming by Radio," *Country Gentleman,* 89 (May 10, 1924), 6ff.

Borg, Walter T. "Clifford V. Gregory and His Writings," *Agricultural History,* 16 (1942), 116-122.

Burlingham, C. L. "Our Own Radio Service," *Breeder's Gazette*, 93 (June, 1928), 3ff.

Butler, Burridge D. "Boys' Clubs and Crime," *The Review of Reviews*, 79 (April, 1929), 74.

Butler, T. D. "What Are Titles Worth?" *Christian Evangelist*, July 23, 1891, p. 468.

Chamberlin, Jo. "Johnstown Remembers," *American Magazine*, 32 (January, 1942), 16ff.

Clark, Neil M. "I've Never Lost Money by Calling a Spade a Spade," *American Magazine*, 111 (June, 1931), 67ff.

Collins, James H. "Putting the Farm on the Ether," *Country Gentleman*, 87 (September 2, 1922), 21.

Farrell, J. "Farm Radio Making Rapid Progress," *Radio News*, 6 (January, 1925), 1143ff.

Gilbert, F. C. "Rural Life Modernized," *Wireless Age*, 12 (March, 1925), 24ff.

Gregory, Clifford V. "The American Farm Bureau Federation and the A.A.A.," in Harwood L. Childs, ed., *Pressure Groups and Propaganda*, Annals of the American Academy of Political and Social Science, 179 (May, 1935), 152-157.

———. "The Master Farmer Movement," *Agricultural History*, 10 (April, 1936), 47-58.

Hurd, William A. "Harvest Time on the Air," *Wireless Age*, 12 (November, 1924), 19ff.

Lord, Ann. "Chicago Broadcasts," *Wireless Age*, 12 (April, 1925), 40ff.

———. "How-do-you-do?" *Wireless Age*, 12 (May, 1925), 34-35.

Mahanay, Stuart C. "Broadcasting Past and Present," *Country Gentleman*, 92 (February, 1927), 143.

Manchester, Harland. "The Farm Magazines," *Scribner's Magazine*, 104 (October, 1938), 25ff.

Parrish, E. V. "Omaha, Its Growth in Ten Years," *The True Voice*, December 5, 1913, p. 16.

Poole, James E. "Confessions of a Broadcaster," *Breeder's Gazette*, 101 (April, 1936), 6ff.

Schapsmeier, Edward L. and Frederick H. "The Wallaces and Their Farm Paper: A Story of Agrarian Leadership," *Journalism Quarterly*, 44 (Summer, 1967), 289-296.

Seeds, Virginia. "Our Big Shindig," *StandBy*, 1 (November 9, 1935), 5ff.

Seeley, Ward. "The Farm Moves Nearer the City," *Wireless Age*, 10 (January, 1923), 24ff.

Shaffer, John C. "Service for City, State and Nation," in *The Spirit of the Union League Club, 1879-1926* (Chicago, 1926), pp. 88-89.

Shipman, Vera Brady. "Behind the Microphone at KYW," *Country Gentleman*, 90 (March 21, 1925), 12ff.

Steele, Harry. "Swing Your Partners," *The Chicago Visitor*, 5 (January, 1933), 34-36.

Taylor, Vernon L. "Doctor John: Pastor to Millions," *Christian Advocate*, July 31, 1952, 7ff.

Thain, R. S. "The Farm League List of Papers," *Agricultural Advertising*, 19 (May, 1908), 51.

True, James. "A Lesson for Manufacturers in the Farmer's Welcome of Radio," *Printer's Ink*, 126 (January 24, 1924), 73.

Wheeler, W. A. "Down on the Farm in 1923," *Radio Broadcast*, 2 (January, 1923), 212-214.

Winters, S. R. "A National College of the Air," *Popular Mechanics*, 45 (June, 1926), 947-949.

———. "One Million Farmers to Study by Radio," *Radio News*, 8 (August, 1926), 104-105.

———. "What Does He Hear?" *Wireless Age*, 10 (February, 1923), 35-36.

H. Unpublished Materials

Anonymous. "A Résumé of the Life of Dave O. Thompson, Sr." Mimeographed report, 6 pp., no date.

———. "Brief History of Radio Station WLS." Unpublished WLS manuscript, dated August, 1951.

———. "Dedication Program," Burridge D. Butler Boys' Club House dedicated by Boys' Clubs of Phoenix, Arizona, November 30, 1952.

———. "Farm Programming at WLS." Undated WLS manuscript.

———. "Illinois Children's Home and Aid Society Fact Sheet." Undated mimeographed report.

———. "Presentation of WLS." Scrapbook prepared by WLS, Chicago, 1928.

———. "Seventeen Years of Farm Service." Mimeographed report by WLS, Chicago, 1940.

Agricultural Broadcasting Company, "Testimony and Exhibits of Agricultural Broadcasting Company, Radio Station WLS, Chicago, Illinois, before the Federal Communications Commission Clear Channel Hearings," Docket No. 6741. Mimeographed and multilithed report in five parts, 1946.

Babcock, Willoughby M. "The *Minneapolis Star*, the *Minneapolis Tribune* and Their Predecessors." Manuscript prepared by Curator of Newspapers, Minnesota Historical Society, March 18, 1955.

Biggar, George C. "A Radiobroadcasting Service for Agricultural Colleges." Speech delivered at the American Association of Agricultural

College Editors annual meeting, South Dakota State College, July, 1924.

———. "Early History of Sears-Roebuck Agricultural Foundation and WLS." Memorandum to Edward J. Condon, June 28, 1960.

———. "Forty Years in the Right Business." Speech delivered at the South Dakota Broadcasters Association Convention, Huron, South Dakota, May 22, 1964.

Blackburn College, Carlinville, Illinois. Dedication plaques at Butler Hall.

Butler, B. D. "To My Mother." Unpublished poem, dated April 20, 1909.

———. "My Mother's 93rd Birthday." Unpublished poem, dated May 20, 1909.

Butler-Morse tombstones, cemetery, Batavia, Illinois.

Butler-Radcliffe-Christopher tombstones, Lot 219, Section M, Cave Hill Cemetery, Louisville, Kentucky.

Church of the Transfiguration, New York, New York. Certified extract from the Register of Marriages, July 30, 1906.

Duermyer, Louis A. "Ashbaugh Outline." Mimeographed report, November, 1939.

Flint, Marjorie. "History of the Illinois Children's Home and Aid Society." Mimeographed report, 1960.

Grand Rapids Public Library, Grand Rapids, Michigan. Dedication plaques at the front entrance of Ryerson Library Building.

Hinshaw, William W., Jr. "The Busey Family in America." Unpublished genealogical charts, no date, 7 pp.

Holland, John W. "Let's Start Something." Eulogy of B. D. Butler, no date, 63 pp.

Holt, Gus A. "Wisdom, Leadership, Service." Mimeographed WLS program policy statement, January, 1935.

Linton, Bruce A. "A History of Chicago Radio Station Programming, 1921-1931, with Emphasis on Stations WMAQ and WGN." Unpublished doctoral dissertation, Northwestern University, Evanston, April, 1953.

Miller, George F. "Boys' Clubs of Phoenix, Inc." Manuscript outlining the development of the program, September 19, 1966.

Moore, A. L., and Sons Memorial Chapel, Phoenix, Arizona. Funeral program for B. D. Butler services, April 2, 1948.

National Committee on Rural Scouting. Minutes for the first annual meeting, May 10, 1927.

Page, Arthur C. "Planning for Rural Program Needs." Speech before the National Association of Broadcasters Program Clinic at Northwestern University, June 28, 1949.

Quebral, Nora Cruz. "*Farm Journal* and American Agriculture, 1877-

1965." Unpublished doctoral dissertation, University of Illinois, Urbana, 1966.

Rowell, Glenn. Untitled speech about early WLS programs for the 40th WLS Anniversary Dinner Program, Chicago, April 12, 1964.

Safford, Harold A. "The Science of Building a Farm Audience." Speech delivered at the Program Directors' Clinic of Broadcast Music, Inc., Chicago, October 23, 1950.

——. "The Woman Broadcaster and Her Station Manager." Address delivered at Association of Women Broadcasters annual meeting, Chicago, March 12, 1949.

St. Monica's Hospital and Health Center, Inc., Phoenix, Arizona. Invoice dated March 30, 1948.

Snyder, Glenn. "Original Policies Built WLS." Unpublished manuscript, July, 1966, 2 pp.

Thompson, Dave O. Unpublished memoirs, prepared by the former *Prairie Farmer*-WLS staff member, 1963, 419 pp.

Union League Club, "A 35 Year Summary of Union League Foundation for Boys' Clubs." Mimeographed report, no date, 15 pp.

Whitfield tombstones, Oak Hill Cemetery, Grand Rapids, Michigan.

Wilson, Allen D. "Agricultural Periodicals in the United States." Unpublished master's thesis, University of Illinois, Urbana, May, 1930.

Winkelmann, David P. "Analysis and Comparison of Selected Agricultural Publications Received in Illinois." Unpublished master's thesis, University of Illinois, Urbana, 1963.

INDEX

297

dation for Boys' Clubs, 259-260; end of active participation in, 261
—and Boys' Clubs (Phoenix): part in formation, 261; donation for club building, 261
—and Boys' Clubs of America: national board member, 260; comparison with Boy Scout program, 262
—and Boy Scouts: Rural Scouting Committee, 262; Lone Scout Department in *Prairie Farmer*, 262
—business philosophy, 72, 202, 273, 275-276
—business skill, 7, 10, 147, 272, 273-274
—and Butler, Ina H.: loss of child, 249; considered adoption of a child, 249; desire for a son, 250. *See also* Busey, Ina H.
—and Butler, Winnie L.: anniversary gift, 252; collecting dimes, 252; Winnie Whitfield Butler Collection of Picture Books in Color, 252; start of Winnie Whitfield Butler Trust, 253. *See also* Whitfield, Winnie L.
—and camping: in Rocky Mountains, 245; companions, 245, 246; equipment, 246; preference for roughing it, 246; experiences, 247-248; typical agenda, 248
—as champion, 3, 18, 65-66, 95. *See also* Butler, Burridge D., disposition of; Butler, Burridge D., and farm people
—childhood: birth, 13; brothers and sisters, 15; moves by family, 16-17; parting from father, 17; early jobs in Louisville, Ky., 19-20. *See also* Butler, Burridge D., education; Butler, Burridge D., immediate family
—and *Cincinnati Enquirer,* 20-21
—and civic leaders of Phoenix, 234. *See also* Butler, Burridge D., and Union League Club of Chicago

—and Clover Leaf Newspapers: founding of *Omaha Daily News,* 30; and Daily News Publishing Company (Omaha), 31; editorial approach on *Omaha Daily News,* 31, 33; to full partnership, 32; to advertising sales office in Chicago, 33; and Daily News Publishing Company of St. Paul, 35; founding of *Minneapolis Daily News,* 37; and *Des Moines Daily News,* 37; and *Kansas City World,* 37; departure from, 40-41; disenchantment with, 3, 53
—and "crown princes": promises to, 264; sequence of candidates, 265-269, 270; reaction of employees toward, 265, 266, 267
—death and burial, 272
—disposition: unpredictability, 6-12; intolerance, 8; domination of others, 8-9, 247; parsimony, 9; desire for challenge, 246, 248; resoluteness, 247; restlessness, 248, 270; paternalism, 250-251; impulsiveness, 264. *See also* Butler, Burridge D., as champion; Butler, Burridge D., and family motivation
—editorial philosophy: statement in 1909, 18-19; stress on campaigns, 95; criteria for embarking on campaigns, 95. *See also* Butler, Burridge D., and Barn Dance; Butler, Burridge D., and KOY, Phoenix; Butler, Burridge D., and *Prairie Farmer;* Butler, Burridge D., and WLS
—education, 23-24
—and employees: unpredictability with, 6-12; freedom allowed, 188; wages, 188, 237; understandings with, 228-229; corrective actions, 229-230; stimulation of, 232-233; criticism of, 234-235; demands on, 235-237; impromptu gatherings, 248; responses to paternalism, 250-251;

Gregory, Clifford V.
—and Agricultural Marketing Act (1929), 137
—and American Farm Bureau Federation: views about its functions, 129; involvement in formation, 129-130; disappointment in, 135; opposition to Grain Marketing Company, 135-136
—appearance, 60
—background, 60
—and Butler, Burridge D.: camping, 245; on employment of son, 250; stock ownership as incentive for employment, 265. *See also* Butler, Burridge D., and Gregory, Clifford V.
—and Chicago Board of Trade, 131-132
—and cooperation among farmers, 125
—and cooperative marketing, 135, 136-137
—death, 152
—disposition, 60, 148
—farm ownership, 133
—farm publication proposed by, 151
—and Illinois Agricultural Association: endorsement of formation, 127; as officer, 127; views about functions of, 127-128; advocacy of new financing plan, 128; departure from executive committee, 128. *See also* Gregory, Clifford V., and Smith, Earl C.
—and McNary-Haugen Bill: aid in getting approval by the Illinois Agricultural Association, 139; open letter to President Coolidge, 139-140. *See also Prairie Farmer* and farm legislation
—and National Council of Cooperative Marketing Associations, 135
—and New Deal: meeting with Franklin Roosevelt before election of 1932, 142; as member

of planning group, 142, 143-144; as candidate for position of Secretary of Agriculture, 143; support of, 144; response from readers, 144-145; endorsement of Roosevelt in 1936, 145; part in writing the Agricultural Adjustment Act (1938), 146
—and *Prairie Farmer*: employment by, 60-61; editorial approach in, 66-71, 83-84, 121, 147, 207, 211-212; relationship with editorial staff, 148; ownership, 150; resignation from, 151. *See also Prairie Farmer*, campaigns
—and radio: predictions in 1922, 169; on WMAQ, 170
—religious activity, 121
—and Smith, Earl C., 139, 143. *See also* Gregory, Clifford V., and Illinois Agricultural Association
—speaking ability, 147
—and Wallace, Henry A., 141
—to *Wallaces' Farmer and Iowa Homestead* and *Wisconsin Agriculturist*, 151-152
—and Wheat Growers Advisory Committee, 134-135
—and WLS: weekly program on, 85; part in purchase of, 173; as officer of Agricultural Broadcasting Company, 174
—writing skill, 60, 141, 185
Gregory, Merrill: employment by *Prairie Farmer*, 250
Griffin, Ind.: in tornado of 1925, 166-167
Ground puppies, 211
Guarantee, advertising: adopted by *Prairie Farmer*, 75-76; usage among farm publications, 76n; by WLS, 179
Guard, Samuel R.: and Sears-Roebuck Agricultural Foundation, 159; recollection of WLS inaugural program, 161; and southern Illinois tornado relief fund, 166,

Agricultural Foundation programs on, 168
WGN, Chicago: popularity of Quin A. Ryan, 162; farm audience in 1928, 173; Amos 'n Andy on, 219-220
Wheat: production incentives during World War I, 106; unfair pricing of in 1918, 108-109
Wheat Growers Advisory Committee, 134-135
White House Conference on Rural Education, 113
Whitfield, I. J., 21, 24
Whitfield, Winnie L.: early contact with Butler, 21; background, 24; disposition, 24; appearance, 24; marriage to Butler, 24-25. *See also* Butler, Winnie L.
WHO, Des Moines: farm audience in 1928, 73
Wilcox, Harlow: on the Angelus, 191; with Fibber McGee and Molly, 220
Wilder, Trulan. *See* Hiram and Henry
Wilksies comic strip: introduced in *Prairie Farmer*, 84
Williams, Anne, 187
Williams, Charles R.: as owner of *Prairie Farmer*, 47
Williams, Jack: with KOY, Phoenix, 236; and Boys' Clubs of Phoenix, 261
Wilson, Grace: pioneer on WLS, 160, 220; request for pay, 216
Wilson, Woodrow: call for volunteer farm help in 1917, 253
Winnie Whitfield Butler Trust, 253
Winninger, Charles: on NBC, 214
"Wireless Man, The," 169
Wisconsin, University of, 266
Wisconsin Agriculturist: consolidation with *Wisconsin Farmer,* 87; in Standard Farm Paper Association, 90; Glenn Snyder on staff, 178

Wisconsin Agriculturist and Farmer: formed through consolidation, 87; in Midwest Farm Paper Unit, 91; loss of advertising, 1928-32, 92; Clifford Gregory as associate publisher, 151
Wisconsin Farmer: consolidation with *Wisconsin Agriculturist*, 87
Wisconsin State Fair, 266
Wiseman, Scotty. *See* Lulu Belle and Scotty
Witter, John H., 259
WJJD, Chicago: farm audience in 1928, 173; transmitter used by WLS, 182
WJZ, Newark, 155
WLS, Chicago
—advertising policy, 179-180
—audience: mail pull, 3, 202; in 1928, 173; sources of mail response, 176; loyalty to performers, 198-199; visitors to studio, 202-203; listening surveys in 1938, 203
—Barn Dance. *See* Barn Dance, WLS
—call letters: selection of, 160, 161
—competitive setting, 198, 202
—editorial policy: uniqueness in 1924, 162; under Edgar Bill, 162; warmth toward listeners, 167; of Butler, 177-178; under Glenn Snyder, 179; for homemaker programming, 187; family spirit, 198, 199. *See also* Butler, Burridge D., and WLS, Chicago
—financial status: in 1939, 5; first profit under *Prairie Farmer*, 203; assets and profit trends, 1929-48, 204; commercial support during depression, 214
—formation: audience reaction to test program, 160; other test programs, 161; dedication program, 161
—fund-raising efforts: southern Illinois tornado relief fund, 166-167; summary, 1925-37, 199;